Moral Dimensions of American Foreign Policy

Ethics in Foreign Policy Series

Edited with an Introduction by
Kenneth W. Thompson

Published for
Council on Religion & International Affairs

Transaction Books
New Brunswick (U.S.A.) and London (U.K.)

Library of Congress Catalog Number: 84-2438
ISBN: 0-87855-967-1 (paper)
Printed in the United States of America

Library of Congress Cataloging in Publication Data

Main entry under title:

Moral dimensions of American foreign policy.

   (Ethics in foreign policy series)
   1. International relations—Moral and ethical aspects—Addresses,
essays, lectures.   I. Thompson, Kenneth W.,
1921-   .   II. Series.
JX1255.M56   1984   172'.4   84-2438
ISBN 0-87855-967-1 (pbk.)

Contents

Introduction

Kenneth W. Thompson

A witty friend once noted that in scholarship as in baseball, you score runs when you bunch your hits. His homely axiom applies to the Council on Religion and International Affairs (CRIA), which has made ethics and international relations its field over the past three decades. It was in 1957 that CRIA began publishing a series of pamphlets on ethics and foreign policy. The organization's unique achievement in assembling this series lies in its refusal to take up causes or prescribe panaceas but, instead, to foster a climate of discussion that has been best described as "an unusually stubborn attempt to think clearly about ethics."

In pursuit of that goal, CRIA's staff and trustees enlisted the efforts of some of the best minds in America—John Courtney Murray, S.J., Hans J. Morgenthau, John C. Bennett, and Paul Ramsey, among others—encouraging them to write and to join in freewheeling discussions of their own and others' work. For a quarter of a century, CRIA's Merrill House headquarters in New York has been a meeting place for people whose presence bespoke unity in the midst of diversity. Continuity of effort is reflected in a rich and varied series of publications unmatched in the literature.

Several of the essays included here—"Ethics and National Purpose," "The Recovery of Ethics," "Moral Tensions in International Affairs," and "Religion and International Responsibility"—are attempts to discern, even in the flux of circumstance, some enduring principles upon which peace with justice might be built. The debate over the moral status of war in general and nuclear war in particular engaged five others, some of them writing within the broad tradition of just-war theory: "Morality and Modern War," "The Limits of Nuclear War," "Modern War and the Pursuit of Peace," "An Alternative to War," and "Just War and Vatican II: A Critique." Two contributions foresaw the emergence of a North-South conflict rivaling in importance the East-West struggle: "Is Gradualism Dead?" and "Foreign Aid: Moral and Political Aspects." Finally, two leading theorists explored two issues that are as problematic today as when they put down their thoughts: "Human Rights and Foreign Policy" and "The Morality and Politics of Intervention."

Hans J. Morgenthau, the teacher and mentor of quite a few of those who participated in CRIA discussions over the years, asserted that the aim of political and moral writings should be to make men wise forever, not clever for a day. These essays meet that test handily. First, they ask the right questions. Second, they have left us with clear statements of the underlying assumptions on which their policy prescriptions are based, offering succeeding generations a resource for addressing the circumstances and contingencies that challenge the future. Distinctions between realism and idealism, prudence and practical morality, power and force; elaborations of conflicting views of international cooperation and development, national interest and interdependence; differing concepts of political morality—all are to be found herein.

The discussions in this volume address recurrent themes and unsolved problems, often anticipating more recent debates. We are told, for example, that Vietnam shattered the political consensus of the early postwar period, giving rise to a new "school" of political history opposed both to the orthodox and the revisionist schools—which I have called "interpreters and critics." It may be, however, that yet more basic differences about questions of power and force in international politics were evident at an earlier stage of intellectual history. Some of these are captured in the present volume in the conflicting assumptions of, say, Murray and Ramsey on the one hand and Bennett and Zahn on the other. If all of political theory is a footnote to Plato, it may not be claiming too much to argue that those who have followed such thinkers as Murray and Bennett have merely elaborated on themes these men first developed.

What we can only guess at is how some of these seminal thinkers whom we celebrate through the publication of an important essay would have modified their positions in the light of changing circumstances. What would John Courtney Murray have said about the Roman Catholic bishops' statement on nuclear war in 1982? What would Hans Morgenthau have thought of Alexander Haig's assertion, when he was secretary of state, that eradicating terrorism took priority over advancing human rights? What is certain is the need to illuminate recent political developments by calling upon "the stubborn attempt to think clearly" of a handful of first-rate minds. The stakes are so high in the nuclear age that to neglect such a resource is nothing short of criminal.

Behind every political decision, Lord Keynes noted, is the work of some academic scribbler. With only a couple of exceptions, the contributors to this volume have not been political actors. But all have influenced generations of policy makers, whether or not those men and women of affairs could name the intellectual heritage upon which they drew. That government leaders often have misunderstood or misapplied certain of these ideas is a further reason for revisiting and reflecting on their efforts today.

The vision for this series was the late William Clancy's; its moving spirit was Dr. A. William Loos, CRIA's second president. The same dedication and skill were brought to the task by James Finn, who assumed duties as general editor in 1961, and by Susan Woolfson and her editorial associates over the years.

Ethics and National Purpose

Kenneth W. Thompson

THE PROVERBIAL "man from Mars" plunged suddenly onto the American continent would be treated to an amazing and confusing spectacle. He would soon discover that whereas leaders and philosophers of earlier civilizations had oftentimes stood in judgment on their people, crying out against individual and collective practices in words enshrined in a historic prophetic tradition — "thus saith the Lord" — most present-day secular and sectarian preachers reject the age-old, persistent and probably inevitable tension between ethics and foreign policy.

He would hear repeatedly that "the United States walks the path of honor alone." He would be told that for us moral force had successfully replaced power politics, selfish interests and agonizing moral dilemmas. He might even be enlisted in a moral crusade. In one word he would be informed that ethics in foreign policy is an accomplishment, not a baffling and heart-breaking problem. Yet our visitor might be excused for noting that ironically enough this national philosophy is being proclaimed in an age of unparalleled conflict, destructiveness, disorder, and strife whose imperatives touch even moral man: at Hiroshima, Budapest, Suez and on the countless battlefields of world politics yet to be.

I believe the starting-point for a discussion of ethics and foreign policy is the quest for a secure vantage-point from which we can perceive that many of our moral judgments are at best premature. Man at root is not only, as for Aristotle, a social and political animal. He is also a moral being. He cannot eschew moral judgments. Yet since his virtue and knowledge are limited, his moral valuations are fragmentary and partial. Moreover, contemporary social scientists like Max Weber have pointed to a hidden and neglected truth regarding moral claims. Since moral men seek moral reasons and justifications for their acts, they are endlessly tempted to invest aspirations, interests and conduct with ethical meaning.

For Weber, men cover their purely selfish pursuits with a tissue of lies and deception meant to convey their virtue. Ideologies are fabricated to justify political conduct to others. It must be said that the notion that an ideal is never more than rationalization is carried too far when men deny the differences between good and bad political ideas or equate the potentially healthy myths of democracy and the demoniac ones of totalitarianism. Yet it is also true that history is strewn with moral claims convincing at the time but seen now as at best a shrewd mixture of good and evil, of aspiration and aggrandizement, of uplift and grosser human qualities. Man's powers of self-deception are seemingly endless.

The Moral Dilemma

At the heart of this problem is a moral dilemma. We are never as moral as we claim to be. This is true of the parent who disciplines the child "for its own good" no less than of the powerful nation who works its will on less powerful, but no less virtuous, states. Even when justice is the goal of a loving father it invariably becomes mixed with coercion, caprice and injustice. The Athenian envoys to Melos, who were perhaps more transparently honest than some of their latter-day successors, said of a powerful rival: "Of all the men we know they are most conspicuous in considering what is agreeable-honorable and what is expedient-just" Centuries later the historian Dicey found that in Western society "men come easily to believe that arrangements agreeable to themselves are beneficial to others."

Nations with few exceptions have seen their cause and supremacy as equivalent to universal justice. Lord Wolseley maintained: "I have but one great object in this world, and that is to maintain the greatness of the Empire. But apart from my John Bull sentiment upon the point, I firmly believe that in doing so I work in the cause of Christianity, of peace, of civilization, and the happiness of the human race generally." Or in 1935 in an early phase of his writings, Professor Arnold J. Toynbee discovered that the security of the British Empire "was also the supreme interest of the whole world." The Archbishop of Canterbury at the time of the Italian aggression in Ethiopia admonished the French: "We are animated by moral and spiritual considerations . . . It is . . . no egoist interest driving us forward, and no consideration of interest should keep you behind." However, more sober historians looking today for the cause of the paralysis of French policy and its failure to act point not to her moral depravity but to a tragic and tangled procession of events that includes our refusal to give guarantees, a pathological fear of Germany, and a plausible but ill-fated attempt to gain security in the Northeast through an *entente* with Italy in the South. As partners in two world wars with the British we perhaps find their claims more plausible than the assertion of a prominent National Socialist in 1935: "Anything that benefits the German people is right, anything that harms the German people is wrong."

Nor is American history lacking in comparable examples. It provides the story of President McKinley, who spent the night in prayer for divine guidance before deciding, as one might have expected, to annex the Philippines. Or President Wilson, who, following the bombardment of Vera Cruz in 1914, assured the world that "the United States had gone to Mexico to serve mankind," and who shortly before our entry into World War I identified American principles and American policies as "the principles of mankind . . . (which) must prevail." We are reminded of De Toqueville's words:

> If I say to an American that the country he lives in is a fine one, aye, he replies and there is not its equal in the world. If I applaud the freedom its inhabitants enjoy, he answers "freedom is a fine thing but few nations are worthy of it." If I remark on the purity of morals that distinguishes the United States he declares "I can imagine that a stranger who has witnessed the corruption which prevails in other nations would be astonished at the difference." At length I leave him to a contemplation of himself, but he returns to the charge and does not desist until he has got me to repeat all I have been saying. It is impossible to conceive a more troublesome and garrulous patriotism.

Spiritual Pride

It should, of course, be obvious that every nation has its own form of spiritual pride, its own peculiar version. Our version is compounded, I would suppose, of at least three factors.

The first derives from the role of the immigrant who had turned his back on the vices of Europe and was making a new beginning. Having shaken the dust of the Old World from his feet, he was anxious to prove that none of its ancient failings were his failings. Their purposes, often sullied by the ambiguities and compromises bound up with national existence in the cockpit of Europe, were not his purposes. And strikingly enough, his affirmations of moral purity — or more specifically, those by which national leaders appealed to his virtue — seemed to be confirmed by early American social history. In the first phases of this history the frontier saved us from the acrimony of class struggle and, later, our superior technology gave new outlets to the ambitious and adventurous. Beyond this we were freed from international responsibility and a European equilibrium of power which British policy and naval power were dedicated to preserve. In such a world, it was natural to assume that domestic policies were more important than foreign policy and that the alliances so prevalent on the European scene were an expensive and pernicious nuisance. These objective conditions have passed but the psychology they inspired lingers on, as in the recent sweeping and indignant denunciations of the exercise of power by European states followed abruptly by our own decision to use force unilaterally if necessary in the Middle East.

Legalism

A second factor shaping the American outlook results from the fact that our prevailing philosophy of international relations has been a curious blending of legalism and rationalism. Law and reason are of course indispensable ingredients of an orderly life. They are precious fruits of the flowering of a free community and the good life. And ultimately peace becomes inevitable only when law and order prevail. However, the tragedy of much of our thinking has been to assume this ultimate end was either realized or shortly realizable and to tailor our words and sometimes our deeds to fit this mistaken assumption.

American lawyers whose influence on our foreign relations has been immense have confused the realities of municipal law with the hopes of international law. They have imposed on the international system burdens it could not bear. If the problem was war, it must be outlawed (the Kellogg-Briand Pact). If the peril was aggression, a legal formula proscribing and defining it was the goal — even though a United Nations Commission recently gave up this task in despair. If states trembled in a state of insecurity, reassure them with security pacts heaped one upon the other! If a state threatened the peace, pass a resolution! All these acts, so frequently a positive force in organized and integrated communities, have on balance weakened the feeble system of international order, for pacts, declarations and formulas at odds with the realities of international life tempt the lawless to reckless adventures and the law-abiding to a whole chain of emotional responses beginning with self-righteousness and indignation, shading off into disillusionment and finally into despair.

Legalists brush aside the limits of international law and the fact that it is still in a *laissez-faire* stage of development. J. L. Brierly, one of the half-dozen lawyers in the twentieth century whose writings have an enduring quality, begins his little classic *The Outlook for International Law* with the following quotation from John Morley:

> Success in politics, as in every other art, obviously before all else implies both knowledge of the material with which we have to deal, and also such concession as is necessary to the qualities of the materials. Above all, in politics we have an art in which development depends upon small modifications. . . . To hurry on after logical perfection is to show oneself ignorant of the material . . . To disdain anything short of an organic change in thought or institution is infatuation.

Then he concludes:

> . . . The part that international law can play, or the conditions on which we can hope to make it one of the pillars of a more stable world, cannot be determined by reasoning in the void or by wishful thinking. Too many people assume, generally without having given any serious thought to its character or history, that international law is and always has been a sham. Others seem to think that it is a force with inherent strength of its own, and that if we only had the sense to set the lawyers to work to draft a comprehensive code for the nations, we might live together in peace and all would be well with the world. Whether the cynic or the sciolist is the less helpful is hard to say . . .

Unhappily for us, historians will search in vain for this modesty and maturity in the legalist approach to American foreign policy. At times the very virtues of the legal approach in a society with effective legislatures and courts have become the vices of international life, e.g. case-by-case diplomacy.

Rationalism

If we have suffered from legalism, the price of liberal rationalism has been still greater. It has been said of the League and the United Nations that they represent an attempt to apply the principles of Lockean liberalism to the machinery of international order. They carry into world affairs the outlook of a liberal democratic society. One rather acute critic has noted in some rational spokesmen the tendency to believe that there can exist a card index of situations or events to be consulted for the appropriate and prescribed action whenever the event or situation turns up. Standardized procedures are valued more than prudence, the perfection of machinery more than political wisdom. Four decades of experience in transplanting liberal rationalism to the world scene have taught that this approach can be full of unforeseen difficulties.

This is not the place to discuss these problems except to suggest that where prestige of states is involved, rational discussion need not necessarily be served by open forums. Mr. Lester Pearson has written with great insight and judgment of the problems of diplomacy in a "goldfish bowl." Moreover, responsible international conduct is not the necessary result of gathering together representatives of some eighty states differing widely in size, in power, and in political, economic and cultural developments. States not affected by events and not required to sacrifice vital interests can more easily strike poses than those whose security is in jeopardy. Nations with limited interests in a question may band together to outvote states whose survival may be at stake. For example, it would be helpful to know how often uninstructed UN delegates on matters of no concern to their government throw their votes capriciously to the support of a resolution for which they would be unwilling to accept direct national responsibility. It would be useful to discover how often states turn to the United Nations when they are unwilling or unable to evolve a viable foreign policy of their own.

To ask such questions is not to detract from the vital and constructive role of the United Nations. However, if this new international institution is to survive and grow, its members must face the hard problems. They must recognize that it provides a set of methods and procedures and embodies certain fundamental aims and goals. However, it can contribute only what its members bring to its affairs in the form of policies, resources and loyalties. It will not, in the foreseeable future, be a substitute for foreign policy, and we should remind ourselves continually of this when we are tempted to drop the hard issues and unsolved problems in its lap.

One observer has argued: "When the government of the United States is asked, What is your policy for the Middle East? and it replies, We shall act through the United Nations, it has only replied to the procedural question and still owes an answer to the all-important question, What is your United Nations policy for the Middle East?" Former Secretary of State Dean Acheson, in a statement to the House Foreign Affairs Committee, declared last year:

It will not do to say that the United Nations will determine policy, make decisions, and enforce them. The United Nations is not a supranational entity with a mind, a will and a power. It is a forum, and no more than the nations which meet there. Nothing more comes out of it than is put into it. If a great nation, like the United States, looks to the United Nations to form American policy, instead of fighting in the United Nations for what the American Government believes should be done, then we have committed an unprecedented abdication of responsibility and power. We deserve what we get. If we believe that we have exhausted our responsibilities when we join in the United Nations to pass resolutions which are defied, and which we have no intention of backing up, we have engaged in a most dangerous form of self-deception.

For modern man, this view of the United Nations or similar conceptions of other cherished institutions are anathema. Rationalism's twin gods are progress and human perfectibility. For Diderot "posterity is for the philosopher what the other world is for the religious." For Comte the advance of human knowledge would eliminate human conflict by "inculcating in all men the same principles of virtue and goodness." For Condorcet progress was such a certainty that he could write his *Outline of the Progress of the Human Spirit* at a time he himself was a fugitive from the guillotine of the French Revolution.

According to the liberal or rationalist world view, evil in history is ascribable to social institutions or ignorance or some other manageable defect in the human environment. It is *not* the product of human nature. Correct the institution and man's problems are solved. The United Nations was designed to rectify the evils of traditional world politics. It was packaged and sold on this basis. Therefore when we have redress to the methods and measures by which states continue to make their way, the rationalist is offended.

Indeed, nothing has been more disabling in America's adjustment to her new world responsibilities than the over-dependence on this liberal rationalist point of view.

Sectarianism

A third source of American pride is the regnant theme of our sectarian religious outlook. Whether for New England Calvinism and the Deism of Jefferson in Virginia, or more recently for much of modernist Protestant and Catholic thought, this land has been identified as God's "American Israel." With all its pessimism about human nature, Calvinism, in the words of Edward Johnson in *Wonder Working Providence of Zion's Saviour* (1650), found here "the place where the Lord would create a new heaven and a new earth, new churches and a new commonwealth." Here the Protestant Reformation had reached its final culmination and here God had made a new beginning for mankind. The Deist's God was nature's God, and Jefferson, whose thought was a blending of religious faith and Enlightenment rationalism, could assert: "Before the establishment of the American States nothing was known to history but the man of the old world crowded within limits . . . and steeped in vices which the situation generates." Superior virtue was an outgrowth of favorable social circumstances and the distinction between Europe and America was an absolute one.

It is the religious dimension of America's pride that brings us to the crux of the problem of ethics and foreign policy. Historically, religion when it has not been used as an instrument of self-righteousness has provided the one firm base from which to view man's moral dilemma. This is true on the one hand because religion almost alone gives the resources for reconciling the majesty and misery of life. It accepts sin and salvation as a datum of life, and at least in its profoundest insights is not forever consumed in proving that through this artifact or that we can escape from the moral dilemma.

This dilemma in foreign policy is but a special, though a particularly flagrant, example of the moral dilemma facing men on all levels of social action. Man cannot help sinning when he acts in relation to his fellow men; he may be able to minimize that sinfulness but he cannot escape it. For no social action can be completely free of the taint of egotism which, as selfishness, pride, or self-deception, claims for the actor more than is his due. Man's aspiration for power over other men, which is of the essence of politics, tends toward the denial of the very core of Judeo-Christian morality. That is the historic precept of respect for man as an end in himself.

The power relation in any ultimate sense is a denial of this respect, for power at root involves the use of man as a means to the end of another man. The full pathos of this appears on the international scene where the civilizing influences of law, morality and mores are less effective than on the domestic political scene. And paradoxically, while nations take this for granted and appraise the power drives of others for what they are or worse, they blind themselves to their own aspirations, which appear as something different and nobler — justified by necessity and ethics. The Founding Fathers were more sensitive to this than some moderns, for it was John Adams who wrote:

> Power always thinks it has a great soul and vast views beyond the comprehension of the weak and that it is doing God's service when it is violating all His laws. Our passions, ambitions, avarice, love and resentment, etc., possess so much metaphysical subtlety and so much overpowering eloquence that they insinuate themselves into the understanding and the conscience and convert both to their party.

Religion has not only contributed the intellectual and spiritual resources for understanding the moral dilemma. It has also at times in Western history check-mated the extravagances of temporal authority.

The struggles between emperors and popes are only the most dramatic expression of the use of a countervailing moral and political power. Probably this resistance has been most successful when the claims of princes and rulers were made in the name of higher moral principles which could be judged by certain accepted moral and legal standards based on an objective external authority. With the passing of the *corpus Christianum* this explicit authority, at least for parts of the world, seems to have disappeared. The substitutes thus far discovered are but pale reflections, for they no longer rest on a substantial moral consensus. It is symptomatic of the times that Ambassador Dillon perhaps indiscreetly reported that the French withdrawal from Suez was due not to the pressure of moral force but to the Russian ultimatum. It may also have resulted from economic coercion and political pressure in the West.

If nations are obliged to consider their own interests, they also must attend to the interests of others. This note is struck in Number 63 of the Federalist papers:

An attention to the judgment of other nations is important to every government for two reasons: the one is, that, independently of the merits of any particular plan or measure, it is desirable on various accounts, that it should appear to other nations as the offspring of a wise and honourable policy; the second is, that in doubtful cases, particularly where the national councils may be warped by some strong passion or momentary interest, the presumed or known opinion of the impartial world may be the best guide that can be followed. What has not America lost by her want of character with foreign nations; and how many errors and follies would she not have avoided if the justice and propriety of her measures had, in every instance, been previously tried by the light in which they would probably appear to the unbiased part of mankind.

The same may be said of other nations as well. Nevertheless, plainly we are groping for new forms of ethical restraint on international conduct and for the rediscovery of old forms of international morality. In conclusion, I may perhaps suggest half a dozen areas in which this may be the case.

Ideals and Realities

First, it seems to have dawned upon even the more cynical among us that there are certain points at which expediency and morality meet. Put in negative and pragmatic terms, we recall the words of the Athenian envoys to Melos: "And it is certain that those who do not yield to their equals, who keep terms with their superiors, and are moderate towards their inferiors, on the whole best succeed." Seen more positively, the Marshall Plan and other postwar efforts are attempts to find points of coincidence between our interests and those of our allies.

Second, we note in the conduct of our relations with representatives of other states that confidence, patience, dignity and restraint comprise the cement without which the sturdiest alliance will crumble. It is too much to expect that nations will show gratitude or lasting affection for one another. Generosity is as likely to produce envy, resentment and contempt as to create goodwill, for no government based on popular support can afford to acknowledge the full scale of its independence on others. Yet there are bonds which can flourish and develop between states which show a decent respect for the dignity and interests of one another. Nor are the personal factors inconsequential. Diplomats may be honest men sent abroad "to lie in the interest of their country," yet they must return to negotiate another day.

One of the factors contributing to peace in an earlier day was the union among members of an aristocratic elite who belonged to the same club, spoke the same language, shared the same values (such as they were) and enjoyed a rough and ready assurance that everyone would keep his word. Even if it were imaginable, no one would wish today to reconstruct the past, yet this aspect of nineteenth century experience contains a profound lesson. Peace is the outcome of mutual confidence and respect. The moral basis for such confidence may be lacking today, say, with the Communist envoys, yet the breakdown of confidence among Western leaders who found they could not trust one another is a more tragic example of the price that must be paid for failure here.

Third, the pathway toward implementing and effecting the values we cherish is a tangled and tortuous road on which we can almost never see the end nor the immediate terrain we traverse. Yet, with halting steps some of our friends have quietly found their way. Austria, following the peace treaty, accepted a neutralist role that was offensive to some in the West who preferred that nations stand up and be counted. It would be hard to prove that her contribution to freedom in recent history could have been any greater had she chosen our directive. Yugoslavia has caused us special anguish, but at the same time set an example for the Satellites that in the long run may be decisive for the West. In much the same way, we face some painful choices in the times ahead. Should we insist that Arab countries accept a new security system as the price of technical assistance? Should we demand that Western Germany retain her membership in NATO even at the expense of reunification? What about our policy toward the Satellites? What is the road to freedom?

Fourth, there are the first faint signs of an emerging set of common values at the United Nations. It is tempting to associate them with those embodied in the Declaration of Independence. The discovery is reassuring that the leader of a great Asian state could share a common universe of discourse with an American President even though they may also share common illusions. The values which have meaning in the practice of the United Nations remain in any detail a mystery. Yet they perhaps involve some appreciation of the principles of justice, of consent of the governed, of peace and of social progress. We can only guess as to the context of these values in practice until we know more than we now do.

Fifth, we have ample proof, it that were needed, that in foreign affairs there is not one ethical principle, but many. Peace is a value but so are security and honor. Freedom from colonialism is a goal but so are order and safeguards against tyranny. Support for the rising colored peoples and the underprivileged of the world is a noble purpose but so is the defense of Western civilization. There is no moral touchstone that can help us judge in advance which goal should be served. Nor can we subordinate all aims to one master goal — for all time. There can be no choice but to view them from the ground on which we stand, members of a nation that we are pledged to serve and defend but whose pretenses and failings must also be judged. The ancients in such a situation called for practical wisdom, and we recall Lincoln's words that he knew no other guide than to do the best he could and would go on doing so until the end.

Sixth, the most hopeful step toward understanding is an awareness that political morality, not morality *in abstract* is what we seek. We have begun to resurrect from the rubble of false philosophies which did not stand the test of time the great perennial truths about politics and morality of which Western civilization is the record. We have learned in the aftermath of two world wars and through the agony of waging the Cold War for peace that we cannot escape the temptations and liabilities of power politics by a simple act of will. We now perceive that we must live in a brutal world and still remain civilized. We must live in an immoral world and make the best of it. Yet even at best we cannot forget that these burdens and temptations are ever with us.

Perhaps the full poignancy of the tension between ethics and foreign policy is seen in the sphere of Soviet-American relations. What do we propose to do about the signs of breakup in the Communist world? Is this a problem where ethics play no role? I think one can look at this problem through the screen of a simple and abstract point of view, a cynical point of view and one which perhaps combines wisdom and morality. The consequences for history are grave and far-reaching. A simple and abstract point of view would prompt us to pursue a policy of active, outspoken liberation. It would revive the boisterous claims and righteous affirmations of the 1952 election campaign. A cynical view would abandon East Europeans to their fate.

Practical Wisdom

Fortunately, we may have a third, less futile or dismal alternative. It has been described by one of our wisest diplomatists as that of liberation through negotiations and disengagement, rather than bloody civil or global conflict. The estimate of Soviet foreign policy on which it is based is, of course, open to debate, for the Russians may be resolved to follow a policy of oppression whenever resistance raises its head. On the other hand, they may conceive it to be in their interest to withdraw from Eastern Europe when they can do so without too much loss of face. A situation that could make this feasible might arise tomorrow, next year or a decade from now. At some time, however, they might consider that Communist prestige could be preserved if, as part of a political settlement, they yield up their claims to base troops in the Satellites for some form of military or political concession from the West, perhaps as part of the creation of a Europe-wide security system. This might conceivably involve the withdrawal of Western forces from Germany and the establishment of a neutralized zone in Central Europe.

Perhaps the prospect of a political settlement is illusory and surely any plan for neutralization would raise serious problems for the West. Yet, the states of Eastern Europe freed from the grinding control of the ever-present Red Army might over time evolve as have other neutral states in the direction of freedom. If so, a policy of restraint would bring victory to freedom over tyranny without the grave risks that other courses of action entail. Thus a prudent policy based on the dictates of practical wisdom might be in the end the most moral course we could follow.

Morality and Modern War

John Courtney Murray, S.J.

THERE ARE three distinct standpoints from which it is possible to launch a discussion of the problem of war in this strange and perilous age of ours that has yet to find its name. My initial assertion will be that it is a mistake to adopt any one of them exclusively and to carry the argument on to its logical conclusions. If this is done, the argument will end in serious difficulties.

First, one might begin by considering the possibilities of destruction and ruin, both physical and human, that are afforded by existent and projected developments in weapons technology. Here the essential fact is that there are no inherent limits to the measure of chaos that war might entail, whether by the use of nuclear arms or possibly by the methods of bacteriological and chemical warfare. Carried to its logical conclusion an argument made exclusively from this standpoint leads towards the position that war has now become a moral absurdity, not to be justified in any circumstances today. In its most respectable form this position may be called relative Christian pacifism. It does not assert that war is intrinsically evil simply because it is a use of force and violence and therefore a contravention of the Christian law of love promulgated in the Sermon on the Mount. This is absolute pacifism, an unqualified embrace of the principle of non-violence; it is more characteristic of certain Protestant sects. The relative pacifists are content to affirm that war has now become an evil that may no longer be justified, given the fact that no adequate justification can be offered for the ruinous effects of today's weapons of war. Even this position, I shall say, is not to be squared with the public doctrine of the Church.

Second, one might begin the argument by considering the present historical situation of humanity as dominated by the fact of Communism. The essential fact here is that Communism, as an ideology and as a power-system, constitutes the gravest possible menace to the moral and civilizational values that form the basis of "the West," understanding the term to designate, not a geographical entity but an

order of temporal life that has been the product of valid human dyna-
misms tempered by the spirit of the gospel. Arguing from this standpoint alone one could well posit, in all logic, the present validity of
the concept of the "holy war." Or one might come to some advocacy
of "preventive" war or "pre-emptive" war. Or one might be led to
assert that, since the adversary is completely unprincipled, and since
our duty in face of him is success in the service of civilization itself,
we must jettison the tradition of civilized warfare and be prepared to
use any means that promise success. None of these conclusions is
morally acceptable.

Third, one might choose as a starting point the fact that today there
exists a mode of international organization that is committed by its
charter to the preservation of peace by pacific settlement of international disputes. One might then argue that the validity of war even
as a legal institution has now vanished, with the passing of the hypothesis under which its legal validity was once defended, namely, the
absence of a juridically organized international community. But this
conclusion seems, at very best, too rapid, for several reasons. The
United Nations is not, properly speaking, a juridical organization
with adequate legal authority to govern in the international community. It is basically a power organization. And its decisions, like
those rendered by war itself, are natively apt to sanction injustice as
well as justice. It is not at all clear that the existence of the United
Nations, as presently constituted, definitely destroys the hypothesis
on which the validity of war as a legal institution has traditionally
been predicated. It is not at all clear that the United Nations in its
present stage of development will be able to cope justly and effectively
with the underlying causes of international conflict today or with the
particular cases of conflict that may arise.

If therefore one adopts a single standpoint of argument, and adheres
to it narrowly and exclusively, one will not find one's way to an integral and morally defensible position on the problem of war. On the
other hand, all of the three standpoints mentioned do derive from real
aspects of the problem itself. In consequence, each of them must be
exploited, if the problem is to be understood in its full scope. This is
my second assertion. It is not possible here to develop it in detail. I
shall merely suggest that there are three basic questions that must be
explored at length and in detail. Moreover, there is an order among
these questions.

The Nature of the Conflict

The first question concerns the exact nature of the conflict that is
the very definition of international life today. This is the first question

because it sets the perspectives in which all other questions must be considered.

I would note here that Pius XII fairly steadily considered the problem of war and of the weapons of war, as well as the problem of international organization, within the perspectives of what he called "the line of rupture which divides the entire international community into opposed blocs," with the result that "coexistence in truth" is not possible, since there is no common acceptance of a "norm recognized by all as morally obligatory and therefore inviolable."

I would further note that the exact nature of the international conflict is not easily and simply defined. The line of rupture is not in the first instance geographic but spiritual and moral; and it runs through the West as well as between East and West. It cannot be a question of locating on "our" side of the rupture those who are virtuous and intelligent, and, over against "us," those who are evil and morally blind. In contrast, it cannot be a question of maintaining that both East and West are so full of moral ambiguities that the line of rupture between them either does not exist or is impossible to discern.[1] In a word, one must avoid both a moral simplism and a moral scepticism in the analysis of the international conflict.

Finally, it is most important to distinguish between the mainsprings of the conflict and its concrete manifestations; or, with Sir David Kelly, between the relatively superficial facts of change in our revolutionary world and the underlying currents of change. Moreover, it is important to relate the two levels of analysis, in so far as this can be done without artificiality.

The tendency of this whole line of analysis, bearing on the nature of the international conflict, will be to furnish an answer to a complex of questions that must be answered before it is possible to consider the more narrow problems of war. What precisely are the values, in what hierarchical scale, that today are at stake in the international conflict? What is the degree of danger in which they stand? What is the mode of the menace itself—in particular, to what extent is it military, and to what extent is it posed by forms of force that are more subtle? If these questions are not carefully answered, one will have no standard against which to match the evils of war. And terror, rather than reason, will command one's judgments on the military problem. This is the danger to which the seven moral theologians in Germany pointed in their statement of May 5, 1958:

A part of the confusion among our people has its source in the fact that there is an insufficient realization of the reach of values that are endangered today, and of the hierarchical order among them, and of the degree of danger in which they stand. On the other hand, from the *Unheimlichkeit* of the technical problems [of war itself] there results a crippling of intelligence and of will.

The second basic question concerns the means that are available for insuring the defense of the values that are at stake in the international conflict. This too is a large and complex question. A whole array of means is available, in correspondence with the multi-faceted character of the conflict itself. It is a matter of understanding both the usefulness and the limitations of each of them, from spectacular "summit meetings" across the gamut to the wholly unspectacular work, say, of agricultural experts engaged in increasing the food supply of so-called underdeveloped nations. This whole complex question of the means of conflict must be fully explored antecedently to the consideration of the problem of war. The basic reason is that otherwise one can give no concrete meaning to the concept of war as *ultima ratio*. Moreover, the value of the use of force; even as *ultima ratio*, will be either overestimated or underestimated, in proportion as too much or too little value is attached to other means of sustaining and pressing the international conflict.

The third and final question concerns the *ultima ratio* itself, the arbitrament of arms as the last resort.

Here we confront the third novelty in the total problem. The present historical situation of international conflict is unique. "Never," said Pius XII, "has human history known a more gigantic disorder." The uniqueness of the disorder resides, I take it, in the unparalleled depth of its vertical dimension; it goes to the very roots of order and disorder in the world—the nature of man, his destiny, and the meaning of human history. There is a uniqueness too in the second basic question posited above, scil., the unprecedented scope of the conflict in its horizontal dimension, given the variety of means whereby it may be, and is being, waged. A special uniqueness resides too in the existence of the United Nations, as an arena of conflict indeed, but also as an instrument of peacemaking to some degree. However, the most immediately striking uniqueness comes to view when one considers the weapons for warmaking that are now in hand or within grasp.

There are two subordinate questions under this general heading of the nature of war today. The first concerns the actual state of progress (if it be progress and not a regress to barbarism) in the technology of defensive and offensive weapons of war. The second concerns the military usefulness, for any intelligible military and political purposes, of the variety of weapons developed. This latter question raises the issue of the strategic and tactical concepts that are to govern the use of these various weapons. The facts that would furnish answers to these questions are to a considerable extent hidden from the public knowledge; and, to the extent to which they are known, they have been generative of confusion in the public mind. In any case, these questions must have some reasonably satisfactory answer, if the moral problem of war is to be sensibly discussed.

Here then are three preliminary lines of inquiry to be pursued before the moral issues involved in warfare today can be dealt with, even in their generality.

A Moral Theory

An initial, not necessarily complete, exploration of these three lines is sufficient to suggest the outlines of a general moral theory. Whether Catholic thought can be content to stop with a moral theory cast simply in the mode of abstractness that characterizes the following propositions will be a further question. In any case, it is necessary in the first instance to state the general propositions. In stating them I am undertaking to render the substance of the thought of Pius XII; but there will be only a minimum of citation, and even of explanation.

1) All wars of aggression, whether just or unjust, fall under the ban of moral proscription.

I use the term "war of aggression" because Pius XII used it.[2] However, he gives no real definition of the term. It seems to stand simply as the contrary of a war of self-defense (whose definition, as we shall see, is more concrete and historical). Expressly, the Pope denies that recourse to force is "a legitimate solution for international controversies and a means for the realization of national aspirations." He seems therefore to be denying to individual states, in this historical moment, the *ius belli* (*compétence de guerre*) of the modern era of the unlimited sovereign state, scil., the right of recourse to war, on the sovereign judgment of the national state, for the vindication of legal rights and legitimate interests. The use of force is not now a moral means for the redress of violated legal rights. The justness of the cause is irrelevant; there simply is no longer a right of self-redress; no individual state may presume to take even the cause of justice into its own hands. Whatever the grievance of the state may be, and however objectionable it may find the status quo, warfare undertaken on the sovereign decision of the national state is an immoral means for settling the grievance and for altering existent conditions.

If this be the correct interpretation of Pius XII's thought, it will be seen that an important modification of the modern Scholastic doctrine of war has been made.[3] The reasons for making it derive from two of the above-mentioned lines of inquiry. First, the immeasurably increased violence of war today disqualifies it as an apt and proportionate means for the resolution of international conflicts and even for the redress of just grievances. Second, to continue to admit the right of war, as an attribute of national sovereignty, would seriously block the progress of the international community to that mode of juridical organization which Pius XII regarded as the single means for the outlawry of all war, even defensive war. In this connection, it would be well to note the observation of M. Gabriel Matagrin:

The preoccupation of Pius XII seems to be much less to determine what might be just in the actual situation of an unorganized humanity than to promote a genuine international organization capable of eliminating war, because the juridical reason for the right of war is the unorganized state of international life.

Pius XII clearly stigmatized "aggressive" war as "a sin, an offense, and an outrage against the majesty of God." Should this sin in the moral order also be transposed into a crime in the legal order? Pius expressly said that "modern total war, and ABC warfare in particular," when it is not stringently in self-defense, "constitutes a crime worthy of the most severe national and international sanctions."[4] I should think that the same recommendation would apply to less violent forms of "'aggressive" warfare. However, Pius XII did not enter the formidable technical problem, how this legal transcription of a moral principle is to be effected. The problem has hitherto been insoluble.

2) A defensive war to repress injustice is morally admissible both in principle and in fact.

In its abstractness this principle has always formed part of Catholic doctrine; by its assertion the Church finds a way between false extremes of pacifism and bellicism. Moreover, the assertion itself, far from being a contradiction of the basic Christian will to peace, is the strongest possible affirmation of this will. There is no peace without justice, law, and order. But "law and order have need at times of the powerful arm of force." And the precept of peace itself requires that peace be defended against violation:

The precept of peace is of divine right. Its purpose is to protect the goods of humanity, inasmuch as they are the goods of the Creator. Among these goods there are some of such importance for the human community that their defense against an unjust aggression is without doubt fully justified.

There is nothing new about these assertions. What is important is their reiteration by Pius XII in today's highly concrete historical context of international conflict. The reiteration of the right of defensive war derives directly from an understanding of the conflict and from a realization that nonviolent means of solution may fail. The Church is obliged to confront the dreadful alternative: "the absolute necessity of self-defense against a very grave injustice that touches the community, that cannot be impeded by other means, that nevertheless must be impeded on pain of giving free field in international relations to brutal violence and lack of conscience."

The harshness of statement in that last phrase marks a new note that came only late (in 1953) into the Pius XII's utterances. I think it fair to say that the gentle Pope of Peace brought himself only with great reluctance, and under the unrelenting pressure of events, to focus on the instant possibility of war, as generated by the essential ethos of the Communist system: "brutal violence and lack of conscience." The focus becomes even sharper after the events in Hungary, and in the light of the Soviet threat to use atomic weapons in Europe if the French and English adventure in Suez were not terminated. These words from the Christmas message, 1956, need to be quoted:

The actual situation, which has no equivalent in the past, ought nevertheless to be clear to everyone. There is no further room for doubt about the purposes and the methods that lie behind tanks when they crash resoundingly across frontiers to distribute death and to force civilized peoples to a form of life that they distinctly abhor. When all the possible stages of negotiation and mediation are bypassed, and when the threat is made to use atomic arms to obtain concrete demands, whether these are justified or not, it becomes clear that, in present circumstances, there may come into existence in a nation a situation in which all hope of averting war becomes vain. In this situation a war of efficacious self-defense against unjust attacks, which is undertaken with hope of success, cannot be considered illicit.

One can almost feel the personal agony behind the labored sentences (more tortured in the original than in the translation). The agony, and utterance itself, are born of the Pope's reluctant realization that, as he had said earlier that same year, there are rulers "who except themselves from the elementary laws of human society." The tragedy in the situation is accented by his further vision that the people over whom these rulers stand "cannot but be the first to feel the need once more to form part of the human family."

The Conditions of War

There is no indication that this reaffirmation of the traditional principle of defensive warfare, to which Pius XII was driven by the brutal facts of international life, extends only to wars conducted by so-called conventional arms. On the contrary, the Pope extended it explicitly, not only to atomic warfare but even to ABC warfare. One cannot therefore uphold the simple statement that atomic war as such, without further qualifications, is morally unjustifiable, or that all use of atomic weapons in war is, somehow in principle, evil.

There are, however, conditions. The basic condition has been stated: "One cannot, even in principle, raise the question of the liceity of ABC warfare except in the case in which it must be judged indispensable for self-defense in the conditions indicated." These further conditions are simply those found in traditional doctrine. But each of them was sharpened to a fresh stringency by Pius XII in the light of the horrors of destruction and death now possible in war.

Briefly, the war must be "imposed by an obvious and extremely grave injustice." No minor infraction of rights will suffice, much less any question of national prestige. The criterion is high, namely, that the nation should "in all truth have been unjustly attacked and menaced in its vital rights."

The second condition is the familiar principle of war as always the *ultima ratio*. Moreover, it is today the extremity of means in a unique sense, given, on the one hand, the new means of negotiation and arbitration presently available, and on the other, the depths of manifold agony into which recourse to the *ultima ratio* may now plunge humanity as a whole.

The third condition is also familiar, the principle of proportion. It invokes a twofold consideration.

First, consideration must be given to the proportion between the damage suffered in consequence of the perpetration of a grave injustice, and the damages that would be let loose by a war to repress the injustice. Pius XII laid some stress on the fact that the comparison here must be between realities of the moral order, and not sheerly between two sets of material damage and loss. The standard is not a "eudaemonism and utilitarianism of materialist origin," which would avoid war merely because it is uncomfortable, or connive at injustice simply because its repression would be costly. The question of proportion must be evaluated in more tough-minded fashion, from the viewpoint of the hierarchy of strictly moral values. It is not enough simply to consider the "sorrows and evils that flow from war." There are greater evils than the physical death and destruction wrought in war. And there are human goods of so high an order that immense sacrifices may have to be borne in their defense. By these insistences Pius XII transcended the vulgar pacifism of sentimentalist and materialist inspiration that is so common today.

Second, Pius XII requires an estimate of another proportion, between the evils unleashed by war and what he calls "the solid probability of success" in the violent repression of unjust action. The specific attention he gives to this condition was immediately prompted by his awareness of the restiveness of the peoples who are presently captive under unjust rule and who are tempted to believe, not without reason, that their rescue will require the use of force. This condition of probable success is not, of course, simply the statesman's classical political calculus of success. It is the moral calculus that is enjoined in the traditional theory of rebellion against tyranny. Furthermore, Pius XII was careful to warn that in applying this moral calculus regard must be had for the tinderbox character of our world in which a spark may set off a conflagration.

A fourth principle of traditional theory is also affirmed by Pius XII, the principle of limitation in the use of force. It may be a matter of some surprise that he gave so little emphasis and development to it, at least in comparison to the preponderant place that the problem seems to have assumed in the minds of other theorists, Catholic and non-Catholic. There is one formal text. After asserting the legitimacy of "modern total warfare," that is, ABC warfare, under the set of stringent conditions already stated, he added:

Even then every effort must be made and every means taken to avoid it, with the aid of international covenants, or to set limits to its use precise enough so that its effects will be confined to the strict exigencies of defense. In any case, when the employment of this means entails such an extension of the evil that it entirely escapes from the control of man, its use ought to be rejected as immoral. Here it is no longer a question of defense against injustice and of the necessary safeguard of legitimate possessions, but of the annihilation, pure and simple, of all human life within its radius of action. This is not permitted on any account.

This is a very general statement indeed. And it takes the issue at its extreme, where it hardly needs statement, since the moral decision cannot fail to be obvious. Who would undertake to defend on any grounds, including military grounds, the annihilation of all human life within the radius of action of an ABC war that "entirely escapes from the control of man?"[5] We have here an affirmation, if you will, of the rights of innocence, of the distinction between combatant and noncombatant. But it is an extremely broad statement.

One finds in the earlier utterances of the Pope, when he was demonstrating the first thesis in the traditional doctrine of war (that war is an evil, the fruit of sin), much advertence to "massacres of innocent victims," the killing of "infants with their mothers, the ill and infirm and aged," etc. These tragedies stand high on the list of the evils of war. In the text cited there is no explicit return to this principle of the rights of innocence when it is formally a question of total nuclear war and the use of nuclear weapons. If there is an anomaly here, the reason for it may lie in the fact that the Pope was forcing himself to face the desperate case. And in desperate cases, in which conscience is perplexed, the wise moralist is chary of the explicit and the nice, especially when the issue, as here, is one of social and not individual morality. In such cases hardly more than a *Grenzmoral* is to be looked for or counseled. In fact, the whole Catholic doctrine of war is hardly more than a *Grenzmoral*, an effort to establish on a minimal basis of reason a form of human action, the making of war, that remains always fundamentally irrational.[6]

Two further propositions in the general theory must be mentioned. The first concerns the legitimacy of defense preparations on the part of individual states. Their legitimacy is founded on two actual facts of international life. First, at the moment there does not exist what Pius XII constantly looked forward to as the solution of the problem of war, namely, a constituted international authority possessing a monopoly of the use of armed force in international affairs. Second, there does exist the threat of "brutal violence and lack of conscience." In this factual situation, "the right to be in a posture of defense cannot be denied, even today, to any state." Here again the principle is extremely general; it says nothing about the morality of this or that configuration of the defense establishment of a given nation. The statement does not morally validate everything that goes on at Cape Canaveral or at Los Alamos.

Finally, the Pope of Peace disallowed the validity of conscientious objection. The occasion was the controversy on the subject, notably in Germany, where the resonances of a sort of anticipatory *Fronterlebnis* were giving an alarming impulse to pacifist movements. Particularly in question was the deposit of nuclear weapons on German soil as part of the NATO defense establishment. The Pope's judgment was premised on the legitimacy of the government, the democratic openness of its decisions, and the extremity of the historical necessity for making such defense preparations as would be adequate in the circumstances. He concluded that such a government is "acting in a manner that is not immoral" and that "a Catholic citizen may not make appeal to his own conscience as ground for refusing to give his services and to fulfill duties fixed by law." This duty of armed service to the state, and this right of the state to arm itself for self-defense, are, he added, the traditional doctrine of the Church, even in latter days under Leo XIII and Benedict XV, when the problem of armaments and conscription put a pressing issue to the Christian conscience.

The Relevance of the Doctrine

The foregoing may do as a statement, at least in outline, of the traditional doctrine on war in the form and with the modifications given it by the authority of the Church today. It is not particularly difficult to make this sort of statement. The difficulty chiefly begins after the statement has been made. Not that objections are raised, at least not in Catholic circles, against the doctrine itself as stated. What is queried is the usefulness of the doctrine, its relevance to the concrete actualities of our historical moment. I shall conclude with some comments on this issue.

I think that the tendency to query the uses of the Catholic doctrine on war initially rises from the fact that it has for so long not been used, even by Catholics. That is, it has not been made the basis for a sound critique of public policies and as a means for the formation of a right public opinion. The classic example, of course, was the policy of "unconditional surrender" during the last war. This policy clearly violated the requirement of the "right intention" that has always been a principle in the traditional doctrine of war. Yet no sustained criticism was made of the policy by Catholic spokesmen. Nor was any substantial effort made to clarify by moral judgment the thickening mood of savage violence that made possible the atrocities of Hiroshima and Nagasaki. I think it is true to say that the traditional doctrine was irrelevant during World War II. This is no argument against the traditional doctrine. The Ten Commandments do not lose their imperative relevance by reason of the fact that they are violated. But there is place for an indictment of all of us who failed to make the tradition relevant.

The initial relevance of the traditional doctrine today lies in its value as the solvent of false dilemmas. Our fragmentized culture seems to be the native soil of this fallacious and dangerous type of thinking. There are, first of all, the two extreme positions, a soft sentimental pacifism and a cynical hard realism. Both of these views, which are also "feelings," are formative factors in the moral climate of the moment. Both of them are condemned by the traditional doctrine as false and pernicious. The problem is to refute by argument the false antinomy between war and morality that they assert in common, though in different ways. The further and more difficult problem is to purify the public climate of the miasma that emanates from each of them and tends to smother the public conscience.

A second false dilemma has threatened to dominate the argument on national defense in Germany. It sloganized itself thus: "Lieber rot als tot." It has made the same threat in England, where it has been developed in a symposium by twenty-three distinguished Englishmen entitled, *The Fearful Choice: A Debate on Nuclear Policy*. The choice, of course, is between the desperate alternatives, either universal atomic death or complete surrender to Communism. The Catholic mind, schooled in the traditional doctrine of war and peace, rejects the dangerous fallacy involved in this casting up of desperate alternatives. Hidden beneath the fallacy is an abdication of the moral reason and a craven submission to some manner of technological or historical determinism.

It is not, of course, that the traditional doctrine rejects the extreme alternatives as possibilities. Anything in history is possible. Moreover, on grounds of the moral principle of proportion the doctrine supports the grave recommendation of the greatest theorist of war in modern times, von Klausewitz: "We must therefore familiarize ourselves with the thought of an honorable defeat." Conversely, the doctrine condemns the hysteria that swept Washington in August when the Senate voted, eighty-two to two, to deny government funds to any person or institution who ever proposes or actually conducts any study regarding the "surrender of the government of the U.S."[7] "Losing," said von Klausewitz, "is a function of winning," thus stating in his own military idiom the moral calculus prescribed by traditional moral doctrine. The moralist agrees with the military theorist that the essence of a military situation is uncertainty. And when he requires, with Pius XII, a solid probability of success as a moral ground for a legitimate use of arms, he must reckon with the possibility of failure and be prepared to accept it. But this is a moral decision, worthy of a man and of a civilized nation. It is a free, morally motivated, and responsible act, and therefore it inflicts no stigma of dishonor. It is not that "weary resignation," condemned by Pius XII, which is basic to the inner attitude of the theorists of the desperate alternatives, no matter which one they argue for or accept.

On the contrary, the single inner attitude which is nourished by the traditional doctrine is a will to peace, which, in the extremity, bears within itself a will to enforce the precept of peace by arms. But this will to arms is a moral will; for it is identically a will to justice. It is formed under the judgment of reason. And the first alternative contemplated by reason, as it forms the will to justice through the use of force, is not the possibility of surrender, which would mean the victory of injustice. This is the ultimate extremity, beyond even the extremity of war itself. Similarly, the contrary alternative considered by reason is not a general annihilation, even of the enemy. This would be worse than injustice; it would be sheer folly. In a word, a debate on nuclear policy that is guided by the traditional doctrine of war does not move between the desperate alternatives of surrender or annihilation. If it means simply an honorable defeat, surrender may be morally tolerable; but it is not to be tolerated save on a reasonable calculus of proportionate moral costs. In contrast, annihilation is on every count morally intolerable; it is to be averted at all costs, that is, at the cost of every effort, in every field, that the spirit of man can put forth.

Precisely here the proximate and practical value, use, and relevance of the traditional doctrine begin to appear. Its remote value may lie in its service as a standard of casuistry on various kinds of war.[8] Its remote value certainly lies in its power to form the public conscience and to clarify the climate of moral opinion in the midst of today's international conflict. But its proximate value is felt at the crucial point where the moral and political orders meet. Primarily, its value resides in its capacity to set the right terms for rational debate on public policies bearing on the problem of war and peace in this age,[9] characterized by international conflict and by advanced technology. This is no mean value, if you consider the damage that is being presently done by argument carried on in the wrong terms.

The traditional doctrine disqualifies as irrelevant and dangerous the false dilemmas of which I have spoken. It also rejects the notion that the big problem is to "abolish war" or "ban the bomb." It is true that the traditional doctrine on war looks forward to its own disappearance as a chapter in Catholic moral theology. The effort of the moral reason to fit the use of violence into the objective order of justice is paradoxical enough; but the paradox is heightened when this effort takes place at the interior of the Christian religion of love. In any case, the principles of the doctrine themselves make clear that our historical moment is not destined to see a moral doctrine of war discarded as unnecessary. War is still the possibility, not to be exorcised even by prayer and fasting. The Church does not look immediately to the abolition of war. Her doctrine still seeks to fulfill its triple traditional function: to condemn war as evil, to limit the evils it entails, and to humanize its conduct as far as possible.

"Limited War"

In the light of the traditional doctrine and in the no less necessary light of the facts of international life and technological development today, what are the right terms for argument on public policy? These are readily reached by a dialectical process, an alternation between principle and fact. The doctrine asserts, in principle, that force is still the *ultima ratio* in human affairs, and that its use in extreme circumstances may be morally obligatory *ad repellendam injuriam*. The facts assert that today this *ultima ratio* takes the form of nuclear force, whose use remains possible and may prove to be necessary, lest a free field be granted to brutal violence and lack of conscience. The doctrine asserts that the use of nuclear force must be limited, the principle of limitation being the exigencies of legitimate defense against injustice. Thus the terms of public debate are set in two words, "limited war." All other terms of argument are fanciful or fallacious. (I assume here that the argument is to be cast primarily in political terms, only secondarily in military terms; for armed force is never more than a weapon of policy, a weapon of last resort.)

I shall not attempt to construct the debate itself. But two points may be made. First, there are those who say that the limitation of nuclear war, or any war, is today impossible, for a variety of reasons—technical, political, etc. In the face of this position, the traditional doctrine simply asserts again, "The problem today is limited war." But notice that the assertion is on a higher plane than that of sheer fact. It is a moral proposition, or better, a moral imperative. In other words, since nuclear war may be a necessity, it must be made a possibility. Its possibility must be created. And the creation of its possibility requires a work of intelligence, and the development of manifold action, on a whole series of policy levels—political (foreign and domestic), diplomatic, military, technological, scientific, fiscal, etc., with the important inclusion of the levels of public opinion and public education. To say that the possibility of limited war cannot be created by intelligence and energy, under the direction of a moral imperative, is to succumb to some sort of determinism in human affairs.

My second point is that the problem of limited war would seem to require solution in two stages. One stage consists in the construction of a sort of "model" of the limited war. This is largely a problem in conceptual analysis. Its value consists in making clear the requirements of limited war in terms of policy on various levels.[10] Notably it makes clear that a right order must prevail among policies. It makes clear, for instance, that the limitation of war becomes difficult or impossible if fiscal policy assumes the primacy over armament policy, or if armament policy assumes the primacy over military policy, or if military policy assume the primacy over foreign policy in the political sense. The second stage is even more difficult. It centers on a *quaestio facti*. The fact is that the international conflict, in its ideological as in its power dimension, comes to concrete expression in certain localized situations, each of which has its own peculiarities. The question then is, where and under what circumstances is the irruption of violence possible or likely, and how is the limitation of the conflict to be effected in these circumstances, under regard of political intentions, as controlling of military necessities *in situ*. The answer to this question is what is meant by the formulation of policy. Policy is the hand of the practical reason set firmly upon the course of events. Policy is what a nation does in this or that given situation. In the concreteness of policy, therefore, the assertion of the possibility of limited war is finally made, and made good. Policy is the meeting-place of the world of power and the world of morality, in which there takes place the concrete reconciliation of the duty of success that rests upon the statesman and the duty of justice that rests upon the civilized nation that he serves.

Toward a Politico-Moral Science

I am thus led to one final comment on the problem of war. It may be that the classical doctrine of war needs more theoretical elaboration in order to relate it more effectively to the unique conflict that agitates the world today, in contrast with the older historical conflicts upon which the traditional doctrine sought to bear, and by which in turn it was shaped. In any case, another work of the reflective intelligence and study is even more badly needed. I shall call it a politico-moral analysis of the divergent and particular conflict-situations that have arisen or are likely to arise in the international scene as problems in themselves and as manifestations of the underlying crisis of our times. It is in these particular situations that war actually becomes a problem. It is in the midst of their dense materiality that the *quaestio iuris* finally rises. To answer it is the function of the moralist, the professional or the citizen moralist. His answer will never be more than an act of prudence, a practical judgment informed by principle. But he can give no answer at all to the *quaestio iuris* until the *quaestio facti* has been answered. From the point of view of the problem of war and morality the same need appears that has been descried elsewhere in what concerns the more general problem of politics and morality. I mean the need of a far more vigorous cultivation of politico-moral science, with close attention to the enormous impact of technological developments on the moral order as well as on the political order.

The whole concept of force has undergone a rapid and radical transformation, right in the midst of history's most acute political crisis. One consequence of these two related developments was emphasized by Panel Two, "International Security: The Military Aspect," of the Special Studies Project of the Rockefeller Brothers Fund: "The over-all United States strategic concept lags behind developments in technology and in the world political situation." This vacuum of military doctrine greatly troubled the members of the panel. But I know from my own association with the Special Studies Project that they were even more troubled by another vacuum in contemporary thought, scil., the absence of an over-all political-moral doctrine with regard to the uses of force. This higher doctrine is needed to give moral sense and political direction to a master strategic concept. "Power without a sense of direction," they said, "may drain life of its meaning, if it does not destroy humanity altogether." This sense of direction cannot be found in technology; of itself, technology tends toward the exploitation of scientific possibilities simply because they are possibilities. Power can be invested with a sense of direction only by moral principles. It is the function of morality to command the use of power, to forbid it, to limit it; or, more in general, to define the ends for which power may or must be used and to judge the circumstances of its use. But moral principles cannot effectively impart this sense of direction to power until they have first, as it were, passed through the order of politics; that is, until they have first become incarnate in public policy. It is public policy in all its varied concretions that must be "moralized" (to use an abused word in its good sense). This is the primary need of the moment. For my part, I am not confident that it is being met.

Notes

¹ This view exists in a number of forms. There is, for instance, the contextualistic morality of Prof. Hans Morgenthau, revealed in his Introduction to E. Lefever, *Ethics and United States Foreign Policy* (New York, 1957). His basic view, never quite brought to philosophical explicitness, seems to be that all moralities are purely "national"; they cannot be subjected to judgment in terms of universal principles. There are also various types of neo-Lutheran theory which see evil as radical, ubiquitous, and inextricable in all human action. In quite a different category there are those who are confused, as well they might be in this age, by the problem of the relations between morality and power; cf., for instance, an intelligent and earnest thinker, Mr. Kenneth Thompson, "Moral Choices in Foreign Affairs," *Worldview* (Sept. 1958). One of today's characteristically confused debates goes on between the "realists" and the "idealists." One school holds that politics is wholly a matter of morality; the other maintains that politics is wholly a matter of power. Both are wrong. But they agree on a disastrous tenet, that between morality and power a great gulf is fixed.

² The concept of aggression is undoubtedly a major source of bedevilment in the whole modern discussion of the problem of war. The recent lengthy attempt to reach a satisfactory definition resulted in failure; cf. Julius Stone, *Aggression and World Order* (Berkeley, Calif., 1958). The concept, I think, is a typically modern one; older theories more characteristically spoke in terms of "injustice." I venture the opinion, merely as an opinion, that the modern prominence of the concept derives from the modern theory that there may be "justice" on both sides of a conflict. Hence the issue of "justice" is proximately decided by "aggression," scil., which nation's armed forces first cross the borders of the other nation. But this military transcription of a basically moral concept is of little, if any, use in our contemporary situation, with its two unique new features. First, today's weapons systems make possible the employment of force at enormous distances without concern for the space between; the concept of "crossing borders" no longer means anything. Second, in view of the striking power of these weapons systems the nation that initiates the attack ("crosses the border") can render the opposing nation defenseless, incapable of exerting a right of self-defense. Consequently, aggression in the older military-moral sense has ceased to be a standard by which to decide the issue of justice in war; it has become simply a technique by which to decide the issue of success. The use of force can no longer be linked to the moral order merely by the concept of aggression, in the modern understanding of the concept. There is urgent need for a thorough moral re-examination of the basic American policy that "we will never shoot first." Under contemporary circumstances, viewed in their entirety, is this really a *dictamen rationis?*

³ For a statement of the modern Scholastic theory, and a critique of it, cf. A. Vanderpol, *La doctrine scolastique du droit de guerre* (Paris, 1919). It would be interesting to have a new study made of this book, which is not without its bias. I also suggest another question. Pius XII seems relatively unconcerned to give an exact definition of aggression. He seems to want to move back into the center of Catholic thought the older, broader Augustinian concept of *causa iusta*. War is not simply a problem of aggression; more fundamentally it is a problem of injustice. It is the concept of justice that links the use of force with the moral order. Would it be correct to say that Pius XII represents an effort to return Catholic thought to more traditional and more fruitful premises? If there is a way out of

the present impasse created by the outworn concept of aggression in the modern sense, it can only be a return to the concept of justice. There would still remain the formidable moral and legal problem of translating *iustitia* into *to iustum*. In politico-moral terms this is today the problem of what is called policy. As a moral problem, war is ultimately a problem of policy, and therefore a problem of social morality. Policy is made by society, especially in a democratic context; and society bears the moral responsibility for the policy made. As a problem in justice, the problem of war is put to the People, in whom, according to good medieval theory, the sense of justice resides, and from whom the moral judgment, direction, and correction of public policy must finally come. As a moral problem in the use of force, war is not simply, or even primarily, a problem for the generals, the State Department, the technologists, the international lawyers. Here, if anywhere, "the People shall judge." This is their responsibility, to be discharged before the shooting starts, by an active concern with the moral direction of national policy. My impression is that this duty in social morality is being badly neglected in America at the moment.

4 Allocution to the World Medical Congress, Sept. 30, 1954; *AAS* 46 (1954) 589. The tradition maintains that the highest value in society is the inviolability of the order of rights and justice. If this order disintegrates or is successfully defied, society is injured in its most vital structure and end. Peace itself is the work of justice; and therefore peace is not compatible with impunity for the evil of injustice. It is pertinent to emphasize these truths in an age in which economic and material values have come to assume the primacy.

5 Around this time (1954) there was a lot of loose and uninformed talk about weapons that really would go beyond human control; there was talk, for instance, of the so-called "cobalt bomb" and its "unlimited" powers of radioactive contamination. It is impossible to know what were the sources of the Pope's scientific information. To my knowledge, he never adverts to the qualitative distinction and radical discontinuity between low-kiloton and high-megaton weapons. The former are not necessarily weapons of mass destruction. Even the latter do not "escape from the control of man"; their blast and fire effects, and their atmosphere-contamination effects, have been fairly exactly measured.

6 I am not for a moment suggesting, of course, that the principle of the rights of innocent life has become in any sense irrelevant to the contemporary problem of war. Still less am I suggesting that Pius XII modified the traditional doctrine in this respect. I am merely noting what I noted, scil., that this principle receives no sharp emphasis, to say the least, in his doctrine. There may be other reasons for this than the one that I tentatively suggested in the text above.

7 When "Washington" thinks of "surrender," it apparently can think only of "'unconditional" surrender. Thus does the demonic specter of the past hover over us, as a still imperious *rector harum tenebrarum*. Thus patriotism, once the last refuge of the scoundrel, now has become the first refuge of the fool. It is folly not to foresee that the United States may be laid in ruins by a nuclear attack; the folly is compounded by a decision not to spend any money on planning what to do after that not impossible event. There is no room today for the heroic romanticism of the apocryphal utterance, "The Old Guard dies but never surrenders." Even Victor Hugo did not put this line on the lips of Cambronne; he simply had him say, "Merde." For all its vulgarity, this was a far more sensible remark in the circumstances. For my part, I am impressed by the cold rationality of Soviet military

thought as described by Raymond L. Garthoff, *Soviet Strategy in the Nuclear Age* (New York, 1958): "The fundamental Soviet objectives which determine political and military strategies may be concisely summarized in one: Advance the power of the Soviet Union in whatever ways are most expedient so long as the survival of the Soviet power itself is not endangered" (p. 5). For the Soviet Union survival is not an issue in war; for us it is the only issue. In Soviet thought military action is subordinate to political aims; with us military action creates its own aims, and there is only one, "victory," scil., unconditional surrender. "The Soviet strategic concept, in the thermonuclear era as before, is founded on the belief that the primary objective of military operations is the destruction of hostile military forces, and not the annihilation of the economic and population resources of the enemy. Thus contemporary American views often diverge sharply from this traditional stand" (pp. 71-72). Finally, Soviet policy envisages the "long war" even after a massive exchange of thermonuclear weapons (pp. 87-91). With us, if deterrence fails, and this massive exchange occurs, that is the end; we have no policy after that, except stubbornly to maintain that it is up to the enemy, and not us, to surrender—unconditionally. There is no little irony in the fact that the Communist enemy seems to understand better than we do the traditional doctrine on the uses of force.

⁸ I use the subjunctive because I do not know how many wars in history would stand up under judgment by the traditional norms, or what difference it made at the time whether they did or not.

⁹ I am not sure that one should talk today in these categories, "war and/or peace," leaving unexamined the question just what their validity is as moral and political categories. The basic fallacy is to suppose that "war" and "peace" are two discontinuous and incommensurable worlds of existence and universes of discourse, each with its own autonomous set of rules, "peace" being the world of "morality" and "war" being the world of "evil," in such wise that there is no evil as long as there is peace and no morality as soon as there is war. This is a common American assumption. Moreover, it would help greatly to attend to the point made by Mr. Philip C. Jessup that we live today in an "intermediate state" between peace and war; he contends that, "if one were accustomed to the idea of intermediacy, it can be argued that the likelihood of 'total war' could be diminished . . . The basic question is whether our concepts, our terminology, our law have kept pace with the evolution of international affairs" (*American Journal of International Law* 48 [1954] 98ff.).

¹⁰ The most significant attempt in this direction was made by Henry A. Kissinger, *Nuclear Weapons and Foreign Policy* (New York, 1957). The validity of his theories on limited war (chaps. 5-7) has been contested on technical and other grounds. The more permanent value of the book may lie in its convincing argument that a vacuum of doctrine, military as well as moral, lies at the heart of the whole vast defense establishment of the U.S. (cf. chap. 12 and *passim*).

Religion and International Responsibility

Robert Gordis

A T THE OUTSET of a discussion of religion and international responsibility, it may be useful to recall the several major approaches
current with regard to the relevance of the ethical content of the Judeo-
Christian heritage to the foreign policy of nations. The oldest and most
widely held and practiced is the one least often articulated. It is that
there is no connection between religious ideals and international affairs.
For this school of thought, foreign policy is exclusively an instrument
for advancing the interests of the state, whose leaders are obligated to
use all the means at their disposal, with no concern for ethical considerations. The classic expression of this viewpoint is to be found in Machia-
velli's *The Prince*, which seeks to train the ruler to manipulate public
affairs in accordance with the practical needs of the hour. Centuries
later, Karl Marx, who defined religion as the opiate of the people, together with his associate, Friedrich Engels, sought to buttress the view
that ethical standards are the instrument by which religion attempts to
enforce obedience to the status quo upon the oppressed groups in
society. It therefore follows that ethical considerations are merely a
façade or a tool, possessing no genuine validity of their own.

Hence, the double-talk of Communism, which employs such terms
as "democracy" "freedom" and "peace" in its vocabulary as conscious
instruments for achieving non-moral ends. And if a philosophy of ethics
is desiderated, "the good" is defined in a dictatorship, whatever its hue
— black, brown or red — as whatever advances the interest of the state,
the race, or the party. In democratic lands, those who adopt this view
of our problem remind us first that politics is the art of the possible, and
second, that in our grossly imperfect world, the possible is always evil.

The Naive Liberal

At the opposite pole from this cynical approach is the naive idealism of the liberal during the pre-World War II period. There is a current tendency which must be guarded against, to over-simplify the liberal position and exaggerate its naivete. Yet it remains true that fundamentally this attitude derived from a strong optimism with regard to human nature and its capacities and, as a corollary, from the belief in virtually automatic progress in history, moving inevitably toward greater justice and peace in international affairs. Hence the liberal placed great reliance upon treaties and covenants openly arrived at, labored for international agreements for limited or total disarmament and greeted with enthusiasm the establishment of the United Nations as the possible instrument for an effective international order.

The ideological sources of the liberal faith are to be found in eighteenth century secular humanism, expressed for example in Rousseau's faith in the fundamental goodness of man, which has been corrupted by the artificialities of civilization, and in Condorcet's doctrine of the perfectibility of human nature. This interpretation of man and of history was reinforced for religious believers by the liberal interpretation of the Judeo-Christian Scriptures. The prophetic concept of history was utilized to suggest that the events of human experience are no meaningless succession of accidental occurrences, no mere aggregation of physical forces and material powers, but the reflection of God's will, utilizing men and nations for the consummation of His purpose. A figure as distant from the philosophers of the Age of Reason as Hegel declared that *Weltgeschichte ist Weltgericht*. When the Kingdom of God was interpreted in purely secular terms, the congruence of the rational humanism of the eighteenth century and the religious idealism of the Scriptures seemed complete.

The idealism of the political liberal, whether derived from secular or from religious sources, suffered major setbacks in the mid-twentieth century. The "war to end war" and "make the world safe for democracy" succeeded in neither objective. The Second World War marked a desperate attempt by the free nations to destroy the manifestations of bestiality deeply rooted in human nature, which, according to liberal optimism, had ceased to exist long ago.

The Fascist and Nazi varieties of totalitarianism were overthrown, but many of their features were absorbed into the Communist state-system, which has proved at least as aggressive and far more successful than Hitler and Mussolini in effectively destroying the hopes of achieving the Four Freedoms for an ever-increasing segment of the world population, at least for the present and the foreseeable future.

The "Realist"

Confronted by the collapse of the liberal vision, many of its former devotees have relapsed into cynical disillusion. Another alternative has, however, found a wide response — that of the "realists" in politics. Many of them are deeply religious spirits and find in the Bible the source both of their ethical standards and of their conception of human nature. Basing themselves on the doctrine of "original sin," they declare that man's weaknesses are the basic constituents of his nature, so that all his activities are at worst evil and at best morally ambiguous. Since the vices of pride, self-assertion, and the will to power inevitably find expression in the area of political activity, politics cannot be reasonably expected to obey the dictates of ethics — the best that can be hoped for is the choice of the least evil of alternatives. Any effort to invoke moral principles in politics must lead to defeat, if not to disaster, because the nature of reality does not conform to the demands of the ethical conscience. Thus Ernest Lefever, in his illuminating volume *Ethics and United States Foreign Policy*, begins with an illustration to which he returns several times:

If December 7, 1941, will live on in American history as a 'day of infamy', November 2, 1956, may well be remembered as a day of irony. On that day our government joined with its arch enemy, the Soviet Union, and Egypt, her willing tool in the Middle East, in condemning our two closest and staunchest allies, Great Britain and France. This act, which helped to destroy the moral and political position of Britain and France in the Mediterranean World, was done in the name of morality. Herein lies its irony.

Obviously, the "realist's" position is far superior to the approach of the unabashed cynic, who begins by surrendering all ethical ideals and thus helps make of human society a perilous jungle in which dangerously armed wild beasts are loose. This "realist" approach is superior, too, to that of the naive idealist, who helps make democracy an easy prey to its undemocratic enemies, and unconsciously furthers the destruction of the ideals he cherishes.

The world-view of the "realist" is compounded in large measure of the attitudes of crisis-theology and of the temper of existentalism. In emphasizing the limitations of reason, the reality of sin and the ambiguities of human activity, and in rejecting the superficial notion of automatic progress in society, these contemporary schools have performed an exceedingly important function. But like most reactions, this reaction to "liberal theology" has gone too far. Reinhold Niebuhr's personal and intellectual integrity has led him to admit that "he has tended to overestimate the frustration which sin imposes and to underestimate the creative possibilities for man in a world which is still God's world, despite the sin and ambiguity of life lived within it."

Unfortunately, this degree of insight is not always matched by those who regard themselves as Niebuhr's disciples. Thus I believe that the "realist" approach to politics, in spite of its virtues, suffers from three basic drawbacks that must be reckoned with.

The Errors of "Realism"

1) Though this is not the intention of its advocates, who are deeply dedicated to idealistic ends, this "realist" approach opens the door to a purely amoral foreign policy. In conceding, nay, underscoring the sinful character of human motivation and action, and in insisting that ethical principles cannot be utilized as instruments of national policy, this school of thought in effect is left only with purely pragmatic considerations as the determining factor in international affairs. Granted these assumptions, what check can be placed upon statesmen and diplomats who declare that their only legitimate purpose is the preservation of the interests of their country and state and who find that the only course that "works" is one unencumbered by idealistic shibboleths?

2) The conception of human nature held by the "realistic" school is not the only possible view. To be sure, in much of the contemporary literature on the subject, it is taken for granted without discussion that the concept of "original sin" is the hallmark of Biblical religion and of the Judeo-Christian heritage. But while this doctrine is eloquently expounded in the Epistles of Saint Paul, it is by no means identical with the Biblical view of man, as expounded in the Old Testament or in the Gospels. Nor is it the "plain sense" of the Paradise narrative in *Genesis,* at least as one component of the Judeo-Christian tradition has understood it for millenia. Not only for Judaism, but for substantial elements in traditional and liberal Christianity, too, neither the intent of the Biblical text nor the realities of human nature compel us to the doctrine

of an ineradicable taint of evil in mankind. Not only in Pelagianism, which the Church officially rejected, but in the systems of theology which it sanctioned, the doctrine of "original sin" was substantially modified, when it was not surrendered.

Centuries earlier, Rabbinic thought, which yielded to no one in its recognition of the elements of imperfection in man, had conceived of men's native endowment as neutral, and saw his instinctual equipment neither as good nor as evil *per se*, the ultimate judgment upon them depending upon the uses to which they were put. In this world-view, man is a battle-ground as long as he lives between two impulses, the good impulse (*yetzer hatobh*) and the evil impulse (*yetzer hara*). There is no disposition to underestimate the power of the evil impulse in its manifold forms, but concomitant with it is the recognition that even this impulse can be an instrument for the service of God.

Thus the great Biblical injunction: "Thou shalt love the Lord thy God with all thy heart" bears the Rabbis' comment, "with both thine impulses, the good and the evil." Anticipating Freud on several counts, the Rabbis are fully aware of the power of sexual desire in human life and of its capacity for working havoc with men's lives. They also express their insight that without "the evil impulse," most of men's functions, such as creative activity, family life and economic pursuits, would cease. According to this approach, human nature is plastic, and any ethical judgment upon its character must follow, not precede, its manifestations in human life.

3) Finally, the realists, it may be suggested, adopt an excessively restricted concept of the nature of ethics and the scope of the ethical virtues. Many of the contradictions they find between ethics and politics dissolve, when the full constellation of ethics is taken into account.

Two Ethical Conceptions

Basically, the Judeo-Christian tradition gives expression to two conceptions of ethics:

The first is the ethics of self-abnegation, which demands the surrender of self-interest, the practice of non-resistance to evil and the offering up of one's life for others as the highest good. It is the ethics which is expressed in the New Testament injunction "Love thine enemy" and it is conveniently, though not with complete accuracy, described as "the ethics of absolute love."

The second conception of ethics is the ethics of self-fulfillment which is generally — and erroneously — referred to as "the ethics of justice." This approach regards it not only as natural and permissible, but as obligatory, for every living organism to strive to maintain its life and function and to seek the maximum expression of its individuality, so long as it does not vitiate or destroy the equal and similar right of other living creatures of the same order of being. The Biblical passage: "Ye shall take good heed of yourselves" (Deut. 4:15) is interpreted in the tradition as a Divine injunction to protect one's life and well-being.

With regard to obligations to others, the ethics of self-fulfillment tends to favor the formulation of concrete principles of conduct rather than of abstract ideals of attitude:

If thou meet thine enemy's ox or his ass going astray, thou shalt surely bring it back to him again. If thou see the ass of him that hateth thee lying under his burden, thou shalt forbear to pass by him; thou shalt surely release it with him.

(Exodus 23,4,5)

In judging of the relative value of these two standards of ethics, several observations should be taken into consideration. Contrary to a general impression, the Golden Rule, enunciated in Leviticus and cited by Jesus as the basic imperative of religion, does not express the doctrine of self-abnegation. As some ethical teachers have acutely noted, it does not command, "Thou shalt love thy neighbor *more* than thyself," but presupposes the love of one's self as a prerequisite and as a standard for the love of one's neighbor. Erich Fromm has emphasized the error involved in equating love of self with selfishness: "The assumption . . . is that to love others is a virtue, to love oneself is a sin. Furthermore, love for others and love for oneself are mutually exclusive. Theoretically we meet here with a fallacy concerning the nature of love. Love is not primarily 'caused' by a specific object, but is a lingering quality in a person which is only actualized by a certain 'object'. . . . From this it follows that my own self, in principle, is as much an object of my love as another person. The affirmation of my own life, happiness, growth, freedom, is rooted in the presence of the basic readiness of and an ability for such an affirmation. If an individual has this readiness, he has it also towards himself; if he can only 'love' others, he cannot love at all . . . Selfishness is rooted in this very lack of fondness for oneself. The person who is not fond of himself, who does not approve of himself, is in constant anxiety concerning his own self."

The insight of the modern psychologist was anticipated by the intuition of the fifteenth-century mystic, Nicholas of Cusa, "I love my life supremely, because Thou art my life's sweetness. . . . For if I ought to love myself in Thee who are my likeness, I am most especially constrained thereto, when I see that Thou lovest me as Thy creature and Thine image."

Moreover, it is significant that only the ethics of self-fulfillment, which is life-affirming, rather than the ethics of self-abnegation, affords a rational basis for regarding oppression as immoral. Political tyranny and economic exploitation, physical and intellectual slavery, are all instruments for suppressing or minimizing the selfhood of their victims. Obviously, these manifestations are evil, only if we believe that the preservation of the self and the fullest expression of human personality are ultimate goods.

Finally, historians of religion have frequently maintained that the ideal of self-abnegation is advanced in the New Testament not as a permanent program for human conduct, but as an interim ethic, at a time when men are poised on the threshold of the advent of the Kingdom of God. However one may evaluate Albert Schweitzer's emphasis upon imminent eschatology as the key to New Testament teaching, it is clear that the early Church anticipated the early end of the human order and the ushering in of the ideal Kingdom. Only in a society living in momentary expectation of a new heaven and a new earth could such a program have been proposed as a program for the generality of men.

When, however, such a consummation is no longer regarded as an immediate eventuality, the ethic of absolute love can serve only as an ultimate ideal for the many and as a voluntary program of action for the very few. One cannot rationally demand that every man conform to the standards of a Saint Francis of Assisi or a Rabbi Israel Bal Shem Tov. The full scope of ethics must be conceived of, not as a point, but as an arc, the lower end of which is justice, representing the minimum standards in our relationship to others, and the upper end of which is love, the ideal goal toward which to strive.

In sum, both types of ethics have their place in the life of the individual. Since life is the supreme good, the ethics of self-abnegation, including its highest manifestation, the act of martyrdom for an ideal goal, finds its justification in the fact that the individual's self-sacrifice ultimately redounds to the enhancement of life for the community. On the other hand, the immolation of a nation or the liquidation of an entire society would have no such beneficial result upon the remainder of humanity. It follows that the only ethic that may legitimately be applied to group aspirations and activities is the ethics of self-fulfillment, which presupposes self-preservation.

The Importance of Our Religious Heritage

To revert to my basic theme, I am unable to accept the dichotomy between the imperatives of the religio-ethical tradition and the exigencies of politics, both domestic and foreign, which the "realist" seeks to establish. As I have noted, my hesitation stems from practical as well as from theoretic considerations. The realist runs the risk of acquiescing in an evil or amoral approach to world affairs. He takes an unnecessarily dark view of human nature and adopts too narrow a conception of the scope of ethics; in both instances his claim to be the exponent of "Biblical religion" is open to question. I therefore would like to propose an alternative view of the relevance of our religious heritage to our international responsibilities.

It is of the very essence of Biblical religion that no aspect of life, including the areas of national and international affairs, is isolated from the Government of God or exempt from the judgment of the moral conscience. To relate our international responsibilities to our religious heritage means, therefore, to walk in the authentic Biblical tradition, and what is at least equally important, to utilize its insights for meeting the crisis of our times: such an approach would prove more successful than the immoral or amoral procedures which govern international affairs today.

Historical analogies are notoriously misleading, but the Biblical experience affords a striking instance of the relevance of ethical standards for a practical national policy. The Hebrew prophets, who were uncompromising in demanding adherence to the ethical principle everywhere in human life, were far more realistic in their understanding of the international scene in their day than all the practical leaders of their time, the kings, the nobility, the military leaders, the international merchants and the statesmen, let alone the common people. From the days of Amos and Hosea through Isaiah, Micah and Jeremiah, the Prophets, and they alone, espoused the doctrine of neutrality for their country, pleading, "In peace and in quiet shall ye be saved, in rest and in confidence shall be your might." From the vantage-point of history, it is clear that the military alliances and diplomatic entanglements favored by the practical men of the age were far more unrealistic than the "perfectionist" standpoint of the Prophets. Had their counsel prevailed, the destruction of the Temple and the state might well have been avoided and the people spared the agony of homelessness and exile.

Eight Pertinent Aspects

In order to indicate the relevancy of the Judeo-Christian religious heritage, the pertinent aspects of the Biblical world-view may be briefly set forth as follows:

1) The world as the handiwork of God and by that token His inalienable possession. The Bible begins with the story of Creation, not because of any primal concern with cosmogony, but in order to justify God's demand for man's obedience to His will. In the Psalmist's words, "The earth is the Lord's and the fullness thereof, the world and they who dwell therein." The social legislation of the Bible gives this doctrine clear-cut legal expression: "The earth shall not be sold in perpetuity, for the earth is Mine and ye are dwellers and sojourners with Me." Man's temporary possession does not constitute ownership.

2) The inherent right of all men, as the children of God, to the enjoyment of the blessings of the world He has created. Justice is therefore an inherent right of man and the alienation or attenuation of the just rights of any group in society is the ultimate sin against God. "The Lord of Hosts is exalted by justice, and God the Holy One is sanctified by righteousness."

3) The law of consequence operates in human affairs, because history is a process governed by God, who may use evil to destroy evil and usher in the good. The forces of evil, such as of Assyria, may in their blindness and arrogance see themselves as their own masters. In reality, they serve as unwilling and unwitting instruments for the achievement of God's purposes in His universe. Immorality must therefore bring on its inevitable doom. "Should the axe boast itself against him that heweth therewith? Should the saw magnify itself against him that moveth it? As if a rod should move them that lift it up, or as if a staff should lift up him that is not wood!" (Isa. 10:15)

4) The interdependence of all mankind and of its destiny. To recognize this truth in ancient times, when means of transportation and communication were primitive and often non-existent, required the vision of

an Amos, who saw all the nations passing in review before God, who holds the scales of judgment equally before all, and makes no distinction in his ethical demands between the kingdoms of Israel and Judah, or between the Hebrews and the world community. The Messianic age, with its burden of weal and woe, will be world-wide in scope. A later teacher, Ben Azzai held that the passage in *Genesis*, "This is the book of the generations of man," which affirms the unity of mankind, constitutes the basic principle of Scripture, taking precedence even over the Golden Rule.

5) The autonomy of the ethical conscience, vis-à-vis the authority of the rulers and the will of the majority. There is no warrant in Biblical thought for the doctrine of the divine right of kings as implying that the king can do no wrong. On the contrary, the unfailing burden of the Scripture is that the kings do little else! The Prophets were equally free from the illusion embodied in the proverb, *Vox populi vox Dei*. The masses as well as the classes, the people no less than their rulers, could and generally did violate the will of God. The function of the prophet was "to tell Jacob his transgression and Israel his sin," for "the Lord God has spoken, who can but prophesy."

6) In tension with the autonomy of the ethical conscience, which Israelite society recognized, however grudgingly, at least for its prophets, stood another principle, the right of the majority to prevail. Implicit throughout the pages of the Bible, this democratic doctrine has its origin in the Semitic background of the Hebrews and is explicated in post-Biblical thought. The existence of a primitive democracy in ancient Israel, embodied in the *edah* or "commonalty," was demonstrated by the present writer and by other Biblical students as well, a good number of years ago. Rabbinic exegesis found the principle that the majority governs in the text of the three last words of Exodus 23:2, which it rendered, "one decides after the majority."

Because of the tension between these two principles, the recognition emerged, not that there was some inherent and mystical virtue in the majority, but that its decision should not be set aside lightly. Ernest Lefever has clearly set forth both the principle of majority-right and its inherent limitations: "Since all men are fallible, self-interested, and morally ambiguous, their decisions, whether in the minority or the majority, reflect their rational and moral frailties. Nevertheless, since one man's interest may cancel out another man's interest, one man's wisdom off-set another man's stupidity, and one man's knowledge make up for another man's ignorance, a majority decision based upon adequate debate may often be wiser than and morally superior to a minority decision." Hence, both principles, the power of the majority to execute its will and the right of the minority to express its dissent and to seek to propagate it, constitute the obverse and reverse of the democratic way of life.

Here an important caveat must be entered. It is often overlooked that the scope of Biblical ethics, largely derived from the Prophets, is not exhausted by them. Within the Biblical canon, Wisdom literature occupies an important place. The Wisdom teachers were by no means isolated from the two other major currents of Biblical thought, Law and Prophecy. Witness the passage in Proverbs (29:18) "Where there is no vision, the people perish, but he who keeps the Law, happy is he." It is noteworthy, too, that the most succinct expression of the Prophetic philosophy of history is expressed in Wisdom literature: "Righteousness exalts a nation, but sin is the disgrace of peoples." (Pr. 14:34).

7) The unique contribution of Wisdom literature to Biblical ethics lies, however, in its emphasis upon realism as a virtue and upon intelligence as constituting obedience to the will of God. For the authors of *Proverbs* and *Ecclesiastes,* the fool is a sinner and the violation of the moral law is folly as well as transgression. The basic approach to life in Wisdom literature was that morality is the best policy. From this identification two corollaries follow — a course of action, however, practical it may seem to be, if it violates the canons of morality, is to be rejected, and conversely, a course of action, however highminded its aims, if it be impractical, is likewise unacceptable, because neither can advance human well-being.

When we include intelligence within the scope of the ethical virtues, as envisaged by Biblical thought, we shall understand the fatal flaw within the school of pre-war liberal idealism. Legalism in foreign affairs, which Lefever defines as "an approach to politics which invests in legal symbols, documents and structures a power and authority which they do not in fact possess," does not fail because of an excess of ethics, but because of a deficiency of ethics, the lack of intelligence.

8) Closely related to the quality of intelligence is the virtue of honesty — both with ourselves and with others. What is taken for granted is often overlooked altogether. We should do well to recall Samuel

Johnson's demand, "Clear your mind of cant," echoed in Carlyle's warning, "Until cant cease, nothing else can begin." Our lack of success in meeting our international responsibilities and in winning "the cold war" is often charged to our "moralism" and our high-minded effort to follow ethical doctrine in an area where it is irrelevant. "Moralizing" is not an excess of morality, but a deficiency of morality, the lack either of intelligence or honesty.

The Question of Morality

Thus intelligence teaches what experience exemplifies — the human situation will often pose a plurality of opposing goals and ends which need to be adjusted to one another. But the contradiction between two ideals is not a denial of their inherent validity. Nor is it an inherent "evil" in the world or in human nature, when men seek to establish a hierarchy of values among them, in order to retain as much as possible of each good. When Lincoln declared, "If I can save the Union by preserving slavery, I shall preserve slavery; if I can save the Union by abolishing slavery, I shall abolish slavery, but I shall save the Union," there was no ethical flaw in his position, merely because he did not seek to achieve all ideal ends simultaneously. The destruction of the Union, already in existence, would have been an ethical retreat; on the other hand, the retention of slavery, which was likewise in existence, marked simply the failure or the postponement of an ethical advance. Lincoln's scale of priorities demonstrated the virtue of intelligence.

The same quality of intelligence offers the clue to a distinction highly important in our day. Expediency means the temporary suspension of a moral principle because of the demands of necessity. Prudence is the reconciliation of two valid moral principles which under given circumstances stand in conflict with each other. Both expediency and prudence are often called for even in an ethically motivated foreign policy. It is, however, the duty of intelligence to recognize the difference. Military aid to Franco, economic assistance to Tito, or cooperation with Saudi Arabia may perhaps be necessary. But to confuse expediency with prudence and to speak of dictators and autocrats as defenders of the free way of life is either an affront to intelligence or a lack of honesty.

A great deal of our idealistic slogans and protestations are forms of self-deception, if not worse. As we have seen, the American position with regard to the Suez Canal crisis in 1956 is frequently cited as a classic example of the inherent conflict of morality and foreign policy.

Here, it is maintained, America's moral idealism compelled it to condemn France and Britain, its two oldest allies, and to demand the withdrawal of Israeli armed forces from the Sinai Peninsula.

That the practical consequences of the American policy offered little grounds for jubilation became tragically clear to nearly all observers, except possibly to some members of the highest echelons in our government. But even apart from the practical results of United States policy in the Suez Canal crisis, was it justified on the grounds of morality? Was our position a sacrifice of material interests on the high altar of morality? This may well be disputed. Egypt had always recognized that she was bound by the Convention of 1888 for the international operation of the Suez Canal. Nasser's unilateral abrogation of the Treaty which had nearly a decade to run and his forcible seizure of the Canal was therefore a clear violation of an international understanding, aside from the injury done to the Canal shareholders. Had Britain and France invaded Egypt in total strength, quickly taken control of the Canal and proceeded to operate it, and then turned the dispute over to the Court of International Justice in The Hague or to a similar tribunal for adjudication, it is arguable that the succession of defeats sustained by the West in the area would have been avoided.

My purpose here is not to assess blame. I am concerned to indicate that the Suez crisis cannot fairly be adduced as an example of the inherent conflict of ethics and foreign policy. It is my thesis that if the qualities of intelligence and honesty are included as they properly should be, within the constellation of moral virtues, the implications of the religious and ethical heritage of the Judeo-Christian are both practical and relevant to our international responsibilities, and we are not compelled to construct our foreign policy simply in terms of power, pressure, and propaganda.

Some Ethical Imperatives

The Hebrew Prophets found as we have seen, not a contradiction, but a confluence between their idealistic aspirations and their realistic understanding, in their doctrine of neutrality for a small, weak state, at best a pawn in the battle of empires for world mastery. I should like to suggest that the sternly practical goals of America as a world power can similarly be buttressed by the imperatives derived from the full ethical tradition of Judaism and Christianity. A few illustrations can be adduced only briefly:

1) *Foreign aid.* The recognition of the interdependence of mankind as a reality will necessarily destroy the illusion, sedulously fostered in many quarters, that foreign aid is a "hand-out" by over-generous, stupid America to the backward and undeserving peoples in far-off regions of the world. Such undertakings as the Marshall Plan and the Point Four Program are therefore not only logical consequences of an ethical outlook, but basic to a practical policy for the United States. Isolationism is neither ethical nor realistic.

2) *International negotiation.* The practice of negotiation with one's enemies is to be recognized, not merely as a practical necessity in a divided world, but as resting upon a profound moral basis. In the first instance, it is the expression of a "decent respect for the opinions of mankind," for obviously there are men and nations who differ vigorously with us in their outlook. Secondly, negotiation between opponents rests upon the truth that there is a common destiny and therefore a common interest binding all men, even enemies, together. We may and should deny the moral right upon which the Soviet system rests, as vigorously as they do ours. Yet in negotiating with Russia, maintaining relations with her and extending cultural and economic contacts, we are not merely yielding to expediency. For the Soviet bloc shares one overriding common interest with the free world, if no other — the desire to survive and be spared the perils of atomic destruction.

To keep the avenues of communication and negotiation open among governments is therefore a moral good of the highest order and the most significant function of the United Nations. Conversely, the refusal to negotiate is the ultimate sin in group relations, not only because it makes impossible the peaceful adjudication of differences and thus increases the incidence of violence and destruction, but because it denies the right of others besides ourselves to live.

In the festering and explosive conflict between Israel and the Arab States, there are tragic issues at stake and the Arab case certainly possesses substantial elements of justice. It is true that the hundreds of thousands of pitiable Arab refugees who live on the borders of Israel left their homes because of the promise made by the five attacking Arab armies that the new State would quickly be liquidated and they would gain rich spoils as the Israelis would be driven into the sea. They were therefore in overwhelming measure the architects of their own tragic fate. Yet their sorry lot in the present and the hopelessness of their future is a crying evil which requires a solution, in which the participation of the Israeli government is indispensable. So too, many of the spokesmen of the Arab states in the United Nations and elsewhere are undoubtedly sincere in voicing their fears that Israel may seek to expand its borders again in the future. In the present atmosphere Israel's repeated denials have not persuaded the Arabs. Israel, on its part, has its own very real grievances against its Arab neighbors. Aside from the fact that only negotiation offers any hope of solving the issues and of dissipating mutual suspicions and fears, these bitter foes do share a substantial common interest. The future of all depends upon the establishment of peace, the reduction of military expenditures, which are draining all these countries, and the economic and cultural development of the entire area.

The perilous status quo in the Middle East is a practical threat to the free world and a moral calamity as well. On both grounds, it should have been one of the objectives of Western policy all along, to use all possible means not to compel a settlement of the issues, desirable as that might be, but at least, to persuade the recalcitrant parties to sit down together and discuss their differences. Instead we permitted the situation to deteriorate steadily. Though it would have been easier to achieve the goal of peace in the Middle East before Russian penetration into the area, it remains indispensable even now.

3) *Civil liberties and integration.* These domestic issues offer another illustration of the confluence of ethical principles and practical policies. During the hey-day of McCarthyism, too many Americans made peace with the indiscriminate hounding of defenseless men and women, though they recognized it as basically immoral. All too often we acquiesced, by observing that one must break eggs to make omelettes, and that national security, which was our paramount aim, might require occasional injustice to individuals.

One would be hard put to it to find a better vindication of the truth of the "unrealistic prophetic faith in the operation of the law of consequence in history. The suppression of scientists and the spirit of free inquiry, the wholesale elimination and resignation of many workers from government services and classified research projects played no little part in the defeats we have sustained in the scientific aspects of the cold war. When Soviet achievements in the field of atomic energy first became known, Americans were assured that our atomic secrets had been transmitted by spies to the Russians, and undoubtedly espionage did operate in America. But no such comforting alibi is available with regard to the launching of satellites, where our achievement continues to limp badly behind that of the Russians. Thus our failure to preserve civil liberties at home led to a tragic debacle in American prestige abroad.

Similarly, our hesitations and evasions with regard to the integration of Negro citizens into American life, by giving a hollow ring to our idealistic claims to love, justice and liberty for all, is grievously jeopardizing our opportunities for winning the uncommitted world to our cause. For Americans at home the sun of freedom shines brightly, in spite of a few dark spots here and there. For the millions of darker-skinned people, yellow, brown and black, the sun itself has been blotted out by the the the spots.

4) *The United Nations.* If we apply the full range of our ethical insights to the United Nations, it is clear, as Lefever has indicated, that it is neither a mere debating society on the one hand nor an international parliament on the other. The United Nations is an instrument for expressing the opinions and interests of the various governments of the world. When these are democratic in character, they reflect in greater or lesser degree the opinions of the masses of the people. When they are totalitarian or autocratic, they are reflections of the constellations of power of the local ruling groups. The United Nations is a voluntary association of sovereign nations who seek to defend their interests without having recourse to the use of force.

The decisions of the United Nations, arrived at by the majority, are therefore of great importance. As we have noted, unless other factors enter into the picture, the opinion of the majority is likely to be more balanced than that of a minority. A numerical majority, however, is not *ipso facto* universally sacrosanct, as we are discovering to our cost. Soviet Russia and its satellites and the Afro-Asian bloc command many individual votes, but reflect very few individual positions. It therefore follows that while the views of the United Nations should not be lightly set aside, a government striving for an ethical foreign policy will not abdicate the exercise of its own conscience in dealing with the problems before it. It is not high-minded morality but an evasion of responsibility to refuse to take a position on controversial issues on the ground that the United Nations will deal with them. On the contrary, it is the moral right and duty of each member to think through the problem at hand and seek to utilize its influence to have its position prevail.

There is obviously room for wide difference of opinion with regard to the judgments I have expressed or implied on various aspects of our international responsibility as a world power. The burden of my paper has been not to defend these positions, but to emphasize that as heirs of the Judeo-Christian tradition, whether in religious or in secularized form, we have no need to compartmentalize our minds and insulate the ethical ideals we espouse from the foreign policy we practice. If we keep before us the full dimensions of Biblical thought and recognize that a vital ethics includes intelligence as well as justice, truth as well as righteousness, we can find in our religious heritage a vital and relevant instrument for grappling with our international responsibilities. Nor need we have any cause to fear the ultimate outcome. We can share Milton's unshakable faith in the victory of truth over falsehood, because we continue to believe in a universe rooted in justice, and flowering into freedom and peace.

The Recovery of Ethics

Paul H. Nitze

Identifying the Issues

O NE LARGE overarching problem and several smaller subsidiary problems emerge from most discussions of ethics and foreign policy. The big problem is the perennial one of the relation between our convictions about what is right, what is good, what ought to be, and our reading of what we can effectively do in the context of the real situation which confronts us in the world. Everyone faces up to this issue in some manner, but the balance is struck at different points and in different ways by different persons.

At one extreme are those who begin with a more or less absolute, clear and ideal conviction of what is right and good (what God wills or requires) and who insist that it is the church's and the Christian's primary duty to preach and to witness to that. To those who take this extreme position, calculations of what is feasible in the real world are largely irrelevant. The focus is on ideal ends rather than on effective means.

It is important to note, however, that the more "idealistic" positions do not ordinarily assume that the results of single-minded dedication to ideal ends imply any tragic choice between the ideal and the feasible. Rather they tend to read the realities in the light of the ideal, and to assume that a sufficiently imaginative effort to achieve those ideals will meet with success. They do not ordinarily say: Witness to these ideals, no matter what comes. Rather, they say: Follow these ideas, and the world will be made over. The insistence, for instance, that we need "massive efforts at negotiation and reconciliation, massive efforts at universal disarmament, massive renunciation of efforts contemplating war" surely implies that what is now lacking is sufficient dedication to the ends of reconcilation and peace, and that an analysis of the objective conditions influencing the attainment of these aims, and of the alternative courses of action which might in fact lead to a more tolerable and desirable situation, is of secondary importance.

On the other side of this issue are those who insist that the consequences in history of *political* action have to be assessed for the moral
quality of that action to be known. They maintain that the intention
alone does not decide the goodness or the badness of *political* acts. An
important corollary of this more realistic conviction is that quite evil
results may follow from quite good motives; that efforts to achieve ideal
ends may not only fail but may produce evils quite contrary to their
intent. This may come about by focusing on one goal where there are
many to be considered and by wishful thinking about the possibility of
achieving that one goal without sacrificing other and perhaps more
important goals. Thus, one might answer those who recoil in moral
horror before modern armaments by asking about United States responsibilities to preserve and carry forward the freedom of our own nation
and that of other nations and our duties to the values and civilization
we have inherited. Will we sacrifice all this as the price of our own
moral fastidiousness?

Those who take a position in most extreme opposition to those who
urge the primary importance of dedication to ideal aims are the group
which seems to equate morality with the care with which decisions are
made. It is their view that if the maximum possible care is taken to
assess all the probable consequences of an act, before acting, one thereby
fulfills the requirements of morality. This group emphasizes the complexity of moral decisions in politics, the importance of careful consideration, the need to consider all the elements of the problem, and the
checks and restraints of diverse views. In its most extreme form this
view appears to deduce the aims of action from the probable consequences of the action and thereby becomes circular in its reasoning.

Obviously, the claim of ideal ends, and of principles ordering or
restricting the means to be used in pursuit of those ends, are essential
to any Christian political ethic. Furthermore, the Christian rejects any
determinism of blind eminent historical forces and discovers both a
measure of freedom for the will to affect history, and a dimension
beyond history in which acts have a meaning greater than their historical consequences.

How can one best summarize the conclusions that seem to flow from
these extreme positions? On the one hand, I find unsatisfactory the
position of those who would concentrate solely upon ends and principles ordering the use of means. On the other hand, I find equally
unsatisfactory the position of those who would look solely to consequences. It appears to me that an adequate approach requires concurrent
consideration of ends and principles, on the one hand, and of the
consequences which are likely to flow from a given line of action in the

concrete and specific situation in which the action is proposed, on the other hand. In other words, I do not reject the extreme "idealist" position and the extreme "realist" position in favor of some middle road. Rather, I think that a more elaborate analysis is needed — one involving *both* a consideration of aims and an assessment of probable consequences.

The Role of the Church

Let me turn now to a different aspect of the same problem. This has to do with the specific role of the church with respect to the problem of ethics and foreign policy.

A case can be made for the proposition that many other people will advocate the claims of practicality and realism and that it is the role of the church to counterbalance these claims by advocating the counter-claim of ideal aims and principles. Thus a person who has arrived at a resolution of the issue of "idealism" versus "realism" similar to the one suggested above may still believe that it is the particular function of the church to advocate one part of the equation and to leave to others advocacy of the other. He may say: There are many groups and persons speaking up for realism, self-interest, and military preparedness; there are also people, such as the President and the Secretary of State, whose special function it is to sort out and judge the various claims that are put forward and who are responsible for decisions governing a foreign policy which takes into account the consequences of its actions; the task of the church is not to do either of these things, but is to urge the ideal claims which otherwise may be overlooked. The church's role is that of the advocate, not the judge. It is history finally that makes the resolution of the many claims; it is the church's role to see that the ideals she speaks for are not absent from the resolution.

To this the reply may be made that though the church's role as to issues of political policy is different from that of a policy-making agency, it still must begin with a realistic awareness of the possibilites of the world before its witness to ideas — its advocacy — can be so oriented as to be likely to advance its own cause. When the church gets into issues of foreign policy, it does not restrict itself to the traditional precepts of Christian ethics, it begins to apply its special background to a specific field of modern existence. As it does so, some regard must be given to the special characteristics of that field; its judgments about reality must be hard-headed and must accord with the truth insofar as it can be discovered; and at least a preliminary attempt must be made to trace the probable consequences of the positions advocated.

In summary of this point, even when one thinks about the special role of the church, it is not possible wholly to get away from the considerations discussed under the first point, the need for an analysis which takes into account both aims and the probable consequences of action.

My own background is not primarily church-oriented. My particular orientation has been toward action and policy making in the business, military and political fields. Those of us with such an orientation are apt to put primary emphasis upon a realistic appraisal of the world as it is and a painstaking calculation of the probable results of alternative courses of action. Our first instinct is to leave to others the discussion of ultimate aims and principles. We tend to feel that common sense gives us a firm enough grasp on proximate aims and principles, and that our job is to get something done and have it work as we intend it to work. We recognize that those proximate aims and principles derive from and are geared into a deeper and more basic system. But we are apt to feel that our forefathers did a very good job of thinking through that more ultimate system and that there is not much use in our tinkering with it. We will give it our full respect, and will be guided by the related precepts for action which have been handed down to us by tradition. Our main job is to act and to act wisely and successfully within that framework.

But then, situations arise in which the proximate aims and principles derived from the system handed down by tradition do not seem to be adequate. They seem to lead to inconsistencies and, in extreme cases, to antinomies when applied to the newly emerging and basic problems turned up by the dynamic and threatening world in which we live today.

In such a world, even the man primarily oriented toward action finds himself forced toward a re-examination of the ends and principles underlying his proximate aims. He turns to the church for guidance. And at that point he may find the church not much better equipped than he to supply the answers that he needs. Both are groping. They start from different initial positions. Neither sees clearly where clarification can be found. It is possible they can help each other. Both churchmen and men of action in the political field can profit from the interaction of each other's ideas. The academician also has something to contribute to the process.

The Problem of Values

Several points which have arisen in recurrent discussions with my students have a bearing on the issue of ethics and foreign policy and merit mention at this point.

At one time much of the new and more advanced analysis of political theory coming out of the academic world in the United States seemed to be based on the thesis that aims and principles — what the behavioristic and positivistic authors referred to as "value preferences" — were somebody else's business and that the political scientist should restrict himself to considering the facts of the real world and the types of action which could be expected to produce given results.

Subsequently a number of writers on the subject of political theory developed a somewhat different approach. In this approach values, in other words, aims and principles associated with a given group or political system, are determined by the need, or in technical language, the functional requirements, of the group or system.

This approach has the virtue of reintroducing values, and thus aims and principles, into the field of political theory. To my mind, however, it suffers from certain defects. In the first place, it tends to underplay the complex interrelations between, on the one hand, individual persons and the values immediately associable with persons and personality, and, on the other hand, the complex structure of groups in which individual persons may participate: the family, the corporation or labor union, the political party, the nation, the church, and the culture or civilization of which they are a part.

There obviously are values, values of survival, of development, of the full actualization of potentialities, associable with the individual person and with each of the groups or systems in which he may participate. To the student of politics the nature of these values, their origin, modification, and relation to the functional requirements of the individual or of the group of which the individual is a member, and with which values are associated, is of interest in throwing light on the nature of the real world which he is trying to understand.

There is, however, more to the problem of values than this. In the first place, conflicts of value arise between personal values and various group values, and between one set of group values and another set of group values. It is often emphasized that the ideal situation is one in which there is convergence and mutual support between these interlocking value systems. The individual may find the opportunity for the realization of his highest potentialities, for instance, within a loving family and as part of a productive business organization operating in a progressive state — the state playing a responsible role in a just international order of some kind.

But convergence and mutual support of the value systems of interlocking and interacting groups do not always take place. Potential conflict is always present. It seems to me that the principal task of ethics and morality is right here; its task is to give some guide lines to the resolution of potential conflict between the various parts of a very complex individual-group structure and of the value systems associated with those parts. Perhaps it would be useful to make a distinction between the concept "value" and the concept "ethical framework." The distinction would be that "values" apply to an individual or to a specific group; "ethical framework" would apply to the broader standards by which conflicts between such values may be resolved.

Interrelated Values

One method of resolving potential conflict is to subordinate or to order the relations between the individual and the various groups, or of one group to another, in a manner depending upon the context in which the issue arises. Thus the individual is expected to subordinate certain of his values to those of the system in which other individuals, as well as he, can survive and have an opportunity to actualize their potentialities. If the context is such that the system as a whole is threatened, he is expected, if necessary, to lay down his life for it. In the political system which has arisen in the modern era, the nation-state is presumed to have a monopoly upon the legitimate use of coercive force. In contexts where the issue of the possible use of coercive force arises, the individual and all sub-groups within the territory of the nation-state are expected to subordinate their actions to those of officials acting on behalf of the nation-state. But in states democratically organized the use of coercive power by the state or its agents is hedged in by a number of restraints. In our country it is hedged by a Constitution, a separation between the executive, the legislative and judicial branches, by the right of *habeas corpus*, jury trial and due process.

Thus in the domestic political scene we have not just a partial subordination of the individual and sub-groups, such as the corporation, labor union, or political party to the state, but an ordering of the relations between them.

I find that it is hard for many of my students to grasp the interrelations between the various elements of a political system. They tend to advocacy of polar positions. They feel that they must choose between dedication to the individual and values associated with the individual, or dedication to the nation and the values associated with the nation. They feel that they must choose between being for the use of force in behalf of the preservation of the integrity of the state, or being against the use of force and for the principle of government solely by consent. They do not easily understand that the individual person and the political order in which he lives are inter-connected as are space and time; that it is hardly possible to speak of one without implying the other.

If the considerations I have been advancing with respect to the arena of political relations within a state have validity, several consequences would seem to flow therefrom for the application of ethics to politics within a state. In the first place, it would seem unjustified to associate morality with the values of any single portion of that political world. It would be wrong to associate the ethical position solely with the values of the individual, the values of the family, the values of the business or the labor world, or the values of the state alone. Neither would it seem justifiable to associate the concept of ethics with an absolute dedication to the use or non-use of a particular type of means, for instance, the non-use of coercion. Morality would seem more appropriately to be associated with a point of view which stands above these immediate political issues and which finds guide lines either in tradition or in the deeper truths revealed by nature and by religion that tend to give point, order and harmony to the resolution of those issues.

International Objectives

International politics presents even more difficulties, as a field in which to sort out the role of ethics, than does the field of domestic politics.

In the international arena, no one has a monopoly of the legitimate use of force and the most basic values may be in conflict — even the values associated with the survival of entire nations or civilizations. There is no executive controlled by a constitution, balanced by a judicial and a legislative branch and subject to the restraints of *habeas corpus* and due process. But even the international arena need not be wholly without order.

From 1815 to 1914, a certain degree of international order was maintained. The balance of power system among the European states preserved a certain degree of stability. England, with control of the seas, could act as a balance wheel. Economic institutions based on the gold standard and centering on the London capital market provided an economic framework within which large portions of the world, including the United States, were able to make tremendous forward strides in developing their economies. Above all, wars were kept limited as to objective and limited in extent.

The two world wars shattered the system which existed prior to 1914. Today the fundamental issue in the international arena is that of who will construct a new international order, appropriate to today's world, to take the place of the one that was shattered in those two world wars.

Until the spring of 1947, we in the United States did not face up to the fact that that was the issue and that we had to do something about it, because no one else had the will or resources to do it. Few of us remember the intense activity of the six months beginning in March 1947 with the Truman Doctrine, announcing our determination to help those willing to fight for their independence. This was followed by the Greek-Turkish Aid Program, the merger of the Western zones of Western Germany leading to restoration of German sovereignty, the Marshall Plan, the Rio Treaty, and the National Security Act of 1947, creating the Defense Department, the Central Intelligence Agency, the National Security Council, and the National Security Resources Board. That intense activity in 1947 was subsequently followed up with the filling out of our treaty arrangements, including NATO and the ANZUS Pact, the Mutual Defense Assistance Act, Point Four, the restoration of sovereignty to Japan and, finally, the decision to intervene in support of the Republic of Korea against overt aggression.

As one looks back on the overall pattern of the actions undertaken in those years, one can ask what is it we were trying to do? I think one can summarize it by saying that we were trying to lay the foundations for an international system which would substitute, in the circumstances existing in the modern world, for the system which the balance of power in Europe, supported and managed by the British — relying on their control of the seas — had maintained during the century following the Congress of Vienna. This new structure had to have its political, its economic and its military aspects. It had to provide for certain overall world-wide functions within which closer regional institutions could be developed. A unique role in this system had continuously to be borne by the United States because we alone had the resources and the will to tackle the job. And while this system was being developed it had to be continously protected against the hostile and destructive efforts of the Soviet-Chinese Communist bloc which was dedicated to the construction of another and antithetical system.

Let us take a look at the main elements of the structure we were trying to erect and to defend while we were erecting it. One important part of the structure was its economic part. This had its world-wide aspects geared into the United Nations structure. The International

Monetary Fund provided an institution looking toward greater stability of the currencies necessary for the financing of the world's commerce. The International Bank for Reconstruction and Development was to provide a pool of capital to flow to those areas needing capital and able to make sound use of it. The General Agreement on Trade and Tariffs was to move toward the reduction of administrative barriers to international trade. These international instruments were reinforced by regional and bilateral actions such as the Marshall Plan, the Organization for European Economic Cooperation, the European Payments Union, the Technical Assistance Program, and the Colombo Plan. And these international, regional, and bilateral approaches were supported by United States economic policies generally consistent with our new role as the world's leading creditor nation and principal reservoir of capital and of technology.

In the military sphere a similar structure compounded of international, regional, and individual arrangements was gotten under way. The heart of these military arrangements had to be strength at the center, strength in the United States itself. The need was early foreseen to give this strength at the center greater flexibility than was provided merely by S.A.C. and its nuclear armaments. It was only as a result of the attack into Korea that appropriations could be secured for anything approaching an adequate effort in that direction. Supplementing United States strength at the center, a major effort was gotten under way to build strength at the periphery through NATO, through the M.D.A.P. program and through our bilateral arrangements with the R.O.K., the Chinese Nationalists and Japan. Finally a German contribution to European defense was sought but ran into very great difficulties. An attempt was made to spread this system to the Middle East through the project for a Middle East Defense Organization — but that effort foundered because of Arab disunity and the strains caused by the Arab-Israeli controversy.

The economic and military measures found their place within a political structure whose broadest aspect was the United Nations Organizations and whose heart and driving spirit were United States responsibility. There emerged a pattern of political relationships characterized by exceptionally close collaboration among the United States, England and Canada, spreading out through close, but not as close, relationships with Germany, France, Italy and Japan, and shading off to cooperation on certain basic matters with the uncommitted but free countries such as India and Burma.

The object was to create a structure sufficiently flexible to house the diverse interests and requirements of the entire non-Communist world.

Even with respect to the Communist world it was hoped that the structure would have something to offer and would, by its attractive power, either draw off portions of the Communist world, as it did in the case of Yugoslavia, or result in a weakening of the bonds within the Communist world, as it did in the case of Poland but failed to do in the case of Communist China.

In 1952 and 1953 only a portion of the United States population was persuaded that an effort as enormous as that entailed in the construction and maintenance, with the United States bearing the principal responsibility, of a new international system was really necessary. Could we not look more to our own interests as a nation and leave to others the worries about an international system? Others thought that so burdensome an external policy would inevitably prove inconsistent with the preservation of our domestic political traditions. Still others thought that, though the aims of our foreign policy might be all right, there must be some easier and cheaper way of going about the business. And there were those who were disappointed in the prospect of an effort extending indefinitely into the future. If we not only had to get such a system going, but then had to keep it going, in spite of the apathy of a large portion of the world and the bitter hostility of another large portion, would we not be at the job forever?

Changes reflecting this national mood were made in the program in an effort to meet the popular objections to the previous program. One result was that public opinion within the United States was consolidated, at least the most serious schizophrenic strains in the body politic were suppressed. But in my view, the program as a whole suffered and our national strategy became less clear in direction and less effective in execution.

To my mind, the most serious modification in our national strategy in the period beginning in 1953 was the decision to emphasize that our first aim was to pursue United States national interests and to play down our interest in the construction of a working international order. The moment we began to emphasize that our policy was directed primarily to the pursuit of United States aims and interests, other nations were forced to look more closely to their own narrow interests. If we were to focus on United States interests, rather than on the creation and defense of a system under which we, along with other independent nations, could survive and prosper, the British were bound to look primarily to United Kingdom interests and the French to French interests.

If the nation, or nations, principally responsible for a given international system appear to lose faith in that system and appear to be following their narrow national interests, the other nations of lesser power are bound to become uncertain in their policy. These lesser powers know they, without the cooperation and leadership of the greater powers, cannot hope to make the system work. They must then decide whether the faltering by the great powers is temporary or whether they must prepare to adjust themselves to some quite different system.

In my judgment, the course of events which ended up in the Suez crisis was in part attributable to this change in our national strategy. It can be argued that the change was largely one of emphasis in presentation and not one of substance. Changes in presentation are likely, however, to result in changes of substance even if not originally intended.

The other modification which seemed to me to be serious was the effort to cater simultaneously to those who wanted a quicker solution and those who wanted a less burdensome effort. We thereby encouraged anticipations and actions which we were in no position to back up. It can be argued that our emphasis upon a policy of liberation had little effect in stimulating the Hungarian uprising. In my view it did have some effect. But it can hardly be argued that we were in a good position to back it up when it did occur.

By the summer of 1957 we had experimented with a series of modifications to that national strategy which had evolved during the period 1947-1952. The modifications, however, had not met with success and we had been forced back by the hard facts of the situation to more or less the same general policy line from which we had started. During that summer the studies of the Gaither Committee and of the Rockefeller Committee reaffirmed that there was no easy or cheap short cut to national survival in today's world; that we needed flexible military strength at the center, that we needed allies in depth and at the periphery, and that, above all, we needed a functioning world political and economic system in which the United States must play a continuing and leading role.

With Sputnik we entered into a new and even more disturbing phase. It is easy to over-emphasize the sputniks. We had known earlier that the Russians were probably ahead of us in the ballistic missile race. We had known from the very beginning that we must count on some time eventually arriving when our technological lead in atomic weapons would be less important, or perhaps of no importance. We knew about Russian economic advances and the percentage of their gross national income which they were putting into defense and the expansion of their industrial base.

The convergence of three separate sets of factors gave a new look to the situation in the fall of 1957.

One of these factors was Sputnik, and the confirmation which it gave to what we had known, but had not really believed, about Russian economic, technological, and specifically missile progress in recent years.

The second was the rapid political recovery which the Communist central authority seemed to have made from the strains which had been increasingly evident during the period prior to the Polish and Hungarian crises. Khrushchev, after the suppression of the Hungarian revolt, had apparently solidified his position within the top leadership; the top leadership had strengthened its position within the Party and the state; and the Russian Communist party had reestablished its authority over all the satellites other than Yugoslavia. One faced the prospects of a long pull before any serious internal political weakening of the opposing forces could be expected.

And, thirdly, the internal political situation in France, India, Indonesia, the Middle East and Africa looked far from healthy.

In such a situation the Russians could be expected to work out some gambit which, in their estimation, was well designed to encourage the divisive factors in the West and to give themselves a good platform from which to pursue their efforts to nail down an international system compatible with their aims rather than ours. The gambit of proposing a summit meeting about Berlin and Germany was admirably designed to do just that.

The resulting debate, which has gone on more intensely in Europe than in the United States, has not been about whether or how we in the West should design an international system which will be attractive to and have a place in it even for countries not behind the Iron Curtain. Under the appearance of debating disengagement in its various forms, including unilateral nuclear disarmament, the debate has been about the question of whether, within the international system proposed by the Soviet Union, there may be a place within which presently independent countries can survive without complete loss of that independence. The alternatives which have been debated have been on the one hand the prospect of nuclear war, on the other hand the prospect of an international order compatible with the aims of the Soviet Union and international Communism but offering, within that framework, coexistence to the West.

The point of this analysis is that the principal issue before the world is what kind of international order will prevail in the future. Will it be one compatible with ideas, principles, and political structures such as those we enjoy in the United States while offering a place within that structure to Communist states? Or will it be an international structure designed by and compatible with the objectives of the Communist states while offering a possibility of coexistence to us and to other states similarly organized? I frankly doubt the possibility of a truly half-way position. I can imagine a system compatible with our ideas under which the U.S.S.R. would have rights and responsibilities as great as those of any other single state. Similarly within an international order basically designed by the Communists I can imagine them granting more or less freedom to the United States and other countries similarly situated. But the essence of the two systems would be quite different. If there is no middle ground, if this really is the issue, if this is what we mean by the struggle for peace with justice, what resources of will and of national sacrifice are we entitled, or obligated, to put into the effort to cause a system compatible with our values to prevail? What risks are we entitled to take with the awful hazard of a nuclear war? Do moral considerations give us any guide lines?

In recent years I have heard the most divergent viewpoints on this issue expressed with clarity and force. One viewpoint is that, in spite of the frictions, inadequacies, and inequities of our system, it is basically humane, progressive, dedicated to truth and to justice and has a degree of validity such that any dedication of will and sacrifice of material benefit necessary to the creation of an international system compatible with its survival is a duty, an obligation, and a privilege which we cannot shirk.

The other view is that any confrontation of will between the Soviet rulers and ourselves over an issue so basic as that of the fundamental nature of the international order which is to prevail in the world, is likely to result in a nuclear war and that the upshot of such a war will be no system rather than their system or ours; and that therefore we should, if necessary, accommodate ourselves to their system preserving for ourselves and others as much freedom as they may permit.

These two positions do not quite meet in direct opposition because those upholding the first view maintain that, if our effort is intense enough, we can prevail in the establishment of a compatible system without having the situation degenerate into a general war. Nevertheless a reasonably precise issue is drawn.

To find grounds on which one can base a firm conviction one way or the other merits the most dedicated application of such capacities as are granted us.

The Implications of Science

In the foregoing section I pointed up only one, in my view the most crucial but still only one, of the multitude of issues posing an ethical problem in the field of foreign policy. Obviously there are hosts of other such problems. Under what types of circumstances, if any, should we continue nuclear tests? Under what circumstances, if any, should we actually use nuclear weapons? Under what circumstances, if any, should we use non-nuclear weapons to enforce our views of what is just and equitable in the relations between nations? Under what circumstances, if any, should we use firm measures to keep our allies from engaging in unjust or imprudent actions? What non-coercive measures are appropriate to what kinds of international purposes? What economic or political sacrifices are we justified in making or requiring of others for what purposes? How should one choose between competing or conflicting political objectives or political groups?

It can perhaps be objected that these questions are too general to permit specific answers. But we still are faced with issues which involve ethical judgments even if we make our questions more specific. The more specific we make our questions the more significant become issues of fact. But even after we have settled all the issues of fact there will remain an irreducible element which poses an ethical judgment.

Others may object that many political questions can be resolved only by the competitive exercise of power and that ethical choice has little place. This objection also falls upon closer analysis.

Werner Heisenberg, the German Nobel physicist who developed the principles of quantum theory, tells a story which illustrates the point. He describes a conversation which he had with a theological student during the revolutionary struggles which racked Germany in 1919. Heisenberg was seventeen years old and was attached to a military unit in Munich during a period when the center of the city was occupied by Communists. Every noon the unit fetched its lunch from a field kitchen in the yard of a theological seminary. Heisenberg describes the discussion with the student as follows:

"One day we became involved in a discussion with a theology student on the question of whether this struggle in Munich was in truth meaningful. One of our group took the stand that questions of power could not be decided by intellectual means, by speech-making and writing; the real decision between us and the others could only be determined by force, he declared.

"Thereupon the theology student replied that the very question of who were 'we' and who 'the others' were obviously depended upon a purely intellectual decision; and that probably a good deal would be gained if this decision were made somewhat more intelligently than was usually the case. We could find no good reply to this argument." Heisenberg ends the story with the comment that perhaps it might not be so bad if we were to teach youth not to despise the values of the mind.

If it is true, as I believe it is, that foreign policy decisions along with political decisions in general involve an irreducible ethical content, how do we go about discovering the relevant ethical framework and how do we describe and justify that framework in terms which commend themselves to belief by the mind of the modern world? Many would say that these are the problems on which theologians and philosophers have broken their skulls for generations, leaving us in the state of intellectual chaos in which we now find ourselves, and that there is little hope that we can do better than to add to the confusion. I take a different view. It seems to me that there is today a convergence of a number of factors which give grounds for hope that rigorous effort can, in the not too distant future, restore a glimmering of light in the existing darkness.

One of these factors is to be found in the developments of modern science and in the implications for philosophy of those developments. One cannot read the more general writings of the leading contemporary scientists without coming away with the conviction that most of the intellectual blocks which classical physics seemed to throw in the path of belief in a meaningful ethic are on the way out. That blind mechanical determinism which flowed from Newtonian mechanics and which seemed inconsistent with ethically oriented and responsible human will no longer finds scientific support. Potentiality is restored to a position of reality. The gulf between mind and matter is no longer in principle unbridgeable. Man need no longer feel that there is an inherent contradiction between his instinctive knowledge that he is a part of a meaningful universe and a cold science, in which he felt he must believe because of its vast success in elucidating so much of the natural world, but which appeared to cut his essential spirit entirely out from that world.

One of the most important features of the development and analysis of modern physics is that, as knowledge expands, the concepts of ordinary language seem more stable than do precise terms of scientific language. The scientific language is derived as an idealization from limited groups of experimental phenomena. Scientific concepts are derived from experience by refined experimental tools and are precisely defined through axioms and definitions. Only through these precise definitions is it possible to connect them with a refined mathematical scheme and derive mathematically the full variety of phenomena possible in the particular field covered by the experiments. Scientific concepts provide a very close fit to the observable results of experiments upon that part of nature accessible to precise measurement and subsumable under mathematically tight deductive systems of scientific concepts. But they may not fit at all with other parts of nature. The concepts of ordinary, natural language, on the other hand, are formed by an immediate connection with reality over many generations. They represent reality over the full span accessible to the human mind, not merely that portion accessible to certain types of precise measurement. Ordinary language concepts may not be precisely defined but they do not lose touch with reality. They may be somewhat modified over the ages. But they are not subject to sudden and complete falsification by a few unexpected results of scientific experiment.

The general trend of thought in the nineteenth century had been toward an ever increasing and widespread confidence in the scientific method and toward a corresponding skepticism with regard to those concepts of the natural language, like mind, soul, life, purpose, duty, justice and God, which do not fit into the closed frame of scientific thought. Twentieth century physics at first increased this skepticism, but then skepticism turned against the over-estimation of precise scientific concepts and finally against skepticism itself. It was finally realized that that part of reality covered by scientific concepts is very limited, and the part not covered by them is unlimited. "Understanding," even of the part covered by scientific concepts must always be based finally upon the natural language. Hence Heisenberg and others conclude that we must be skeptical about skepticism with regard to this natural language and the essential concepts referred to by it. In this way the door is reopened which seemed to be shutting on the possibility of an ethical view of the world not in contradiction with the modern world of science.

Similarly, the climate of belief with respect to all fundamental ideas of philosophy, the concepts of ontology, epistemology, of logic had shifted from that which pervaded much of the nineteenth century and much of this century. No longer do people look at one askance if one says that logical positivism is an inadequate approach to the sum total of reality. Today the writings of a man such as Charles S. Peirce, which received little public attention during his lifetime, are republished and widely commented upon. As confidence in the completeness of our understanding of the material structure of the universe has declined, the stature of the concepts of relation and of mediation has risen to a point where the reality of general ideas, such as duty and justice, is on a par with the reality of the concepts of atomic particles and of simultaneity and of position. And our confidence in our ability to know about and to reason with respect to these general ideas has similarly been restored.

The second factor which seems to me to converge in indicating that one can have grounds for hope that progress can be made in discovering an ethical framework commending itself to belief by the mind of the modern world is the factor of need. I do not mean to imply that merely because something is needed, it is possible. Rather my point is that when the need is not evident and immediate people are apt not to take the pains to get to the bottom of difficult questions. For many generations it appeared to Americans that this country was getting along very well indeed. Our founding fahers had wrestled with the basic question of the relationship of politics to fundamental philosophic and ethical concepts and had produced the United States Constitution. The political institutions which flowed from the Constitution might need minor modification from time to time, but there was little need to rethink the basic philosophic ideas behind them. That had been done and the results were obviously good. Any one who might try to tackle the extremely difficult job of thinking the problems through afresh must be some manner of crank. Today the context has changed. The future no longer looks obviously good. To tackle the job of thinking through to fundamentals does not today convict one of being a crank.

The third factor which impresses me is that ideas and ways of approaching the problem of politics and ethics are now being exchanged among those thinking and writing in this field which offer the prospect of clarifying and simplifying the analysis. These ideas may not be new. Most useful ideas are not novel. But in combination they suggest, to me at least, the possibility that a major step forward can now be made toward clarity and understanding.

"We" and "They"

Let me mention a few of these ideas. First there is the idea that one of the basic questions of politics is that of the "we" and the "they." In any particular context, who is it that is considered to be "we" and who is considered to be the "they"?

Second, there is the idea that any individual participates in an overlapping system of a number of such "we" structures. Third is the idea that associated with each individual and with each group with which he is affiliated there are over-lapping systems of value which are connected with his purposes and the purposes and the functional requirements of each group.

Fourth is the idea that over and beyond the values of any particular array of groupings of human beings there exists an ethical framework which has objective validity, of which men can aspire to have some degree of understanding — not perfect, but approximate — and which can give a measure of insight and guidance to those who seek it.

An important thing about these four ideas in combination is that they make possible a distinction between the values associated with the purposes and interests of an individual and the groups with which he is associated and the ethical framework pursuant to which ethical judgments as between conflicting value systems are to be judged. The fourth idea, the idea that it is possible to rise above both individual value systems and socially formed value systems and obtain some approximate insight as to the nature of an objective ethical framework over and above those value systems is obviously closely related to the traditional concept of natural law.

Let us briefly examine the problems of ethics and foreign policy in the light of these four ideas. To be specific let us assume we are looking at the problem from the point of view of the Secretary of State of the United States.

The Secretary has certain individual distinctions of personal character and personal ambition. He has duties and obligations to the State Department organization which he heads and which looks to him for leadership. He is a member of the executive branch of government, at present operating under a mandate to the Republican Party and a Republican President. He takes his oath of office to uphold the United States Constitution and the faithful execution of the laws.

Even in this highly simplified description of the Secretary's relationship to "we" groups internal to the state, we see a complex of interrelated interests, duties and responsibilities — in short, values. Conflicts of values associated with these different groups arise daily and must be brought into convergence or resolved on some basis. In this context, the primacy of values associated with the nation can be presumed generally to take precedence over those associated with the Secretary as an individual, with the State Department as an organization, or with the Republican-controlled Executive as a branch of government. Nevertheless, even at this level, the harmonizing, integration and concurrent pursuit of multiple values are involved.

When we proceed to the next level and consider the interplay of value systems on the international scene — from the standpoint of the American Secretary of State — we run into similar complexities. The Secretary has a primary obligation and responsibility to the interests of the United States as a nation-state; at this level the people of the United States are the "we", and all other peoples are the "they." The Secretary, in representing the coalition system and alliance systems of which the United States is a leading member, has obligations and responsibilities to a much wider "we" group of nations and peoples. If the thesis advanced in Section V of this paper is accepted, the thesis that a principal task of United States foreign policy is today the construction and defense of a world system of order to replace that shattered in the two world wars, then the values to be pursued by the Secretary of State include those associated with a "we" group virtually coterminous with mankind as a whole.

We have now reached a level of complexity which does not lend itself to simple methods of analysis. Not only are the value systems associated with each "we" group complex; we now have over-lapping "we" groups of expanding comprehensiveness to deal with.

At this point a few general observations on value systems appertaining to an individual nation-state may be pertinent. No single value — such as survival, security, power, wealth, prestige, respect, influence or freedom to actualize its potentialities without unwanted outside interference, can be posited as the supreme value in relationship to which the other values are to be regarded merely as means. Neither are principles ordering the relationship of means to ends to be regarded as absolutes. What is involved is a complex of interrelated values and principles which in the aggregate define the direction and character of the energy comprising the nation-state. The politician may be able to deduce and define with reasonable precision the interests of a state at a given time in history, in a given context and in the light of currently accepted general values for the state. But judgment concerning the adequacy or rightness of those general values of a nation-state requires a process more akin to aesthetics than to deductive logic or to the scientific method.

Furthermore, the values to be maximized are indeterminate as to time. They are not merely to be assessed over the immediate present or in their relation to some future point in time. They are to be integrated over an extended period including the present and the indefinite future. Looking back over other states in past historical eras, one should not assess the values actualized, for instance, by the Athenian city-state merely for their contribution to later civilizations, nor slight them because the Athenian city-state did not indefinitely survive. It is only reasonable to judge that the actualization of values by the Athenians had a component of worth in itself.

What has been said above with reference to the nation-state applies with perhaps even greater force to the values to be associated with Western civilization, with the free world, and most generally, with mankind of today and of the indefinite future. And the values associated with each of these are not identical with, although at many points they may converge with, the values associated with the United States as a nation-state.

VIII. The Ethical Framework

Earlier in this paper it was suggested that the concept "ethical framework" be distinguished from the concept of value systems associated with particular groups or even a limited system of interrelated groups. It was suggested that the phrase "ethical framework" be reserved for those approximate insights into objective value standing above earthbound value systems. Such insights, at a minimum, can be said to relate to the traditional idea of natural law; at a maximum, they can be said to relate to the insights of religion.

Being myself innocent of any theological training or discipline, I prefer to restrict myself to the minimum approach, that relating to natural law and philosophy.

I suggest that the following points have a bearing on the problem of finding some applicable content for such an ethical framework.

The first is the presupposition that the universe and that life are purposeful.

Professor Arnold Brecht of the New School for Social Research has recently re-emphasized the point that the entire structure of the scientific method depends on accepting the presupposition of consubjectivity, the acceptance of the real identity of an object observed by several persons. The scientific method cannot by its own method prove that consubjectivity exists. It accepts this presupposition on grounds of common sense.

That the universe and life are characterized by purpose similarly cannot be proved by the scientific method. The common sense grounds for accepting this ethical presupposition, however, seem fully as solid as those for accepting consubjectivity.

The second point is that the general direction of that purpose is not wholly beyond the insight of man. Common sense again rejects the proposition that if the universe is purposeful that purpose is trivial. It is possible to conceive of highly trivial conceptions and then of less trivial and still less trivial conceptions. A highly trivial conception, for instance, would be that the purpose of the universe is to maximize on a given day the production of bathtubs. A less trivial, but still basically trivial, conception would be that the purpose of the universe is to maximize the material satisfactions of mankind over the span of existence of mankind. If any distinction can validly be made between degrees of triviality, the general direction in which the non-trivial is to be found is, in principle, established.

Third, mankind has in the past developed non-trivial approaches to the question of the meaning and purpose of the universe and of life. The approaches by each of the great cultures have differed but none of them has been trivial. That of modern Western civilization — which has now spread to form at least a major component of the approach of most of the world — is based upon the accumulated experience, insight and wisdom of the Judeo-Christian, Greco-Roman and European cultures. One generation after another has added, adapted, tested for error, reconciled theory with practice and practice with theory. The resulting structure may be complex; it may not be wholly consistent; it may not be fully adequate to today's world; but it is not trivial. From it does emerge a sense of direction, an aid to understanding, a sense of the beautiful and an insight into values transcending those of individual, of class, of nation, of sect, or of generation — in other words, a framework of reason, of aesthetics and of ethics.

The fourth point is that the human will can be effective only at the margin. Freedom is not absolute either for individuals or for nations. Much is determined by forces beyond our control, by events of the past which are irreversible, by accident or chance. At any given moment in time the margin of freedom left us may seem so small as to make it hardly worthwhile to exercise our will one way or the other. But the narrow margin of today becomes the foundation of the broader possibility for tomorrow. Over time the margin of freedom — of the possible — expands geometrically. The decision of today makes possible, or forecloses, ten decisions of tomorrow.

Fifth, the accumulated wisdom and experience of the past do not always give unambiguous precedents for decisions and actions at the relevant margin of freedom of the present. A new integration of general purpose with the concrete possibilities of the present may then become necessary.

Sixth, changes in degree may, at some point, move so far as to become a change in kind. The most difficult issues of foreign policy and ethics arise where changes of degree become so great that they cross this boundary line and fundamental changes in past policy seem to be indicated.

Let us examine a currently important foreign policy issue in the context of the ideas suggested above. Are any of those ideas relevant, and, if so, how and to what extent?

As an example, let us consider the circumstances, if any, under which the deployment and possible use of nuclear weapons might be justified.

Western civilization and its antecedent cultures have not taken the view that the precept of the Sixth Commandment was to be taken as an absolute. The values of achieving or maintaining freedom, diversity and cultural growth and of combatting tyranny, reaction and cultural stagnation or death have been generally considered to overweigh, at least under certain circumstances, the strong presumption against the taking of life. There has been much debate about the circumstances under which the important values are so threatened as to justify action involving the loss of life and much debate about what can be done to reduce the chances of such circumstances arising. But, except for absolute pacifists, the major point — that there may be such circumstances — has been agreed and has been the basis on which foreign policy has been conducted and judged from time immemorial.

There have been, from time to time, changes in the degree of destructiveness of weapons and of war. These changes have, up to now, generally been considered not to have invalidated the major point. But, with the advent of nuclear weapons in volume, we are faced with a new issue. Has the change in degree now become one of kind? At the extreme of the possible it may very well have become such. The release of the full potential for destruction of the nuclear weapons presently available in national stockpiles could amount to virtually total destruction.

Our consideration of an ethical framework suggests that the values, even the most important values, associated with any partial group of mankind, say the United States or the U.S.S.R. as nation-states, must be presumed not to be ultimate. A course of action likely to lead to general destruction cannot, therefore, be justified in support of those values.

That there are no conceivable circumstances under which the deployment and possible use of nuclear weapons would be justified does not, however, necessarily flow from the same premises.

The argument is made that the whole purpose of a policy of nuclear deterrence is to prevent nuclear weapons from being used. The thesis is that nuclear deterrence both makes possible the preservation of the values of freedom, diversity and cultural growth and makes the general destruction of a nuclear war so unlikely as to make the risk tolerable. Some would argue that no risk of so important a stake is tolerable. At a minimum it is clear that the risk must be reduced below its present magnitude. Can that be done? This is largely a question of fact rather than a question for ethical judgment. I believe it can, with great effort, be done — that by, say, 1965 we can so design and construct our nuclear defense system that no rational purpose could be served by the Soviet Union in initiating nuclear war and that, thereafter, little purpose would be served by either side in further accelerating the nuclear arms race. At such a time, if it has not earlier been possible, agreements on the control and regulation of armaments still further reducing the risk of nuclear war should, in my opinion, be possible.

An analysis of the reasons for the inherent instability in the current weapons confrontation between the U.S.S.R. and the U.S. and the technical considerations which lead to the belief that this inherent instability can be radically reduced over the next few years is not appropriate for inclusion in this paper. The point relevant to this analysis is that an assessment of the facts, of feasible possibilities, and of probable consequences of alternative courses of action is an essential element in judging any important issue of foreign policy and ethics.

But the even more important conclusion is that the meaningful analysis of foreign policy cannot even be begun unless we have some idea of an ethical framework from which the analysis can derive its **relevance.**

The Morality and Politics of Intervention

Manfred Halpern

It is not inevitable that men should ask whether it is moral to intervene in the internal affairs of other nations. To some, it has obviously become a mere question of posture—how to keep a straight face while intervening, how to smile piously when discovered, and how to win converts during the moral upsurge that should accompany the exposure of others in the great game of intervention. Some are convinced that the Communist world represents a menace so evil that any action against this threat, as long as it is successful, is by definition moral, or else merely a problem of techniques.

If the question of morality is evaded by the technicians of power and the secular crusaders, the meaning of intervention is often obscured by traditional preconceptions. Only at first glance does "intervention" seem an obviously identifiable act carrying obvious consequences. In a world built upon national sovereignties and jurisdictions and the equality of independent states, any state that intervenes in the internal affairs of another undermines the institutional and legal foundations on which its own existence rests. This is a truth of great consequences to which we shall have to return. But it is not the only truth. Intervention, which by its nature subverts the foundations of the existing international system, takes place in a system which is by its nature fundamentally unstable. States in fact are not equal: nations can exploit the rules and opportunities of the present international system to enlarge their power over others and so risk death on a vast scale. We live at a time when intervention, by subverting the sovereignty of national independence, may further undermine the only rules of the game that now maintain order, yet when only intervention may be able to restore the free operation of these rules, save freedom in a nation or, indeed, help to create a more secure and more freely interdependent world order. In our world, intervention can be moral or immoral, or simultaneously illegal and justifiable. The morality of intervention is determined both by the principles it creates or destroys and by the contingencies of circumstances. Intervention therefore involves a realm of morality in which a discussion of principles is essential but in which no discussion of principles has relevance for the next act of intervention or nonintervention until the circumstances surrounding that act have also been discussed.

It is an illustration of the unstable character of the present international system that there is no agreement on the definition of the
two acts most likely to destroy the sovereignty, independence and
equality of any participant of the system, or perhaps even the system
itself—namely, aggression and intervention. That is not to say that
there is no agreement whatever. There is enough agreement to make
the system endure; not sufficient agreement to make it stable. Nonetheless, to say that intervention is interference (falling short of aggressively
crossing the frontiers with military force) in the internal affairs of
another sovereign state is almost to obscure the question. We live,
more now than ever, in an interdependent world. Almost everything
that a powerful nation does (or almost everything that a weak nation,
like the Congo, is powerless to do) vitally affects the internal affairs
of many other nations.

A great power intervenes in the domestic realm of other states
when it says yes and when it says no; indeed by its sheer existence.
By our very model of life we set an example for the Russians which
stings Khrushchev to competition and not a few of his citizens to an
emulation subversive of the official ideal of Bolshevik Man, even if
not directly of the Soviet government. We intervene when we say no
to the Aswan Dam, without which Egypt's standard of poverty would
further deteriorate; we intervene correspondingly when we say yes
to the Volta Dam in Ghana.[2]

It has been said that if the American economy sneezes, the world's
economy, and especially countries depending on the export of a single
raw material, catch pneumonia. A socialist is entitled to say that
deliberate nonintervention by governments in their own richer and
more powerful domestic economies may cause as much suffering,
not only at home but abroad, as the deliberate exploitation of poorer
and weaker foreign economies. The capitalist recognizes the potency
of such economic intervention in the affairs of other sovereign states
both when he opposes and when he supports selective foreign aid.
Intentions alone do not keep actions from being interventionist. The
Western democracies' intention not to intervene in the Spanish Civil
War was one of the crucial factors intervening in favor of General
Franco's victory.

Intervention may include propaganda, espionage, discriminatory
economic policies, assistance to legitimate governments in their domestic
tasks[3] no less than aid to subversive movements, and support or denial
of support to governments or their opposition in domestic crises where
such foreign support might prove to be decisive. There is no validity
in confining the term only to those actions which the *legitimate* govern-

ment of the country considers to be intervention. In an age of social and colonial revolutions, any prudent government will be as sensitive to the reactions of the future rulers of Angola or Iran to intervention and its consequences as to the reactions of the present ruling regimes. In trying to distinguish intervention from other actions that have consequences across frontiers, one can only set outer limits: intervention is any action, beginning with deliberate or remediable interaction among nations, that significantly affects the public internal realm of another sovereign state and which stops short of aggressive crossing of international frontiers.[4] Intervention is action along a continuum of possible choices. The range of alternative courses once men have decided to intervene (or indeed, not to intervene) is far greater than is usually thought of when men debate intervention. Our political and moral responsibility in the realm of intervention is therefore far greater than we usually assume.

Several objections may be raised against so broad a definition of intervention. Certainly it would not be helpful for USIA to speak of such constructive American policies as the application of the Truman Doctrine in Greece and Turkey, or our successful efforts to deter the French from deposing in 1951 the nationalist-minded King of the then French Protectorate of Morocco, as a policy of intervention. To refer to American policy publicly as a "diplomacy of involvement" may be no less accurate, but more agreeable, reserving the harder word "intervention" to describe the actions of unfriendly nations. In the present clinical discussion, a single term is more fitting for describing this singular form of national behavior.

A more profound and substantive objection may be raised, namely that giving such wide compass to the meaning of intervention will tend to undermine precious distinctions between coercion and persuasion in international diplomacy. These distinctions are vital, but they do not take the simple form often ascribed to them. No serious great power tries to persuade another nation unless it means to convince. Whether it wins its case or strikes a bargain depends not merely on the soundness of its arguments but also on the coercive weight of power that each interested nation experienced or wished to avoid experiencing. In international affairs, coercion begins at the moment of persuasion. There is only one important exception, namely where two nations have agreed on overlapping national interests in a situation in which one nation is not invidiously dependent on the other. In all other cases the crucial distinction in international relations does not lie in the separation of power and persuasion, but in the difference among the means and ends of power and persuasion—or among types of intervention (discussed below). It still makes a considerable difference whether the coercive component in intervention is assassination and terror or whether it is a deliberate reduction in economic aid. Men who in the present world order are inclined to draw a fundamental contrast between persuasion and coercion in international affairs tend to become either impotent idealists or else seeming realists who hand over to the technicians of power any problem not yet solved by discussion. Those who know that persuasion and coercion are inseparable in the uses of authority may require experts in covert activities and armed combat, but they have no need for men who specialize in power, or else in morality.

The Relevance of Morality to Intervention

At this point, some may be ready to respond to the complex interrelationship of power and morality by relaxing into moral ambiguities or, which is the same thing, platitudes. Others may be content to trust instead to individual moral leadership, forgetting that the same man who rightly would not read another individual's mail must find standards by which we would enthusiastically break another nation's code. A man who would not hesitate physically and immediately to avenge an insult to his wife's honor may not act with similar assurance when a hundred million dead become the price of avenging a nation's honor.

Complexity must not deter us. The need for wisdom has grown: intervention is likely to become more common than ever before precisely as we succeed, through military technology, in making gains through outright aggression less probable, even while the conflict between ourselves and expansionist Communism remains unresolved. Under these terms also, the danger of uncontrolled intervention escalating into unintended but destructive aggression rises—but so also rises the price of nonintervention whenever Communist nations are already intervening. The greater our power and our responsibility, the greater the need also to find a valid and moral code for our actions in history.

There is no obvious synthesis between morality and intervention. It is a cruel simplicity that makes a virtue of necessity or a necessity of virtue. To balance the demands of morality against the demands of victory in order to strike a mere compromise is almost bound to frustrate action and damage morality. Nor is morality merely an added decoration or only an ultimate grace: morality, especially when it serves to strengthen lawful stability or stabilizing change, has obvious practical consequences. These we ignore at our peril whenever we are tempted to gain only the practical results of power, and imitate the tactics of conflict management developed by Communists or sometimes attributed to them by our our own secular crusaders who compliment Communists beyond reason by believing them to be omnipotent and omnipresent in conspiracy and subversion. Surely the problem deserves to be resolved in terms of choices based on our own values of world order.

Nothing is easier than to state the solution in abstract terms: we must choose the right means for the right ends, and then apply our full force to achieve our goals. But what can this mean in practice? I would attach myself to a view voiced for about two and a half millenia: morality is not the highest value, and neither is power or knowledge. What matters is the best and most relevant relationship between these three—a union which in its contemplative aspect may be called wisdom and in its active phase, justice. Nothing is more difficult, nor more necessary, in practice.[5]

Let us see just how difficult it can be. On July 14, 1958, the State Department in Washington received a telegram from the President of Lebanon requesting the landing of American forces within twenty-four hours in order to save that country's political integrity and independence. The issues seemed clear enough. The President of Lebanon had been the only Middle Eastern leader to endorse the Eisenhower Doctrine, which committed the U.S. to come to the aid of any Middle Eastern country which requested assistance "against armed aggression from any country controlled by international Communism." Here, explained President Eisenhower, was a government that had been democratically elected, and that was now threatened by subversion armed and encouraged from outside. Here, as the State Department briefed the press, appeared to be a clear-cut case: we must demonstrate that we are ready to support our allies when they need us. American inaction, especially at a moment when pro-Western leaders had just been overthrown in Iraq, could result in the dominance of the Middle East by Soviet or Nasser imperialism "assuming," as American officials pondered, "that these are or could remain separate." In a recent prize-winning series on Communism, *Life* recalled our Lebanese intervention as a major demonstration that we could stop Communism in its tracks.

The real story, however, does not begin in July 1958. Early in 1957, Lebanese President Chamoun faced the bitter truth that during the preceding decade, the birthrate had shifted the balance of power in his country. In 1943, when Christian Arabs were still the majority in the country, the Moslem Arabs and the other minorities had agreed that Christians would always assume the position of President, Foreign Minister, and Commander-in-Chief of the Army while Moslems would always assume the office of the Prime Minister and the Speaker of Parliament. All other positions in the state were similarly frozen on the basis of sectarian strength. By 1957 it had become clear to everyone that Moslems were turning into a majority, and that most Moslems and an appreciable number of Christians were being attracted to Nasser's neutralist, socialist, and authoritarian Arab nationalism.

Chamoun was unwilling, in a state founded upon ten Christian sects, three Moslem sects, and several "others," and hence viable, if at all, only by compromise, to strive for a new bargain consonant with the changing situation. He might have eased the transition to a system in which Moslems would have gained more responsibility or to a secular state in which all jobs are indiscriminately open to all men of talent, and in which Lebanese Christians, thanks to their superior education and prosperity, would have remained at least equal in influence for a long time to come. Instead, in order to make up in foreign backing for what he had lost in domestic support, he agreed to the Eisenhower Doctrine. Then, in order to perpetuate the status quo, Chamoun rigged the 1957 election enough to give himself that two-thirds parliamentary majority required to amend the constitution so that Parliament could re-elect him for a second six-year term.[6]

When the majority had thus been deprived of the effective use of the ballot while the country, hitherto neutral in intra-Arab conflicts, was being transformed into a pro-Western bulwark against the spread of neutralist Arab nationalism, the opposition resorted to bullets and the civil war began. Into this civil war, Nasser soon sent arms, money, and men, and we, after several months, our own armed forces.

One other fact has to be mentioned. Most politically active Lebanese believe that there is conclusive evidence that the Lebanese President and Foreign Minister, though they failed to consult other members of their government, had from the start acted in concert with CIA. The American intervention in Lebanon seemed to them, as to most other observers, to be part of American efforts after the Suez Crisis of late 1956 to stem the growing influence of Nasser's neutralist nationalism. This naturally raises a major question to which we shall have to return: does our knowledge of Middle Eastern forces and trends suggest that it is a moral or necessary use of American power to intervene against neutralist nationalism?

By July 14, 1958, however, there were some additional issues at stake. By the day the telegram arrived, UN observers had already succeeded in materially reducing the level of UAR intervention in Lebanon; the Commander-in-Chief of the Lebanese army, who had used his Christian-officered, but Moslem- and Christian-manned army to umpire the civil war rather than to fight the opposition, was already laying the groundwork for the compromise that would end the war and make him President. It had also become evident that we had be-come progressively less eager to have Chamoun cash the blank check we had given him—calling for the intervention of American troops. On the other hand, the telegram was sent a few hours after a coup in Iraq overthrew the only Arab government bound to the West by a defense pact. Since no one in Beirut or Washington had anticipated this coup at this moment, nor knew much about its main actors, ignor-ance conjured up fears and fears led some to think about being close enough, if necessary, to intervene in Iraq.

In addition to seeming new dangers, those who had to answer the telegram now also had to face fundamental and conflicting moral issues only distantly related to their original intentions. Could they, seeing the Lebanese situation itself now closer to solution, afford to say no, and so let it be said by our allies in NATO and elsewhere that when it comes to a showdown, the U.S. is likely to have second thoughts? How reliable would that make us as an ally? Who would trust our pledge in the future? Yet should the United States now add a larger, more dramatic commitment to support a status quo that had already been undermined by the kind of forces against which Marines lack adequate weapons—birthrates and nationalism? What would have been a wise and just decision?

We chose to land troops. The troops fired on no one; the American mediator who entered in their wake strengthened and secured the compromise that had already been in the making. But our landing of 10,000 troops in a country half the size of New Jersey also had various other consequences. The compromise brought about the departure from his country of the all too pro-Western Foreign Minister, Charles Malik, gave the rebels the Premiership, but under the firm neutral leadership of the new President, General Chehab. The compromise has also led to a new, yet deeply frustrating deadlock among Lebanese factions. As a result, little has been done since 1958 to resolve the imbalance between political structure and political reality which helped to produce the civil war.

The case must be summed up in paradoxes. We concluded that our international status demanded our intervention at a time when we were beginning to feel that the situation in Lebanon itself no longer required it. We demonstrated to the world the solidity of our commitment to our friends, by intervening with immediate, well-coordinated, and major force, but we also exposed to the world our incapacity to airlift more than 10,000 troops to more than one trouble-spot at one time.[7] The com-promise solution we helped to fashion left our closest friends without further power, so that other Middle Eastern governments could draw various valid lessons: the United States, whether in a right or wrong cause, will not deny itself the use of force and therefore must always be reckoned with; it will employ its horses and its men in its own national interests, and not necessarily in trying to put even an apparently pro-Western Humpty Dumpty together again. Even so, the Humpty Dumpties on our side may still take comfort: we do not use our strength to make structural changes; we merely put others on top of the wall. A UN resolution propounded with remarkable unanimity by all Arab states (presumably the kind of unity which we had earlier viewed with reserve) provided the basis on which our forces agreed to leave Lebanon. And contemporary Lebanese governments find it more difficult to act on advice for dealing with their still searing problems of social change than the pre-1958 government with whom we so eagerly agreed to repress the problems of change.

I have dealt with the Lebanese intervention in such detail because no wise and just action is ever hypothetical. Unlike our interventions in Cuba or Laos, the Lebanese case also is neither familiar nor (oddly enough) controversial, and hence may most easily lead to fresh insights. For from this one example (with suitable footnotes to other similar actions), we shall be able to raise most of the relevant questions and, possibly, conclusions for the general problem we are considering.

Needless to say, I consider most aspects of our intervention in Lebanon as an unhappy demonstration of American power, morality, and knowledge. Our difficulties stem from failures in each of these three realms of power, morality and knowledge, and from the faulty connections we fashioned among them.

The Relevance of Knowledge to Moral Intervention

To begin with knowledge, we have scarcely begun to develop theories of social change that would allow us to understand the fundamental revolutions now in progress in the world, and hence to develop doctrines of intervention relevant to the politics of modernization.[8] Khrushchev has a theory. It is a dogmatic one, and it has led him into error as often as not. But he has a theory which sensitizes him to the great fact of rapid historical transformation that constitutes the modern age. It makes him more aware than we are to the probability that governments owing their power to deadlocked sectarian parochialism or to absentee landlords are not long for this world. Communists are not responsible for having started the revolution of modernization and Khrushchev is dogmatically wrong about the inevitability of the next stage of social development. But if we compete against his partially correct theory about social change with no theory at all, he may well turn out to be right about the next stage as well, not because of his theory but because of our errors and omissions.

Lacking a theory that would help us understand the transformation of societies, we have tended to play for possible lucky breaks in history, though the breaks have not always come or do not always linger. Or else we have tended to be hard-headedly manipulative, but without a sense of theory or ideology. We are the inventors of a new kind of revolution—the hit-and-run revolution. We help make it and go home and leave the politics of social change, that alone can justify and fulfill a revolution, almost entirely to others who have even less appreciation of the problems of social transformation than we do.

We are not entirely without knowledge. If we do not yet possess a major theory about social change as broad in its concerns and as related to action as Marx's, but a hundred years younger and less dogmatic (for it would lead to mischief merely to look for a counter-creed), we still have available a number of insights that would form part of any such theory. One such proposition, for example, is that improved administrative efficiency, economic amelioration, and political concessions offered by a regime that is morally and politically isolated from the most important newly emergent classes cannot preserve political consensus has broken down, the price of political stability in modern times is to overcome the moral and political isolation between ruler and ruled. This certainly requires, among other things, economic and administrative progress but these cannot substitute for political enterprise that goes to the root of the matter. Another proposition is that the longer repression succeeds in postponing the political adjustments to the transformation of a society's structure and values, the more likely it is that the more extreme and violent elements will gain leadership of the opposition. From these propositions alone it would follow that you can, if you must, use Marines to intervene, in a rebellion affecting a change in top personnel. You can not, even if you try, use Marines effectively to intervene in a revolution that is transforming what men believe, how they live, and how they relate to each other.

The revolution of the peoples of the underdeveloped areas to build institutions that would put them in command rather than at the mercy of the forces of modernization is more searing than any that ever confronted the West. It takes place, for the most part, in the face of fewer resources and skills, greater poverty and population pressure, and in societies that were, until a few decades ago, sure of their ancient truths and traditions. They are now driven by the pressure of sheer needs and new aspirations and the pain of backwardness and powerlessness in the presence of the industrialized nations to pass through their revolution in telescoped time.

If we have failed to understand the dimensions of the forces now transforming Asia, Africa, and Latin America, and viewed them frequently from the shallower perspective of cliques and personalities struggling for power, the fault has not only been in the inadequate state of our intellectual knowledge. The experience that would make us receptive to such knowledge has until recently been lacking. Our own society has been in the midst of constant change, but we have always, barring one civil war, been able to maintain a consensus on our basic social, economic, moral and political values and institutions. We have been able to pay so much attention to the individual because we could afford to take our institutions for granted. We are only beginning to experience the pain of bafflement and frustration that comes from living in a world changing both hopefully and dangerously, and certainly quickly and seemingly beyond control. We are coming to recognize that our institutions are not yet adequate to maintain peace, eliminate ignorance, bigotry and poverty, deal with the sheer growth of the number of people, facts and institutions, master technology, and preserve and spread beauty. We are only gradually becoming interested in the theory and practice of social change.

We cannot yet effectively capitalize on our knowledge in this field because we have so far invested much more in power than in the knowledge on which the prudent and effective exercise of power must be based. We intervene about as often in the internal affairs of other nations as the USSR, but the world is (and we ourselves ought to be) harder on us when we do. Since intervention, when it involves duress, is normally neither a legal nor a democratic exercise, we must have better reasons, founded on better values and sounder knowledge when we intervene than are offered by Communist dogma.

One reason for our intervention is, of course, partly beyond our control: we cannot be secure in a non-Communist world where domestic political life is in turmoil or guided by dogmatic or cynical adventurers. Within limits, the USSR can prosper from such instability. But not all burdens which this invidious problem imposes on us are inescapable. Had we really explored the roots and implications of neutralism when we intervened against it in Lebanon and Laos? Have we explored all mechanisms by which internal conflicts can be insulated from the cold war?

Our lack of knowledge and foresight about problems of Asian, African and Latin American stability in which we have an intrinsically greater stake than the USSR also often forces us into intervention against our expectations. We often fail to anticipate crises. Yet there is a world of difference between the range of choices and the decisions one can make when one is aware of the forces and trends of history and the decision at a moment of crisis—when you are no longer free to pick the issue but when you must say yea or nay. On July 14, 1958, we were no longer free to say nay in Lebanon and break our word, yet many were the options we had before that day.

The position of the United States in world affairs, for the sake of power and morality alike, puts a premium on adequate knowledge. Yet the institutional barriers remain high against overcoming our historical ignorance and preconceptions about our rapidly changing world. Until very recently, we were governed by a generation whose education did not include knowledge about that majority of the world which lives in Asia, Africa, and Latin America. A large number of our policy-makers are lawyers, and many lawyers tend to see history as moving from case to case, instead of as a ceaseless trial that can sometimes be made to move in one direction rather than another but that has no final solutions. We are also, as a people, so action-minded that many of our best and most devoted policy-makers are seldom tempted enough, and therefore seldom find time enough, after their intense preoccupation with the evils that are sufficient unto the day, to think about the relevance of their actions to the long-term forces and trends of history. The machinery they have built over the years reflects their predilections. It swarms with facts; it seethes (if not always productively) with action, but few parts of State or CIA are smaller than those whose task it is to devote themselves, full-time, to long-range analysis and estimates.

Knowledge, however, bears an effective relationship not only to power but also to morality. One major reason why there is not yet a controlling international sense of morality is that the world does not yet share a single structure of knowledge, values, and sanctions. This moral deficiency in turn demands and perpetuates a hierarchical inequality of knowledge in each nation. This is an issue of intrinsic yet unavoidable danger. Precisely on the most vital questions of power, where emotions most require the discipline of knowledge and life itself may be at stake, knowledge can least of all be prudently shared with others who will certainly experience the consequences of action. Just prior to intervention and war, security is likely to dictate the greatest restrictions, even within the government itself, on men's "need to know."

Granting all this, I believe nonetheless that we have let secrecy hinder the application of knowledge and advice so far that both morality and power have suffered. This is worth saying especially since all the pressures are still moving in the direction of narrowing the spread of knowledge and the range of debate: witness President Kennedy's pleas for voluntary press censorship after the Cuban intervention. As long as rivalries among independent sovereignties force citizens to accept an inequality of knowledge about questions of security, it remains all the more essential to insist that the leaders of our nation persist in constant exchange with the moral and political consensus of their community. Yet their isolation from that consensus is proceeding apace. We are, as a nation, approaching the moral disability of the international system as a whole. Differences in power positions are leading to growing differences in knowledge, values, and sanctions available to different segments of our community.

The fact that the community can no longer arrive at a sense of wisdom and justice because it lacks adequate knowledge and power in the crucial fields of subversion, weapons technology, and social change in strange civilizations makes its notions about the morality of intervention often impractical or else seemingly relevant only because its maxims survived from an earlier age when our institutions were being created and knowledge, power and morality were still more closely entwined with each other. Compensations for this weakness are possible but they are seldom brought into play. Our leaders do not, on the basis of their own special knowledge, take much more time to lead the discussion that could clarify our national purpose than they now take for clarifying the historical and moral context of their acts of intervention. On the contrary, they sometimes feel impelled right up to the moment of intervention to speak enthusiastically against it.[9] Congress seems to have yielded its legislative and educational power on fundamental national issues to the Supreme Court, but the Supreme Court will not be able to guide us with equal strength on foreign affairs. Congress has a watchdog committee over the Atomic Energy Commission which can transform matter but still neglects to appoint a similar committee over CIA which can transform men and history.

Most of the press west of the Potomac is of little help in discussing and clarifying issues that could lead to intervention. Bipartisanship among our political leaders helped turn the failure of our intervention in Cuba into a numbing celebration of national unity before the discussion had scarcely begun, and inhibits debate on Laos or Vietnam. In contrast to democratic Britain, we also suffer from a peculiar form of patriotism. While the British Parliament sharply debated the merits of the Suez invasion of 1956 while it was in progress, and similarly argued British troops landings in Jordan contemporary with American landings in Lebanon in 1958, the Speaker of the House of Representatives, Mr. Rayburn, effectively stopped debate in Congress during the Lebanese intervention by saying that "in times like these we had better allow matters to develop rather than make remarks about them." Though our national interest had become deeply involved, our survival as a nation was not at stake in Lebanon. Why then should the noble sentiment of patriotism turn into a crippling disease of eye, ear, nose and throat? Is a Congressional, instead of a parliamentary, system doomed either to irrelevance or irresponsibility in the conduct of today's foreign affairs?

The top decision-makers are thus usually left to pursue the national interest, especially in the field of interventions, without any lively, free, or constant touch with the moral and intellectual consensus of the nation or its most representative institutions. What is more, this relative isolation of the decision-makers from the community's consensus, rendered painless by the community's widespread stereotyped acquiescence, persists in institutionalized form almost to the pinnacles of power. Few are the experts in government who are consulted prior to an intervention. What is publicly known about our intervention in Cuba in 1961 illustrates this. Considerations of security, curbing the security-cleared government official's access to information, may well at times have harmed our security.

It is my impression that there are very few among our experts at intervention who are not hard-working, intelligent, imaginative, and courageous far above the average of men. It is also my impression, however, (and this one more likely to be erroneous than the first) that just as the Office of War Information during World War II tended to attract an unusually large number of men who responded to the grandly heroic, hopefully liberal, and victory-promising aspects of the war, so CIA has attracted a core of men similarly attuned to one aspect of their task and their age. They know they are engaged in a cold war without foreseeable end, in an institution which reflects America's recent reaction against its long infatuation with idealistic legalism and its tough-minded discovery of the morality of power. They are involved in a task that must avoid publicity as much as possible, engaged in acts they would not countenance as citizens in their own country, blocked from discussing their problems with anyone but their immediate colleagues, under attack more often from the liberal moralist than the rightist actionist. They have rejected the ideological historicism of their enemy, but they have not yet developed a systematic understanding of their own concerning the forces of history. It is not surprising, therefore, that CIA should have attracted to its ranks of expert interventionists especially the technician of power and the energetic but doctrineless conservative. They are not the only kind of person working at CIA, but their presence inhibits that concern with the linking of knowledge, morality, and power that insures, as far as it can be insured by man, wise and just intervention.[10]

We have been fortunate so far that at the very top of power, in the Presidency, and often close to it, the country has been blessed ever since our final initiation as a world power—during the months preceding our entrance into World War II—with leadership of intelligence and morality. If the actions and interventions of this leadership have not always lived up to expectations, it is in part because our leaders are human and not omnipotent. It is in part also because they have been most intimately in touch with two, not entirely helpful, collections of men. On issues of intervention, the broad American constituency acquiesces in any seeming success against Communism and is most erratic in the interpretation and punishment of what it, or some segment of the public, considers failures. (Compare the public's reaction to China, Cuba, Lebanon, and Congo.) The other group, the President's most immediate advisers on intervention, have labored under the limitations which we have been describing, affecting the state of the art and constituting a profession more skilled in surgery than in the problems of disease. The final responsibilities of the President cannot be lessened, but under present circumstances, the handicaps under which any President must decide on intervention are dangerously high. A wiser American consensus on the merit and uses of intervention has become a necessity for clarifying and sustaining that final decision which only one man can make in each concrete case. Informed public discussion of at least the fundamental issues and types of intervention is essential to this end. But discussion is no longer a simple task. It could easily make intervention of any kind more difficult to carry out. It could arouse public pressure for crusades in behalf of moralism. Practice and passion have outrun discussion. Whatever the perils, there is no way of creating a relevant consensus except by discussion.

Types and Uses of Intervention

As one contribution to such a discussion, I should like to examine several types of intervention and ask to what degree each might be wise or just.

Counter-intervention: No other kind of intervention is as easy to justify. It is an action designed to help free a country from the interventionist manipulations of another power and so enable it to regain its sovereign integrity and independence—that is, to stand free again of all interventions. It is coercion intended to create options rather than, as in the Soviet intervention in Hungary, to foreclose them.

Easy to justify, it is not at all easy to do well. For while it is not unreasonably difficult to define the point at which intervention becomes imperative, it is most difficult to help create that degree of internal stability which makes it prudent again to end intervention. Intervention involves, clearly, not merely a manipulation of power but a sharing in the historical trials of others.

Intervention Through Indirect Imperialist Rule: Though its advocates may wish to call it "preventive intervention" it closely resembles the form of colonialism known as "indirect rule." We intervene to impose rulers who promise to be resolutely anti-Communist, but we leave them otherwise free to pursue any domestic policy they please. This indirect imperialist form of intervention has caused the United States more harm than any other kind of initiative we have undertaken, in particular because—for a number of good reasons—it can usually be counted upon to produce the very dangers we most feared when we first embarked on such adventures.

The initial argument raised in favor of indirect imperialist intervention is normally not confined to the reasonable proposition that if the USSR or its agents are about to intervene, why let the USSR gain the initiative—why wait until the legal government can no longer seek our aid and we are forced to embark on the more difficult path of helping to organize a counter-revolution? Such clear and present danger would justify *Pre-emptive Intervention.* (And the final justification of such a pre-emptive purchase of time is, of course, what constructive use we make of it.) The argument for indirect imperialist intervention goes further. It does not trust the existing government, one composed, say, of Laotian neutralists, to invite our aid *if* pressed by the USSR or its agents. It does not trust Mosadeq of Iran or Kassim of Iraq to know when or how to stop short of opportunistic collaboration with local Communists. Or, in the form of an Anglo-French argument, it does not trust Nasser to keep the Suez Canal open or run it efficiently. One could readily list more examples: it has been our favorite form of forceful intervention, and it has almost inevitably backfired. Why?

It was founded, in part, on insufficient knowledge. In an Asia, Africa, and Latin America that have a highly sensitive pride in their new nationalism, the danger that neutralist nationalists might willingly yield to Soviet control has usually been less than we have feared. On the other hand, the danger that "pro-Western" regimes, by stifling popular nationalist and reformist impulses, would sap their internal support has been far greater than we usually anticipated. We have also tended to underestimate the readiness and effectiveness, as in the Congo, or in Syria between 1954 and 1958, with which nationalists will turn to whichever great power did not intervene first for countervailing force against the original transgressor. The results might have been much worse, had it not been possible to mobilize UN intervention to counter national interventions which the U.S. did not support, as at Suez, or about which it had second thoughts, as in the Congo.

Indirect imperialist intervention has been pernicious morally because it has invariably been invoked against nationalist neutralists instead of Communists, apparently on the devil-ridden notion, happily on the decline since about 1960, that those who are not with us are against us. It has thus obscured the moral distinction between our sense of world order and that of the Communists, all the more so since the USSR has, from about 1951, based its foreign policy on the premise that those who were not against it were potentially for it.

In the realm of power, indirect imperialist intervention has therefore alienated rather than won people. It has never been truly preventive. In no instance—neither in Iran nor Lebanon nor Laos or in other places not to be mentioned—has power been devoted to the creation of that dynamic stability that might produce a resilience and immunization to subversion by extremist forces. In the future, indirect imperialist intervention may prove even less pertinent as an exercise in power than before. Given the state of the international Communist movement, not every local Communist coup may be automatically interpreted as a Moscow initiative. It may be a new thorn in Moscow's (or Peking's) side. Yugoslavia may not be the only Communist nation we can afford to live with.

Precautionary Intervention: This involves a kind of action which our government and our people have least discussed. Let me, for the moment therefore, merely outline some of the pros and cons of such intervention.

Among the most significant examples of how we failed to intervene in time are Hitler's Germany three decades ago and Algeria, where French colonial policy had reached a dead end more than a decade ago. Today the most foreboding case is probably the Republic of South Africa. Our own moderate southerner need not fear: there is an obvious distinction between a policy intent upon achieving rapid equality, with deliberate speed, and a policy bent on perpetuating and deepening racial inequality. There is a technical strategic question (there usually is)—can we defend ourselves successfully against missiles looped around the South Pole without the cooperation of the Republic of South Africa? But there is also one obvious estimate to be made: within the next few years, the Republic of South Africa is going to be a bloodier battleground within the free world than Algeria, because the Republic has no imperial overlord that can act as final arbiter, because the white settlers do not have an obvious place to which to return (though there are available areas for emigration), and the grievances of the non-Europeans are obviously worse than in Algeria. Do we intervene now or after the bloodbath starts? Do we insist on a solution now, or after the Communists gain greater influence among the Africans, and other African nations also covertly intervene?

The objections to such intervention can be phrased in terms applicable to both the Republic of South Africa and to other similar areas. Is the United State to intervene in the domestic affairs of countries with which we have satisfactory foreign relations? Are we to intervene wherever men are oppressed and exploited? Do we not establish a mischievous breach in international law if we proclaim our right to overthrow tyrants who, however brutal at home, trespass on none of their neighbors? After all, we do not intervene against Communism because it is tyrannous but because it is expansionist and threatening us. If precautionary intervention from outside seems prudent, should it not be reserved for the collective action of the states of the region or, when that appears infeasible, the United Nations?

The contrary position is not destroyed by these arguments, however. The various regions of the world suffer from various limitations in handling precautionary intervention by agreement among their constituent states. Neither Asia as such, nor any important subregion with it, possess the requisite unity for this kind of joint positive action. Africa might be able to act in unison, but only against European, not African, leadership on that continent. The Americas cannot act without us, and might not act with us. UN action, affected by these differences among and within regions, therefore depends powerfully on the response of the United States. What do we stand for in the world? We no longer, to be sure, intervene to collect our debts. Some of our best friends are now our debtors. But shall we only intervene against tryranny which expands abroad, and take obviously milder measures against other evils, so that we seem to become champions of the status quo while the USSR makes itself the champion of racial equality and the abolition of poverty and exploitation?

I am not yet sure how to resolve all these questions, in principle. When it comes to practice, however, I am certain that the gassing of millions of human beings, or the official suppression of elemental human rights to millions of others because of the color of their skin must not be placed beyond remedy as a "domestic issue." I must confess that I liked very much the last paragraph of President Kennedy's letter answering Chairman Khrushchev's protest against our Cuban intervention: "I believe, Mr. Chairman, that you should recognize that free people in all parts of the world do not accept the claim of historical inevitability for Communist revolution. What your government believes is its business; what it does in the world is the world's business. The great revolution in the history of man, past, present and future, is the revolution of those determined to be free."[11] But the letter ends at that point, and the operating clause that would show how this statement could be made effective is missing, just as it was from the Cuban intervention in the Bay of Pigs.

I think it may be possible, however, to distinguish among (1) countries which, despite tyranny (or its obverse, instability), are yet some distance from internal warfare involving extremists, or foreign adventurism inviting aggression; (2) countries which, like Ataturk's Turkey, have chosen an authoritarian road that is intended to lead to democracy; and (3) countries like the Union of South Africa, Iran or Jordan, which are clearly heading for the kind of catastrophic internal or external explosion which will make intervention by outside powers unavoidable. In the first two categories, the United States might well undertake the kind of joint precautionary and constructive diplomatic and economic measures that constitute *Intervention in Partnership,* even though the disparity of power and needs between the collaborating parties seldom permits this kind of partnership to proceed without friction. In this sense, the "Alliance for Progress" with Latin America is an agreement giving the United States and other participating states the right to create effective pressures for altering the social, economic, and political structure of Latin American states for the sake of ultimately putting an end to tyranny, instability, and poverty. In the third category of countries, is not the real choice between precautionary intervention and subsequent intervention under much more unfavorable terms? Our little-publicized but morally and politically sound intervention against the Trujillo dictatorship soon after our Cuban fiasco demonstrates our ability to act prudently and effectively in the realm of precautionary intervention.

There are other forms of intervention. One is equivalent to bear-baiting without invitation in other people's gardens, as when, for a time, we subsidized Chinese Nationalist troops on Burmese soil—but it would not be rewarding to explore further in that direction. Another is constructive, though it seldom earns credit in the short run, as when we inject ourselves powerfully as arbiters in disputes that touch us only because they divide two countries friendly with us. Espionage is also a form of intervention when it involves entering without permission into areas, on the ground or in the air, that fall under the national jurisdiction of other states. This kind of intervention, having the commendable purpose of expanding the world's knowledge, is based upon rules of the game implicitly agreed upon among the nations. As an activity, it damages the international system less than adultery damages the institution of marriage. Like adultery, it damages the formal system of intercourse whenever the culprit is caught or insists on publicly championing his right to adultery. That was our compounded sin in the U-2 incident. Unlike adultery, which can damage most by the act itself, that is, by betraying love and trust, no love or trust are present to be undermined in the international system, a vital point to which we shall return in our conclusion.

Toward the Limitation of Intervention

Surely it is a symptom of the aberrant state of the world that the preceding section might well have been entitled, "Toward a Wise and Just American Intervention in the Internal Affairs of Other Nations." I submit that such a discussion is necessary, but I cannot bring myself to suppose that it would be wise or just to stop here. No state has the sovereign right to intervene in the internal affairs of another sovereign state. It is not merely a contradiction in terms but an attack on the very system on which the freedom of every nation rests. It cannot be dismissed as a "mere" breach of international law. It undermines the very structure of a world order which is most imperfect, but in whose survival we have a far greater stake than does the USSR, for unlike the intended Communist international system, the present international order contains the actuality of national freedom and the potentiality of voluntary collaboration.

We have two choices especially worth discussing. We can accept the world as a jungle in which right and wrong do not apply but only survival matters, and we concentrate on improving the skill and thrust of our power. Since we are still in a jungle, it would be foolish not to do so. Since we do not want to remain where we are, since our very lingering is likely to spell our doom, we must also act to limit the terms of the competition and enlarge the effective power of law.

At the moment we are doing badly. We accept as inescapable the proposition that the challenge posed by the USSR gives us the right and duty to intervene, and that we can deny the same right of intervention to the USSR by threatening to escalate the kind of forces we shall enlist in the fray.[12] To ease the burden and danger of our vigilante activities in a lawless world, we have tried several methods. We have tried to explain to the world the superior justice of our cause. Most people might well grant that ours is a better country to live in than the USSR, but the appreciation of the justice of our cause has often been marred by the kind of interventions by which we have tried to translate justice into practice and by our talk, perhaps justifiable on other grounds but certainly far more frightening than any uttered by the USSR, about the risks we would take in behalf of justice. And though some are tempted, there is an attitude toward the justice of our cause which we cannot afford to adopt. "Intimidation," Trotsky wrote, "is a powerful weapon of policy, both internationally and internally. . . . The revolution works the same way: it kills individuals, and intimidates thousands. . . . 'But in that case, in what do your tactics differ from the tactics of Tsarism?' we are asked by the high priests of Liberalism. . . . You do not understand this, holy men? We shall explain it to you. The terror of Tsarism was directed against the proletariat. . . . Our Extraordinary Commissions shoot landlords, capitalists, and generals who are striving to restore the capitalist order. Do you grasp this—distinction? Yes? For us Communists it is quite sufficient. . . ."[13] Should means no longer matter to us, justice will become a remote question.

We have also tried to ease our burden by emphasizing order above social change, taking care to improve the repressive machinery of other governments, and through economic aid, to diminish the political violence which often topples rulers in rapid succession in Asia, Africa and Latin America. We have often neglected, however, to develop the political enterprise by which they and we might limit the international consequences of such internal warfare. By giving priority to order, we found it more difficult to seize such political initiative, for while it is true that control of rapid social change itself requires strong, stable authority, such resilient stability is unlikely to arise in most underdeveloped areas until many more fundamental changes have taken place.

In a similar vein, we have championed world law without adequate study of how law might play a constructive role in a rapidly and fundamentally changing world. Our concept of law is fit largely for a world in which political conflicts no longer touch the very purpose and character of life. We have, moreover, failed to live up to international law which we have helped to shape.[14] For example, we agreed in Article 15 of the Charter of Bogata (1948) that "no state or group of states has the right to intervene directly or indirectly, for any reason whatever, in the internal or external affairs of any other state. The foregoing principle prohibits not only armed attack but also any other form of interference or attempted threat against the personality of the state or against the political, economic and cultural elements." In Article 16, we agreed that "no state may use or encourage the use of coercive measures of an economic or political character in order to force the sovereign will of another state or obtain from it advantages of any kind."

It is true that in subsequent treaties we and the Latin Americans agreed on collective intervention against the encroachments of Communism in this hemisphere, that we and they could not agree on effective action against Guatemala and Cuba, and that we therefore had no alternative, as our government saw it, but to proceed unilaterally against a danger condemned in principle by collective agreement. I would not worry so much about such a few, somewhat ambiguous breaches of law—hope, patience, and fortitude have sustained the international system as much as law, and these are not as gravely damaged yet by such actions as is the law—except that I foresee no end to such breaches, and it is this which makes me fearful. We have already reached a dangerous point. After our Lebanese intervention, our Secretary of State, forgetful of the origins of our travail, thought of asking for a UN resolution against "indirect aggression," but relented when he remembered how vulnerable we would be both in the debate and through the intended law.

One may sympathize with those who would judge our record in this field with some forebearance, pointing out that our nation has only recently arrived fully as a world power. (Our interventions prior to World War II had an impact only on our immediate region and only an indirect effect on the world order.) But one must not sympathize too long, for we shall not be given much time to learn our lessons. It is imperative to move on, if not yet to world government, at least into a system based on self-restraint, constructive forms of intervention, and a broader overlap of national interests.

I do not think such a movement is impossible. Self-restraint would mean, for example, rejecting Edmond Taylor's recent proposal in *The Reporter* for "encouraging and explicitly accepting responsibility for the revolutionary forces behind the Iron Curtain. . . . We should oppose only premature and uncoordinated insurrections."[15] It would mean curing ourselves of the anxious and dogmatic aggressiveness that has caused us to intervene against neutralists and authoritarian socialists in usually unjustified fear of the next stage in their development. It would require us not to treat every Communist challenge—as in 1961 in Cuba—as an issue of survival, and not to turn any confrontation that could affect survival into alternatives that must lead either to complete victory or complete defeat.

Such a strategy would also involve forebearance when non-Communists challenge the status quo. Imposing the high standards of

American political comfort on the rest of the world, we have scarcely paused to be surprised by how the passing of traditional society has been accompanied by far less violence in most of Asia, Africa and Latin America than during a similar period in Western Europe. But we must not expect this historical transformation to be an entirely peaceful event, nor prepare to intervene whenever it is not.

We shall have to be more tolerant of violence connected with the end of the system of colonial domination than with violence threatening the system which governs the relationship among independent states. (India's usually justifiably high ideals have often fallen short of India's sometimes justifiable and sometimes unjustifiable practices. Our reaction to Goa, however, was an idealistic exaggeration unmindful of the distinction I have suggested.) I believe we should insist that the arbitrary and artificial frontiers drawn by Europeans for African and Middle Eastern states must not be altered by direct aggression, but forebearance of a kind unjustified in Europe may also be in order when such kindred peoples intervene, short of aggression, in each others' affairs. We need neither to become involved in their rivalries nor protect them from such excesses in their attempts to achieve unity. Counter-intervention would be justified, however, to keep other great powers from exploiting such rearrangements.

Above all, we need to rid ourselves of the erroneous notion that whenever a privileged Western position in Asia, Africa, or Latin America is lost, the USSR correspondingly gains. The conversion of a pro-Western nation like Iraq to neutralism is not a loss to the West. On the contrary, it usually rids the West of a discreditable relationship and in bringing about a neutralist state, creates a situation with which we, by virtue of our sense of world order, can live but which the USSR is pledged to alter. Whether our subsequent relationship with a former client state is satisfactory or not depends on our mutual ability to transform our relationship by cementing overlapping national interests and enhancing such a country's internal stability.

That brings us to the second major task in moving toward a more lawful world, namely finding more constructive forms of intervention. Self-restraint may be helpful in reducing instability and tension within the international system as a whole, but it cannot prevent or cure the internal conflicts within countries of the non-Communist world that incite the interventions of the great powers. We also need to develop wiser and more just forms of precautionary and counter-intervention.

A number of possibilities may be suggested. Diplomacy, and at worst, the threat of unilateral intervention, may be employed for the specific purpose of persuading the reluctant smaller nations of a region to act or even intervene collectively themselves in order to avoid the intervention of a great power. This, after much waste motion, was the final outcome in Lebanon when all the usually disunited Arab states agreed not to intervene, and even more effectively and with greater dispatch in Kuwait where the Arab states agreed collectively to protect that country against Iraq intervention. Increasingly it may be possible to parlay the threat of great power intervention, as in the Congo, or earlier in Lebanon, into UN intervention.[16] Since great power intervention is initially masked in most instances, and there is no international law-enforcement agency that can investigate and act in time, the counter-intervention may have to be initiated by the United States. But such action should from the first moment be accompanied by a pledge to withdraw as soon as a UN or regional peace force can take its place while those employing force under the duress or discipline of a great foreign power withdraw their threat.[17] An international police force should therefore be organized so as to be in constant readiness.

Precautionary intervention could also be internationalized to a considerable degree. Societies that are already deeply split politically and therefore are unwilling to become dependent on a single great power should be helped in larger (and not merely technical) measure through the UN.[18] Aid from the USSR should also be welcomed, even for joint projects, for what counts is not the source of the money and not even the prestige it earns for a foreign power, but the constructive use to which it is put inside the country.

Neither our self-restraint nor more constructive forms of intervention will help, however, unless the USSR reciprocates in like fashion. Is there any hope that the two powers might develop and enlarge an overlap of national interests in the realm of intervention? It is just such reciprocity that finally creates international law. Fortunately, such an overlap already exists to a significant degree, though amid the sound and fury we have paid little attention to it.

We are now operating on implicit rules that keep the USSR from intervening in sufficient measure within the Western community and the Western hemisphere to make it the decisive force in placing its local men in power and protecting them there. We have accepted the same restrictions within the Soviet satellite area. This does not mean that the Soviets or the West refrain from intervening in each other's realm in a great many other ways. But Hungary and Cuba indicate the limits of the game with precision. In October 1962, it had clearly become necessary to take bold measures to remind the USSR of these tacit rules as they affect Cuba. Moscow agreed with no resistance and little delay. We, however, offered only to pledge ourselves not to undertake an outright invasion.

In the uncommitted but hitherto non-Communist areas of the world, the USSR is willing to take risks, but not as many as we do in intervening. We have never been deterred from intervention in these areas by fear of the Soviet reaction. By contrast, in several instances where the USSR had excellent opportunities for assisting Communists in seizing control (as in Iran in 1953, Syria in 1955-58, and Iraq in 1958-60),[19] the USSR restrained itself for fear of the international consequences. It is also noteworthy that the USSR no less than the smaller states in the UN agreed that it would be better, even after the murder of the undoubtedly popular Lumumba, to let Congolese fight each other as Congolese rather than as great power puppets. Nor are these instances accidental. One of the chief conflicts between the USSR and China concerns the risks the USSR does not think it prudent to take in assisting "national wars of liberation."

What can we do to harden and to multiply the number of these restricting rules of the game? The first (there is no avoiding it) must be to keep ourselves strong enough to convince the USSR, and increasingly also China, that the risks of intervention on their part remain too high to allow them to take chances. Secondly, we must take diplomatic initiatives to reduce the incitements to intervention. It might be useful to explore, for example, whether it might help to agree to neutralize the Middle East—outlawing all foreign military alliances and foreign bases, agreeing on limitations of arms shipments to the area, and on collective steps from outside to prevent any border from being changed by military aggression.[20] Such steps might lessen tensions within the region, allow a major shift of local resources from military preparedness to projects that could enhance economic, social, and political stability, lessen the dangers flowing from actual Communist involvement in locally endemic *coups d'etat* from reaching the dimensions of a serious crisis, and restrict the possible need for counter-interventions to those more generally acceptable to the international community—namely to keep neutrals from being subverted from their neutrality.

It would indeed serve to improve international order for us to help all non-Communist states, whether neutralist or not, to cope with the unbalancing forces of uncontrolled social change and so help them lay foundations on which to build independent and responsible foreign and domestic policies. However much we might prefer a policy of close alignment, it might be acknowledged that the great majority of neutralists in Asia and Africa have demonstrated both the will and the skill to make sure that both the West and the Communist bloc remain on hand competing for advantage among them, each ensuring that the other shall not gain predominance in the area. The interplay of these countervailing forces, and the extraordinary nationalist sensitivity of these new states to any new form of colonialism constitute powerful new forces at work since the 1950's in restricting the intervention of the great powers. The weaker nations of the world are thus for the first time beginning to help define the rules of international relationships.[21]

Among diplomatic initiatives, it might also be worth exploring whether our explicit acknowledgement of the status quo in Eastern Europe might have two worthwhile consequences. It could help to institutionalize the rules of the game of intervention. It might also have more fundamental consequences. By diminishing our pressure on Eastern Europe, we make it harder for the foes of relaxed controls within the Communist world to justify their position, and thus we might help ultimately both to ease the pressures within the Soviet elite for adventurous interventions abroad and ease pressures for conformity among the satellites. Accepting the status quo might thus make changes in the status quo more likely—and thus become a most constructive form of intervention.

The USSR is unlikely in the foreseeable future to accept our conception of international order. Though the threat which Soviet behavior thus raises for us may tempt us to copy Soviet techniques, it behooves us to work harder by far instead to attain standards of world law and justice to which the uncommitted might be won, and which the USSR could ignore only at the cost of incurring international sanctions.

This task is no longer as easy as it might have sounded in the 1920's. Today it is painfully apparent that the demands of international law and international justice do not yet coincide, in part because the old historical order which set our present standards has become dangerously fragile, in part because our present standards are not shared by our principal adversary, nor even by all the rest of the world. To argue that in such a world our self-interest and what we hold to be our superior values justify our intervention, however coercive, as long as it succeeds, is to risk the attainment of the surer morality based on law for the sake of morality based on power. It would certainly lead to a conflict with the USSR in which no holds were barred except on grounds of inefficiency, and hence the present difference in values between us would cease. To argue, on the other hand, that until intervention achieves in the international order that lawful status which it now possesses in all domestic societies, there should be a moral and political presumption against intervention abroad, is to champion law at the expense of justice and ultimately to threaten law itself. Let us observe and insist on respect for national sovereignty, and try to resolve conflicts in bargaining among these sovereignties. But if national sovereignty is threatened, or itself clearly threatens peace, freedom or justice, wisdom demands intervention, but in such forms as will best enhance these values and improve the opportunities for the growth of an international order in which these values could endure.

God, Man, and the Purpose of Intervention

This essay must not end, however, without speaking of two elements which have so far been ignored in this analysis of the morality of intervention. We have talked only about national states. We have said nothing about the human being as individual and nothing about God.

The Austrian writer Kraus gave the last line in one of his plays to God, who, contemplating the destruction of the world proceeding under his eyes, declared, "I did not will it." A recent writer in *worldview* has wondered whether nuclear death might not save more Christian souls for eternal life than life under atheistic Communism. I hesitate to conclude that any man could know God's earthly preferences with such precision. We have been given the capacity to distinguish life that is based on loving one's neighbor from life based on killing him or being indifferent to him. This is the core of our knowledge and of our guide to action; the rest is deduction, induction, or dogmatic assertion. We also know how fragile, uncertain, and even absurd this knowledge is, for God has obviously left himself free not only to love but to destroy.

I have therefore spoken in this essay only about our responsibility to act wisely, justly, and with love. I think it is most fortunate for the potentials of justice in international relations that this responsibility arises whether one believes in God or not. It would be fearful it it were not so, for the world which is unlikely to be converted soon to the same view of intervention is even less likely to be converted soon to the same theology. Some men also know how this fits in with God's plans, but I believe that our inescapable ignorance on this subject imposes (as does faith in God) the added responsibility of humility in international relations.

If we commonly err by confusing God's will with our concrete aims in foreign policy, we usually also err by ignoring the existence of concrete individual human beings in discussing the justice of foreign interventions by the abstract collectivity known as the nation-state. If law is not yet an alternative to force in international relations, and indeed requires force, law cannot rest on force alone. The moral individual, however, will not be content with justice; he will prefer a world in which public authority establishes an area of security and justice in which love becomes possible. Instead, he is often confronted by the essential idiocy of politics in which, to take a recent example, his family is shelled only on odd days on an off-shore island that has no military value in preparation for interventions which neither side is in a position to pursue. He knows that interventions are concerned with issues of national power far more often than with poverty, tyranny, or exploitation. As if in compensation for this neglect of the daily concerns of most men, his national leaders make policies based in part on estimates of the personal sincerity or trust or goodwill of a Nasser or Eden as if international relations already allowed for more than the identification and enhancement of common national interests. What we share with any rational leaders, whatever their personal morality, is a common interest in the right of their nations to establish foundations which will allow them (and all other nations) to pursue responsibly independent foreign and domestic policies. In such a common interest lie the potentials both for public justice among nations and personal dignity and love among individuals within nations.

The technicians of power, having shrewdly rejected the illusion that national and individual morality are automatically the same, stop short and do not see that the unfinished task is to relate national purpose to the kind of international justice that gives security and freedom for justice and love to develop among individuals. Indeed, they tend through the prestigious position of their manipulative power to diminish the citizen's concern with love, till he feels embarrassed by the very mention of it in a context of power. In the insecure world in which we live, national loyalty and solidarity have become more precious to most peoples than justice and love. Still, the existence of a nation, any nation, is not justified except as it and its interventions preserve and enhance the individual's capacity to be wise, just, and to love. Mere security can most cheaply be purchased by surrender.

NOTES

[1] I am deeply indebted to Ernest W. Lefever, Washington Consultant to the Council on Religion and International Affairs, for first inviting me to explore these ideas under the intellectually hospitable and rewarding auspices of the Council; to Robert E. Osgood, Robert C. Good, John Courtney Murray S.J., Robert C. Tucker, Arthur Hertzberg, Robert Gordis, William A. Lybrand, Samuel P. Huntington, Kenneth W. Thompson and William Lee Miller, who served as Chairmen or first Discussants during Council consultations; and to the board of trustees and the staff of the Council, and to more than fifty

government officials, men of religion and scholars who joined for several intensive hours in Washington and New York to discuss an earlier draft; and to Gregory Massell, Thomas P. Thornton, and Betsy Steele Halpern, who read this paper at various stages. The ideas offered here owe much to their criticism and suggestions even if, at times, this revision may only serve to clarify and sharpen differences of opinion. Needless to say, I speak for no one in this essay but myself.

[2] Robert Batchelder has raised the question of what responsibilities the American government ought to accept when a private U.S. corporation establishes a plant abroad which, by virtue of the scope of its activities in an otherwise underdeveloped country, not only dominates that economy but sets in motion a social and political transformation which the local government is too weak to guide into channels conducive to domestic welfare and national independence. On the more limited question of the rights of private companies abroad, the U.S. government has for several decades now adhered to the policy that each nation has the right to nationalize foreign property provided it pays fair compensation.

[3] For example, agreeing to the holding of a Summit conference because, among other reasons, it may benefit the British conservatives in a forthcoming election, or training the Iranian police in more effective techniques of coping with anti-government activities.

[4] It may be argued that the threat of aggression, and even aggression itself, may constitute intervention. The U.S. has repeatedly moved military forces into Caribbean states for the sake of altering their internal policies without, however, staying long or taking sovereign title to the countries involved. The question is difficult to decide. The British army "intervened" in Egypt in 1882 and stayed for seventy-four years without taking title to the country. Is it therefore merely to be called "intervention"? This ambiguity illustrates the difficulties of defining the most desperate encounters nations may have, and how readily intervention can shade into the ultimate kind of force.

[5] Rabbi Robert Gordis has suggested that morality is the highest good since, unless it includes honesty and intelligence, it is simply moralism. I do not put it this way because I want to make sure that we explore anew the power and knowledge that have become part of our morality.

[6] Oddly enough, Chamoun had become President in 1952 after helping to overthrow President Khuri—a man who had greatly increased the number of enemies by his attempt to amend the Constitution so that he might serve an additional six-year term.

[7] Our military mobility has much improved since that time.

[8] I have dealt with this issue specifically in relation to "Perspectives on U.S. Policy in Iran," published in the SAIS Review (Washington), April 1962. This and the next two paragraphs are largely drawn from that article. A more extended analysis of the politics involved in the revolution of modernization may be found in my studies, The Politics of Social Change in the Middle East and North Africa (Princeton: Princeton University Press, 1963), and "The Social Revolution," in The Developmental Revolution in the Middle East, edited by William Polk (Washington: The Middle East Institute, 1963).

[9] Mr. Nixon, one of the earliest and strongest advocates of intervention

in Cuba, in retrospect perceives only the electoral ironies that arose from his having declared on TV in August 1960, while preparations for the invasion were under way: "We would lose all of our friends in Latin America, we would probably be condemned in the United Nations and we would not accomplish our objectives."

[10] Readers of the *New York Times* and *Time* before, during, and after the Cuban intervention should have no difficulty recalling evidence for this view. We seemed to have lacked adequate knowledge about a country 90 miles from home or at least failed to utilize knowledge that was available; we ruthlessly manipulated men and groups among Cuban exiles; we gave unconcerned support (or pragmatic and instinctive favoritism) to ex-Batista or pre-Batista men, rather than men willing to deal with discontent which Castro had exploited. Had we insisted on the military success of this particularly ill-conceived venture it would have been a moral and political tragedy.

There are also men at CIA who have produced major and imaginative projects in what will be defined below as constructive precautionary intervention. Their successes, by nature, evolve slowly and lack the drama of failure. It is my impression, however, based on inadequate knowledge, that the failures at intervention deserve the greater weight of attention.

[11] *New York Herald-Tribune*, April 9, 1961.

[12] The following quotations illustrate our position. On our right to counter Soviet interventions: "Let the record show that our restraint is not inexhaustible . . . This Government will not hesitate on meeting its primary obligations which are to the security of our Nation." (President Kennedy, "The Lesson of Cuba," *Department of State Bulletin,* 1961, Vol. 44, p. 659.) On the USSR claiming the same rights: "If you consider yourself to be in the right to implement such measures against Cuba which have been lately taken by the U.S.A., you must admit that other countries, also, do not have lesser reason to act in a similar manner in relation to states on whose territories preparations are actually being made which represent a threat against the security of the Soviet Union. If you do not wish to sin against elementary logic, you evidently must admit such a right to other states." (Mr. Khrushchev's Message to President Kennedy, *ibid.,* pp. 664-65.) On escalation: "We are resolved," said Secretary of Defense Robert S. McNamara, "to continue the struggle in all its forms," coping with Soviet long-range ballistic missiles armed with nuclear warheads as well as subversion and indirect warfare, "until such a time as the Communist leaders, both Soviet and Chinese, are convinced that their aggressive policies, motivated by their drive to communize the world, endanger their security as well as ours." (*New York Times,* January 20, 1962.)

[13] Trotsky, *Terrorism and Communism 1920;* (English Translation, *Dictatorship vs. Democracy: A Reply to Karl Kautsky,* New York, Workers' Party of America, 1922, pp. 54; 57-59.)

[14] I am greatly indebted for insights into the relationship of international law to the politics and morality of intervention, and for information, to three articles by Professor Richard A. Falk (Princeton University), namely "The United States and the Doctrine of Non-Intervention in the Internal Affairs of Independent States," *Howard Law Journal,* June 1959, pp. 163-89; "American Intervention in Cuba and the Rule of Law," *Ohio State Law*

Journal, Summer 1961, pp. 546-85; and *Law, Morality and War in the Contemporary World* (New York: Frederick A. Praeger, 1963).

[15] *The Reporter,* September 14, 1961.

[16] What cannot be used as an effective threat, however, is collective intervention by NATO in the non-European and non-Communist areas of the world. Those who would neglect the UN in favor of NATO do not appreciate the limited usefulness of common action by the white partners of a military alliance in the rest of the world.

[17] It will be noted that I speak only of intervention against elements employing *force* under the duress or discipline of *great* foreign power. Threats from smaller nations can surely be handled in less spectacular ways. In restricting counter-intervention to a reply against force, I should like to reject the other alternative with entire clarity. If, as a result of an inadequate performance by democratic forces in India and the West, for example, Indians turn to Communism in a free election, I would not for a moment regard the forceful reconversion of India into a Western colony as a morally justifiable or politically prudent alternative.

[18] For a discussion of problems of political therapy involved in UN intervention, see Manfred Halpern, "The UN in the Congo," *worldview,* October 1963, pp. 4-8.

[19] For detailed documentation of this point, see my essay on "The Middle East and North Africa," in Cyril E. Black and Thomas P. Thornton (eds.), *Communism and Revolution* (Princeton: Princeton University Press, 1964).

[20] Between 1956 and 1958 the USSR several times publicly indicated its interest in such a proposal.

[21] In the realm of intervention, as one insightful member of the Department of State has pointed out, these new rules of the game demand far more skill and prudence than the old. For example, for a great power patently to extend support to any local faction, whether in the government or the opposition, may in this highly nationalist environment turn out to be a Kiss of Death. In a world in which the Soviet bloc has become an alternate source of support and supplies, we may not always be able to afford to let a country which refuses to abide by the conditions of our aid suffer the consequences. But the more moral and more useful course of action has also become clearer: it is no longer enough to pick a strongman and intervene on his behalf. The politics of social change demand intervention in behalf of *programs* relevant to societies already in rapid transformation.

The Limits of Nuclear War: The Do-able and the Un-do-able

Paul Ramsey

The writing of this paper was begun in the context of a deeply distressing event. For seventeen years of the nuclear age no leader of the Western world indicated any doubt that military policy should be based on President Truman's judgment that an entire city is a legitimate military target. The "massive" deterrence of the Dulles era, when the United States still had a monopoly of atomic weapons, has now been supplanted by "balanced" deterrence from hopefully invulnerable bases. Arms control and measures to lessen the danger of surprise attack and of accidental war have been proposed, and conventional and "unconventional" military capabilities have been strengthened. But during these years there appeared to be no crack in the official acceptance of cities as targets for total destruction.

Then in June, 1962, Secretary of Defense Robert McNamara delivered the commencement address of the University of Michigan. In this speech, which had the approval of President Kennedy, he said: "The United States has come to the conclusion that, to the extent feasible, basic military strategy in a possible nuclear war should be approached in much the same way that more conventional military operations have been regarded in the past. That is to say, principal military objectives, in the event of a nuclear war stemming from an attack on the Alliance, should be the destruction of the enemy's forces, not of his civilian population."

Instead of a chorus of "Amens!" from the millions of decent citizens of this country, Christian and non-Christian, hardly a single voice was raised to say, "*That* is certainly the upper limit of what we ever want done in our behalf, if for no other reason than that it is clearly the upper limit of what can ever be done in defense of anything." Hardly a "civilized" person was reminded by the Secretary's words that the proscription of direct attack upon a whole society is the oldest and most well-established rule of civilized warfare. Hardly a Christian was reminded by the Secretary's words to seek from his own traditional teachings practical wisdom for the direction of public affairs. Hardly any of the leaders of religious and public opinion stepped forward to support the most significant change (or suggestion of change) in military policy in nearly two decades of the nuclear age.

Instead, the opinions expressed were stereotyped and evidenced as much inertia as can exist in the vast and sprawling defense establishment which McNamara is struggling to subdue and direct. Perhaps resistance to McNamara's proposal was to be expected from our allies.[1] When we think of the magnitude and complexities of our interlocking systems of defense, "doctrine" is almost bound to lag behind realities. It is not surprising, therefore, that C. L. Sulzberger reported from London that this novel "nuclear defense theory, based on counterforce rather than countercity strategy . . . produced confused reactions in Europe," or that he concluded two weeks after the policy was announced: "It is now dead."[2] Yet it is surprising, and most distressing that individual leaders of opinion manifest not much greater freedom to explore "new" doctrine.

Instead of support for this or any other effort to limit the nuclear holocaust for which the two great powers now stand ready, one heard only sterile protests that our leaders were again trying to make us grow "accustomed" to the idea of fighting a nuclear war. Instead of applauding the announcement as a policy of definitely *limited* feasibility, the public widely regarded it as simply one more assertion of the limited *feasibility* of nuclear war. Even the *Christian Century* damned with faint praise — because the editors apparently know in advance that any thoughtful effort to un-target the cities is bound to prove impossible. It will show "the essentially unmanageable nature of these weapons," and direct us again with single-minded attention to "the importance of preventing any war from starting."

"So vast is the destructive capacity of nuclear weapons that their effects could not be confined to military objects," said the *Century*, sweeping aside any distinction between effects that cannot be confined and deliberately enlarging those effects by targeting on cities. "Would the United States," it asked rhetorically, "be prepared to remove military installations from the vicinity of its great cities, where some of them are now located?" — as if war plans must now and for the future be ruled by the stupidity of Congressmen who secure the location of missile bases in their districts near large centers of population where there is an unemployment problem; and as if the fact that Tucson, Arizona and Plattsburg, New York and Omaha, Nebraska and Colorado Springs,

---

[1]*The New York Times* reported (August 9, 1962) that Franz Josef Strauss, West German Defense Minister, " 'is giving up hard' on a strategy based largely on nuclear weapons." Herr Strauss apparently believes not so much in a credible fight-the-war policy as in deterrence that "begins at the battle line" with tactical nuclear weapons and goes to the grave line, by means of massive nuclear weapons targeted mainly on cities.

[2]*The New York Times*, July 9, 1962.

Colorado are now legitimate military targets means that this must necessarily remain the shape of modern war. "In making his proposal Mr. McNamara has rendered a service," the *Century* concluded, "but probably not the one he intended to render. What he has really done — or so we hope — is to strengthen the argument of the Committee for a Sane Nuclear Policy that the only safe way to manage nuclear weapons is to abolish them as one step in a plan of complete disarmament."[3]

The Alternatives of Policy

So far public opinion in this country seems to ignore the difference between 25,000,000 dead as the probable result of all-out counterforce warfare and 215,000,000 dead as a result of all-out countercity warfare between the great powers.[4] We seem to turn away from any effort to make counterforce nuclear war, if it comes, fall far, far short of all-out. So, in addition, do we gloss over the qualitative moral distinction between tragically killing or sacrificing human beings as an indirect result of knocking out military targets (counterforce warfare) and the murderous policy of deliberately killing them in totally devastating countercity warfare. The only ground for hope is that our leaders who must make the decisions will not be so irresponsible. Richard Fryklund reports, at least, that the shift to counterforces strategy has been in the making for the duration of this administration, and he always writes of the decision in the past tense.[5]

Still, this is a decision that will have to be not only our actual policy but our *declared* policy. More than once it will have to be declared, and massive manifold actions will have to be taken in accord with it, if there is again to be a well-understood boundary and a mutually accepted limit in the conduct of war. This will require the support of an informed and morally sensitive people. When one asks why the just conduct of war is the last thing people want to talk about or to believe possible, or why they do not demand that governments make only limited nuclear war possible (if there is to be nuclear war) or limited war (if there is to be war at all), the answers are hard to give except in terms of a breakdown of the tradition of civilized politics that is without parallel.

Yet these distinctions among possible strategies have long been made by weapons analysts. Glenn H. Snyder, for example, discusses at

---

[3]Editorial, July 4, 1962.

[4]C. L. Sulzberger's report, *op. cit.*, of the estimates on which McNamara's policy shift was based. These, of course, are very uncertain figures.

[5]*100 Million Lives: Maximum Survival in a Nuclear Age*, New York: The Macmillan Co., 1962. The Pentagon studies and debates go back to early 1960.

some length the choice between "all-out counter*city* retaliation" and "all-out counter*force* retaliation," and also between "*limited* counter*city* retaliation as a bargaining tactic" and "*limited* counter*force* retaliation."[6] And Herman Kahn's latest book spells out in some detail the difference that exists and *can* be drawn between "Counterforce plus Counter-value," "Straight Counterforce," "Counterforce and Bonus," and "Counterforce plus Avoidance" in the choice of strategies.[7] Moreover, two other such books have recently appeared: one analyzes "limited strategic warfare";[8] the other, based in part on interviews with highly-placed Pentagon officials, offers a reporter's analysis of a "No City" strategy (Kahn's "Straight Counterforce" or "Counterforce plus Avoidance") in contrast to "Pure City," "Cities Plus" or "Devastation" war-plans.[9]

Thus, there stands on one side Countervalue warfare; Pure City, Cities Plus and Devastation war; controlled or unlimited Countercity retaliation; Counterforce plus Countervalue or Counterforce and Bonus; and limited strategic city reprisal. These all aim at civilians, except for the sort of "countervalue" warfare which proposes to allow time for cities to be evacuated. On the other side stands Counterforce warfare; No City war; controlled or unlimited Counterforce retaliation; Straight Counterforce or Counterforce plus Avoidance. Only Counterforce plus Avoidance may be called a just way to conduct war, since traditional and acceptable moral teachings concerning legitimate military targets require the avoidance of civilian damage as much as possible even while accepting this as in some measure an unavoidable indirect effect.

This paper defends the thesis that counterforce nuclear war is the upper limit of rational, politically purposive military action. Two ways are commonly taken to avoid this conclusion, and another uncommonly. Those who magnify the difficulty and undesirability of adopting a policy of making just war possible usually do so because:

(1) they believe that general disarmament is about to be accomplished and therefore no plans should be made for the use of any weapons, nuclear or other; or else because

(2) they believe that balanced deterrence can be stabilized and kept perfect enough to insure that nuclear weapons will never be used except in their non-use for deterrence.

---

[6]*Deterrence and Defense*, Princeton, N. J.: Princeton University Press, 1961, pp. 68-79.

[7]*Thinking about the Unthinkable*, New York: Horizon Press, 1962, pp. 65-68.

[8]Klaus Knorr and Thornton Read, eds., *Limited Strategic War*, New York: Praeger, 1962. In this volume, this concept includes both limited strategic city reprisal and limited strategic attacks on forces.

[9]Richard Fryklund: *100 Million Lives: Maximum Survival in a Nuclear War.* New York: The Macmillan Co., 1962.

In these two schools, extremes meet. They are brothers under the skin who believe so strongly in peace by disarmament (whether unilaterally or by treaty or by technical contrivance by which the weapons will neutralize themselves) that as a consequence they see no need for thinking about the upper limit of sanity in the actual use of nuclear weapons. The conclusion that "Pure City" is the only way in which nuclear war can ever be fought, or the judgment that "Pure City" is the aim the weapons *should* have, is thus "the favorite [strategy] of influential civilians whose eyes are actually on disarmament rather than defense,"[10] or who, at least, find it impossible to be active on two political fronts at once. And not only civilians.[11] Even Prussians are pacifists of this new breed. So Franz Josef Strauss, West German Defense Minister, explained why he did not want even to *discuss* plans that actually exist for controlled fighting in Europe by saying that the inevitable outcome would be that "the credibility of the deterrent is weakened. . . . And if we do not have a deterrent that is credible, the only alternative is war as an element of policy."[12]

Therefore, no steps *should* be taken to plan to fight war justly against forces if you believe that peace by deliberate disarmament can soon be achieved; and no such steps *need* be taken if you believe that weapons technology can keep the nations permanently disarmed and no future rational decision-maker need ever decide to fire these weapons. Most, if not quite all, of the arguments against counterforces warfare (its instability, for example) have absolute peace as their premise; and the latter is, one way or another, believed to be a genuine, and the sole, option today.[13] There is an inner logical connection between indigenous American pacifism and the Strategic Air Command with its motto, "Peace is our profession." "Pacifistic deterrence" has been our policy, our hope and our faith. Only if fighting a possible war is understood to be a governing purpose of a military establishment will inherent limits in the design of war seem choiceworthy. It is always easier to plan murder and mutual suicide, and somehow despairingly more pleasant too, than to plan for defense and the survival of the nation.

10Fryklund, *op. cit.*, p. 42.

11Cf. General Pierre Gallois: *The Balance of Terror: Strategy for the Nuclear Age.* Boston, Mass.: Houghton Mifflin Co., 1961.

12*The New York Times,* March 1, 1962.

13For this argument in expanded form, see my "Dream and Reality in Deterrence and Defense," *Christianity and Crisis,* vol. xxi, no. 22 (Dec. 25, 1961), pp. 228-232; "U.S. Military Policy and 'Shelter Morality,'" *worldview,* vol. 5, no. 1 (Jan., 1962), pp. 6-9; "Correspondence," *worldview,* vol. 5, no. 3 (March, 1962), pp. 6-9; "Turn Toward Just War," *worldview,* vol. 5, nos. 7-8 (July-August, 1962), pp. 8-13; and *War and the Christian Conscience,* Durham, N. C.: Duke University Press, 1961.

There is no way to avoid thinking about militarily feasible and politically purposive warfare. Against the first of these positions, it must be said that nuclear weapons and armaments in general are unlikely to be scrapped soon, if ever. Against the second, it must be said that "balanced" deterrence and invulnerable weapons-systems do not preclude the need to think about believable fight-the-war plans. Instead, the opposite is the result. The more the great powers think they have achieved for the moment a nearly automatic neutralization of nuclear weapons, from bases it will take years to find a way of attacking, the more the world is prepared for local war, for conventional and unconventional war. The more, too, will it seem possible to make a controlled use of tactical nuclears, and after that to expand the war to controlled attacks upon an enemy's strategic forces and then to engage with him in a cold-blooded exchange of a few cities.

The third, and more uncommon way, of going around or beyond counterforces warfare is to envision a slow-lobbing intercity exchange as, under some circumstances, the decision of statesmanship. It is this proposal of "limited attacks on cities," or "controlled countervalue" war or "Counterforce plus Bonus civilian damage," which should be examined in depth. In doing so, I shall regard the limited exchange of cities as a lower limit of Pure City or of unlimited Countervalue war, and not as simply a variant or upper limit of controlled (or even all-out) Counterforces warfare. Those analysts who fail to note here an essential distinction have failed to observe the point at which, in making a courageous effort to "think about the unthinkable," they themselves began to think about the un-do-able.

Herman Kahn's latest book, *Thinking about the Unthinkable*, bears in its title reference to the contribution for which we are all indebted to him and to other weapons analysts. Some actions and events have been termed "unthinkable" because they are unpleasant to consider, or because they disturb our customary ways of thinking, or because we are weak in our determination to overcome the problem and submit it to the most rigorous rational analysis. Other proposed actions, however, are "unthinkable" in the far different and deeper sense that they are morally or politically "un-do-able." Properly to think about the unthinkable requires that we be open to the possibility that such effort will lead beyond the mere delineation of many possibilities for choice and action, which are distinguishable only extrinsically and in terms of consequences. That man is not quite resolute in thinking about the unthinkable who does not know that he may one day think something that is, in and of itself, un-do-able. He has not much confidence in his own powers of rational analysis who does not know that he can perfectly well think the "unthinkable" which will remain unthinkable in the sense that it is, for human agency, un-do-able.

A first illustration of this is to be found in what analysts say about policies based on the "rationality of irrationality." There is a point where a fundamental irrationality of at least some of these policies becomes evident in the fact that, we are told, one must irrevocably "commit" himself to doing them. That is to say, there are some actions that cannot be *done* at the time they are to occur. For them to occur, human agency and rationality must be placed in suspense at the time of occurrence. One must get himself bound by some artistic contrivance, or, better still, by acting as if he were a force of nature, before the event happens or before the (wrongly termed) "action" is to take place. "Committal strategies" cannot, in the extreme instances, be located in the ethical and political sphere. Instead, ethics and politics are abolished by the adoption of such strategies, for the simple reason that they put human agency out of commission. They are designed to do precisely this.

In this day when action and the principles of right action have been so far reduced to techniques, Aristotle's distinction between "making" and "doing" reasserts itself at the heart of any consideration of "committal strategies." "Making," he said, always has "something beyond itself" as an objective, whether this be a poem, a physical artifact, a weapons system or a social system. In contrast, in ethics and politics, "the very well-doing is in itself an End."[14] Right and wrong doing are to be found in the nature of moral and political agency itself, and not first of all in any of its external results. Of course, from any "well-doing" a lot of "making" results. Even so these are not the same.

The fundamental questions of ethics and politics have to do with "the very well-doing" that in and of itself is an end and norm of action. This question is simply avoided by schemes that plainly annul human agency at the place and time of an event's occurrence. Extreme "committal strategies" cannot be the result of an exercise of practical reason which Aristotle rightly called "doing." As un-do-able actions, they can only be contrived by "Art," an exercise of practical reason properly called "making"; or, we might say today, as a consequence of social "engineering." Today, those who manage to think the un-do-able actionable, accomplish this in large measure by virtue of what Jacques Maritain calls a "merely artistic view of politics" and of military conduct.

I once improved on Herman Kahn's use of the game of "Chicken!" as an analogy to the game of deterrence. The driver who wants to make *certain* he will win this game (to "deter" the other driver and force him to pull over before their vehicles collide) can do so by being the *first*

---

[14]*Nichomachean Ethics*, 1140b.

to strap his steering wheel and communicate to his opponent that he has done so and now *cannot* pull over even if he wanted to do so.[15] This is how one must contrive to do the un-do-able. He must effectively rule out human choice and agency at the time a totally irrational action is to be produced. He must get himself totally committed, and he is not totally committed if any "doing" remains to be done. Neither at the time of deterrence *nor before* has he made a human *political* decision, or chosen means apt to political ends if used, or put forth a political deed. *Before*, he did an *artistic* thing, beautiful to behold, whose whole meaning was to rule out choice and to make the exercise of political wisdom impossible at that later moment. This is the only way to think, and to think how to do, the un-do-able.

Now I find Kahn saying this same thing more clearly than in his earlier book, in which he stated that "Doomsday" deterrence machines would be unchoiceworthy (un-do-able) even if they might work. Or, rather, I find him stepping back and forth across the line between the unthinkable that has not yet clearly been thought and the unthinkable that, the more you think about it *with political judgment*, is inherently un-do-able. Out of his own writings our present point can best be made, namely, that this line exists between right and wrong political choice, and it is not one to be discovered merely by calculating numbers killed or saved or by engineering the values marched by in various scenarios. It is, rather, in the mind and judgment of the observer stimulated by "War and Peace Games" to think about "doing" and what is worthy to be done, as a just man would make the choice and perform the deed. Scenarios and "War and Peace Games" are altogether to be praised for what they can do to enlarge our knowledge of actual and exceedingly complex cases moving, as they must, through time. They stimulate the imagination, and if in no other way the opposing "team" insures that no fact or riposte or consequence is neglected.[16] This has always been the service of actual or hypothetical "cases" in moral and political

---

[15]In John C. Bennett, ed.: *Nuclear Weapons and the Conflict of Conscience.* New York: Chas. Scribner's Sons, 1962, p. 166.

[16]Litigation in our law courts and our "adversary" procedure are also ways of re-enacting the case and making sure that all the relevant facts will be found and brought to bear upon the decision. Here, however, members of the jury, deciding as to the facts of the case, also bring their sense of justice and injustice to bear on it; and rules of law, in which they are instructed by the judge, are not only positive laws "making" right but also depositories of collective judgment as to the justice or injustice of similar cases, and judge-made law provides a growing edge of decision-making in which the justice or injustice of a specific aggregation of personal and impersonal facts is determined. It is one thing to mount procedures apt in determining facts and for thinking the unthinkable action one is enabled and almost forced by these procedures to think through concretely. It is another thing to judge that the unthinkable is criminal. War and Peace Games-men should remember this.

reasoning: they require and enable informed concrete decision to be made. But, in an earlier age, this exercise was for the purpose of illuminating and stimulating *judgment* concerning what is to be done or not done, and not only to enable a man to think something about some "unthinkable" situation that might possibly face him in the future. Since Herman Kahn has probably run through more scenarios than anyone else, and since he is also a moral man concerned with the conduct of politics and war, it is helpful to observe him making judgments concerning the to-be-done and the not-to-be-done.

Before examining his position, I will insert here the opinion that the morality of war, and distinctions between just and unjust, rational and irrational, human and inhuman conduct, would be clearer in Kahn's writings if these distinctions were not trammelled from the beginning, and turned into seemingly *technical* judgments only, by the conviction he shares with most modern men that since war as such is immoral, no *moral* judgments can be made concerning the way it is conducted. In short, if there is no distinction to be made between killing and murder in the calculated (*vs.* wanton) acts of war between nations, then only technical questions remain to be solved. For example, the *numbers* the computers tell us will be dead will be the only basis for choice between, say, counterforces warfare and limited strategic city exchanges for bargaining purposes.

"Rationality of irrationality" policies cannot be said to be useless in politics. It was certainly true that, in the case of many delegates to the U.N., "the apprehensions created by Mr. Khrushchev's boorish actions in the General Assembly outweighed their dislike of such behavior," and that these delegates became "more disposed to go along with Soviet demands."[17] Nevertheless, *extreme* "rationality of irrationality" policies obviously become irrational again. For a nation to go to *total* committal policies is obviously to step over the line into action by contrivance, despite the fact that the action is politically un-do-able. Total committal to irrational action turns diplomacy or statesmanship itself into a Doomsday machine whose parts are erstwhile people.

This, it seems to me, Kahn now says more clearly. He spells out more fully what it would take to deter irrational action by irrational action. One must say convincingly, "One of us has to be reasonable and it is not going to be me, so it has to be you."[18] "One of us has to be responsible and it isn't going to be me, so it has to be you."[19] Now, how can this be done effectively, and effectively communicated? The enemy

---

[17]Thomas J. Hamilton in *The New York Times,* Oct. 30, 1960.
[18]Kahn, *op. cit.,* p. 78.
[19]*Ibid.,* p. 130.

has to be convinced you are "stark, staring mad"[20] or

> totally reckless, oblivious to the danger, out of control. These objectives can probably be met best by getting into the car drunk, wearing very dark glasses, and conspicuously throwing the steering wheel out of the window as soon as the car has gotten up speed.[21]

The side using this tactic tries to act like an unreasoning force of nature or, at least, a rigid human being. It tries to point out, implicitly or explicitly, that, "One does not argue with a hurricane, one seeks shelter in a cellar or suffers the consequence. Why then do you argue with me?" This tactic is particularly effective upon bystanders.[22]

Yet Kahn knows that this cannot be *done*, certainly not by a free society or by a government responsive to the will and responsible for the weal of a free society. He writes that

> thermonuclear threats . . . must look and be both prudent and rational. We cannot go around threatening to blow up a major portion of the world, or attempt to get our way by looking insane and dauntless. These strategies might be available to a totalitarian nation. They are not available to us, a democratic nation in a democratic alliance. Strategies overly dependent on resolve, on committing first, on extreme use of the rationality of irrationality, are not likely to succeed if attempted by the West.[23]

And immediately after one of Kahn's most extreme statements of how "best" to play this game of deterrence by total committal, he writes:

> If we must play the game, we should play it soberly, with clear vision, and in full control of both our capabilities and our emotions, even if doing this results in serious competitive disadvantages. We must do this in order to have both the appearance and reality of responsible leadership.[24]

In both the foregoing passages, Kahn plainly calls for never *being* or *appearing* to be totally committed to action that is so irrational it can never be politically done by free and present decision. Certainly, the upper limit of the politically do-able would be to appear to have strapped the wheel or thrown it away, but not actually to do so. Given the *deterrent* value of "this *appearance* of irrationally inexorable commitment," one would want to provide for the possibility of revoking the apparently irrevocable, since "if deterrence fails . . . it would then be

---

[20]*Ibid.*, p. 79.

[21]*Ibid.*, p. 45. Also see p. 188. "The youthful degenerates' game would be a better analogy if it were played with two cars at an unknown distance apart, travelling towards each other at an unknown speed, and on roads with a fork or two so that one is not even certain that he is on the same road as his opponent" (*ibid.*, p. 187).

[22]*Ibid.*, p. 179.

[23]*Ibid.*, p. 124.

[24]*Ibid.*, pp. 188-9.

irrational to carry through the commitment."[25] There may even be "some advantage in not using too extreme a 'rationality of irrationality' strategy," because, if you neither are nor seem to be totally committed, the enemy may actually do only what *he* can do purposefully, then and there at the time of action.[26]

Still there are passages in his recent book in which Kahn seems to hold open for adoption strategies which he himself has plainly stated ought never to be chosen, and which, his own analysis makes clear, *cannot* be "done" except by "making" ourselves do them (if that is to be called "doing"). He writes, for example, "*It can make sense* to commit oneself irrevocably to do something in a particular eventuality, and at the same time it may not make sense to carry out the commitment if the eventuality occurs."[27] Yet far more frequently, as I have shown, Kahn says *this cannot make sense*. Certainly not the actuality of it, and likely not the appearance either. This is not surprising, for we should have known all along that rational purposive action cannot contradict itself, or ever be "made" to do so. "Making" cannot take the place of "doing," nor contrivance replace responsible decision in the moment of action, nor can Art supplant Politics, if men remain men.

War as a Test of Wills

Policies of extreme committal to irrational behavior are only one illustration of where one is driven when war is regarded as primarily or exclusively a trial of wills or a test of resolve. There is no end here, no limits. Limited strategic war involving controlled city exchanges or limited countercity retaliation *as a bargaining tactic* offer another illustration of war in which the sides aim to "prevail" by demonstrating resolution. This, too, is "unthinkable" in the sense that the more you think about it the more it will seem manifestly "un-do-able." But first, a word should be said about war as a trial of wills in contrast to war as a trial of strength.

In war as a trial of wills, what one side does is determined primarily by its calculation of what the other side expects of it, or what is required for its resolution to be broken. Analysts in our day have developed an entire science of purely voluntaristic games of strategy simply by abstracting the encounter of the wills and minds of the

---

[25]*Ibid.*, p. 68.
[26]*Ibid.*, p. 69.
[27]*Ibid.*, p. 45 (italics mine).

combatants (always a significant aspect of military engagements) from other factors. Put aside for purposes of analysis are considerations of war as a resort to a controlled collision of bodily forces, war as a trial of physical strength, or war as the challenge and response of national entities each with concrete policies to be defended or effected. Where will and resolve are at issue, the question is not what would I do if I were the enemy seeking to enforce some definite national policy by possible resort to arms. The question is rather: What would I do if I were he, wondering what he should do if he were wondering what I would do if I were he . . .? In the determination of radically voluntaristic policy, the focal point is each side's expectation of what the other expects it to expect to be expected to do. Such is the result of our present-day attempt thoroughly to "spiritualize" the conduct of war. Such is the result of trying to elevate war from being a trial of strength directed toward some controlling objective, and of transmuting it into a test of resolve which has no other purpose than to prove who wins in a battle of wills. There is no limit or end to this. One is guided only by "what he expects the other to do, knowing that the other is similarly guided, so that each is aware that each must try to guess what the second guesses the first will guess the second to guess and so on, in the familiar spiral of reciprocal expectations."[28]

Much of the language of the foregoing paragraph presupposes that a nation's strategy is framed as a *response*, though an empty response that takes shape only, or mainly, in terms of what it expects another (so far) empty expectation to expect of it. You have the same conflict of wills, each empty and formless until it is filled by the other, if it is supposed that one is on the "offensive," trying to "bargain" with the other, to break his resolution, or to deter him from further action. Thus, the determination of strategy takes place almost wholly within a meeting of the wills and resolves of the combatants, in the sense that what each must be willing to do in order to "win" is determined by what the other is willing to do. This goes on to mutual destruction, or until one gives up and turns away, or until the strange notion comes to the mind of one or both of them that warfare has no limit or purpose unless it is predominantly a trial of strength.

American voluntarism was the source of this nation's confidence in deterrence. "The strategy of deterrence has assumed that this requirement of an ever triumphant will could be satisfied, if only because strength of will must somehow be proportionate to nobility of purpose. If our heart is pure, our hand will be steady, or at least steadier than

---

[28]Thomas C. Schelling: *The Strategy of Conflict.* Cambridge, Mass.: Harvard University Press, 1960, pp. 54, 57, 87.

the aggressor's." "To convince the adversary that we would act in the manner threatened, it is indispensable to convince ourselves that we would so respond. As long as we believe, others will believe. As long as others believe, they will not act. The key to a successful strategy of nuclear deterrence lies wholly within ourselves."[29] So, deterrence is a technical contrivance for doing what religion never could accomplish and the Christian religion never proposed (i.e., banish the *use* of force from human history), backed by an infinitude of correct anticipations of our anticipation of an enemy's anticipations, and so on.

The same American voluntarism is the source of our confidence in extreme "rationality of irrationality" policies, and it also has given birth to the thought that it is feasible and proper to fight a war of controlled countercity retaliation *as a bargaining tactic*. The question is not primarily whether cities can be deliberately exchanged with coolness and control enough to prevent this from at once becoming a spasm of countercity devastation. To this there is a prior question: whether exchanging cities for bargaining purposes and to play on the will of the adversary and break his resolve has not already transgressed the limits that are clearly present when war is understood as a trial of the actual military strength of nations. War as a test of the limitlessly variable "strength" of resolve may go as high as strategic city exchanges. War as a test of real strength to defend or effect objectives can and will go no higher than counterforces warfare. A nation determined to play a game of wills to the end, and resolved to will in accord with the internal "rationality" of a radical voluntarism, never will discover that there are any limits in resolutely willing to win this game of hostile wills in conflict. Not here is to be found any *ratio* in the *ultima ratio* of the arbitrament of arms. A nation comes upon no boundaries in this upward spiral, so long as proper acts of war are believed to arise not primarily out of concrete policy but out of contending wills. Unfortunately, in this, a commander can show his resolution in no other way than by proving he is willing to sacrifice one or more of his own cities; and he must reduce the enemy's cities to rubble as a means of getting at his resolution. This is the very definition of the unjust conduct of war.

Fighting a war has its obscure *ratio* only when the conduct of war is subordinated to the civil life and purposes of a nation, to its concrete civilization, values and policy objectives. The will to fight and the manner of fighting must be governed and controlled by the pre-eminence of society, and the effectuation or defense of its policy, over the use

---

[29]Robert W. Tucker: *The Just War: A Study of Contemporary American Doctrine.* Baltimore, Md.: The Johns Hopkins Press, 1960, p. 185.

of armaments. This relationship is lost sight of when war becomes a matter of one will "prevailing" over another, and the destruction of an entire city is made a mere means of "demonstrating" resolution, or is used to "symbolize" one side's willingness to go higher unless the other "chickens out."

Although analysts of the strategy of abstract conflict of wills would probably regard themselves as cool-headed rationalists in comparison with the warm-blooded "engagement" and passionate "involvement" recommended by contemporary existentialist philosophy, these schools are nevertheless brothers under the skin. The latter abstract from the structures of the person and the substance of inter-personal relationships and concentrate attention on only an *aspect* of the meeting of person with person, namely, the limitless capacity of self-consciousness to include in its consciousness the other's consciousness which in turn is determined only by its consciousness of the first person, and so on *ad infinitum.* Some existentialists reduce inter-personal relationships to a trial of wills or a test of resolution to "prevail," just as some analysts have pictured conflict between groups or nations. This is the secret meaning of the statement that countervalue warfare can, as a test of wills, have only *quantitative* limitations. This really means that there are no limits, except that quantity of destruction which will cause one side to give up first. If there had been more resolution to continue fighting (as there certainly might have been) the quantity would have been higher. No *ethical standards* are to be discovered for *inter-personal* behavior unless encounters between persons are imbedded in the nature of the persons and their good. No *political* limits are to be discovered for inter-national relations unless encounters between groups are imbedded in the structures of civil societies and their good. The wills and resolves of men must come down from aloft, they must return from their self-transcending "freedom" and limitless transcendence of the other in order to find that there are some things they are *bound not to do,* by the very nature of personhood, the very nature of political society, and the "natural justice" of warfare that is a purposive trial of strength with some controlling objective in view. The controlling goals in warfare may, of course, be "political effects objectives" which range far more widely than "battlefield objectives."[30] But surely, that contest is no longer "war" which has become a mere will to become demonstrably more resolute than someone else, by means that are not basically intended to insure that choiceworthy political effects will follow.

---

[30]Cf. Morton H. Halperin: *Limited War in the Nuclear Age.* Center of International Affairs, Harvard University, June, 1962, draft of an unpublished book.

War as a Limited Strategy

Analysts who now have managed to think this "unthinkable" thing — limited counterpeople war — give evidence in what they say about it that in this they have begun to think about the "un-do-able." It is instructive that, in his recent book, Herman Kahn leans away from Controlled City Reprisal toward Controlled Counterforce even more than seemed to be the case in his first and major work, *On Thermonuclear War*.[31] He finds greater difficulty thinking about situations in which an exchange of cities might seem justifiable in actual execution, and (most significantly) he states with substance and at length the political reason opposed to *doing* in this regard what he and other analysts have *thought* with some exactitude while playing war games. The same judgment — that controlled inter-city warfare is actually an un-do-able plan of war — finds support also on almost every page of the latest study specifically devoted to *Limited Strategic War*.[32] To be sure, none of these analysts recommends such a war; they say only that "limited strategic war is a *possible* war; to fight and prepare for such a war is a possible strategy."[33] My contention, however, is that even such a statement by a researcher goes too far, or not far enough toward decision. It is a possible war and a possible strategy in the sense that one can think of it after having not done so before: it is thinkable and possible in this sense. But it is not a strategy that can be chosen and put into effect by rational statesmanship, least of all by the government of a free society.

---

[31]Princeton, N. J.: Princeton University Press, 1960.

[32]Edited by Klaus Knorr and Thornton Read. Published for the Center of International Studies, Princeton University, by Frederick A. Praeger, New York, 1962, with chapters by each of the editors, and by Herman Kahn, Herbert D. Benington, Morton A. Kaplan, Arthur Lee Burns, Clark C. Abt & Ithiel de Sola Pool, and T. C. Schelling. My discussion of this volume of essays of necessity ignores significant differences among these authors.

[33]Knorr in Knorr and Read, *op. cit.*, pp. 5-6. "Limited strategic war" entails *long range* exchanges; and this may mean (1) limited attacks on strategic *forces* or (2) limited strategic attacks on *cities;* and the latter in turn may mean attacks (a) on *evacuated* or (b) on *populated* cities. In commenting on a volume of essays which analyses all these possible types of war under the heading of "limited strategic war," I cannot avoid using the term "limited strategic war" mainly to mean controlled counter-populated-city exchanges, which I deny is a plan of war at all possible to be done. At the same time it should be clear that I mean to allow that "limited strategic war," in the other senses, may possibly be done and justly done. Certainly, limited attacks on strategic *forces* conforms to the principles of *legitimate* military conduct. While unthinkable in one sense, such a war is not un-do-able. One has to be more cautious, however, in describing the conditions under which "countervalue" warfare that engages in exchanges of cities allowed to be evacuated might be do-able, or could be a possibly legitimate military action.

1. Limited nuclear attack on populated cities is only a limiting case of general nuclear war, and partakes of the same insanity. The fact is that weapons-analysts are only able to think of a war of controlled city exchanges as a *possibility for choice* by almost forcibly channelling their not inconsiderable intellectual powers in this direction, by resolutely concentrating their attention upon all-out general nuclear war as the *only* alternative to the one they are considering at the moment. This means that they first think of unlimited attack or unlimited retaliation, and then and by the aid of that unspeakable horror they manage to think of a limitation just short of that as possibly choiceworthy and do-able. Thus, Kahn writes: "*If the only alternatives are* between the all-out mutually homicidal war and the city exchange, bizarre and unpleasant as the city exchange is, it is not as bizarre and unpleasant as complete mutual homicide — even if a confusing and obsolete doctrine seems to make the latter the more conventional response. *It is precisely the value of this model that it jars me into adjusting intellectually* to the changed character of modern war."[34]

Klaus Knorr writes that limited strategic retaliation is "absolutely speaking, a calamity" so great that "a rational person will consider it only if all available alternatives are appreciably worse."[35] To be sure, he seems to believe that there may be a *number* of alternatives that might be worse; and he even implies that, if strategic forces become more stable and invulnerable, this *might* be a form of war frequently resorted to. I suggest, however, that this can be done, or genuinely considered only if the *sole* alternative is to go higher still, i.e., to go rapidly to all-out counter-city retaliation. This, at least, is what Knorr's conclusion seems to mean: "From every conceivable point of view it looks like a bad war and a bad strategy. But the question remains whether the available alternatives may not be, or may not come to be, more absurd and worse; and the possibility cannot be ruled out that *our* choices, *and* our opponent's choices, may become as absolutely bad as that implies."[36] It was probably the short distance between the greatest use and *this* "least undesirable" use of nuclear weapons that produced the first significant attempt to procure for this nation a wider range of choices: McNamara's move toward counterforces warfare. Significantly, in his concluding comment on these essays, T. C. Schelling

---

[34]*Thinking About the Unthinkable*, p. 134 (italics added). Or see p. 133: "The comparison should be made with the destructive all-out war, and the reader must fully understand that, *at least in our model*, this destruction really is total. Everybody is killed. Nobody is left. In these circumstances I believe one could expect the decision makers to prefer the controlled city exchange to the all-out war."

[35]Knorr and Read, *op. cit.*, p. 11.

[36]*Ibid.*, p. 30.

writes: "the concept of limited reprisal is something that a rational decision-maker can invent or discover in five minutes, once he is in a situation in which general war is an appalling prospect, a local tactical campaign is ineffectual, and inactivity and withdrawal are intolerable. It takes an act of intellect to *exclude* this kind of strategy from consideration. . . ."[37] It also takes an act of intellectual surrender to base strategy on city exchanges without making every effort to procure for ourselves other alternatives.

2. Whenever another pair of possible wars is in mind — when the analyst contrasts limited countervalue or countercity warfare with limited counterforces war — it seems very clear that the latter is choiceworthy for far more than quantitative reasons. Countercity or counterpeople warfare is bizarre, whether it is limited or unlimited. Doubtless there are distinctions to be made according to whether such war (fought between commanders proving their resolve by means of their cities and people) is partially or totally destructive, whether one of the contending wills seeks to bargain and to prevail over the other in measured terms or goes all-out against that other will. There are distinctions of objective importance in comparative damage to the societies and in the number of casualties. But, in addition to these *quantitative* comparisons, there is also a *qualitative* distinction between countercity and counterforce which soon discloses itself in the midst of cool calculations of one-city-for-one or five-cities-for-one; and one cannot remain content with saying, "fifty cities is a lot to lose" nor contemplate for long actually *doing* the fighting of a war in which "Both A and B will run out of cities before B runs out of missiles."[38] So there are qualitative reasons to recommend that, as an upper limit, nuclear warfare limited to counterforce be designed, if there is to be nuclear war, and for as long as there remain any nuclear weapons.

3. The Knorr and Read volume reveals quite clearly the abyss of infinitude and illimitability into which strategic city exchange has already plunged. To this there are no real boundaries; and to speak of "quantitative" limitations is misleading and dangerous language. Even the understandings reached during the fighting will be arbitrary ones, maintained only by encounters of resolve. The bargaining is not only over survival or prevailing. It is also over "the criteria of behavior permissible in the nuclear age;"[39] such war is "a contest to define the rules of the game"[40] while the game is being played. The "teachers"

---

[37]*Ibid.*, p. 257.
[38]Cf. Kahn, *op. cit.*, pp. 138, 142.
[39]Kaplan in Knorr and Read, *op. cit.*, p. 149.
[40]*Ibid.*, p. 154.

must themselves be "learning" what they are going to will this war to be.[41] As Thornton Read puts it: if "strategic punishment is limited voluntarily," then it not only influences bargaining but is itself "also a subject to bargain about"; "when punishment is limited by the will (rather than the capability) to inflict it, every tactical engagement becomes an individual case of tacit bargaining."[42] An aspect of war that has always been present in it has now become its whole content: war now has to be "conducted according to rules that are themselves subject to tacit bargaining,"[43] for example, whether the cities exchanged are equivalent or accepted by the other side as an indication of equivalent or greater resolve. The expression Read uses, "a pure punitive contest," is itself probably too retrospective. This strategy is, on the contrary, primarily prospective: one side is teaching the other "strategic foresight." In contrast, punishment has an appositeness and may have limits, which are not to be found in war whose purpose is to convince your opponent that you have irreversibly passed (by slow motion, to be sure) to higher levels, because you are irrevocably committed to "appositeness *plus*" following each exchange. The side wins which first effectively communicates the fact that it will take two cities for one.

What then can Kaplan mean by saying that "limited strategic re-taliation depends on and appeals to the inherent rationality of the players"? He means: "It induces them to think in cooperative rather than in strictly competitive ways. . . ."[44] But the writers of other essays make abundantly clear that this spiritualizing of conflict into cooperation only means "shared intimidation";[45] and only the optical illusion suf-fered by voluntarists and idealists can encourage one to imagine there must be more limits than in limited conventional war.[46] The more the players are lion-hearted and resolved to prevail, the more obvious it becomes that there are no boundaries to be found simply by pooling intimidation. On the contrary, each contestant must strive to demonstrate to the other that he is inexorably going higher. No matter how slow the pace up the scale of "value" exchanged, that side wins which appears most like an ascending force of nature. The "heart of the problem" for each contestant, once limited strategic retaliation has begun, is that he must "by individual examples . . . achieve the credi-bility of *an irreversible trend.*"[47]

---

[41]There are "probably intolerable 'expenses' of the educational program." Burns in Knorr and Read, *op. cit.*, p. 168.

[42]*Ibid.*, pp. 82, 84, 86.

[43]*Ibid.*, pp. 82, 84, 86.

[44]*Ibid.*, p. 158.

[45]Knorr and Schelling in Knorr and Read, pp. 21 and 247.

[46]Kaplan in Knorr and Read, p. 159.

[47]Abt and de Sola Pool in Knorr and Read, pp. 220-21 (italics added).

The way to win such a war is to get in the car, cold sober, with 20-20 vision and with the steering mechanism in perfect working condition, but with an accelerator so contrived that it will press itself very, very slowly to the floor unless and until the car's radar picks up a beam which tells it that the other car has pulled off the road or that its driver has retarded its speed. T. C. Schelling's comment at the end of this volume is worth noting, concerning a "mistake that one can be seduced into," and, he seems to imply, one made by some of the contributors. This is the supposition that "to conduct war in the measured cadence of limited reprisal somehow . . . gives it rational qualities that it would otherwise lack." Instead, writes Schelling:

> The situation is fundamentally indeterminate as far as logic goes. There is no logical reason why two adversaries will not bleed each other to death, drop by drop, each continually feeling that if he can only hold out a little longer, the other is bound to give in. There is no assurance that both sides will not come to feel that everything is at stake in this critical test of endurance, that to yield is to acknowledge unconditional submissiveness.

It is cold comfort that the foregoing statement is preceded by the sentence: "Even if this kind of warfare were irrational, it could still enjoy the benefits of slowness, of deliberateness, and of self-control"[48] — except that here Schelling inadvertently makes backhanded reference to another kind of rationality in the conduct of war than the "rationality of irrationality." A slow lobbing value-for-value war, like deterrence by threat of massive retaliation, can best be conducted by providing in advance for making an increasingly "choiceless choice."[49] This can be done, at the time and in the increasingly un-do-able fashion it has to be done, only by "making" oneself actually or apparently less and less the doer of it.

4. The fact that controlled city exchanges are an "un-do-able" way to conduct war becomes evident in the fact that Kahn can think this "unthinkable" only by thinking of its being done *once*. "It is, in fact, hard to imagine a 'controlled' city exchange or similar limited Counter-value attack being used more than once in two generations," he writes. "If used once, the shock might be sufficient to cause drastic and irreversible changes in the international order that would make repetitions unlikely."[50] He lists the objections against limited general war in order of increasing importance, and places last the objection that "surely

---

[48]Knorr and Read, *op. cit.*, p. 255. Also see Knorr, p. 5: "Only in a crudely descriptive and arbitrary sense would it be possible to say where limited strategic war ends and 'unlimited' general war begins."

[49]Cf. Benington in Knorr and Read, *op. cit.*, p. 123.

[50]Cf. Kahn, *op. cit.*, p. 63.

even if it worked once or twice it will eventually escalate into all-out war, and that would be the end."[51] Whereupon Kahn comes down heavily on the side of this objection:

> It is, in fact, inconceivable to me that such a system could continue. The objection is less to the strategy than to the model of two nation states both armed to the teeth, both regularly playing a version of the juvenile game of chicken, and yet both somehow expecting the system to last for a long time. I do not believe that this is possible. The proper, possibly the only, way to view this type of controlled war is as an attempt to use what influence one has, while one has it, to "vote" on the system which replaces our current deterrent system with its negotiation and resolution of disputes and political objectives against a background of threatened mutual homicide. One possible effect of a controlled exchange might be a heightened sense of crisis and danger plus a greater realization of the two nations' mutual interest in developing a better system — this could end in a détente.[52]

Surely this says as plainly as anything can that Controlled Nuclear Reprisals against cities is not a proper form of war at all. Into this none of the definite objectives of a nation are extensible at the time of the action. The scenario describes a critical *transition* from City Reprisals to purposive action. In itself, it cannot be politically *done*. If it is thinkable as being done once only before another line of action takes its place, and if city exchanges cannot even be done once with the expectation that the system is going to last for a long time, then the task of statesmanship is to think through such a critical transition without engaging in it and to initiate action that can continue, if need be, in behalf of definite policies.

If what Kahn supposes is what happens, let this not be called a plan of war among others that can be drawn up. It is rather a catastrophe that exceeds all the limits of warfare, for the purpose of teaching ourselves, and the world, a lesson that might have been otherwise learned simply by taking a little thought *within* the limits war now has, as a just barely purposive extension of politics. For the scenario which begins "the morning after" city exchanges is as follows:

> . . . the President of the United States might send a copy of this book [Granville Clark and Louis B. Sohn, *World Peace Through World Law*, Cambridge, Mass.: Harvard University Press, 1958] to Premier Khru-

---

[51]*Ibid.*, p. 133. Some contributors to the Knorr and Read volume seem to believe that limited strategic war may frequently be used in an era of balanced and invulnerable missile bases. But those who suggest this are using the term "strategic war" to mean strategic counterforces warfare. Thus Morton Kaplan writes that he "tends to believe that, *unless limited strategic nuclear war reaches the city-busting stage*, it can probably be used at least several times." (Knorr and Read, *op. cit.*, p. 161, italics added.)

[52]*Ibid.*, p. 135.

shchev, saying, "There's no point in your reading this book; you will not like it any more than I did. I merely suggest you sign it, right after my signature. This is the only plan that has been even roughly thought through; let us therefore accept it. We surely do not wish to set up a commission to study other methods of organizing the world, because within weeks both of us will be trying to exploit our common danger for unilateral advantages. If we are to have a settlement, we must have it now, before the dead are buried."[53]

Instead of even once doing the unthinkable which is "un-do-able," it might even be possible to think in another (habitually) unthinkable direction: "serious, tough-minded study of world government or other 'alternatives' might even result in a scheme's being devised that could be negotiated without the pressure of war,"[54] or rather without contriving a catastrophe illegitimately called "war" to "make" ourselves think politically. In any case, it is significant that most of the viable war plans Kahn runs through in his recent volume (in settings that are more imaginable in real political encounters than the *one* model that can ever give countercity reprisals an apparent choice-worthiness) are controlled counterforce, or this *plus avoidance* of civilian damage, even when this seems to sacrifice some military advantage!

5. Finally, there are internal considerations, as well as external ones, why even limited city exchanges must be judged politically un-do-able, especially by the government of a free society, un-do-able even once in the expectation that such a system will continue:

> If every time a hard decision has to be made, a major portion of the country has to be risked; if every time a country's diplomat walks into a hostile conference room, every man, woman and child feels threatened; if every time a nation stands firm against aggressive probes, panic seizes the hearts of many of its citizens, then many citizens will simply adopt an attitude of denial or apathetic fatalism. Others will call for "peace" at any price with such intensity that their governments will have to get out of their way. There may even be some who will say, "Better a fearful end than endless fear." Responsible political life is likely to suffer disastrously as a result of a combination of apathy, denial, and hysteria. The trouble with "negotiating" in this atmosphere is that, to put it mildly, it is not likely to produce thoughtful, considered suggestions or programs. It will instead invite blackmail and deception by the government which is in better control of its people, and irresponsible rigidity or destabilizing weakness by the government which cannot manipulate its people.[55]

This says as plainly as anything can that war-plans based on the premise that civilian lives and property are to be sacrificed indiscrim-

---

[53]*Ibid.*, p. 148.
[54]*Ibid.*, p. 150.
[55]*Ibid.*, pp. 214-15.

inately or made the object of attack in planned city exchanges, however controlled, are imaginable only in a world in which legitimate political activity has already been strangled. Men, cities, and politics have already been put to death, in thinking this unthinkable thing that is also, in and of its very nature, politically "un-do-able" conduct in war. This is not a surprising conclusion, since the "natural justice" of counterforces warfare defines the upper limit of the use of force which is politically justifiable.

To this reader, the most interesting chapter in the Knorr and Read volume is that by Clark C. Abt and Ithiel de Sola Pool on "The Constraint of Public Attitudes." This is an inquiry into whether the strategy under consideration can "satisfy the constraints of the politically possible."[56] This, happily, is "not, in any rigorous sense, a researchable subject,"[57] except by means of speculative scenarios. The response of people, and particularly of a people who have a measure of influence on their government's decisions, to city exchanges is in no sense comparable to their reaction to the destruction of an entire town by a natural disaster, nor even to their probable reaction to damage of the same magnitude that may be the unavoidable side-effect of counterforces nuclear war. To speculate about what their reaction will be is, I believe, to speculate about the rudiments of the "just war doctrine" that still makes its presence felt.

The most these authors seem able to say in behalf of a countercity war-plan is that "the strategy may still be worth planning for if it can be a contingency policy, available for use if public opinion turns out to tolerate it. . . .[58] Even the idea of folding this war away in a contingency plan is not actually supported by their findings of probable fact. It is true that during the time of actual execution one possible public reaction counterbalances another. Perhaps the people in threatened cities "would channel their fears and anxieties into the direct self-protective actions of evacuation rather than into civil protest."[59] Perhaps, on the other hand, "substantial portions of the people living in the cities threatened with prompt counter-reprisals, *if given time to make their opinions known on the matter,* would be violently opposed to the United States' initiation of limited reprisal against Novosibirsk."[60]

The question, however, concerns civil protest not only during the execution of this strategy, but also *before, during,* and *afterward,* unless

[56]Knorr and Read, *op. cit.*, p. 199.
[57]Knorr in Knorr and Read, *op. cit.*, p. 23.
[58]*Op. cit.*, p. 204.
[59]*Ibid.*, p. 215.
[60]*Ibid.*, p. 214.

politics has already been put to death before cities and people are. Statesmen cannot long remain, if they ever are, isolated from the civil life it is their function to serve. Therefore, "the major inhibition felt by the President would be his *perception* of what public opinion was likely to be *after* the crisis." To be prepared to fight a counterforces war requires a "community" fall-out shelter system, correlated with private shelters. To be prepared to fight a countercity war, however, would make it rather dangerous for the statesman to allow the people thus to congregate, since "large communal shelters in cities might be the scene of considerable political agitation that might have both immediate and long-term effects."[61] People must be isolated from one another if a decision-maker is to be sufficiently isolated from them to make this a do-able policy. Free political life would have to be put to death if this is the way a nation's survival is to be engineered. This analysis is revelatory of the inherently non-political character of this supposed strategy. It means that "many of the problems that may result from the adoption of a policy of limited retaliation could arise if the policy were even considered with sufficient seriousness for people to believe that it might be undertaken."[62]

So there they stand, these "spiritualized" conquerors, each seeking to "prevail" by throwing cities to rubble, as wealthy dandies in San Francisco used to fight their "duels" by throwing gold dollars into the Bay until one of them had the will to do so no longer. It is evident that the people of one of the selected cities will have to be put out of politics before they can knowingly agree to their own government's arbitrary resolve to use them in this game of tit-for-tat. And it would be *their own* government's resolve and not that of the enemy alone, since if this game stays limited everything will depend on the enemy's attacking no more cities or cities only a little larger than those we have "signaled" him to take out by our own immediately prior choice of targets from among his cities. This is a war that is supposed to be fought slowly up the range of the "value" we and the enemy have agreed to place on cities in order that the sacrifice of them will, in turn, effectively signal the enemy our determination to go somewhat higher than he.

So there they stand, these "spiritual" warriors, as they engage in a war of nerves, each saying to the other, "There, you see, one of us

---

[61]*Ibid.*, p. 215.

[62]*Ibid.*, p. 237. Under this strategy, the relation of the people of our cities to their government domestically is the same as the relation of a smaller ally to an alliance thinking of adopting this policy, if the ally is apt to be offered as target or more of a target. See, in Knorr and Read, Arthur Lee Burns on "The Problem of Alliances."

has to be rational, and since it's not going to be me, it has to be you, or you first." This war of "value for value"

> can be regarded as a late and perhaps last desperate move in the *economization* of war and world politics. Arms and men are more or less scarce means having alternative uses; resources such as cities, fertile countrysides, and even stable social systems are in one aspect, economic goods—as implied in the strategic term countervalue. [63]

The people of a country cannot knowingly accept their complete inclusion in this process of the *economization* of politics by which they themselves are reduced to the status of values in exchange. No government responsive to their will or responsible for their weal can conduct war in this fashion. In contrast, the civil damage collateral to actually fighting a counterforces war will seem rationally directed to some purpose, and is intended to be, even if the damage proves as extensive or more. As with massive or balanced deterrence, so with value-for-value war that has none but the quantitative limits which the weakness of one side's resolve may allow: these war-plans are intrinsically intolerable. Both are tolerated only because people don't think about them or because people who think about them stand several steps back from thinking through the actual doing of them, or because they think grimly that, if only we have these wars in preparation and are strong enough in our will to use them, why, then none of them will ever have to be used.

On the other hand, no one should blink the fact that the transformation of "political man" into "economic man" may have proceeded so far in the contemporary period that it has become an irreversible trend in this civilization. Then modern man will sooner or later destroy himself. This will be because of his merely quantitative evaluation of human life and of ethical and political conduct, because of the economization of politics, and his lack of capacity for political agency and for making sound political judgments concerning the do-able and the inherently un-do-able. These things increasingly characterize all of the realms of decision. This leads, in international relations, to a nation's unquestioning acceptance of the supposed rationality of countervalue warfare.

Suggested Policy Decisions

The "just conduct" of war proscribing deliberate direct attack upon non-combatants, and the primacy in war of weapon-to-weapon

---

[63]Burns in Knorr and Read, *op. cit.,* p. 170.

trials of strength over a contest of wills, are not of course immediately *constitutive* of policy decisions or war plans. But these are *regulative* of such decisions, so long as war remains in any measure a definite purposive political act.

I will venture here to suggest a series of policy decisions which seem to me imperative at this hour for the free world's security. These suggestions are put forward .with a great degree of reluctance, since I do not believe that ethico-political analysis extends so far beyond providing regulative moral guidance. Not every decision, not even every important decision, is an *ethical* decision, and many exceedingly important choices are the business of statesmen and of experts other than the moralist. Still, with the aid of other experts the following suggestions can be made for steps that need urgently to be taken. None of these decisions waits on international agreement. Each must be *declared* policy, and each can at least begin to be put into effect by "unilateral initiatives."

1. This nation, and other nations of the West, need increasingly to procure forces for sub-conventional and conventional warfare, and at the same time to repair in public consciousness a doctrine of the possible and just use of such forces. Of course, it may be said about conventional forces that we lost that "arms race" with the Russians long ago, or rather never sought seriously to enter upon it. It is also true that the strength needed for conventional warfare would require a change of heart in that "economic man" who bears the name of the free world taxpayer. He must be told in no uncertain terms that his unexamined reliance on deterrence of total war by threat of total war and mutual homicide policies are themselves of a piece with his unwillingness to prepare for any real trial of strength. He must be told that he is in mortal danger precisely because at every level of warfare he is so completely non-political and unpurposive. Hoping to banish the use of force by threatening unusable force, he only banishes usable force and pulls the nerve of action. It is an ominous weakness in the West that the enemy can heat a crisis to almost any temperature knowing that the West will be no better prepared after the event. Men will be called up, it is true, but we now give a crisis-maker the luxury of knowing in advance that very soon the *status quo ante* will be restored.[64] The free world taxpayer must be awakened from the dream of deterrence; and he must be told that we cannot make unjust, inter-city warfare measur-

---

[64]On the same pleasant summer evening in August 1962, the "Seven O'Clock Report" showed film and the voices of reservists complaining how useless their call-up was ten months ago, and a commentator's analysis of the evidences that Russian military might was being mobilized in support of another Berlin crisis about to be created.

ably more of an impossibility without making just or counterforces warfare again a possibility. This means, first and foremost, strength in conventional arms; and there is no analyst who does not say that NATO could match the mythical Russian "hordes," and the whole free world could do this at every point of probable vital challenge.

If religious opinion has any influence on public opinion, and that in turn on high-level policy decisions, then a false Christian identification of the peace of God with the peace of the earthly city must bear a share of responsibility for this nation's reliance on war that can never under any circumstances be fought, and its simultaneous abandonment of the sort of war that can be used. No churchman can condemn the one without condemning the other. He cannot in good conscience oppose the present reliance of the U.S. on massive weapons unless he also confesses that, during the period we developed this reliance, a general "Christian" pacifism contributed to it and to our present design of war by a sweeping opposition to a more equitable and universal military service. In 1948, for example, it required only a one or two-man social action lobby of the Presbyterian church and a few telephone calls to prominent Presbyterians in Oklahoma to determine the vote of one representative which was decisive in Republican caucus in bottling up a universal training bill in committee and in insuring that it never reached the floor of Congress for debate.[65]

2. This nation should announce that as a matter of policy we will never be the first to use nuclear weapons—*except* tactical ones that may and will be used, against forces only and not strategically against an enemy's heartland, to stop an invasion across a clearly defined boundary, our own or one we are pledged by treaty to defend. This would make it unambiguously clear that tactical nuclear weapons will be used if need be against any invasion, even by conventional forces. The threat would be believable, because of the clearly declared limits which state that the use of nuclear weapons will be defensive only and that not even in reply to an invasion will we first use nuclear weapons

---

[65]See R. Morton Darrow, "The Church and Techniques of Political Action" in *Religion in American Life*, ed. by J. W. Smith and Leland Jamison. Princeton, N. J.: Princeton University Press, 1960, Vol. II, pp. 186-7. The author considers only the technique of making religious opinion politically effective, not the substance of the matter.

After a nuclear war, the survivors may well ask concerning the complicity of the churches and "peace" groups in the assistance our government gave to the enemy in killing people he did not want to kill—by locating missiles near populated cities and by failing to construct a national system of community fall-out shelters. If this question is asked, the answer can only be that such resulted from the effort good people of the previous age made never to grow accustomed to the idea of nuclear war, from their resolve instead to avoid war altogether, and from the natural kinship between their views and *pacifistic deterrence*.

"offensively" against an enemy's territory or his strategic forces. This would make it unnecessary for the President of the United States constantly to warn off a possible invasion of Europe by words that allow the possibility of our initiating the use of nuclear weapons, and possibly an offensive strike against Russian cities or against her strategic bases. This proposal may be called the right of first defensive use of nuclear weapons against invading forces, or a commitment to use nuclear weapons first only over one's own territory.

This proposal has been made by Paul Nitze,[66] and more recently by Leo Szilard[67] and Thornton Read.[68] While Szilard's formulation should be looked at to see the significance of the inclusion of this policy decision among the tenets of a Council for Abolishing War, the fuller and sounder analysis by Thornton Read affords us the clearest way to elaborate further the meaning of this second policy proposal. Thornton Read has written most eloquently and forcefully concerning the value of preserving the distinction between conventional and nuclear weapons as such, of preserving the fear the people of the world have of ever again crossing this boundary, and of channelling this fear into a proposal for neutralizing nuclear weapons in a system of international sanctions against their use.[69] Without even invoking the danger of escalating from tactical to massive nuclear weapons, he has satisfactorily demonstrated the essentially escalatory character of tactical nuclear weapons themselves, because of the relation of their weight to their fire power in comparison with conventional explosives, a relation which places a great gulf between conventional and tactical nuclears as possible instruments of controlled warfare.[70]

Thornton Read does not lightly find virtue in a proposal involving a possible first use of tactical nuclears. The fact is that he can do so only because he thinks it may be possible to link legitimate first use of tactical nuclears with another well-understood limit, namely, national boundaries, which may serve as a focus of agreement concerning the rules of conflict. This is his proposal for defensive first use in or over one's own invaded territory. Such a declaration of policy is, of course, a positive assertion of legitimacy which requires, and makes it possible

[66]*East-West Negotiations.* Washington Center of Foreign Policy Research, 1958, pp. 28-36.

[67]"Are We On The Road to War?" *Bulletin of the Atomic Scientists,* April, 1962.

[68]"The Proposal to Use Nuclear Weapons Over One's Own Territory," Unpublished paper, Center of International Studies, Princeton, 1962.

[69]*A Proposal to Neutralize Nuclear Weapons.* Center of International Studies, Princeton. Policy Memorandum No. 22, Dec. 15, 1960.

[70]"Counterforce Strategies and Arms Control," Center of International Studies, Princeton, March, 1962 (unpublished); and Knorr and Read, *op. cit.,* pp. 72-77.

to declare, that not even to stop a massive conventional invasion will we use nuclear weapons offensively first. *This possibility we now hold ambiguously open* for ourselves, in order to "strengthen the deterrent." Yet in view of the destruction an offensive first strike over an enemy's territory would immediately let loose over own own, it has become increasingly unbelievable we will ever employ it for any of the definite military or political objectives involved in recent crises. Thus, the proposal is that we publicly renounce that first use of nuclear weapons which we can really mean to renounce, while asserting a defensive first use of tactical nuclears tied to the repulsion of an invasion across a conventionally defended boundary.

> National boundaries have the same sort of clarity and symbolic significance as the distinction between conventional and nuclear weapons. Crossing the nuclear threshold has, in fact, been compared to crossing a national boundary. Both limits are unambiguous and both are the focus for strong feelings.
> The proposal to use nuclear weapons defensively combines two sharp and unambiguous discontinuities in the spectrum of violence and says that crossing a clear-cut geographical boundary justifies the opponent in crossing the equally clear-cut discontinuity between conventional and nuclear weapons.[71]

It may also be added that the qualitative discontinuity between counterforce and counterpeople warfare is tied in with boundaries, if nuclear weapons are ever justifiably used. The side using nuclear weapons justifiably would have every incentive to limit their destructiveness, and to maintain sufficient conventional forces either to hold the border or to slow an invasion so that civilians could be evacuated from between the lines. Moreover, "the region that is fair game for a nuclear attack is not only clearly defined and small in area; *it does not even exist until the aggressor creates it.*" The objective in this use of tactical nuclears will not be "victory" but defense strictly understood as sealing the border. "At the border there would be a discontinuity in the life expectancy of enemy soldiers. In crossing the border residual life expectancy would drop from, say, fifty years to fifty minutes. This would establish a powerful incentive not to cross and would create serious problems of morale for the aggressor."

This is certainly a clear case of "just conduct" in a first resort to nuclear weapons. It is counterforces warfare, surrounded by the additional limitation of the aggressor-defender distinction. And it allows "bargaining" and an encounter of wills in which rules of warfare may

---

[71]Thornton Read, "The Proposal to Use Nuclear Weapons Over One's Own Territory" (Unpublished). Subsequent undesignated quotations are also from this document.

be agreed to, created, preserved or enforced. Here the aim is not "to bind a potential violator through his sense of honor" but "to influence his behavior by creating in his mind expectations as to how we will respond." This is its superiority over a simple proscription of aggression.

At the same time, in contrast to our present policy which admits the possibility of a first initiation of nuclear warfare over his territory, "the advantage of the more restrictive rule is that it is more credible" and therefore more likely to deter, more likely to bring about tacit agreements to limit nuclear war and to restrict it to forces. The point is to "emphasize the distinction between the defensive and the offensive use of nuclear weapons so that it becomes a focus of expectations comparable to the nuclear-conventional distinction." Breaching the latter distinction may serve to enforce the former. This proposal is, therefore, also a struggle over the rules of warfare. "An aggressor having superior conventional forces would try to establish the rule that nuclear weapons should not be used at all. The defender would want to establish the rule that nuclear weapons could be used defensively but not offensively." But this is far removed from a limitless struggle of empty wills, each only reflecting the other.

Before going on to my third point, a comment may be inserted here concerning Leo Szilard's formulation of this proposal that "*America could and should adopt the policy that, in case of war, if she were to use atomic bombs against troops in combat, she would do so only on her own side of the prewar boundary.*"[72] Against the objection that it is an odd war, indeed, in which weapons with the greater destructive side-effects are reserved for use over one's own territory, Szilard gives the obvious answer: "I do not know to what extent West German cities could be spared by a judicious tactical use of atomic bombs by American forces, but I do know that if America were to use bombs beyond the pre-war boundary, West German cities would be destroyed by Russian bombs." In comparison with "the simple pledge renouncing the use of the bomb" altogether, the proposed commitment "would be easier to keep and therefore it would be a more believable pledge" (though Szilard does suggest that "it would be possible for Western Europe to build up within five years conventional forces to the point where it could renounce the use of atomic bombs against troops in combat in case of war").

To announce unilaterally, as Szilard proposes, this limitation upon any first use of nuclears requires us also to renounce unilaterally "*plans which call for a first strike against Russian rocket and strategic bases*

---

[72]*Op. cit.*

in case of war" and to renounce *"the policy of 'deterring' Russia, with the threat that America would resort to such a first strike in case of war."* The "general *deterrent"* would be given up; and in urging this surely Szilard is correct when he says that America would not "lose much by giving up the threat of strategic bombing because the deterrent effect of such a threat is negligible unless the threat is believable," which increasingly it is not. A *second* strike, however, should be maintained, as a threat and a promise, in case *"American cities or bases are attacked with bombs, or if there is an unprovoked attack with bombs against one of America's allies."* Szilard's use of the word "bomb" for all nuclears is inexact, of course. He probably means to justify an attack first upon the strategic *forces* of an enemy who has used tactical nuclears offensively on the territory of our allies. If so, the above statement amounts to a crucial point yet to be considered in Read's rule for restricting legitimate use of nuclears to one's own territory, namely, that any violation of this rule will, for the first time, make offensive strikes legitimate over the enemy's territory. Szilard's present proposal shows that when a powerful intellect (even though his mind is the mind of a scientist) focuses attention on the grave problem of war today, he will be driven to follow the lineaments of the just war doctrine in his policy proposals.[73] Something like this is what anyone will come up with if he focuses attention on how we are to "back away from the war to which we have come dangerously close," and to which we still stand too dangerously close.

---

[73]Szilard's mind wanders from the problem of concrete political and military policy, and his political objectives "which must be pursued in the next couple of years" turn into "steps" which must be taken toward a more lofty goal, and are of value only if they lead to this goal. These policy proposals, which surely are worthwhile in themselves to limit war, are only "in order to make the present danger of war recede to the point where attention could be focused on the task of abolishing war."

No one would deny that attention must be given to this task, but it must be political reason and political action which attend to it. Unfortunately, in Szilard's case, it is "scientific" reason instead of the political reason he exercised in the concrete proposals. These are all set in the context of the formation of a "Council for Abolishing War." This Council is to have "fellows (who are all scientists)" and would elect a board of directors, on which "membership would not be restricted to scientists." A panel of political advisors, of course, would be assembled. The scientific Council would by these means formulate two sets of objectives. "To the first set belong those objectives which can not be attained at the present time through political action because it would take further inquiry, and perhaps even real research to know, in concrete terms, what needs to be done. To the second set belong those objectives which can be pursued through political action because it is clear what needs to be done [presumably Szilard's concrete policy proposals]." A *political* movement will be brought into being to enable us to back away "from purposeless warfare. *Scientific* research may then tell us how to abolish it altogether." Thus, "the combination of a few per cent of the votes and the sweet voice of reason might turn out to be an effective combination."

3. In the foregoing, we have bracketed for the moment the question whether the first use of tactical nuclears only between the front line and the border crossed is a rule we want simply for the five years needed to mount adequate conventional forces, or whether this self-imposed rule of war should be regarded as a permanent part of justifiable resistance to conventional invasion in a nuclear age. Should the United States have as its ultimate goal the preparation of conventional defense so that as soon as possible it can accept a prohibition of *any* first use of nuclear weapons?

73(*Continued*)

A conversation between Szilard and Polanyi is not, I think, untypical of this sort of reasoning. Polanyi said that, since it might be suicidal for people to be *overly* generous, "perhaps the rule ought to be 'Be one per cent more generous to people than they are to you.' This should be sufficient . . . because if everyone were to follow this rule, the earth would, step by step, turn into a livable place." [An alternative name for Szilard's Council is "Council for a Livable World."] To which in reply Szilard summed up the phenomena in human nature and politics which theologians have always called the boundless "sin" of man, by saying, "each is bound to think that he is 30 per cent more generous than the other;" and he proceeded to slay this with a rule: "Perhaps if we were to stipulate as the rule of conduct 'Be 31 per cent more generous to others than they are to you' such a rule might work." Everywhere in this article Szilard describes the men he wants in his proposed Council and movement as men who have an adequate "historical" point of view, meaning (I think) men who believe the bomb has completely changed the nature of history and of politics; and who are as a consequence resolved to reconcile the nations by rules and abolish war by additional research in the time provided by concrete political proposals. This is exceedingly *un*historical and *non*-political reasoning.

This may seem needlessly harsh on that great man and generous spirit who is Leo Szilard. I have already paid tribute to his concrete proposals as disclosing the very anatomy of just and rational conduct in war. But one cannot forget the fact that Szilard was also the first to propose that *countervalue* warfare be planned and, if need be, put into execution. ("Disarmament and the Problem of Peace," *Bulletin of the Atomic Scientists,* October 1955, pp. 297-307.) Once he also speculatively proposed a variant of Kahn's Doomsday deterrent machine: cadres of Russian demolition experts under New York City and an American demolition team under Moscow, to make certain neither side can ever fire their massive weapons because neither *can* want to, and because both are now *bound* to want peace. ("The Mined Cities," *Bulletin of the Atomic Scientists,* Dec. 1961, pp. 407-412.) To such proposals the ascendency of the scientific mind in politics almost invariably comes. (For an excellent study of scientific advisors in government, the undeniable political character of their "scientific" advice, and the additional confusion introduced by the fact that they often fail to acknowledge this, see Robert Gilpin: *American Scientists and Nuclear Weapons Policy.* Princeton, N. J.: Princeton University Press, 1962.) Such proposals are in play because of the ascendency of "making" over principles for the guidance of political agency and inherent in proper "doing." One must question, not the present proposals themselves, but whether they are soundly grounded. Is not Szilard and the "scientific" mind generally just a special case of the modern mentality which out of limitless passion for peace on earth might be willing to design and do unlimited war? Was it because he simply became convinced his former proposals could not be "made" to work or because he began to think politically that Szilard wrote his recent article? Does *he* understand that his concrete proposals were born out of the morality of war's conduct which has validity in a multi-national world long before and apart from the descent of peace?

The more one thinks about a policy of using tactical nuclears defensively, and unilateral initiatives to try to govern war in this fashion, the more it seems a possible choice for the nations of the world. At least they would be forced to ask whether it is only for the time being that security for the free world and the peace of the entire world could be based on this proposal. If this first use of nuclear arms can be tied to the resistance of aggression across well-understood and conventionally well-defended boundaries, will not free world security and world peace be less in danger? Will not this be better than an absolute distinction between conventional and nuclear explosives as a basis for the peace-keeping machinery of some future international organization? Or, on the contrary, ought we to begin now to strengthen conventional forces with a view to placing all nuclear weapons in a class by themselves as illegitimate weapons (like bacteriological weapons) which may be possessed to deter their use by an enemy but never used first even in self-defense?[74]

In whichever way this question is decided, it is of great importance that freedom-loving and peace-loving people realize that to renounce the first use of any weapon is a matter more of what they do than of what they say. "To the extent that the Communists are unable to defeat the conventional forces of the free world without resorting to nuclear weapons, the practical effect will be our renunciation of the first use of nuclear weapons."[75] This means that at the moment we may have simply presented the Russians with the ability effectively to renounce the first use of tactical nuclears in the European theater.

4. Nuclear capability must be maintained for use in counterforce strikes over an enemy's territory. These strikes would have a dual purpose: first, to prosecute the trial of strength and destroy or decrease an enemy's forces and the force he can muster on the battlefield; secondly, to punish any violation and thus to enforce if possible the rule which we declare by word and by action we have imposed on ourselves, namely, that while defensive first use of tactical nuclear weapons is legitimate, not even in answer to this will we tolerate the use of tactical nuclear weapons offensively over the territory of another nation. Both these purposes indicate that nuclear weapons over an enemy's territory should first be used against *tactical* objectives, munitions dumps, supply lines, bridges, etc. If *nuclear* weapons are used to do this, their

---

[74]There is an excellent summary of the arguments for eliminating *any* first use of even tactical nuclear weapons from Western military policy in Halperin, *op. cit.* He, however, does not explicitly consider the possibility of tying first use to a self-imposed and announced policy limiting the use of nuclear weapons to one's own invaded territory.

[75]Henry Kissinger, *The Necessity for Choice.* New York: Harper, 1960, p. 91.

use will both prosecute the war and be a signal that the right to do this was granted when the enemy first used nuclear power offensively across another nation's boundary. The reasons for the limitation of these retaliatory strikes to tactical targets, however, will have to be declared again and again and communicated to both the enemy and neutral nations.

If *tactical* targets are clearly the objectives of an answering offensive use of nuclear weapons, the distinction Thornton Read makes between these two uses may be a little too severe:

> The defensive use is primarily to act on the opponent's capability, to deny him territory. The offensive use is rather to act on his will, to punish him and to communicate to him our resolve and our determination not only to defend our territory but to uphold the two rules he has violated, namely the rule against conventional aggression and the rule against the use (or first use) of nuclear weapons against another nation's territory.[76]

Acting upon his will is, of course, important, perhaps now of added importance, but one is still engaged in war to deny him territory and cause him to withdraw. Moreover, in acting upon his will one is doing so by just and limited counterforce means, and with the objective of achieving possible political effects in societies that may endure beyond the conflict.

5. We come now to the No City strategy discussed in the first parts of this paper. The statement of U.S. policy that McNamara presented in his University of Michigan address, if carried out, would place as wide a "firebreak" as possible between a war of exchanges involving strategic forces and counter-city strategic warfare. There should also be a "firebreak" between conventional and tactical nuclear warfare— by, for example, not equipping the same troops with both types of weapons—and another between strikes against tactical targets and strikes against strategic forces.

We ought not to say at once that, in the nuclear age, "a main consequence of limited war, and a main purpose for engaging in it, is *to raise the risk of general war.*"[77] Since "general war" ambiguously embraces both attacks on an enemy's strategic forces and attacks upon his cities, this implies that a main purpose of engaging in any form of limited war is to indicate that we are prepared to go to massive retaliation against cities. This is to regard the main purpose of any of the forms of limited war as a simple trial of wills. We ought rather to say that one of the consequences and one of the purposes of limited con-

---

[76]*Op. cit.*, p. 29.

[77]T. C. Schelling, "Nuclear Strategy in Europe," *World Politics*, Vol. XIV, No. 3 (April, 1962), p. 421.

ventional or tactical nuclear war is *to raise the risk of counterforce strategic war*. A nation which first makes use of tactical nuclear weapons to resist a conventional aggression, for example, says by that action that it may be finally willing to use strikes against the enemy's homeland tactical targets or missile bases to impose on him its self-imposed rule that nuclear weapons are to be used only defensively and to punish any violation of this limit. The latter is clearly one purpose of nuclear war at the first level. Its main purpose is to seal the border and defend the country. Its main purpose, in any case, is not to raise the risk but to preserve a limit.

Moreover, the risk which the defender raises is still counterforces warfare and not the mutual destruction of societies. The will to fight "counterforce plus avoidance" can be signalled to the enemy, can work to keep war limited and enforce tacit or declared agreements about the rules of war in international law, *only* if one is able to fight such a war marked off as clearly as possible from "general war." One must have the ability to carry limited counterforce warfare to the enemy's own territory in order to bargain effectively about the limits and rules by which war is to be fought.

6. Just as it would be wrong to say of unconventional, conventional, or tactical nuclear war that it is *nothing but* deterrence during the war, so it is also wrong to say that a No City Strategy "is nothing but deterrence during a war." Counterforce strikes over an enemy's territory, and preparations to limit war to this, do replace the assumption of massive general deterrence policy (so far as it is possible to deter a rational enemy *before* the war starts) with the assumption that "it surely is possible to deter that rational enemy from going to city destruction even if the war starts."[78] Such deterrence during strategic strikes against forces is only an aspect of even this war, whose principal purpose is to enforce *lower* limits, punish violations of them, and in any case decrease the enemy's military capability and affect the balance of power in the world after the war is over.

Still, all forms of limited war, including counterforce strikes over the enemy's territory, do have this additional purpose of reducing his will to fight, or to fight in certain ways, by indicating our possible willingness to go higher still. The capstone of this system, which includes war at any of the lower limits in a nuclear age, is finally the deterrence of city destruction by the threat of city destruction. Thus, Fryklund sums up the No City Strategy that may now be in the making:

---

[78]Richard Fryklund, *op. cit.*, p. 89.

We adopt publicly a weapon-against-weapon strategy and concede that there are no targets in Soviet cities worth destroying at the cost of our own cities. At the same time, we emphasize that if the Communists start blasting our cities, we will use our hidden invulnerable forces to wipe out their cities. To make the decision easier for the Russians, we see to it that none of our cities or suburbs contain important military targets.[79]

Even if we can say that the Russians and the West have equal reason for policy decisions based on the judgment that "no matter what happens it doesn't make sense to start hitting cities," there stands in the background and in support of this the fact that in the nuclear age city destruction seems to be deterred only by the threat of city destruction in reprisal. Thus, McNamara went on to say, in his University of Michigan policy statement:

> The very strength and nature of the Alliance forces make it possible for us to retain, even in face of a massive surprise attack, sufficient reserve striking power to destroy an enemy society if driven to it. In other words, we are giving a possible opponent the strongest imaginable incentive to refrain from striking our own cities.

This question of continual massive deterrence, to which any consideration of limiting policy decisions seems inevitably to be driven, is my concern in the following section.

The Justice of Deterrence

In the foregoing, I have argued that the No-Cities or Counterforce plus Avoidance policy is the only just and sensible way to conduct war; that weapons analysts have sometimes overlooked the distinction between the unthinkable that has simply not yet been thought and the unthinkable that is un-do-able when thought about; that war as a trial of wills disconnected from trials of strength becomes an abysmal and unlimited conflict of resolutions; that current discussions of "general" war or "limited strategic war" need to distinguish more clearly between long-range attacks on strategic forces and strategic attacks on cities; and finally I advanced tentatively a gradation of policy decisions designed to set "firebreaks" between the steps in increasing violence, up to the No-Cities or strategic Counterforce policy. We need now to take up the moral and practical questions involved in "deterrence during the war," which at every stage seems necessary to keep war limited.

I shall argue that none of the virtues of the limiting policy decisions for which a case can be made, or of war considered only in the

---
[79]*Ibid.*, p. 97.

context of constant massive deterrence, can invalidate the distinction between the do-able and the politically un-do-able.

It is frequently contended that "both prudence and international law" permit and make it "desirable to carry out reprisals in kind," and that the only question remaining once an enemy strikes one of our cities is how to determine the equivalence to be exchanged moment by moment in countervalue war.[80] Whatever may be the rule of reprisal in international law today, this can hardly be said to settle the question of the justice — the natural justice — of reprisal in kind (or in *some* kinds). If it is unjust for an enemy to destroy our society, the fact that he does or tries to do so first cannot make it any less of an injustice for us to destroy his. William V. O'Brien's judgment concerning this "pernicious institution of reprisals" seems to me to be irrefutable:

> Few rights are more solidly established in the law of nations than the right of reprisal, and few principles have done so much to gloss over immoral behavior with an aura of legality. . . . This exceptional right [of reprisal in kind] applies to all the laws of war. It is supposed to serve two purposes: it provides a sanction for the law and it tends to restore the balance upset when one belligerent uses illegal means.
> Obviously, this kind of "legality" is ridiculous. . . . If bombing cities were really contrary to the law of nations, violation of the law could not affect the legal obligation to refrain from such bombings.[81]

Such a law of reprisals can only be described as a product of an age of legal positivism where justice has become something men and nations "make." No wonder they suppose they can make "just" an act that before was "unjust," or unjust when *first* done. With no sense of the difference between the do-able and the intrinsically un-do-able, the nations may well agree that a certain weapon or plan of war should never be used, unless, of course, it is. That excuse must today be called radically into question.

It can be shown that the traditional limits upon the "just" conduct of war were a product not so much of man's sense of justice as of "social charity" determining, in crucial situations in which the use of force cannot be avoided, how force can be directed to the saving of human life.[82] From this point of view — from the point of view of concrete Christian charity — even more than in the context of the natural justice surrounding killing in war, this so-called law of reprisal in kind, if it is proposed as a sovereign and all-embracing rule for conduct, must

---

[80]Thornton Read, "The Proposal to Use Nuclear Weapons Over One's Own Territory," (unpublished ms.) p. 28.

[81]"Nuclear War and the Law of Nations," in *Morality and Modern Warfare* (ed. by William J. Nagle). Baltimore, Md.: Helicon Press, 1960, p. 140.

[82]See my *War and the Christian Conscience,* chapter three on "The Genesis of Non-Combatant Immunity."

itself always be condemned. Pure reprisal between persons or between nations will appear especially heinous to a just or Christian man. Neither in inter-personal nor in international relations will a Christian accept the reduction of moral and political agency to this attempt to gain an empty victory of one will over another. Instead, if he is properly instructed and sensitive to the requirements of a love-informed justice, he is apt to call such punishing reprisal of will against will the very epitome of sin and of injustice.

The injustice of the law of reprisal is perhaps hidden from view in impure cases where actually *doing* the reprisal in kind seems clearly connected with accomplishing some definite purpose. In this way an almost self-enforcing system of diplomatic immunity is maintained, and restrictions are imposed upon the travel of Soviet citizens in this country roughly equivalent to those imposed upon American citizens traveling in Russia. Almost all the laws of war in the past have been enforced, to the extent that they have been enforced, by creating the expectation of reprisal in kind. The race toward increasing irreconcilability between actions of nation-states seems to be slowed down by *doing*, on occasion, the expected reprisal in kind, even if in itself the action has no reconciling power.

But then, it ought to be observed that many of these enforcements, which seem to warrant reprisal in kind, involve actions which are not *malum in se*. In a great many kinds of action the nations can "make" right what they want to, and enforce rules they agree to by reprisals in these kinds. What was not inherently wrong when first done but only legally proscribed, can be legitimately done in reprisal. The possibility of massive nuclear retaliation against the society of an enemy who struck first has made clear that the rule of reprisal in kind was never an all-embracing rule for the conduct of men or nations. *This* kind of reprisal can only be justified by a very immoral "moral" system, or by a positivism that seeks to "make" right in the second place what was ruled to be wrong in the first.

To the argument from justice and the argument from charity may now be added a third argument against ever *doing* the reprisal in kind that is now in question. Today the irrationality and purposelessness of pure punishment is laid bare, and the spiritualization of war into a contest of resolves is exposed as the most *abysmal* of all wars we could contemplate. One can still contemplate it, but it cannot be done except as an act that no longer has political purpose. Such reprisal would be a choiceless choice, an act without a definite end to be attained. For it can no longer be said that reprisal in kind — the kind we are speaking about — will "restore the balance when one belligerent uses illegal means," or defend freedom or civilization, or hold back from destruction any life worth living, or even that it will enforce a lower limit of warfare.

It remains only to be asked whether actually *carrying out* this reprisal in kind is really necessary in order to "provide a sanction" for the lesser laws and rules of warfare which it is urgently necessary for the nations of the world to impose on themselves and one another.

Clearly, staged limitations upon the conduct of war, each stage separated from another by a "firebreak," depend on deterrence during war, and finally upon the hidden and not so hidden *possibility* that one's own cities may come into range. The threat that one's society as a whole and that of the enemy may be subjected to capital punishment seems necessary at the crucial point, to support the rule against the capital punishment of any society as a means of war, and to insure that this limitation is observed.

Shall we say this is to be compared to what must be done by any society which wishes domestically to abolish capital punishment for crimes? An exception has to be made in the case of treason in wartime and in the case of anyone who in resisting arrest shoots a policeman in his execution of the law. He has not only killed a man; he has also challenged the whole structure of the law, and precisely that law which seeks to order human relationships without capital punishment. For that, capital punishment is not likely to be abolished. Shall we say, then, that the nation which resorts to bombing without avoiding civilian damage as much as it can and instead begins deliberately to strike cities has challenged the laws of civilized conduct in war at such a fundamental point that such a society can be justifiably put to death? That nation has, in fact, violently attacked not only another whole people, but also a central part of the whole system by which, it is hoped, counter-society warfare can be abolished now that it has been invented. Is it not just, then, to exact the supreme penalty under these circumstances?

The objection to this line of reasoning, and one that is fatal to it, is that the analogy does not hold. In the case of enforcing the law, even the law which has abolished capital punishment, by *carrying out the deterrent threat* maintained in the minds of potential "cop-killers," the one put to death is the person who threw down the gauntlet to the whole administration of justice. In the case of strategic warfare against a whole nation, however, to do this would be to destroy indiscriminately people who were not "unjust aggressors" as a means of getting at their government (which, in turn, is now a useless endeavor). If this is like anything in the world, it is like shooting the children of the criminal who shot a policeman, or of a soldier who turned traitor in wartime. John Bennett's conclusion here seems to me unavoidable: "We must not deceive ourselves into believing that we could ever justify the use of megaton bombs for massive attacks on the centers of population of another country no matter what the provocation."[83] If a first strike, it would be both wicked and foolish. If a second strike, it would still be wicked and foolish — supremely foolish because when one comes to the actual doing of the act of reprisal in *such* kind it is already abundantly clear that the limitation upon war one hoped to "sanction" can no longer be preserved by the proposed sanction. It would be an act of pure purposeless punishment and retrospective vengeance. One simply cannot argue, as do the proponents of the various forms of limited war, that limited war must be *made possible* today and then say that illimitable inter-city warfare becomes less than an irrational absurdity *because committal to do this* is for the sake of deterrence *during* the course of limited war.

Any politically viable solution of the problem of war today requires that we finally employ a distinction between the *possibility* and the *certainty* of illimitable city destruction; and in deterrence during the war that we carefully discriminate between the *appearance* and the *actuality* of being partially or totally committed to go to city exchanges. The reader should recall at this point the discussion in the first section of this paper of Herman Kahn's contention (or admission) that while the appearance of irrationally inexorable commitment may have its uses, one would need in actuality and in advance to provide for revoking it. A nation ought never to be totally committed to action that is so irrational it can never be done by free, present decision; and even to *appear* to be totally committed may itself be altogether too dangerous. A nation ought not to communicate to an enemy that it might go to city exchanges without at the same time communicating some doubt about it, if it wants both to remain and to seem to remain a free agent with still some control over its destiny and the course of world politics. The *appearance* of *partial* commitment, or the *appearance* of *possible* commitment, may be enough of a commitment to deter an enemy.

I would be willing to consider adding to the stages of military decision set down in the previous section yet one more. A statesman might consider ordering one of the enemy's cities to be struck after a warning allowing time for civilians to be evacuated. That would be an act of countervalue warfare in which human beings have not been economized; and there may be some argument for it to be found in

---

[83]*Nuclear Weapons and the Conflict of Conscience,* New York: Chas. Scribner's Sons, 1962, p. 101.

the changed nature of much property today in comparison with the period when both civilian property and civilian lives were surrounded with moral immunity from direct attack.[84] Whatever be the correct judgment of this possibility, the arguments against ever actually engaging in a war of nerves by means of populated cities cannot be withdrawn. Deterrence will have to be accomplished by the deterrent effect of the *possibility* and the *appearance* of the possibility that the sanction of city exchanges will be invoked, or not accomplished at all.

I propose, first, to discuss the moral issues in preserving such a national posture, and to conclude with some remarks upon technical questions concerning the feasibility of limiting war under the deterrence of a possibility we do not intend to carry out. In approaching the moral issues involved in appearing to be willing to do something that is wrong, I shall make use of a volume of essays by British Roman Catholics[85] who follow the anatomy of the just war doctrine to a conclusion altogether different from mine, namely, nuclear pacifism.

It is never right to do wrong that good may come of it. Nuclear weapons have only added to this perennial truth the footnote: it can never do *any good* to do wrong that good may come of it. Neither is it right to *intend* to do wrong that good may come of it. If deterrence rests upon intending massive retaliation, it is clearly wrong no matter how much peace results. If weapons systems deter city exchanges only because and so far as they are intended to be used against cities, then deterrence involves a "conditional willingness"[86] to do evil, and evil on a massive scale. Granting that deterrence deters before or during the war, and that it supports peace or the control of war, that alone cannot justify it. It would be justified "if, and only if, in employing this threat, we were not involved in . . . *immoral hypothetical decisions*."[87] The distinction between murder and killing in war, or between directly killing combatants and directly murdering non-combatants, posits an ethico-political principle that can only be violated, never abrogated. "Nothing, not even the alleged interests of peace, can save murderousness from evil",[88] and nothing, not even the alleged interest in deterrence during war for the control of war can save the *intention* to commit murder from being evil. Does reliance on nuclear weapons for deterrence hypothetically commit us, here and now, to murder, there and

---

[84]See Thornton Read: "Counterforce Strategies and Nuclear Weapons," p. 48 (unpublished).

[85]Walter Stein, ed.: *Nuclear Weapons and Christian Conscience.* London: Marlin Press, 1961.

[86]*Ibid.*, p. 23.

[87]*Ibid.*, p. 36 (italics mine).

[88]*Ibid.*, p. 36.

then?[89] If so, such deterrence is wrong, and can never be anything but wickedness. This conclusion would seem to follow from the comparatively simple moral truth that "if an action is morally wrong, it is wrong to intend to do it."[90]

This is surely a correct "finding" as to the moral law. The authors of these chapters, however, intermix with this a certain "finding of fact" which may be questioned. They assert that "deterrence *rests*, in the end, on the intention to use nuclear weapons," not that in some or many of its forms it *may* or *might* rest on either present murderous intention or on a "conditional willingness" to do murder. No wonder the conclusion follows: if this is the case, deterrence "cannot but be morally repugnant for the same ultimate reason as is the use of the weapon held in reserve."[91] The following statement of the case is a better one, and by accenting the first word the fact to be questioned can be stressed: "*If*, then, we find that 'having' nuclear weapons involves intending to explode them over predominantly civilian targets, no more need be said; this intention is criminal, just as the action is criminal."[92] This is the matter of fact that needs to be determined — whether it *is* so, and must or should remain so if it is now the case — before we can know how the moral prohibition of intending to do wrong is to be applied in an assessment of deterrence policy.

The authors of these essays systematically fail to show that there can be no deterrent effect where there is no intention to use nuclear weapons. They underrate what is pejoratively called "the argument from bluff," while admitting that if this deterred and if this is what deters there would not be an implied "conditional commitment to total war."[93] These essays are remarkably sophisticated, and at many points suggest their own answer. "Having an H-bomb," for example, is no simple matter. It is not only that "having an H-bomb," differs from having a gun "in respect to the nature of the object possessed." One can "have" one or both these instruments with subtly but significantly different ways of "having" them. There is then a considerable difference "in respect to the nature of the 'possession' of the object" that has to be taken into account.[94] The question of whether "possession" of massive nuclear weapons is reducible to the crime of "using" them over civilian targets, and the question of whether "having" or "posses-

---

[89]*Ibid.*, p. 125.
[90]*Ibid.*, p. 71.
[91]*Ibid.*, p. 78 (italics mine).
[92]*Ibid.*, pp. 73-4 (italics mine).
[93]*Ibid.*, p. 32.
[94]*Ibid.*, p. 75.

sion" implies a criminal intention to use them murderously, or a conditional willingness to do so, cannot be answered without first exploring a spectrum of "havings" that may be possible, and indeed desirable. This further exploration of the nature of the "possession" of nuclear weapons which may be possible will determine whether deterrence by means of them before or during any war can ever be judged legitimate.

The technical possibility of deterrence before and during war can now be indicated, as can its compatibility with the moral prohibition of both the use and the intention to use nuclear (or any other) weapons in direct attacks on centers of population.

1. The collateral civilian damage that would result from counterforces warfare in its maximum form may itself be quite sufficient to deter either side from going too high and to preserve the rules and tacit agreements limiting conflict in a nuclear age. In that case, deterrence during the war and collateral civilian damage are both "indirect effects" of a plan and action of war which would be licit or permitted by the traditional rules of civilized conduct in war. To say that counterforce strikes over an enemy's own territory are licit or permitted is to say that one can morally intend and be "conditionally willing" to engage in such a war. Whether one positively should ever do so depends on the conditions. Collateral civilian damage is certainly an unavoidable indirect effect and, in the technical sense, an "unintended" result of something a nation may and should make itself conditionally willing and ready to do. The deterrent effect, of which we are now speaking, is then, as it were, an indirect effect of the foreseeable indirect effects of legitimate military conduct.

One can certainly "intend" to deter in this fashion, and oneself be similarly deterred. Not knowing the tyrannies future history may produce one cannot say whether the one effect of successful resistance to them will justify the direct and the indirect costs. Still we foreknow that these costs may be very great indeed. This is to say that, at least to a very great degree, perhaps a sufficient degree, nuclear warfare is a design for war that is inherently self-limiting upon rational decision-makers without their having to intend to use these weapons directly to murder cities and civilians.

This is not at all a matter of "double-think about double effect."[95] To justify "possession" for the sake of deterrence one does not have to invent possibly legitimate uses for nuclear weapons, such as their use against a ship at sea. Many a military installation in the nuclear age

---

[95]*Ibid.*, p. 57.

is fifty or more miles in diameter.

2. In respect to the nature of the weapons we possess, there are two possible uses which cannot be removed. The dual use the weapons themselves have — the fact that they may be used either against strategic forces or against centers of population — means that *apart from intention* their capacity to deter cannot be removed from them. This means that there may be sufficient deterrence in the subjectively unintended consequence of the mere possession of these weapons. No matter how often we declare, and quite sincerely declare, that our targets are an enemy's forces, he can never be quite *certain* that in the fury or in the fog of war his cities may not be destroyed.

. This is so certainly the case that the problem of how to deter an enemy from striking our cities ought not for one moment to impede the shift to a counterforces policy and to the actual intention to use nuclear weapons only against forces. We should declare again and again, and give evidence by what we do, that our targets are his forces rather than his cities. Since it is morally repugnant to wage war without renouncing morally repugnant means,[96] this should be speedily done, and communicated as effectively as possible to the enemy. Still, without any hesitation or ambiguity on our part, the weapons themselves will continue to have deterrent effect because they have ambiguous uses. They always *may* be used over cities; and no enemy can *know* that this will not be done. Was McNamara's reserved use of massive nuclear weapons for retaliation in case Russia strikes our cities really necessary, or his declared policy of conditional willingness to do this? Was not this aspect of his speech mainly needed to reassure domestic public opinion which is still so far from supporting any steps toward a counterforce strategy and away from pacifistic maximal deterrence?

Similar conclusions can be reached from an analysis of the "familiar spiral of reciprocal expectations" which is an important aspect of war in the nuclear age. This spiral not only threatens to be illimitable, but it serves as a built-in dampener, which no deliberate policy nor any intention can remove. This is the truth in T. C. Schelling's contention that in the nuclear age all forms of limited war raise the risk of general war, whether intended or not. The point here is not the "threat" of general war because of some technical or human failure or some mistaken calculation. The point is rather that in a nuclear age all war raises a risk of general war by an apparent *possibility* of a *politically irreversible trend*. War creates this risk which we share with the Russians. They can never "be confident that even the lack of resolution sometimes

---

[96]Cf. *Ibid.*, p. 82.

attributed to the United States could guarantee that general war would not result." "It is our sheer inability to predict the consequences of our actions and to keep things under control, and the enemy's similar inability [or our reciprocal doubt whether the other is in control], that can intimidate the enemy," and ourselves.

If war is no longer a matter of making no threat that does not depend on our ultimate willingness to *choose* general war, it is no longer a matter of having to put forth acts or threats that involve a conditional willingness to choose general war.[97] If war is sufficiently threatening, a good case can be made for the proposition that massive nuclear weapons should never be intended for use against societies. The nations of the world *should* and *can* devote all their attention and intention to making only just or counterforces war possible. A single great power *can* and *should* do this, since the other ominous possibility will always remain in the background as a shared and unintended threat.

3. Only now do we come again to the suggestion that the distinction between the *appearance* and the *actuality* of being partially or totally committed to go to city exchanges may have to be employed in deterrence policy. In that case, only the appearance should be cultivated. If the first two points above do not seem to the military analyst sufficiently persuasive, *or able to be made so,* then an *apparent* resolution to wage war irrationally or at least an *ambiguity* about our intentions may have to be our expressed policy. This is a matter, not of the nature of the weapons themselves, but of the manner in which we possess them — the "having" of them that is necessary for deterrence during justifiably conducted war.

The moralist can certainly say to the decision-maker that it can never be right for him to do such a thing as attack an enemy's society, or for him actually to intend to do so, or under any conditions to be willing to match his resolution against that of the enemy by means of populated cities. He can point out to the statesman that it can never be right for him to contrive to "make" the un-do-able intention irrevocable, or to have the intention of doing so. He can even point out where the military analyst will be found saying the same thing about the irrationality of total committal to an irrational act of war, or even of appearing quite unambiguously to be totally and irreversibly committed.

But the moralist must be careful how he rushes in with his ethico-political principles mixed with an assortment of findings of fact and various arguments *ad horrendum.* He must be careful how he spells

---

[97]See T. C. Schelling, "Nuclear Strategy in Europe," *World Politics,* Vol. XIV, No. 3 (April, 1962), pp. 421-424.

out his *moral* guidance for deterrence policy. For, on a sound solution of this problem the security of free societies may well depend in a nuclear age which is also an age of "megacorpses,"[98] "deracination from humanity,"[99] and of "unparalleled moral landslide."[100] The moralist must be careful how he disparages the so-called "argument from bluff" to a morally licit form of deterrence; and he should examine whether the reasons *he* uses to dismiss this argument are telling *moral* ones or rather technical judgments he has gathered to fulfill a prejudice.

Some Further Questions

The crucial question for the moralist is whether deterrent effects that flow from a *specified kind* of studied ambiguity concerning the intention with which a nation holds nuclear weapons in reserve are *praeter intentionem* (besides or without the actual intention to attack cities) as surely as are the first two types of deterrent effects we have analyzed. To say and to act as if we might go to city exchanges is certainly a form of deception. But, if this can be done without intending to make irrational immoral use of nuclear weapons, and even with the intention that our weapons be not so used and with the intention of revoking what had never even the appearance of total committal, such deception cannot be said to be based on the criminal intention or conditional willingness to do murder. The first thing to be said then, is that the intention to deceive is certainly a far cry from the intention to murder society, or to commit mutual homicide.

The second thing to be said is in connection with the moral problem of *deception* in politics and in wartime. A moralist need not slur over the fact that in all sorts of ways deception may be an evil, just as he need not slur over the fact that the killing of combatants is evil (though certainly not wicked). But having said this, it must then be pointed out that there are deceptions and deceptions. Or rather, the word "deception" ought perhaps to be reserved for any denial of the truth to someone to whom the truth is due, or permitting him to gather from you a false or inadequate impression concerning the exact truth which, in some sense, "belongs" to him. If this is a fair statement of the moral rule, then an experienced finding of fact must be that there are many situations in both private and public life when withholding the "truth" or even communicating an inadequate representation of the "truth" is

---

[98]One million dead bodies.
[99]Walter Stein, ed., *op. cit.*, p. 31.
[100]*Ibid.*, pp. 125-6.

not a lie. Relative to this, there is a teaching of long standing in the Western tradition about the virtues of a military commander, to the effect that there is nothing wrong with his having military secrets provided he does not pretend that he has none. It would be extremely difficult to support the judgment that an effective reservation about the use of the weapons we possess, or an intention that they not be used over cities, in any sense belongs to an enemy, or that this information is due to be given him.

Finally, a moralist must raise the question of whether this truth is not owed to the people of an enemy nation, if not to their military commanders. In answer to this, it goes to the point to say that this may be necessary to save *their* lives as well as those of our own civilians. Or (worse than their death from the point of view of an ethics that does not place supreme value in mere physical existence) it may be necessary in order to save them (and ourselves) from a measure of complicity in their government's conditional or actual willingness to save them by doing mass murder, or from the *tragedy* (not the *wickedness*) of actually being saved by murderous intention (if a wrongly willed deterrent worked) and some of them from the tragedy of living on in a world in which their lives have been spared in the midst of the greatest possible wrong-*doing* by a government which in remote degrees of participation was still their own (if the shared intentional risk does not work). So the question resolves itself into the question of whether it is ever right to withhold the truth in order to save life, to save from moral wrong-doing,to save from sheer tragedy. Does the truth that might well be "fatal" in all these senses "belong" to them? Is it "due" to be given if it can be? Do we "owe" them a true report that will unambiguously quiet their fears by effectively communicating to them (if this *can* ever be done) that we have no intention of engaging with their government in inter-society warfare under any circumstances? I am so far from believing that one ought readily to justify this deception that it seems to me that the first two types of deterrence must, if at all possible, be made to work. Still, if deterrence were based on a cultivated ambiguity about our real intentions, and if "deception" in an objectionable moral sense would thus in some measure be perpetrated, it would still be an intent to deceive and not an intent possibly to do murder.

Perhaps we should say that we ought to be conditionally willing to strive for this ingredient in deterrence, that is, on the condition that it is necessary to deter and to save life. I do not grant to a physician any right to withhold from a patient knowledge of his true condition; but then I also do not believe that learning the truth about his condition can be demonstrated to be so nearly fatal as, in our present supposition, it would be for an enemy government and population to learn that we do not intend to attack people. A better analogy might be the following one. If you were trying to save a man out on the ledge of a building, threatening to commit suicide and to take you with him, would you withhold from him, and have an obligation to withhold from him, any blandishments, including "daring" him to join you inside for a duel to the death by "Russian roulette" at three paces, with no intention of ever carrying out this dissuasive dare or threat?

The military and political analysts I have consulted do *not* reject as infeasible the sort of "possession" of nuclear weapons for deterrence which we are now discussing.[101] If it is thought to be infeasible now, then the "system" may have to be studied and perfected so that it can be done. For this may be one of those customarily "unthinkable" things which, the more you think about it, will prove to be technically and politically "do-able." If needed, it should be developed in many a scenario. It is on balance, I believe, morally "do-able," as city-busting is not, however much you think about it. Whether this ingredient in deterrence can be adopted and exercised by a democratic society is, of course, a serious question. It requires of a people a mature "ethic of restraint, limits and silence,"[102] not moral protest always, much less punitive fury or he-man morality; and a reliance on the morality and rationality of their political leaders not to be expected or (on any policy decision not so crucial) desired in a free society. For this reason, if for no other, all our attention and intention should doubtless be directed toward adopting, declaring and implementing a policy of counter-forces warfare, with the deterrence that policy affords. This is the doctrine which should form the consciences of free men today; and if their consciences are thus formed, it may then be possible to add to counterforce policy this last type of non-murderous deterrence.

Then it may be possible to put, not nuclear weapons as such, but the inter-city use of nuclear weapon into a category by itself, so that, while the capability still exists, the intention to attack cities will recede into the background so far as not to have actuality. Things as strange have happened before in the history of warfare. Tribes living close to death in the desert have fought cruel wars. They even used poisoned arrows, and certainly to a limited extent they fought one another by

---

[101]Halperin, *op. cit.*, for example, develops at length the distinction between "communication policy" and "action policy."

[102]Cf. Kenneth Thompson in "The Nuclear Dilemma—A Discussion," *Christianity and Crisis*, Nov. 27, 1961.

means of direct attack upon women and children. But they knew *not to poison wells!* That would have been a policy of mutual homicide, and a form of society-*contra*-society warfare that would have removed the possibility of any more bloody cruel wars, not to mention peacetime pursuits. In refraining from massive well-poisoning, or in keeping that ambiguous, did these tribes, in any valid or censorable sense of the word, still "intend" to poison wells?

An Alternative to War

Gordon Zahn

In the long-awaited conclusion of a treaty banning nuclear tests in the atmosphere and in underwater and outer space environments, we may have reached a significant turning point in world history. The agreement, limited though it is, might be a sign that men are now ready to abandon the callous disregard for human life which might otherwise prove to be the final bitter fruit of human civilization. But, however much we may hope that this is the case, our optimism must be tempered by the memory that not too long ago leaders on both sides of the cold-war battle lines were proclaiming their readiness to match test with test regardless of the globe-circling pall of potentially lethal fall-out each new round of tests would have loosed. We have seen this callousness in operation before — in the technological triumphs of two murderous world wars and the atrocities made possible by these "advances," to cite an obvious example. We have seen it, too, in the horrifying spectacle of Hitler's "Final Solution of the Jewish Question," and its echoes are still encountered all too often when people, here or in Germany, quibble about the exact number of millions of persons so exterminated — as if the enormity of the crime lay in the calculation and not in the fact that there were men who were prepared to destroy *any* number of other men to achieve the goals set by their perverted ideals and dreams of a future and, in their eyes, better world.

There are men among us today, and they are legion, who are prepared to destroy other men in pursuit of other goals, admittedly more laudable and reasonable in our eyes. Some of them are ordinary men plagued by insecurity or fretful with impatience; others are distinguished political, military, and even scientific leaders. Dr. Edward Teller, for example, assures us that in a nuclear war it would be probable that no more than 10% of the American population would be wiped out; and Ernest Lefever, calculates the possible loss at 20% of the earth's population (with the additional note that most of this would occur north of the Equator). Converting these percentages to absolute numbers, we find therein a willingness, however reluctant, to prepare for a war that would, in one instance, kill approximately 18 million Americans and, in the other (a more meaningful expectation in that it apparently takes into account the enemies of a victorious America and any other nations which happen to be in the vicinity of combat), the even more impressive total of more than 700 million.

No one will question whether the aims and purposes motivating the nuclear optimists are more laudable than those of the Nazis — they most certainly are. But one must ask whether or not *any aims and purposes* can justify the inhumanities these men are prepared to support. Christian Geissler, referring to the tragic history of Auschwitz and Hiroshima, made the point in these words: "Anyone whose mind is capable of developing (and this means, for future use) justifications in the presence of such calculated mass murder — or, to be more specific, for the planned and willed burning of 200,000 people; anyone whose mind can in any sense entertain justifications here instead of seeking to use these to effect the most stringent correction of our moral sensibilities by holding these happenings before our eyes as the horribly certain consequences of the organized misappropriation of better human capabilities — such a mind is corrupt, its thinking is infected by the genocidal habits of thought of the fascist."

Geissler's judgment lends chilling immediacy to Albert Schweitzer's warning: "Increasingly there is lost the consciousness that every man is an object of concern for us just because he is a man; civilization and morals are shaken and the advance to fully developed inhumanity is only a question of time."

Perhaps it is no longer "a question of time." Perhaps we have already "advanced" to "fully developed inhumanity" when we reach the point at which a nation's scientific genius foresees a weapon which will destroy all vestige of human life and leave undamaged the buildings and other material objects in its area of destruction — and when that nation's journalists and senators join in the chorus demanding that this be accomplished posthaste. What more ultimate expression of the disregard for human life can be imagined? What more ghastly reversal of values than this which proposes to destroy God's proudest creation and carefully preserve the passing creations of human technology?

It is all too clear that man's frantic pursuit of security through violence has led us to this dead end where, like the strange and unnamed animal of Kafka's *Burrow*, we find ourselves the captive of our own fear-created devices. Indeed, the simile is apt in more ways than one if we but consider the suburbanite hard at work digging the family fall-out shelter and loudly proclaiming (with the nodding approval of the professional theologian) his right and intention to man a machine gun at its entrance, if necessary, to repel any threatened invasion by his neighbor's children. We have mastered the arts of violence to the point that we now have it within our power to destroy the world and annihilate its population. And in the process have we not destroyed the very hope of security we had sought and jeopardized the continued existence of ourselves, our potential enemies (and friends), and — the cruelest injustice of all — the generations, if any, still to come?

The Proposed Alternative

This total failure of total violence to provide the security we crave presents us with what is at once a pressing need and a great opportunity to develop some alternative means to achieve the security we desire and to preserve the values we hold dear. More than this, it provides us with a definite hint as to the direction this alternative must take if it is to offer any hope of success. Instead of contributing further to the denigration of man, a new approach to security must recognize and rest upon the concern for man — *any* man, including our potential enemy — just because he is a man. We must resolve that if, in the words of John XXIII, "individual human beings are and should be the foundation, the end and the subjects of all the institutions in which social life is carried on," these institutions can never be given absolute priority over the worth of these individual human beings. Therefore, our means of defense must be so organized and our policies so developed that they find their effectiveness in the identification and exploitation of the essentially human qualities and capacities in ourselves and the potential enemy and not in the continued effort to destroy the greatest possible number of "them" at the least possible cost to "us."

Such an alternative presents itself in the complex of ideals and techniques usually covered by the negative term, non-violence. At least one can say that a growing number of serious-minded men are beginning to consider it as a possible alternative. In his coldly analytical survey of the positions represented by the unilateralists and their opponents, who favor maintenance of nuclear parity, Walter Stein rejects both as ultimate answers to the problem facing us. The answer, he insists, is the creation of "a radically new international order"; but this merely raises for him the new problem of how such an order is to emerge from our present world state of "mutual anathema and terror." It is necessary, he insists, to *will* the means to make this possible, and he goes on to say:

> I have argued that to will the means of peace in our situation is to be ready to bear very great risks indeed (though we cannot, anyway, avoid very grave risks of one kind or another). In effect, we should have to be prepared for unilateral risk-taking (or the equivalent of unilateral risk-taking—whatever the diplomatic formalities) and so ultimately for non-violent resistance.

Thomas Merton, too, reaches the conclusion "that we must defend freedom and sanity against the bellicose fanaticism of all warmakers, whether 'ours' or 'theirs' and that we must strive to do so not with force but with the spiritual weapons of Christian prayer and action. But this action must be at once non-violent and decisive. Good intentions and fond hopes are not enough."

Thus, through non-violence our real and absolute defenselessness in the face of the new instruments of total destruction can be converted into power, a kind of power which could prove far more effective in the final reckoning than any breakthrough in megaton potential or in the accuracy and range of the instruments of delivery.

Non-violence is not to be dismissed as a passive surrender to or a defeatist compliance with the putative violent aggressor; instead, it is a form of concerted activity which is intended to generate the power to compel an opponent, negatively, to desist from an actual or anticipated program of action ("passive resistance") or, positively, to institute a program of action desired by the party utilizing it. To risk a slight terminological difference with Merton as he is quoted above, I would insist that non-violence, like violence, constitutes *force* and should be so regarded in any consideration of its merits as a policy alternative. It represents a contest of will and spirit in place of our present tests of the relative strength of the material resources and supporting technology of the combatants. As such, its advocates would insist, non-violence is a more ultimate kind of power, one which ranges above and beyond the more limited potentialities of violence. Gandhi and his followers called it "soul force"; the Christian pacifist speaks of the "power of love," of a "charity" that can overcome the world.

In its essence, non-violence, since it rests upon the force of the "soul" and the practice of the virtue of love, is a personal act. To this extent, then, one might object that it does not lend itself to the group activity such as would be required in the context of a national defense alternative. But this is at most a paradox and certainly not the disqualification such objections might suggest. The same paradox may be seen in the practice of violence: the "army" attacks or retreats, but in reality it is the individual members of that army who strike or fall back as the case may be. Yet one must admit that there is a vital difference between the two — the individual can be conditioned to perform unthinkingly acts of violence; the efficient practice of non-violence, however, must involve a deep personal commitment and, in its most perfect form, requires of its practitioners a degree of self-mastery and dedication customarily associated with religious immolation. Non-violence on the group level, then, does not arise from welding an assortment of separate individuals into a functioning collectivity but, instead, from creating a community of committed persons and inspiring them into concurrent but always responsible and intentioned patterns of behavior.

In its statement, this might suggest an impossible ideal. Admittedly, it has rarely, if ever, been perfectly attained. Yet significant victories have been won through the application of non-violence by groups, and some of these victories have been quite recent.

The dramatic series of successful assaults upon long-standing patterns of racial discrimination and injustice which have taken the form of "sit-in", "kneel-in", and even "wade-in" demonstrations has demonstrated its effectiveness. Negroes are now eating at lunch counters from which they were formerly excluded; elsewhere they are now able to enjoy the use of the beach facilities from which they had been driven by hate-inspired mobs. Of course, the scope of these victories may be discounted in the context of a proposal that such techniques be tried on an international scale; but two important points must be noted.

In a very real sense, the "Freedom Riders" and other non-violent demonstrators have incited an astonishing degree of *fear* in those who seek to uphold the threatened patterns. This is reflected in the anxiety with which whole communities have organized to speed them out of town and in the haste with which the discriminating restauranteur closes up shop when word of their approach reaches him.

The other significant aspect is the as yet unmeasured gain — and the most essentially relevant to the underlying rationale of non-violence —the extent to which these visible accomplishments have been made possible because many of those who previously had accepted and defended the patterns of exclusion and discrimination have been forced to question and reject them. Such a re-assessment and conversion may usually be traced to the convert's inner reactions of admiration for the dedication and personal bravery of the demonstrators or of revulsion against the coarseness and brutality evidenced by the die-hard defenders of segregation. It is precisely these reactions *inspired in the other* that constitute the critical mass of the weapons of non-violence and which have made possible the earlier and more extensive victories recorded in the early Christians' conversion of the pagan Empire and Gandhi's successful campaign for Indian independence. The non-violence alternative is keyed to a universalistic identity with and concern for the humanity inherent in all men, including the potential aggressor. And this, in turn, is expected at some point to trigger a reciprocal response in the opposing party; to fan, so to speak, the spark of human decency which, no matter how low it may burn in individual men for a time, cannot be extinguished completely or forever.

With the fall-out from past series of bomb tests (some of which could have destroyed the world's greatest city in the flash of an instant) still presenting its lingering threat to mankind's health and well-being, it may seem utterly unreasonable to propose as a counter-measure a set of techniques associated in the public mind with a handful of college students at a drugstore counter or a few hundred fanatics sitting in a London street. Again, the barbed wire and the concrete blocks of the Berlin wall, not to mention the tanks and well-armed men behind it, seem to present a situation totally invulnerable to the fasts and spinning wheels of any number of frail old men. If these were indeed all that non-violence did propose, I fear that few, if any, reasonable men could be induced to give it even a passing moment's consideration as a possible alternative to the present quest for ever greater and ever more effective destructive potential which seeks to assure, if not the desired advantage over all likely enemies, at least a continuation of the balance of terror which today holds them (just as it holds us) in check.

The sad truth, however (and this too must be granted by our "reasonable men"), is that this balance of terror is only a sometime thing and, even when achieved, is self-defeating since, by definition, the enemy's terror finds its counterpart in our own. This situation necessarily provokes each to attempt to undo the balance, to gain superiority by some breakthrough. Or, failing this, it creates the kind of continuing tension and strain which could lead one party or the other into the panic of desperation in which the hidden terrors of tomorrow become far worse than the known terrors of today and the attempt is made to break out of the confining circle whatever it may cost.

To this point in time, of course, the balance has not been destroyed and everything has not, as yet, gone "boom." This fact has comforted many and has been interpreted by them as proof of the efficacy of the so-called "deterrence" policy. It is difficult to justify the comfort or to accept the interpretation. A far more plausible illustration might be that a favorable enough calculation has not yet been produced by the computers serving either of the potential combatants; if true, this would be more a matter of each "biding his time" instead of being effectively "deterred." At whatever point the expected gains can clearly and certainly promise to outweigh the expendables, the "deterrence" will vanish completely.

That the situation is one of each biding his time until he is in the more certainly advantageous position may be seen in the threats and counterthreats relative to atmospheric nuclear testing before the recent treaty was concluded. Both major atomic powers loudly proclaimed their concern over the effects of such tests — yet both maintained they were prepared to continue them to whatever point was necessary for each to gain or maintain the desired *advantage*. Thus, the United States boasted of its superiority but insisted it had to test because the Soviet tests threatened to reduce or remove that superiority; for their part, the Soviets insisted that the threatened resumption of American testing would have obliged them to initiate a new series of tests to further perfect their monster bombs; and so on and so on. Even now, after the test-ban treaty has become a reality, it is significant that arguments for its ratification by the Senate had to stress the fact that the agreement will *preserve the advantage* we claim.

Seen in this light the maintenance and expansion of national nuclear arsenals is every bit as much — and, properly speaking, much more so — a policy of incitements as it is one of deterrence. Perhaps the most terrifying fact of all (and this is the final refutation of the deterrence thesis) is the manner in which the "expendable" allowance keeps pace with the annihilation capacity of the new weapons. There are already minds which are not only able to entertain justifications for the incineration of 200,000, 6 million, 18 million and 700 million, but have actually reached the point of justifying the possible extermination of human life altogether rather than expose future generations to the risk of Communist domination. This disordered theology—which is remarkable if only in the implied suggestion that God would be helpless in dealing with a Communist victory and the world order it would bring — certainly introduces a framework which would remove the last suggestion of "deterrence" as far as our own leaders and their policies are concerned.

Our situation is, therefore, one in which we have the *actuality* of total destruction at our command without the security it was to have brought us. It is in such a context that the *potentiality* of non-violence as an alternative deserves thoughtful consideration. And that potentiality is not to be measured in terms of scattered hundreds of people protesting air-raid tests in New York City or Polaris bases in Scotland. Instead, it offers a two-fold advantage: first, the immediate reduction in the fears of the potential enemy would make possible a relaxation of tensions and open the way to a new association based on confidence and, in time, trust; second, his recognition that any attempt to exploit the changed situation through violent aggression would be rendered futile by a nation mobilized and trained in the use of civil disobedience and total non-cooperation would impose a note of prudent restraint upon him.

At least such is the argument for non-violence. This is to say that a whole new set of "rules-of-the-game" would be developed for future tests of international power. As these rules now stand, the losers in wars, having matched violence with violence to the limit of their ability, are expected to acknowledge their defeat once it is accomplished and to accept the consequences of conforming to the demands imposed upon them by the victors. The new set of rules would be altogether different. They would envision a situation in which the violent aggressor would probably — though *not* automatically, nor even necessarily —win the initial victory over the opponent committed to non-violent defense.

But that victory would soon be revealed as a hollow and altogether meaningless prize in the face of a total and disciplined refusal on the part of the victim population to recognize the victor's power or conform to his will. For the victor there would be no "spoils."

Such a formulation effectively destroys the false dichotomy of the current "red-or-dead" controversies. It now becomes possible to conceive of a nation refusing to make the choice in favor of death for its population (and 700 million others!) and, at the same time, refusing to become "red" just because Communist officials supported by Communist troops attempt to take over. The answer lies in converting the tempting fruits of a violent victory into the bitter reality of an unmanageable liability.

In the process, of course, the refusal to conform or cooperate would cost the lives of many who would be sacrificed as victims of terror or reprisal actions. And this number would undoubtedly be far greater at the hands of soldiers who are products of a totalitarian regime and schooled in total obedience and total commitment to a perverted ideology than was the case, let us say, for imperial forces called into action to subdue and repress colonials who were only demanding rights similar to their own. Even so, however, there would be a limit, a limit set by the fact that no amount of indoctrination and no system of psychological formation, however intensive they may be, can completely unmake a man in the sense of changing his essential human nature. At some point, even the totalitarian automaton will have to react as a man; and this will be, for him, the breaking point. Only so many trains will run over so many bodies before the trains stop running altogether; only so many hostages will be executed before the executioners refuse to shed more innocent blood. Perhaps it is starry-eyed idealism to speak of such limits; but to deny that they exist and that they must ultimately be reached would be a denial of the very dignity and humanity of man, the recognition of which we claim as the hallmark of our way of life and the justification of its defense.

But does not the very willingness on the part of the advocates of non-violence to contemplate the possible toll in lives to be taken before this point is reached constitute a parallel to the callous disregard for human life for which the nuclear optimists have been censured? In purely quantitative terms, this objection might hold some semblance of validity, but it fades away when the comparison is set in qualitative terms. There is a vast difference between millions of lives destroyed by others in the pursuit of some objective and the readiness on the part of even an equal number to suffer the loss of their own lives rather than surrender the ideals to which they have committed themselves. The difference, and it is a critical one, arises from the recognition that it is better to perish as the victim of the inhumanity of others than to save oneself (or one's nation) by making others the victims of our own inhuman acts.

Prerequisites for Non-violence

Thus non-violence, too, involves a test of breaking-points; but they are of a vastly different order than those now presented by war. Just as the militarist frames his plans in the assumption that a point can be reached at which his opponent will surrender because he can no longer endure the horrors visited upon him, so does the advocate of non-violence assume that a point exists at which the perpetrators of horror will break under the strain of the persecution they are ordered to prolong. The hypothetical all-out conflict between the violent aggressor and the non-violent resister would, in a very real sense, be a test of the upper and lower reaches of the human spirit. The advocate of non-violence is an optimist in that, trusting in the spiritual nature and destiny of man, he is confident that the capacity to love and to bear whatever sacrifices such love may entail is greater than the human capacity for evil — though, in his optimism, he will freely grant that as yet the full depths of that capacity for evil may not have been plumbed.

Because of this, the advocate of non-violence must not stop with his optimistic act of faith. Instead, he should recognize and insist upon a preparedness and training equal to that now devoted to transforming the ordinary man into a brutal killer who can callously perpetrate a Lidice or Hiroshima. Indeed, their importance is magnified and complicated by the fact that, whereas the perpetrators of such violence can be especially selected and trained for designated tasks, a successful demonstration of non-violence would rest upon the full-scale participation and support of the general population. True, the content and direction of the training program will be different: instead of developing the baser potentialities of human nature (the bayonet training with recruits encouraged to growl and snarl like animals as they assault the dummy is a case in point), the program will have to aim at developing the higher spiritual potentialities which will enable the individual to accept and withstand whatever suffering and terror his passive resistance might bring upon him. But in this effort, conscious organization and planning, firm discipline and a strenuous formation framed in terms of ethical and religious commitment are essential.

The preparedness programs now devoted to building and maintaining the highest possible level of violence potential would have to be duplicated to implement a non-violent defense policy. The arguments for conscription, for massive budget outlays — in short, for everything associated with the preservation of today's balance of terror— are pre-mised on the unchallengeable logic that a nation cannot wait until the enemy moves to organize a successful defense of its rights. The ordinary man, whether he be the friendly young clerk at the supermarket or the teacher called from his classroom, has to be "made over," has to be taught to understand and use the modern weapons of war and, most crucial of all, must be conditioned to a level of virtually automatic and certainly unquestioning acceptance of the fact that he is expected to kill other human beings — and risk being killed by them.

It is not much different for non-violence. The same clerk would have to be trained in the techniques of civil disobedience and non-cooperation; he would have to learn to submit to the orders of those given the responsibility for planning and directing the total campaign; and he would have to be prepared to endure not only the prospect of his own death but, much more difficult perhaps, the violent death of others about him without resorting to retaliatory violence and thereby betraying the cause to which he has been called. In the one case, a con-scious and calculated effort is made to transmute the civilian into the professional killer by bringing to fullest flower the brutality latent in the animal nature of man and stunting or at least controlling the softer sensibilities and spiritual inclinations of human nature. In the other, the effort would be made to transmute the civilian into the non-violent "warrior" by bringing these latter capacities to the threshold of self-sacrificial fulfillment and controlling to the point of elimination, if pos-sible, that part of man's nature which is ever too ready to repay evil with evil and answer each assault upon him with another and stronger assault on his own part.

The truly astonishing successes that have been scored in the struggle for racial equality, first on a limited scale in Montgomery but since then on a nation-wide scale, by individuals and groups who operated largely on a basis of personal commitment with no formal training and a mini-mum of organizational discipline and direction, show that it can be done. The larger scale success of the Gandhi revolution, with its *Vidvapiths* and *Ashramas* serving as training centers, offers even more impressive confirmation. The superficial dramatics of the fasts unto death and the marches to the sea should not be permitted to hide the hard core of theory and tactics, the planning and timing of each new move, and the inflexible insistence upon obedience that received its clearest illustration when effective demonstrations-in-progress were abruptly terminated because some of the demonstrators had sullied the entire effort by per-mitting themselves to be provoked into violence.

Nevertheless, even with its success, the Gandhi movement must be regarded as little more than a primitive experiment in the use of non-violence. Since his time, startling discoveries have been made in the behavioral sciences which have unlocked many of the secrets of motivational control and provided many valuable insights into the dynamics of morale. Many of these findings were made (and employed) in the course of World War II when the nation's resources of psychological scholarship and talent were mobilized and given the task, among others, of selecting and preparing the candidates for the "special service" forces. There is no doubt but that this same professional experience and these same tools could be utilized in selecting the types of individuals best suited for positions of leadership in non-violence and in developing the educational and training programs through which the necessary mass participation in the civil disobedience and general non-cooperation demonstrations must be achieved.

Assuming that the radical shift in defense thinking implied in this proposal is possible, can one imagine that it is at all likely? The answer, once again, would appear to be a resounding negative if the issue is seen only in the context of the present situation. For it is not enough that non-violence be recognized as a kind of force which could be effectively organized and employed as an alternative to violence. It is quite clear that other prerequisites must be met before this possible alternative can be converted into a likely or preferred alternative.

These additional prerequisites consist, in the main, in a serious reexamination and revision of present value orientations. In some cases, the revision would involve downgrading and deemphasizing — even *eliminating* — some of our most revered values; in others, it would require the introduction of new values or the emphasizing of values already present but not given the priority they would have to have.

Foremost among the latter is a meaningful acknowledgment or reaffirmation of the personal competence and responsibility of the individual member of society to make a rational assessment of a situation and the behavior it requires of him. This is, of course, one of those values to which we in America regularly give lip service but which, when the chips are down, we all too regularly ignore. In issues involving international tensions or conflicts — or, for that matter, the policies and programs of the national leadership as they may contribute to those tensions and conflicts — this ideal image of the competent and responsible individual as citizen is not taken seriously by any significant segment of the population. On the contrary, an impressive body of arguments and rationalizations is developed to deny the applicability of this image in a time of stress.

It is taken for granted that the individual citizen must ride along with the decisions of his government and loyally and manfully do as he is told because, in the first place, he does not have access to all the relevant facts and, in the second, even if he *did* have such access and *did* come to a contrary conclusion, it would be futile if not treasonable for him to take an open stand against his government. How many men fought and died on the battlefields of World War II — on both sides — convinced, if they gave any thought at all to the question, that there was nothing else for them to do? How many cities were laid waste by bombs loosed by men who believed war to be immoral and inhuman but who "had their orders" and never gave a thought to the possibility of refusing to take part in an activity they judged sinful? I have talked to such men in America; and one of my most touching interviews in Germany was with a woman whose last recollection of her fallen son was the sorrow he expressed, not over the dangers he himself was leaving to face, but over the knowledge that he was leading the men under him into battle for an unjust cause.

The common denominator in both instances is the unchallenged assumption that once a citizen's duty is defined for him by his nation's leaders he has no valid choice but to obey. Somehow, if this pattern is ever to be broken, each individual must be convinced that he has the right and the competence to judge what is asked of him on the basis of the information that is available to him and that he can have some impact upon the course of events, even if he must stand alone. Until this more exalted image of man is incorporated into our thinking, it is futile to expect widespread support for a program of non-violence; for, in the last analysis, since the effectiveness of its means lies in the moral strength of the individual, the success of the whole program is always likely to depend upon that individual standing firm in a situation of extreme personal stress.

But this is only part of it. Once the individual is accorded the *competence* to observe, judge and act for himself, it must be just as forcefully affirmed that he has the *responsibility* to do so. Accepting this value and making it effective in shaping the behavior of men would eliminate the sad mockery of a prudence behind which so many have sought safe haven in times which should try men's souls. Too often merit is found and a false satisfaction taken in keeping one's own record clean by not performing (if we can help it) the actions we have judged adversely — but at the same time, making it possible for these same actions to be performed by others less scrupulous than we merely because we choose to "sit tight" in silence and avoid "sticking our necks out." One might suggest that it is this kind of thinking, much more than the fanaticism of the true believer, that ultimately provides the surest guarantee of success for our modern totalitarian tyrannies; certainly, to the extent that it represents a kind of elevated hypocrisy, it is the more reprehensible.

Yet, as recent history has shown, this is all too often the course of action that is excused, justified and even praised, while the unfortunate deviant who does stick his neck out is likely to be pitied at best, more probably scorned, and sometimes even resented by those who regard his deviance as a possible incitement to reprisal against the whole group.

Geissler, in the article quoted earlier, sees the hopes of mankind resting on just such an awareness of responsibility. "It is, however, to be strictly demanded of each man in the future that he, together with all other men and without any conditions whatsoever limiting their liabilities, make himself responsible for that which has happened upon this earth, which is happening today, and which is going to happen in the future." It is as simple as that; and he who tries to bow out or who counsels resignation to "the inevitable" in a very real sense betrays human solidarity, betrays mankind itself. And just as this personal responsibility devolves *upon* every man, it is a responsibility *for* every man. Hebrew religious literature contains a passage summarizing it nicely: For him who saves even one life, it is as if he saved the whole world; for him who destroys even one life, it is as if he destroyed the whole world.

These values are already present in the total system of democratic values to which we claim to adhere. Our belief in the dignity of the human person is regularly proclaimed and periodically defended by a resort to arms. But if this means anything at all, it should mean that we must grant to human reason the ability to make a sound and independent assessment of a given social situation and to the human will the freedom to consent to or reject the decision reached by others — even though these "others" be in the majority or occupy the positions of temporal authority and power. By the same token, our whole complex of values centering around and depending upon the concepts of universal human solidarity and the brotherhood of all men, the values from which we draw our image of ourselves as our brother's keeper, provide a foundation upon which a more effective appeal to personal responsibility could be based. The shameful fact that we usually modify and occasionally suppress these values in our surrender to a "prudent realism" which gives the benefit of every doubt, no matter how great, to those in authority; or that we tend to be concerned with the needs of our brothers only after we have made sure of generously providing for our own — these facts merely express a hierarchical ordering of values that must be changed if non-violence is to have any chance at all of developing into an acceptable alternative to violence and war.

Strangely enough, at this point in the argument the two contrasting systems of force tend to converge. The question must be raised whether, even with these recommended revisions in the present value system, it would be possible to train our supermarket clerk to perform his assigned tasks in a non-violent program of resistance. Might he not, in the exercise of the competence which is his, decide in favor of some attempt, however hopeless, to beat back a threat against his own personal or his nation's rights and security? Might not his sense of responsibility make it impossible for him to witness the slaughter of others, including perhaps those most dear to him, without resorting to violence against the killers? Indeed, is it not unnatural to expect any other reaction from the ordinary man?

This is, again, the argument positing an automatic self-interest calculation on the part of the human animal inclining him to defensive or even retaliatory responses whenever those interests are threatened. It was countered before with something of an affirmation of faith in the higher capacities of the human spirit as being at least as "natural" to man as the brute capacities exploited in the training for and use of violence. It might be well to turn this argument about now and relate it to the more familiar war situation. For once we have granted to the individual a real measure of competence in making difficult (and not automatic) behavioral decisions, on what basis can we assume that he could ever be induced to abandon the quiet security of his civil pursuits and expose himself to the inconveniences and the grave and imminent dangers of war in defense of an abstract ideal when all that would be involved was a compliant surrender to the obviously lesser demands of the enemy? The "quislings," experience has shown, often have an easy and profitable time of it.

Even the consideration of his responsibility to others dependent upon him might argue that our clerk should avoid at all costs anything which would involve him and them in such apparently senseless risk and sacrifice. It should not be necessary to add, in this connection, that the growing certainty of mutual destruction in nuclear warfare strengthens both of these arguments considerably. The oft-cited law of self-preservation, if it is a "law" and if it applies at all to the question of war and peace (and I am not sure that it does) would have to work both ways; and, if anything, it can be maintained that it would operate most immediately in the form of preserving one's self by not getting involved in the dangerous business of war in the first place, by not fighting.

But, of course, it doesn't work that way. When the call goes out, the overwhelming majority of service-eligible men answer it. It is not enough to explain this by positing a pleasure-pain calculation in which the threatened sanctions of non-compliance are adjudged more certain or more painful than the risks involved in answering the call. Instead, the usual, and better, explanation is found in what might be called "the ascetic ideal" as exemplified in the glorification of the soldierly life and the *Heldentod,* the heroic death in battle, and in the whole mythology of a nation united in dedicated sacrifice. The "convergence" referred to above lies in the fact that it is precisely this same ascetic ideal, albeit with an altogether different content, which lies at the heart of the theory of non-violence.

The ascetic ideal is manifested in the belief that sacrifice and suffering can be borne and even sought as a positive good, as a chosen means to a desired end. To say that it still has some currency in the military ideology is not to deny that its actual impact as a determinant of behavior has greatly weakened: the scramble for deferments or, failing this, for the safer assignments suggests that few men are really eager to offer their lives and substance for the nation's welfare or glory. Despite this, however, it still has status as a verbalized good; our clerk will almost certainly find much compensatory ego-satisfaction in the assurance (an assurance repeatedly confirmed for him by all his associates) that the risks he is forced to take, however hesitantly or unwillingly he takes them, are somehow associated with a cause so much bigger than he that it can ask even the supreme sacrifice of his life. There is no reason why this same process could not be employed to win his acceptance of the risks and hardships associated with the non-violence alternative once he were convinced that they would serve the same or even higher goods and offer a greater likelihood of success.

The same or even higher goods. Can national survival be assured by non-violent means? I would go beyond a merely affirmative answer to that question and suggest instead that, given the present stage of development of military technology coupled with the certainty that both the major potential enemies possess a lethal retaliatory or "second strike" capability, national survival is possible *only if* some such alternative is developed and soon. But are there higher goods that could be called into consideration? Again the answer must be yes, though this is admittedly a far more sensitive area of decision. One such higher good, the advocate of non-violence would insist, is the continued existence of mankind itself. The Teller-Lefever optimism notwithstanding, any course of action which contemplates the destruction of a major part of the world's population and most, if not all, of its greatest accomplishments simply can not be countenanced — even were it the only means by which the national good might be defended. And the human spirit itself must also be recognized as such a higher good. If it does not profit a man to gain the whole world at the cost of his immortal soul, it would certainly not profit him to gain or protect his claim to a fragment of the world at that price. Thus, any course of action that involves the dehumanizing of the actor or his victim or both (something modern war, even pre-nuclear war, clearly does involve and perhaps, if one follows Gandhi's formulation, even violence in general involves) may not be justified by the attainment or preservation of any material good or even of spiritual goods of a lesser order.

Political freedom and national sovereignty cannot be viewed as ultimate goods. Goods they are indeed, and goods that are to be sought and defended at every legitimate opportunity and by all legitimate means. But should the occasion ever arise that such defense would involve the sacrifice or surrender of these greater goods, such defense simply could not be justified. The advocate of non-violence would insist that the practice of violence has reached such a point, and it is for precisely this reason that he is so insistent upon the urgency of the need to consider the alternative he proposes as perhaps the last remaining hope for the effective defense of those lesser goods which might otherwise be lost because the only means available at the time of showdown are those which may not be utilized. That there is some support for his reasoning in recent events may be seen in the fact that the successes non-violence has registered and is registering today have all involved the winning or the preservation of political freedom and human rights in situations where a resort to violence could not have been successful.

But granting the legitimate claims of these higher spiritual goods to precedence over the material goods of national and physical well-being, might one not say that we are engaged in the preliminaries to an ideological conflict in which, should the Communist enemy gain predominance, these same spiritual goods would be ignored, denied, and ultimately crushed? The question is a troubling one in that it represents the most telling objection to the proposals for non-violence. Yet it, too, is in the end an unsound objection. The battles of the spirit will be waged most effectively by the weapons of the spirit, and certainly these battles are not to be won by surrendering or abandoning (or even suspending) the very spiritual goods and values we propose to defend. If we accept for ourselves the standards and the means advocated and maintained by the enemy, we will have become the enemy — and the battle for the spirit of man will have been lost. We cannot honestly claim to be engaged in a struggle for the preservation of human dignity and all the other ideals we proclaim if we are ready to treat the human beings who happen to live in the enemy cities or even wear the enemy uniforms as so many calculable and expendable units to be destroyed.

To this point, then, the argument can be summarized as follows: since the quest for national security through violence has worked us into a corner where a resort to the means of violence now available to us would most likely provoke our own destruction and, with it, the destruction of a significant part of the world's population, the techniques of non-violence being proposed as an alternative would present — assuming, of course, they were given the benefit of a degree of acceptance and official support comparable to that lavished upon the techniques of violence — the only reasonable hope for escape from that dilemma. Such a change, however, would require certain crucial changes in our contemporary value structure, including, among others, a more exalted estimate of the personal competence and responsibility of the individual and a firmer commitment to the ascetic ideal which alone can sustain the kind of sacrifices non-violent resistance would probably demand. This would also imply a diminished emphasis upon the goods of political freedom and national sovereignty when these come into competition with or threaten the more universal goods of the human spirit and the continued existence of humankind upon the earth.

The Role of the Churches

In essence, non-violence rests upon individual commitment and individual readiness to act according to that commitment, regardless of the cost such action might entail. This is to say that any policy or program based upon its techniques must be personalist rather than collectivist in approach and actualization.

However, if non-violence is to succeed in winning respectful consideration as an alternative to the present pyramiding of means of total destruction which has produced nothing more than a highly tenuous balance of terror; and if, having won such acceptance, it is to have any prospects of victory in a future test of strength with an opponent using or threatening to use the means of violence, it must be organized and employed on a mass scale. This means that it is not enough to base the movement on the support won from deviant individuals who have been attracted to it. These people who are always ready to demonstrate their individuality and independence by "going against the stream" whatever personal sacrifice this may involve are often heroic figures and fully deserving of honor·and support. But non-violence as an instrument of successful international policy requires something else, a situation in which the desired behavior is produced by conformity to, not deviance from, the value orientations of the general society. In short, the flow of the stream itself must be changed, and to accomplish this the movement must somehow avail itself of the influence and resources of one of the major social institutions charged with the task of creating and transmitting the values by which men live and act.

Of the several institutions of society which share this important function, it would appear that the religious institution would be the one most responsive to the appeals of non-violence. It alone is sufficiently detached, in theory at least, from the controls and the essentially worldly aspirations and concerns of general society. Unlike the school, for instance, which is always and almost completely the servant of whatever social order exists and, therefore, more resistive to any proposed value changes, the church — and this is stated in the Christian frame of reference with which the writer is most familiar though, he is confident, the same would hold true for the other world religions as well — regards itself as the servant of an Authority far superior to and independent of the particular secular order in which it operates at any given time or place. Furthermore, the religious institution declares its values to be the ultimate values, the fixed standards by which all others are to be judged and confirmed. It matters little that the social scientist might argue with this assertion and be able to demonstrate that, in actual practice, all religious organizations tend to be much more deeply bound to "the world" than their spokesmen are aware or care to admit and that even their value orientations (and certainly the application of them) are at times little more than reflections or rationalizations of the "social imperatives" as they are defined by the temporal authorities and by the human beings who constitute the living membership of these churches. Such findings — and they can be all too easily verified — merely show that the religious institution is not what it claims to be, not that it cannot become what it says it should be.

Its vulnerability to the appeals of non-violence relate to what this writer would propose as the true self-image of the churches and the correct definition of their proper role. For one thing, the value changes suggested here show a very close fit to the values proclaimed by virtually all religious bodies. There is, for example, the matter of demanding priority for spiritual goods and the concern for the supernatural rewards or punishments earned by one's daily acts. Such a position obviously offers a "built-in" advantage for a movement which would seek a new ordering of values in which the goods of political freedom and personal survival are replaced at the head of the list by a commitment to the welfare of all men, including the populations of "bystander" nations innocently drawn into the vortex of nuclear destruction and even those of enemy nations. The Christian churches need but turn to their own history to see such a value orientation in operation: their Founder was Himself a citizen of an occupied nation, and the Caesar whose image was on the coin was the foreign oppressor. In such a context the "give unto Caesar" instruction, which has since been elaborated into a blanket order to obey any national call to arms, could more convincingly be interpreted as a call to resistance (to non-violent resistance when other Scriptural texts are taken into account) to those demands of Caesar which go beyond his rightful due. This is the interpretation which seems to have prevailed throughout the catacomb era of Christian history, a period in which the goods of personal and national survival — and political freedom as well — were nowhere near as ultimate as they have come to be in the thinking of the majority of Christians who now seem prepared to accept virtually any extremes of violence to preserve them.

Similarly, the universalism which would replace the particularist nationalism or other ethnocentric attachments is fully in keeping with the value systems of the major world religions. Christianity again provides a clear illustration. Structurally in some cases and historically in all, the Christian churches have been international and supranational in scope and appeal. They should, accordingly, be particularly sensitive to the destructive devisiveness of nationalism as a force in human affairs. Again, the verb form is important: one of the tragedies of the long history of Christianity is the scandalous degree to which the responsible leadership of most, if not all, of the Christian churches have been seduced by nationalistic ties and sentiments. This, too, is unfortunately a point of similarity with the other world religions; but the scandal is at its greatest when the vision of all men as the children of God redeemed through the saving graces of Christ's sacrifice is somehow forced into reconciliation with a situation in which the different nations and races of men stand poised behind barriers of prejudice, fear and hate, ready and all too willing to destroy one another.

The religious definition of man offers other points of agreement with the definition proposed by the advocates of non-violence. Perhaps more than is true for some of the other world religions, the Christian heritage has always stressed the overriding importance of the individual, seeing in him a creation in God's own image and the direct and personal object of divine concern. It is unfortunately true that this heritage has not always and unfailingly distinguished itself in its willingness to trust that individual to determine his own course of action according to the lights of his own conscience; but there are hopeful signs that religious leaders are becoming more aware of the need to accord the faithful such a broadened scope of competence. Such a trend obviously offers great encouragement to those in the non-violence movement. As far as the other crucial dimension of human action is concerned, the insistence upon personal moral responsibility for one's actions has been a much more consistent element in Christian teaching. It follows, then, that once the broadened scope of individual competence is granted, the redefinition of individual responsibility included as one of the required changes in our present value orientation will be an almost automatic result.

But to complete the set of prerequisites offered above, this redefined responsibility would have to be expressed in terms of what has been called "the ascetic ideal." It is here that the religious institution should prove most vulnerable to the non-violence program and its rationale. To draw our illustration again from the Christian heritage, one finds repeated evidence not only of a readiness to suffer the loss of all earthly good in preference to losing or sacrificing spiritual goods; but, in addition, the more positive note is added that such hardships and sufferings, even unto death, are to be regarded as a privilege to be welcomed. From the early martyr who rejoiced that he might be ground by the teeth of lions into flour for the Bread of Life down to the Austrian peasant, Franz Jaegerstaetter, who just before he was beheaded in 1943 for refusal to serve in Hitler's unjust war effort thanked God that he was given such an opportunity to serve Him — between these two the ranks of Christianity's heroes or "saints" have always been filled by men and women who embraced the ascetic ideal with a sense of total commitment. Their names and deeds are given public honor in the feastdays of the liturgical year, in the inspirational tales used for the instruction of children, and in many other forms of special recognition and devotion by the faithful.

It should not be impossible, it should not be too difficult, to induce the leadership of the religious communities to place more explicit emphasis upon the ascetic ideal behind such hallowed martyrdom and to be much more rigorous in awakening in their membership the awareness that they, too, must be prepared to evidence that ideal in their own behavior when and if the occasion should ever arise. And let us be quite clear on this: the acceptance of non-violence as an alternative to war would undoubtedly present such an occasion to an untold number of these believers.

In the fullest sense of religious asceticism, however, this somewhat grim expectation becomes at once a token of endurance and confidence. The practice of non-violence as the only form of resistance to the unjust aggressor-oppressor may indeed require generations of sacrifice and suffering before the victory is achieved. Here again, only in terms of the religious promise with its duration confounding the short-term reckoning by which we mark the course of human history can we expect to make sense of the full potentiality of non-violence. The first great temporal victory of Christianity required centuries of persecution before it could be achieved; perhaps at least an equal period of trial and purification must be endured before that victory can be regained. Yet such endurance is possible because the victory is assured. Here, again, non-violence as an alternative to violent reactions rests upon a confidence born of a total act of faith in the ultimate vulnerability of evil and the certain invincibility of the good. We have been told that the gates of Hell will not prevail; and in this divine assurance the religious advocate of non-violence finds the rationale for the program he offers as the key to a moral and effective defense of the values we hold.

But men must believe that the gates of Hell will not prevail before they are willing to undergo the crucial test. In this connection, whatever difficulty will be encountered in inspiring the necessary depth and scope of awareness and conviction will lie not so much in the weakness of man but, more likely, in two self-imposed restraints that have served to undermine the influence of religion upon modern society. The first is a hesitancy on the part of responsible church leaders to formally and actively involve themselves in political or social questions which appear to be only indirectly or peripherally related to morality or in issues which do not touch upon the institutional interests of the church. Since the tendency has been to continually sharpen the distinction between sacred and secular concerns and force an ever-widening gap between them, we thus face a situation in which the religious institution is virtually isolated from those issues of paramount importance to mankind. As a result, we encounter the almost incomprehensible paradox of formal high level church pronouncements on relatively trivial matters (sex in movies or on book covers, financial assistance in the form of school bus or lunch programs, etc.) and a crashing silence on the proposed development of the neutron bomb.

The second restraint, in a sense the pragmatic extension of the first, is the frank unwillingness on the part of church leaders to impose what may be regarded as "too great a burden" or "impossible demands" upon their faithful lest such "excessive" expectations cause a drop in active membership or be reflected adversely in some of the other statistical indices of religious behavior. Actually this attitude may be the most serious problem of all in that it represents a betrayal or abandonment of the ascetic ideal — and with it the betrayal or abandonment of much of the Christian heritage. It suggests that, before the religious institution can assume its proper and leading role in converting the general population to the new value orientation required for the non-violence alternative, the institution must itself be re-converted — or, at least, re-awakened — to those value affirmations and beliefs which, in its time of origin and its times of greatest glory, have always made it an institution for the transformation of society and not what it has tended to become, an instrument of accommodation and conformity to the secular *status quo.*

The tragically short reign of Pope John XXIII may have marked a major break with this tradition. If, as he declared in his momentous *Pacem in Terris,* "it is hardly possible to imagine that in the atomic era war could be used as an instrument of justice" — obviously the only basis on which war could be a permissible option for the Christian — we may look for some effort on the part of the most powerful segment of the Christian Church to break away from its centuries-long and generally futile fascination by the so-called "just war" and lead the search for some effective and legitimate alternative to war itself.

The Prospects

Thus far this essay has outlined the nature of the defense alternative proposed by the advocate of non-violence, the new value orientation this alternative would require, and the part the religious institution — especially as it is represented by the Christian churches — could be expected to play in bringing about these essential value changes. One other question of central importance remains: even granting that the non-violence program would constitute a more *moral* form of defense policy, does it hold sufficient promise of being *effective* to warrant its adoption by practical men in preference to the more familiar defense polices based on violence?

It is immediately obvious that the proposed alternative can claim no victories on a scale comparable to the violent clashes of the major world powers. However, since it has never been put to such a test, one can say that it has a record of no failures at this level — a rather impressive recommendation for it when compared with the consistent and ever more devastating pattern of failure registered by violence and war. The issue, then, may be stated in terms of a choice between a possible failure and a proven failure in determining long-term security and survival possibilities. This statement would apply as much to the so-called "limited war" as it does to the world-consuming conflicts of the past two generations. In a real emergency, whatever "limits" may be set at the outset will always prove flexible enough to permit whatever course of action the military or political leaders may propose as the only remaining alternative to defeat, thereby reducing the "limited war" concept to little more than an attractive and conveniently disposable cloak for the nuclear holocaust it supposedly circumvents.

The argument is sometimes advanced that this is too pessimistic a presentation of the possibilities. After all, one might say, the period since the close of World War II offers abundant illustration of violent engagements that did not escalate into full-blown nuclear war. Korea, Vietnam, Laos and even Berlin are often cited to prove this point. The argument is challenging — but not necessarily convincing. If we are right in viewing all of these as tentative probings and responses to probings on the part of the two major world powers (and their supporting blocs) in what has been termed "the cold war," it would seem that the fact that nuclear weapons have not been employed could be interpreted just as easily as a sign that neither power has found it appropriate *as yet* to take that step. The fact that these contacts have been "limited" up to this time merely testifies to the fact that neither contestant has yet been forced to the point of acknowledging defeat. The spokesmen for the radical Right have made it clear in their attacks upon the so-called "no win" policy that they, at least, are dissatisfied with this situation; should they succeed in winning a broader base of support, the emptiness of the "limited war" concept would soon become evident.

The policy of nuclear deterrence, too, while tempting in its formulation, holds no real promise as an alternative to the kind of World War III which would claim the horrifying toll contemplated in even the most optimistic estimates advanced by its proponents. An empty threat with no intent to follow through with the use of nuclear weapons under any conceivable circumstance simply will not deter. Yet once any such intent, however faint or however simulated, is admitted, it necessarily opens the way to the same grim progression described in connection with the limited war concept; for we cannot hope to convince a potential enemy that we will actually use the bombs "as a last resort" without convincing ourselves as well. And "the last resort" will always prove to be much more imminent than we thought.

The "close-call" at the time of the Cuba emergency, generally taken as incontestable proof that deterrence works, also illustrates the imminence of "the last resort." No one can deny, of course, that both major powers were forced to a level of circumspection in their actions because their leaders took the possible effects of a nuclear exchange into account; to this extent, it was a success for the advocates of deterrence. However, in another very important sense, it reveals a distinct failure — and a shocking measure of hypocrisy. The failure lies in the fact that the American action was specifically predicated on a readiness to escalate the limited Cuban threat into a full-scale and world-wide nuclear exchange. And there was no wave of horrified protest; on the contrary, it was generally taken for granted that our military forces would have no alternative but to use whatever means were available and might have been required to bring about the stated objective of dismantling and removing the missiles.

This is where the hypocrisy comes in. For that objective represented an official repudiation of the logic of deterrence *for others*. Weeks before the installation of the missiles, evidence had been accumulating of another projected invasion of Castro's Cuba with either direct or indirect American involvement. Under the circumstances, the defenders could have covered their island several times over with the kind of "defensive weapons" enumerated as permissible by the President; but, it should have been obvious to everyone, this would have merely delayed a foregone conclusion and made it somewhat more costly for the invasion forces. The only kind of weapon by which the Cuban government (and the Soviet ally committed to come to its assistance) could have hoped to deter its giant adversary would be precisely the kind of weapon involved in the controversy. If Polaris missiles in the Mediterranean are "defensive" against Soviet threats to "bury us" and our NATO allies, Soviet missiles in Cuba have to be recognized as "defensive" for that nation, subjected as it was (and still is) to the threat to its security from the North. Let this argument not be misinterpreted: I firmly oppose the installation of missiles *in Cuba or anywhere else;* and I was, as a result, most happy to see them dismantled and removed. And it is possible for me, as an opponent of the deterrence theory, to take this position and be consistent, whereas it should be something of a logical embarrassment for the advocates of such a policy to offer a convincing explanation of why sauce for the goose should not also serve as sauce for the gander.

Cuba was just one illustrative incident. Before and since then leading representatives of the military and those who have joined them in the frank espousal of pre-emptive war, or who see the nuclear bombing of North Vietnam military centers as a solution to our difficulties in the Near East, have given evidence enough by their impatience that "the last resort" is really always just around the corner. In one of his major policy addresses, President Kennedy warned against extremists who offer what he described as the false dichotomies of choice between "appeasement or war, suicide or surrender, humiliation or holocaust." One may agree with his warning and yet, at the same time, regret that his defense of his administration's foreign and defense policies reveals a comparable failure to recognize *any alternative to violence itself* in maintaining a strong position between these false dichotomies. It is proposed here that such an alternative must be found and that it does, in fact, exist. The alternative of non-violence represents neither weakness, nor appeasement, nor surrender, nor humiliation. Instead, it represents a new kind of force, a power to compel and to defend. Gandhi described the difference in 1932 as he prepared to enter upon his famous fast unto death: "Violent pressure is felt on the physical being and it degrades him who uses it as it depresses the victim, but non-violent pressure exerted through self-suffering, as by fasting, works in an entirely different way. It touches not the physical body, but it touches and strengthens the moral fibre of those against whom it is directed."

Seen in this light, non-violence becomes a real option, the only option, its advocates would insist, holding promise of ultimate success; for if even one nation — our own — could be awakened to its promise and be prepared to pursue it, the world could finally be freed from the vicious circle of violence in which it is now locked and the way opened to a security based on those greater and surer kinds of force incorporating a power which until now we have not dared to consider, much less exploit. Instead of continuing our present descent to total inhumanity, we would be making a significant and long-overdue turning in the direction of a renewed act of faith in the humanity of our potential enemy — and ourselves.

For we are dealing with something far more profound than a mere difference in policy options. Our question ultimately concerns our basic conceptions of man. Is man, after all is said and done, a creature whose behavior is finally controlled through promises of physically satisfying rewards and threats of violently induced pain; or is he something greater, the deepest wellsprings of whose behavior contain forces responsive only to the power of love and recognition of common identity? If we deny the latter possibility, we deny many of the core values upon which we base our claims to a preferable way of life and, indeed, our hopes for any future advance for humankind. The non-violence alternative takes these values seriously enough to propose them as the foundation of our defense action. The belief that all men share a common humanity which cannot be totally or permanently suppressed; the corollary that every man (including the Roman tyrant, the Buchenwald guard, the Communist oppressor, yes, even the indifferent RAND theorist at his computer) has a "breaking point" beyond which his participation in patterned inhumanity cannot be forced; and, finally, the confidence that a disciplined, large-scale exercise of the moral power of sacrificial "love" or "soul force" will most surely bring him to that breaking point and thereby negate whatever power of violence he may have at his disposal: these deserve a far more receptive hearing than they have received from those supposedly committed to the defense of the West and its Judeo-Christian foundations.

If, as history has demonstrated, the way of violence demands an ever more thorough-going renunciation of this common humanity and its implications for our own behavior, coupled with a callous ignoring of the humanity of the enemy, it should be rejected as a policy option not worthy of consideration. Otherwise, in the process of "defending" these most cherished values we may find ourselves forced to abandon and betray them in our total surrender to the inevitably destructive logic of violence.

Its advocates, then, regard non-violence as the most effective and most promising defense policy. There are, of course, no guarantees. The mounting of a well-conceived and disciplined campaign of civil disobedience and non-cooperation against an opponent using the means of violence might end with total victory for the latter. But grim as this prospect admittedly is, even it could be preferable to the kind of world promised us as the aftermath of a Third World War — for victor and vanquished alike. At least such a defeat would leave us with the hope that civilized mankind spared from the near-total destruction nuclear war would have brought will be able to make a new start toward the freedom and dignity that is temporarily suppressed. And throughout the "dark ages" imposed by the victor, they would find the way lighted for them in that upward struggle by the inspiring memory of the sacrifices made in heroic testimony to the imperishable and indestructible spark of goodness to be found in every man just because he is a man.

Moral Tensions in International Affairs

John C. Bennett

An Affirmation

Those responsible for policy in international relations, as well as American citizens generally, usually seek to preserve some harmony between their moral convictions and their decisions and actions in this field. It may be that in practice morality is often not an independent factor but a source of rationalizations which are much used when decisions and actions have to be defended, but I do not take a cynical view of this matter and do not press this as being a full account of the relations between morality and discussions of foreign policy. There are in the background commitments to morally significant goals and values and at least there are limits to the willingness to make use of means which are dishonest and cruel. This is true in general and in many cases those responsible for the most difficult and most ambiguous decisions are extremely conscientious and struggle with great sensitivity with the unresolved conflicts between what it may seem necessary to do or to accept as policy and personal moral convictions.

I begin with this affirmation of what may be in large part an unexamined assumption and yet is a real and operative one—an affirmation that, in spite of all of the difficulties encountered as we move into the area of actual choices, we do not in principle separate morality and foreign policy. Denunciation of the policies of our adversaries in moral terms may be in part ideological self-deception and in part propaganda, but there is an element of sincere commitment to moral values involved which we may believe to have no place in our adversaries' scheme of things. But I shall devote the first part of this paper to a statement of the actual difficulties in relating national decisions and acts in the sphere of foreign policy to morality. I refer here both to explicitly Christian or Jewish morality and to a humanistic morality that takes seriously a concern for a universal human good. Fortunately the area of overlap between the effects of these three sources of moral inspiration is very great.

Obstacles to the Emphasis Upon Morality

The first of these obstacles is a current revulsion against what is often called "moralism" in the attitudes of nations. There has often been a good deal of what sounds like cant in Anglo-Saxon expressions of foreign policy and this has often taken the form of self-righteous idealism in American expressions of foreign policy. There has been a tendency to cloak the stance of the United States as a nation with high democratic ideals, to turn our national objectives into a righteous cause and to divide the world between good nations and bad nations. This has not been all hypocrisy by any means and there has been enough truth in our claims to make self-righteous self-deception relatively easy, but this tendency has generated far too much pretentiousness in our attitudes toward ourselves and too much fury in our attitudes toward our adversaries. The psychology of the crusade or of the holy war has sometimes made impossible prudent limiting of objectives and realistic distinctions among those in the opposite camp. The attitude toward neutrals during the first half of the cold war was in part a result of this habit of drawing our own moral lines without first seeking to understand the motives of other nations. It is very difficult to negotiate with "the devil" and a moralistic view of foreign policy usually produces devils on the other side. The revulsion against moralism may cause many critics to be afraid to relate morality to foreign policy, but this is a mistake since this very revulsion is itself favorable to a more sensitive understanding of morality, one that sees humility as an essential national virtue and that is influenced by openness to the neighbor, even though he be an adversary.

Second, the details of foreign policy, mixed with all of the details concerning national security, come to belong to the province of the expert who is immersed in technical problems that may be far removed from moral considerations. His interest in the technical problems may stem from moral commitments at some stage. He wants to preserve American power for reasons that are at least partly moral, but the details of this process of preserving relative power in the world are themselves so demanding and yet so morally neutral that it may be difficult to keep in mind the original objectives of policy or to be open to new moral criticisms of them in a changing situation. I say of these details that they are "morally neutral." It may be debatable as to whether the discussion of power which is the power to annihilate is morally neutral in itself, but certainly the measuring of relative power in a world of competing powers does have this morally neutral element. There has developed in recent years a science of deterrence which is partly a matter of this measuring of units of power and partly a matter of reasonably informed guessing about the psychological responses of the adversary. Universities and governments have spawned semi-scientific studies in these areas which have little day-by-day contact with moral considerations.

A third very profound difficulty in the way of making moral judgments paramount in many situations is that those concerned about policy may have two or more objectives which have significant moral sanction but objectives that are in some measure of conflict with each other. When this is the case there may be no overriding moral criterion by which these conflicts can be adjudicated. The obvious cause of this difficulty is the tension, if not conflict, between such current objectives of policy as peace and freedom. The most sensitive policy makers may well be committed at the same time to the prevention of general war and to the preservation of as large an area of the world as possible in which nations are free to choose their own social systems. There may be some self-deceptions on our part in regard to the preservation of this freedom to choose, and yet there has been a real threat of Communist expansion and our nation has had responsibility to maintain power to limit it. This power and policies affecting its use may at times involve risk of war, as in the Cuba crisis of 1962. The case is often made that peace was here actually served by the risk of war. But perhaps peace was served just as much by the restraint (including mutual face-saving) with which both sides acted in the crisis. Valid objectives which can be morally defended may actually be in conflict at least provisionally, and at the moment of crisis the estimate of the comparative claims of these objectives may be most difficult.

What is needed is great practical wisdom that includes commitment to both objectives but which also involves a tactical resourcefulness that cannot be understood fully in moral terms. At the end of the day we may discover that the competing objectives are far from being in real conflict. Indeed so far as these two objectives—peace and freedom—are concerned, we cannot in the end have either without having the other. If we do not avoid a general nuclear war, there is not likely to be the social health necessary for the institutions of freedom. If peace is imposed only by superior power it may well provoke revolts that will destroy it. The only security for our major values is that somehow we find ways of serving all of them together. But, again, the adjudicating of moral claims here is most difficult. Men of equal moral sensitivity may differ about priorities, and arguments between them are usually stalemates until the topography of the problem is changed by history.

In what follows I shall first discuss briefly three areas in which we may see most clearly the relevance of moral convictions to international affairs. Then, I shall discuss three major problems: (1) the relationship between morality and national interest; (2) the need to make distinctions between moral goals and American ideology; (3) the limits of violence with special reference to nuclear deterrence and the possibility of nuclear war.

Where Relevance of Morality Is Most Evident

The long-term objectives of policy—broad criteria that determine these objectives.

However we may become bogged down in the technical discussion of means and however we may be inclined toward cynicism when we hear moral preachments in the context of international affairs, almost all of us who give thought to these issues in this country do take for granted moral criteria concerning objectives in policy. There are problems of priorities among the criteria about which there may be serious differences of opinion among us, and we often come up against very serious moral dilemmas that may be so bitter that we might prefer to forget the moral dimension altogether. Yet even in these latter cases, we do prefer the lesser evil for moral reasons and we do experience real distress because of the moral ambiguities in all choices. Professionally, those close to policy-making may avoid making this distress fully articulate.

I think that there is a quite widespread moral consensus molded by the Biblical tradition however much it may be secularized. We do lip service and more than lip service to a humane ethic that is based upon a sense of solidarity with all persons, an ethic that is at least touched by a response to the *agape* of the Bible. I put this cautiously in order to avoid claiming too much but there is also danger of claiming too little. That this humane ethic is related to our vexing social problems is shown by the various ways we state concerns for order or peace, justice, freedom, the openness of society to sources of truth that transcend it. Justice is generally seen both as fair treatment in relation to existing laws and institutions and as a dynamic raising of the level of life of those who are poor and oppressed, as the transforming of laws and institutions. These values can be related more directly to the domestic structures and policies of our own nation than they can be related to international affairs. But we cannot be morally indifferent to what happens within other nations and we favor international structures that make peace more likely and that tend to promote humane goals. Many of these are well expressed in the United Nations charter and are embodied in various organs of the United Nations. There is, for example, a breakthrough for a dynamic view of justice in the recognition that in non-self-governing territories "the interests of the inhabitants of these territories are paramount."[2]

The growth in moral awareness comes usually with the capacity of neglected and oppressed people to call attention to their grievances and to exert pressure on those who have been complacent in their strength and favored position. We see the truth of this in the fact that white Americans become really concerned about the civil rights of Negroes when the latter have become articulate and have gained power to bring pressure. Conscience is educated by this pressure but it has its own reality and makes its own contribution to the response to pressure.

In relating these moral objectives and criteria to international affairs we find ourselves deflected by many things—by the rightful claims of prudence when we must adjust one objective to others, by the sovereignty of other nations in dealing with their own populations, by the dilution of concern for people at a distance, by the immediate claims of our own national interest, and by the pressures of special economic interests in our own country that may seek to preserve a kind of economic colonialism abroad which as a nation we reject in principle. These many ways in which moral purpose is deflected do not nullify it, but they create serious moral dilemmas and they are the source of much real and much apparent national hypocrisy.

National self-criticism.

There is ample room for moral criticism of the nation. Nations tend to make themselves absolute, to allow national interest to be the ultimate criterion for policy while they use the ideals of a universal morality to defend that interest. It is, therefore, always important for citizens to be critical of national policy. Often moral self-criticism is made difficult because of the tendency of those who make policy to claim that they are the pioneers of public opinion while the public passes responsibility to the policy-makers who are presumably better informed and in a better condition to judge. Someone must break through this vicious circle and give a fresh lead to public opinion. President Kennedy was beginning to do this in his American University address in June 1963. Was this what former Assistant Secretary of State Roger Hilsman was trying to do in his San Francisco address on the Far East in December of that year?

The self-deceptions of national pride continually need to be deflated and the temptations of nations to abuse power need to be exposed. In an open society in which freedom to criticize is safeguarded and in which institutions that are independent of the state are encouraged to be themselves, this type of national self-criticism should be expected. One of the effects of the separation of church and state should be the preservation of the church's freedom to criticize the state from its own vantage point as the interpreter of the transcendent will of God and as itself a universal community that includes people on the other side of every international conflict.

One of the most revealing episodes in the life of President Kennedy which I have heard was told on a T.V. broadcast the Sunday after his death by Dr. Franklin Clark Fry, a leader of Lutheranism in this country and the Chairman of the Central Committee of the World Council of Churches. Dr. Fry had gone with a delegation from the World Council of Churches to see the President to present to him a message to heads of states from the New Delhi Assembly of the World Council. This message included a section on nuclear tests. This was early in 1962, before the United States had resumed nuclear tests. When Mr. Kennedy read this section, he revealed his own dilemma and inner conflict on this issue and evidently spoke with great feeling about it. One of the Americans in the delegation said to him: "Mr. President, if you do resume tests, how can we help you?" The President turned to him and said: "Perhaps you shouldn't." This was a very different reaction from the common one of seeking more church support the more one feels uneasy about one's decision. Kennedy had respect for the distance between church and state and did not want the church to be a mere moral echo of the state even though, as a representative of the state, he may have felt shut up to a course of action that gave him moral distress.

I think that those who represent churches should understand the limited alternatives between which policy-makers must often choose and that policy-makers should welcome the possibility of criticism from a standpoint that transcends their own. The existence of such sources of criticism in a nation may in the long run make new alternatives available. In discussing particular problems I shall give more content to the kind of moral criticisms that those who make policy in the United States today should expect, but here it is enough to emphasize this context in which morality may be relevant.

Preserving the possibility of morally sensitive personal living with people in other nations.

It is only in an open society that this dimension of morality can be made explicit. In an open society the relations between states do not supplant personal relations which have a morally independent basis. However, the policy of states can have the effect of favoring or limiting these human relations across national boundaries. There are differences between the morality of states and the morality of private persons but these should not be allowed to be so separated that there is no inter-action between them. One of the morally intolerable aspects of war is that it turns people into destroyers of their neighbors on the other side of the conflict. Human relationships are made impossible by this political situation. One very admirable episode in recent French history was the organized revulsion in France against the use of torture by French troops in Algeria. Policies of state that cause the citizen to defy his own moral sensitivities in dealing with other persons because of a political relationship with them are especially repellant.

I think that we have usually solved this problem in this country by having an ethic of war which has permitted great barbarities toward people, especially toward people at a distance, and an ethic of peace which in principle enables us to deal with persons as persons regardless of political relationships. The ethic of war was put in brackets and it was assumed to be exceptional. This neat division between an ethic of war and an ethic of peace has been lost in a time of cold war, revolution and civil conflict, but policy-makers and citizens still have a responsibility to reduce to a minimum the practices which corrupt or destroy personal relations. I do not know what is done in our name by our government's secret agents and there seems to be here a moral underworld below the acknowledged ambiguities and compromises of international relations which—whether necessary or not under present conditions of conflict—should not be allowed to go without moral re-straints. The citizen should be able to know that some trustworthy persons are in a position to insist on the preservation of moral limits in this underworld. The existence of this underworld was acknowledged officially at the time of the shooting down of the U-2 plane over the Soviet Union and then the question arose: how much should the people of the upper world lie to keep the two worlds separate? How much does such lying corrupt the upper world?

One of the consequences of the cold war that needs to be kept under moral scrutiny is the absence of relationships between Ameri-cans and the people of China and Cuba. This utter denial of human relationships across these boundaries is itself a great evil and not to be accepted complacently as the result of some political necessity. I am not interested in raising the Chinese or the Cuban issues here and I am only illustrating a broader problem, but the utter denial of human contacts is a sufficient reason to insist that everything possible be done to overcome the frozen positions on our side that contribute to the situation.

I shall only mention a few other illustrations of this dimension of morality in international relations. One is the moral problem of being a citizen of a rich nation in a poor world where most people remain hungry. The Peace Corps gets much of its remarkable support because it is a way of dealing with this problem, but it can be an escape from the problem unless it causes the nation to take with full seriousness the contrast between the so-called northern and southern nations and to strive to find ways of narrowing the gap. Perhaps one effect of the Peace Corps will be the influence which those who have participated in it exert on national policy in the next period. Another illustration is the encouragement of freedom of the mind in international associations. Scientists should be encouraged by government to put loyalty to truth above obedience to the national will. This should be true of all forms of intellectual life. The moment that political policies begin to restrict the possibility of this intellectual faithfulness, they become a danger signal.

Another example is the role of the international civil servant and of those who perform international functions amidst the conflicts of nations. One of the tests of the moral maturity of a nation and of the moral sensitivity of its policy-makers is the acceptance as a matter of course of the principle that a citizen is more than a citizen of the nation and that his wider responsibilities may cause him to take action that appears at the time to be against his nation. Judges or arbitrators who can go against the wishes of their government are the fruit of a finer form of patriotism than those who recognize no duty beyond the duty to their own state. As a theologian, I put special emphasis on the role of the world-wide church in relation to the nations and upon the dual citizenship of the members of the church. I take this dual citizenship very seriously and put the loyalties not to the church as an institution but to that which it represents above loyalty to the state or the nation. There is a world of difference between governments which make a place for this kind of dual citizenship and those which reject it or look upon it as potentially a form of treason.

Major Politico-Moral Problems

Morality and national interest.

Thought on the relationship between morality and national interest should move between two poles. One pole is the recognition that government is a trustee for the national interest broadly understood. It can stretch the ideas held in a nation about its true interest very far, but there are limits to this process. Those who represent government or who as legislators or other elected officials represent the citizens cannot be guided fully by their private idealism. This sets limits, for example, to the role of a convinced pacifist in government at least in relation to foreign policy. A pacifist might in theory function as the representative of a nation in which the citizens were mostly convinced pacifists, but such a nation does not exist and it is not likely to come into being at any time in the future. There may be nations which choose to avoid having defense establishments, but they will depend upon their more powerful neighbors that have an interest in defending them. They may be guided by a prudent guess that there is more national security in avoiding the possession of the kind of power, especially nuclear power, that would tempt other nations to attack them directly, but this kind of prudence is not pacifism. Also, we should recognize that national interest is itself a good as far as it goes. The real welfare and security of 200,000,000 Americans is a part of the good of humanity. National interest needs to be distinguished from the powerful private groups that may be able to use government to defend their interest as though they were identical with the national interest. This confusion often bedevils our relations with some Latin American countries.

The other pole is the recognition that no morally responsible person who is controlled by Christian ethics, Jewish ethics or secular humanistic ethics can make national interest supreme whenever it does come into conflict with a broader human interest. It is difficult for any citizen or policy-maker to live in sight of these two poles at the same time but there are at least two considerations which may help him to do so.

a. National interest often has considerable moral value as a limiting concept. This is something that I have learned from George Kennan and Hans Morgenthau. A nation that crusades for moral ideas that are not supported by national interest is likely to throw its weight around too much. We can see this in the case of the Communist nations and we breathe a sigh of relief when there are signs that the Russians are concerned about their national interest rationally understood more than about world revolution. Russian national interest may tempt the Russians to do some aggressive things to round out their empire or to safeguard their security against all future threats, but it will prompt them to avoid great risks to what they already have; it will set limits to ideological crusading. A nation guided by a prudent sense of national interest may at least be willing to settle down and accept limits to its power. *Prudence* may be the chief word. A prudent avoidance of the greater evil may be the most relevant morality in many international situations.

Suppose that our country decided that it had a moral commitment to unify such nations as Germany or Korea or Vietnam and that, regardless of the consequences, this was the national duty. Probably if we embarked on such a crusade, there would not be much left of any one of the nations to unify. Probably much the same thing can be said of all morally supported efforts to liberate nations under Communist rule. It would destroy the candidates for liberation in the process.

b. A second consideration is that it is a mark of human solidarity that there are wide areas of mutuality of interest between nations. I am not suggesting that under all conditions this exists, but it is true of the relations between our own nation and many other nations with which we deal. There are particular conflicts of interest, especially in the sphere of trade, between our country and, for example, Japan and the nations of Western Europe, but the United States has an overriding national interest in the economic health of those same nations. We have an interest in all that makes for peace and political stability and for the long-term economic well-being of other nations. I believe that we have an interest in the essential well-being of the Soviet Union. Instead of trying to starve out Communism where it is established, we would do better in our own interest to help Communist nations to get into the more stable and moderate stage of Communism. I know that this goes against our Cuba policy and our China policy. But I doubt if we would be better off if either of those countries were thrown back into chaos and civil war with years of political anarchy and economic misery ahead or, in the case of Cuba, with a return to a rightist tyranny. We might score a victory over Communism by encouraging such things to happen but we would be in no position to control events, to establish a viable order that would also be more free. We would take our chances with chaos, followed, in all probability, by new tyrannies, and these new tyrannies would probably be less able than Communism to solve basic national problems, the solution of which is a precondition for a more free society.

I think that the moral problem raised by the government's responsibility for national interest often becomes manageable if we stress mutuality of interest in dealing with other nations. This is especially true of nations to which we give economic aid. We do this not out of generosity but out of a wise caring for mutual interests, but there are generous impulses in the doing of it. In fact, if there were not many Americans who really care about what happens to other nations we would probably not be able to discern the real mutuality of interests which we share with them. Our national leaders who are most admired abroad seem to embody all of these attitudes in their own persons. I felt that this was true of President Kennedy when I saw how much genuine grief there was in the world at the time of his death. He was faithful to the national interest but he made people in other nations feel that he cared about them. And there was something else about him and there is something else about any other national leaders who arouse this feeling abroad; there is a real desire for a world community in which all nations have a better life together. *To be able to live in such a community is itself an American national interest.*

There is another phase of this matter which may point beyond national interest altogether and yet not entirely if we are flexible enough in our understanding of it. I have in mind the following passage by George Kennan: "We should conduct ourselves at all times in such a way as to satisfy our own ideas of morality. But let us do this as a matter of obligation to ourselves and not as a matter of obligation to others."[3] I do not think that this contrast will hold. Our obligation to others must surely be a part of any morality that creates an obligation to ourselves. Perhaps what is meant is that the citizens of a nation need to be able to live with their consciences. This is not very different from W. W. Rostow's emphasis on doing what fits our national style as a humane nation.[4] This involves concern for others for our sake in part, but also for their sake.

The freeing of morality from American ideology.

Now that the world is changing so fast it may be easier to distinguish between the essential moral issues and a rather frozen position on what might be called the level of ideology in this country. I am not using ideology as the expression of a class interest or as the expression of a purely national interest. I am using it to refer to convictions with which the nation has become identified, including familiar political and economic ideas which are fused with moral commonplaces into a fighting creed which is no longer in touch with the realities of the situation. Ideology as I use it involves rigidity more than it does the passion which is often associated with the concept of ideology.[5] There is an American ideology which makes difficult a real openness to the experiences of nations whose historical situation is entirely different from our own. I have in mind the freezing of our public opinion by a moralistic anti-Communism that refuses to make distinctions between Communist nations as human communities that are themselves no longer consistent embodiments of the Communist ideology. American anti-Communism has some elements of a mirror image of what Communism is believed to be. I also have in mind a tendency to identify our moral criteria concerning what is universally good for man with our own political and economic institutions.

There is need of a more sophisticated combination of ultimate moral criteria, that have a touch of the absolute, with a great deal of cultural and institutional relativism. Reinhold Niebuhr has expressed this second need of greater openness in the following passage: "We are in the strange predicament that, as the leading exponents of the 'open society', we introduce a stubborn insistence of our own kind of openness (including the alleged virtues of the free-enterprise system) as the only basis for a free society." He speaks of our "fanatic protagonism of a non-fanatic culture."[6]

An editorial in *The New York Times* caught this ideological conditioning very well in the following words: "What should be avoided [in dealing with Latin America] is a know-it-all, self-righteous, dogmatic, emotionally anti-leftist and complacently pro-rightist attitude."[7]

I believe that Pope John XXIII has done a great deal to deliver the Catholic world and hence a large part of our country from this too ideological approach to Communist nations. His encyclical, *Pacem in Terris*, while it does not speak directly of Communism or Communist nations, does open the door to fresh thinking on this subject, and events which accompanied the encyclical make it probable that he had Communism and Communist nations in mind. (What Pope John has said is entirely in line with the positions often expressed by the World Council of Churches.) I refer especially to the following passage from the encyclical:

> It must be borne in mind, furthermore, that neither can false philosophical teachings regarding the nature, origin and destiny of the universe and of man, be identified with historical movements that have economic, social, cultural or political ends, not even when these movements have originated from those teachings and have drawn and still draw inspiration therefrom. Because the teachings, once they are drawn up and defined, remain always the same, while the movements, working on historical situations in constant evolution, cannot but be influenced by these latter and cannot avoid, therefore, being subject to changes even of a profound nature. Besides, who can deny that those movements, in so far as they conform to the dictates of right reason and are interpreters of the lawful aspirations of the human person, contain elements that are positive and deserving of approval.[8]

Here is an open door and there could be many arguments as to exactly what the terrain is on the other side. But certainly there is here a very different approach from the single-track anti-Communism that bolts all doors leading toward a nation or a movement which has a connection with Communism. It enables us to ask with some openness in what direction a nation with a Communist regime is moving. The present spectrum in the Communist world is such that the United States is justified in having a policy that is dictated by the distinctive characteristics of each nation in the bloc. This is different from the common tendency to condemn all of these nations moralistically or in terms of religion in advance.

An editorial in *The Commonweal* boldly stated in the following sentence a relevant truth which I have seldom before seen in explicit form: "Communism within Russia should be looked upon as an experiment that deserves a chance to succeed."[9] Our national policy is now certainly based upon that idea though no politician running for office could say it in his campaign! There is ambiguity in the use of words in this area. We can say that a nation that has changed so much that such a statement can be made about it is no longer Communist. The important question is whether we believe that it is possible for changes to take place in a nation that claims to be Communist without a direct, deliberate, conscious displacing of Communism. I believe that there can be an erosion of Communism, to borrow a word from George Kennan, without its explicit displacement and that there has to be a similar erosion of the American ideological position if we are to see what is taking place.

The second aspect of the change in ideology to which I have referred is our willingness to be open to the political and economic experiments in other nations even though they do not conform to our standards. I realize that we are not dogmatic about all of our institutions. We do not insist that a new African state establish an equivalent of our "rules committee" in the House of Representatives. Our carefully preserved governmental stalemates would not bear good fruit in the new nations! Yet I doubt if there is a sufficient realization that nations that must deal with competing tribalisms and that must in a few years accomplish in terms of economic development what it took us generations to do under vastly more favorable conditions will have to have a much larger socialistic ingredient in their economies than we need here and will have to have governments more authoritarian than we approve for ourselves. This is where the institutional relativism comes in. There is a spectrum of political types between what we may regard as totalitarian government along the lines of Stalinism or along the lines of a terroristic personal dictatorship of the Trujillo type at one end, to the most free and reliable constitutional democracy at the other. We must expect all varieties here and be thankful for any distance that a nation travels from the totalitarian end of the spectrum. Government is an extraordinarily difficult and precarious matter and to bring our own democratic yardstick to every national political experiment is foolish and unfair. This is even more the case with our yardstick of free enterprise.

What I say about the new nations of Asia and Africa applies also to nations that are moving away from Stalinism. As they move toward the center of the spectrum our tendency is to apply to them the democratic yardstick when it is quite irrelevant to their experience. When we think of the desperate difficulty that Latin American nations have in developing stable governments or in improving the conditions of the masses of the people, again we need to have a greater openness. Radical revolutions may sometimes be required. We should not be critical if the movements which are dynamic enough to inspire such revolutions make Marxist noises. We have a clear interest in their being free from control by Chinese or Soviet Communism, but the pattern of policy dictated by our American ideology is to reject such movements because of our own *a priori* bias—and then the nation involved gets pushed to a more dangerous form of the left or to the far right. I realize that any mention of a particular nation arouses a fierce debate among us, but sometimes the fierceness of the debate is a sign of the ideological conditioning to which I have referred.

Unless our morality can be freed from our ideology in the sense in which I have used the word, we can expect it to be one of the factors which cause our minds to be unable to deal with the changing realities. Much fresh thinking is needed here to relate moral convictions to what is possible in terms of constitutional development in various nations and cultures. There are forms of tyranny and of cruelty that are wrong everywhere, and freedom of the mind and spirit is always a great good. But the relating of order and justice and freedom to the needs of nations which require revolutionary change and which have no unifying traditions and which have had no experience of success with free institutions calls for more humility and more imaginative sympathy than we find it easy to show. Such humility and such imaginative sympathy are highly moral traits that are inhibited by the moral dogmatisms that are the results of combining morality with ideology.

Morality and the nuclear dilemma—the limits of violence.

The threat of nuclear annihilation makes many of our other problems more dangerous than would otherwise be the case. It greatly reduces the margin for error in our decisions. It creates the most harassing moral dilemma. If I were a nuclear pacifist I could suggest an absolute solution of the basic problem, but I cannot do this. Nuclear pacifism is not a possible position for the government of the United States; moreover I question the moral adequacy of a policy of unilateral nuclear disarmament on our part because it would leave the whole non-Communist world vulnerable to all sorts of pressure or blackmail from any power that still would possess nuclear armaments. I do not see how we can consent to the existence of a nuclear monopoly in any nation or alliance of nations. It does not take much reflection to come to accept the idea that it would be undesirable for us to have such a monopoly however much we may be confident of the reliability of our own virtue.

The scaling down of nuclear power and the control of it by international authority should be our goal but even this goal should not be accompanied by illusions. In a reasonably well-organized world community there would still be the danger of a civil war to seize control of the instruments of nuclear power. This would be a possibility on the international stage similar to the seizure of the centers of military power in a national civil war. Before there is an orderly approach to some humanly possible multilateral control of nuclear power, we must hope for more steps like the partial test-ban treaty which was the fulfillment of a unilateral initiative of President Kennedy's when he announced that this country would have no more tests in the atmosphere. In this paragraph I have tried to suggest the ultimate danger and the general direction of hope. At the same time I have tried to indicate the precariousness of the best measures that can be taken. I should much prefer the comforting assurance that must be the possession of those who have absolute answers and more secure institutional solutions!

In the present situation we face the literally terrible dilemma involved in the program of nuclear deterrence. The dilemma is easily stated: there is need of nuclear power in the non-Communist world (in as few hands as possible—and this suggests other dilemmas) to deter the use of Soviet nuclear power, but if nuclear weapons are used in a general nuclear war they are likely to destroy all that the program of deterrence is intended to defend. At this moment the governments of both the United States and of the Soviet Union are realistic about this situation and because of this the world is somewhat relaxed about the danger of nuclear war. But the dilemma remains. Sometimes the depth of it is not grasped because of the facile assumption that our deterrent will certainly deter the other side. While this might be true if history were subject to rational control, there is no security against the danger of escalation from a minor to a major conflict, and this is especally true if several nations become involved.

I believe that we were morally badly prepared for the decisions that may be forced upon us in the nuclear age because of the moral deterioration that set in during the Second World War when we assumed that any degree of violence was permitted if it made victory more likely. The mass destruction of German and Japanese cities before the use of the bombs on Hiroshima and Nagasaki prepared the way for the moral acceptance of unlimited violence. The idea of "the just war" as a limitation on means or the idea of limited war was hastily abandoned under stress.[10] Now it seems to be taken for granted that if worst comes to worst, the annihilation of the adversary's centers of population is an expected strategy which neither state nor church has morally rejected in advance.

Those responsible for strategy are caught in a trap. They prefer to keep military operations limited in any war, to limit the weapons, the terrain of battle, and the targets. But increasingly both sides are making their bases invulnerable so that the only way to hit the enemy a sufficiently destructive blow may be to bomb cities. It is ironical that in the strategic jargon "limited deterrence" seems to mean the aiming of missiles at cities. It seems to be assumed that actually this is a more limited operation because to seek out most of the hardened or the mobile bases would cause a saturation of the country with bombs, leaving it a flaming wreck. To threaten the destruction of a limited number of cities might do that "unacceptable damage" which would cause any rational government to avoid provocation or aggression.

The dilemma of deterrence becomes all the more intolerable morally when it means that the most reliable way of preventing war in this context is to encourage both sides to keep their retaliatory power invulnerable knowing that, if the deterrence should fail, the war would be fought against populations. I believe that the moral rejection of counter-peoples' war is fully sound as it has been set forth by Professor Paul Ramsey following an ancient tradition of just and limited war. I should make less of the distinction between combatant and non-combatant than Professor Ramsey does,[11] though there is still some substance to it. But I think that any use of violence that destroys most of the people together with the fabric of community and the nation's recuperative capacities is beyond all moral limits.

We and our policy-makers are in a moral trap. When this is the case, it is the part of wisdom to examine all of the assumptions that have brought us into the trap. There may be time to get out of it because of the present lull, but this cannot be done by some one spectacular movement. Rather it will call for a reconsideration of the nature of the present Communist threat, and for many specific efforts to reduce the area of tensions—including some willingness to admit that the Soviet Union and its neighbors in the East have reason to oppose any policy of ours that seems to them to bring West Germany nearer to the possession of nuclear weapons. Many specific initiatives to control the arms race and to create zones free from nuclear weapons will be necessary.

I suggest two major changes in attitudes, assumptions, and expectations:

The first is that we should emphasize more than we do the intangible or qualitative consequences of nuclear war. It is not enough to estimate the number of casualties, for it remains possible to say that it may be our duty to take the casualties for the sake of freedom. But in all probability freedom would be a casualty of nuclear war for a longer time than it would be a casualty of Communist power. The changes under Communism make the old "red or dead" contrast quite meaningless today. Polish "red" is different from Chinese "red." We in this country have a responsibility to prevent people from becoming either "red," in some new Stalinist form especially, or dead. But the choices are less simple than they were fifteen years ago when we learned to use these slogans. Seeing the issues in this way is a cure for nuclear recklessness in general and in particular for the habit of mind that assumes that any confrontation with the Soviet Union should be accompanied by ultimate threats. The rhetoric of an earlier period suggested that we were thinking of the risk of annihilation versus the risk of a permanent centralized Stalinist slavery, and that Americans were quite ready to choose the former risk not only for themselves but for hundreds of millions of people who never had a chance to choose.

Today the alternatives have changed and this rhetoric is less often heard, but there is need of a new rhetoric in much lower key that prepares the nation for more limited contrasts and risks. In addition to the new rhetoric, actual programs of deterrence need to be less tied, not only to nuclear weapons, but also to all forms of overt military resistance. Military defeat need not mean surrender to tyranny; rather it might be the beginning of resourceful resistance at many levels. Several of the Eastern European nations have shown that it is possible to resist Soviet tyranny after American rhetoric had condemned them to permanent slavery.

My second suggestion is that we abandon the assumption that at some stage in a conflict it would be permissible for the United States to be the first to use nuclear weapons. The possession of nuclear weapons to deter their use by the other side has justification, but if we were to use them first and so initiate the nuclear stage of a war, we would take upon ourselves the terrible responsibility for all that may come from such a war. So far the discussion of this matter has been carried on in strategic rather than moral terms. It may be debatable as to whether our government should announce the policy of avoiding the first use of the weapons. Perhaps for the present we should take advantage of the uncertainty in order to make the deterrence of any major attack by one country upon another with conventional weapons more effective. Whatever is done or not done is likely to leave us in an untidy state in this context. But when the chips are down, anything would be better than for our nation to be the one that initiates the nuclear stage of a war, making itself a nation of destroyers as well as a nation of the destroyed, and ending most of the continuities of corporate human life perhaps in the northern hemisphere. Even those who argue with a degree of relativism concerning better or worse consequences of choices should be able to draw the line absolutely at being the ones responsible for such monstrous deeds.

I believe that most of those who insist on the possible first use of nuclear weapons as a matter of policy do so in the conviction that this very insistence will prevent the occasion from arising in which it might, on their terms, be necessary to use the weapons. For this reason the devastating effects of even small nuclear weapons in such places as middle and eastern Europe are insufficiently emphasized. One of the best statements of the effect of the use of nuclear weapons on a limited scale in Europe is to be found in a book by one of the chief advocates of a tough policy in relation to the Soviet Union in Europe, Dean Acheson. He says of a limited nuclear war in Europe: "Our allies would see at once that the proposed strategy would consign them to a fate more devastating than would be compliance with the demands of the Soviet Union. The merit of this strategy, they would be told, would lie in its avoidance of 'all out' nuclear war, but it would seem to be all-out enough for them, even though designed to restrain the major participants from battering each other with hydrogen bombs."[12] Mr. Acheson, when he wrote those words in 1958, put his trust in the effect of our "all-out" nuclear deterrent combined with conventional NATO forces in Europe, attack on which would be an attack on the United States and would thus expose the Soviet Union to our full strategic nuclear power.

The reason for drawing the line at the use of even tactical nuclear weapons is not that they are more evil in themselves than equally destructive conventional weapons, but that they are likely to cause escalation of a conflict until it becomes an all-out nuclear war. Professor Henry Kissinger, who was one of the first to emphasize the role of tactical nuclear weapons in Western strategy, in his book *The Necessity for Choice*, draws back to some extent from this because of the difficulty of avoiding full escalation of the conflict if once the line between conventional and nuclear weapons is crossed. He says: "The dividing line between conventional and nuclear weapons is more familiar and therefore easier to maintain—assuming the will to do so—than any distinction within the spectrum of nuclear weapons."[13] In view of these considerations and in view of all that I have said about the qualitative effects of nuclear war and about the great difficulty in nuclear war of avoiding massive attacks on populations, our nation should not under any circumstances be the one to initiate the nuclear stage of a conflict. This would be a moral choice which we could not defend on the basis of any political advantage.

The distinction between low-yield tactical nuclear weapons and conventional weapons of comparable destructiveness may be more psychological than technical, but it is a fact of overwhelming importance for political and military decisions. Perhaps the temptation to disregard this distinction will come in Asia rather than in Europe—if only because there is military conflict in Southeast Asia—while the danger of Soviet aggression in Europe is now regarded as minimal. Reckless words have been uttered about the use of nuclear weapons to defoliate the jungles in Viet-Nam. In Asia also there is danger of escalation, but there is another dimension to the use of nuclear weapons in Asia that is in part a result of our use of them on Japan. It is a dimension of moral horror and of resentment at the thought that Westerners should so readily think of Asians as the targets for nuclear bombs. To use these bombs on Asian jungles might result in some local military advantages but in its moral and political effect it would be catastrophic. Our claims as defenders of freedom could hardly survive such a catastrophe; we would stand out as the most feared representatives of ruthless power. Here one can see with great clarity how technical and strategic decisions can be disastrously self-defeating if they are not controlled by political wisdom informed by moral sensitivity.

This paper has been limited to a consideration of some of the moral dilemmas that we confront in the world as it is. I have not discussed the kind of changes that we should seek in the political structure of the world because that is a vast subject in itself. Work for these changes is an essential part of our moral responsibility in international relations. The achievement of radical disarmament would create new moral opportunities for actions. At least we could live with less fear and act without the risk of total war. On the other hand the problems of power would remain because any possible scheme for disarmament would still leave some nations much stronger than others. Indeed, the idea of general and complete disarmament is really no more than a propagandist slogan because if that were to take place it would expose the present powerful nations to the pressure from the nations with the largest populations. But radical disarmament, including total nuclear disarmament, represents a reasonable goal, however difficult it may be to achieve it and to maintain it. A world that has taken some steps toward arms control on the way to radical disarmament would be in a very different condition, probably with a much more favorable moral climate for the relations between nations, than a world that is engaged in an uncontrolled arms race. We may be thankful that at the present time we have at least reached the stage where we are somewhere between these two worlds. We should take full advantage of opportunities to press forward on this front. Here the moral imperative and technical understanding must interact continually when political decisions are made.

I have not dealt with the role of the United Nations in its present form or as it may be strengthened. Again a very large part of our moral responsibility in international relations is in this area. The United Nations even now can provide important resources for limiting or overcoming .international conflict. This is clearest in those situations where the super-powers are not centrally involved as in the Near East and in the Congo, but even in conflicts between the United States and the Soviet Union the United Nations may help to create situations favorable to stability and may invent ways of saving face and of expediting settlements. In the Cuban crisis of 1962 the United Nations did help to gain time and to save face and thus to prevent the ultimate conflict. The overcoming of the most threatening conflicts of the cold war would give the United Nations new horizons for development for it presupposes cooperation between the great powers.

Any adequate discussion of ethics and international relations should give great attention to the development of international institutions. But such discussion cannot take the place of the consideration of the kind of moral issues which I have emphasized and which are very urgent. The logically most adequate institutions would not of themselves alter the location of real military or economic power or the power of populations. Legal restrictions upon national sovereignty would not cancel these realities. As I have said earlier, civil wars to capture the centers of international decision could take place within a world community under law and under institutional controls more effective than the United Nations as it now exists. Often world law and institutions of world government are presented as though they were fully dependable solutions of the problems of international relations. We should reject illusions in this regard while emphasizing the moral responsibility to work toward these goals of world order. As we move toward them we shall discover that many of the old problems which I have discussed will reappear in new forms and that new problems of relating order and freedom will appear on a world scale. Whatever the new difficulties, movement in this direction will offer new opportunities for solving many of humanity's problems, including the problem of survival.

NOTES

I am greatly indebted to the Council on Religion and International Affairs and especially to its representatives in Washington, Ernest Lefever and William O'Brien, for the invitation to prepare this paper and for making possible the extraordinarily stimulating and informative consultations at which it was discussed. I am grateful to the fifty academic experts and government officials whose knowledge and experience of the actual subject matter of international affairs greatly exceeds my own but who were willing to discuss the issues raised in this paper, most particularly to those who served as Moderators or first Discussants during these sessions: Robert C. Good, Edmund Gullion, John K. Moriarty, James E. Dougherty, Alain E. Enthoven and William H. Lewis. I learned much from these discussions and I came from them with deep admiration for the intellectual openness and the moral sensitivity of many persons who live close to the dilemmas of military policy and of foreign affairs. I am also grateful for the illumination that came from a discussion of this paper in a session with the Board of Trustees of the Council on Religion and International Affairs.

[2]Article 73

[3]*Realities of American Foreign Policy* (Princeton: Princeton University Press, 1954), p. 47

[4]*The United States in the World Arena* (New York: Harper, 1960), pp. 528 ff.

[5]See Daniel Bell, *The End of Ideology* (New York: The Free Press of Glencoe, 1959).

[6]*The Structure of Nations and Empires* (New York: Scribner, 1959), p. 295.

[7]April 19, 1964

[8]*Pacem in Terris*, Part V, Par 159

[9]April 17, 1964, pp. 101-102

[10]Recent discussions in Britain and the U.S. concerning the bombing of Dresden indicate that there are sober second thoughts on this subject. These discussions have been largely provoked by David Irving's recent book *The Destruction of Dresden* (New York: Holt, Rinehart & Winston, 1964).

[11]See especially his *War and the Christian Conscience* (Durham: Duke University Press, 1961), *passim.*

[12]*Power and Diplomacy* (Cambridge: Harvard University Press, 1958), p. 98.

[13](New York: Harper and Row, 1960), pp. 82-83.

Foreign Aid: Moral and Political Aspects

Victor C. Ferkiss

The United States has been engaged in massive programs of military, economic and technical assistance to other nations for more than sixteen years. Since the inception of the Marshall Plan in 1958 it has spent more than eighty billion dollars in providing such assistance. The Agency for International Development, the current successor to a whole series of foreign aid agencies, has some 15,000 employees, and sister organizations such as the Peace Corps employ thousands more. Foreign aid activities seem to have become a permanent aspect of American foreign relations.

Yet each year the foreign aid program comes before Congress in the form of legislation, and each year it is the occasion of heated debate —debate not merely about details or even the size of expenditures, but about such basic issues as the utility, effectiveness, and fundamental philosophy of our aid program. It is clear that foreign aid is neither unequivocally accepted nor fully understood either by the Congress or by the people of the United States as a whole. After sixteen years we have no consensus on a philosophy of foreign aid or on its place in American foreign policy, and the debate over fundamentals goes on.

Indeed, in recent years the tempo of the criticism of foreign aid has increased rather than declined. Not only have ordinary citizens and their legislative representatives been ever more critical of the cost and effectiveness of the aid program, but important academic and intellectual voices have been raised to question the basic rationale of the program. Is it really a useful means for countering Communist aggression? Is it really useful in helping to build a world in which American ideals will have a chance to flourish? Is it really a meaningful expression of America's humanitarian desire to help our less fortunate brother nations? The passage of time has stimulated this re-examination of the purposes and effectiveness of foreign aid by turning what many were ready to accept only as a temporary stopgap measure into a permanent burden. This questioning has also been encouraged by what to many appears to be a growing détente in the Cold War, at least in so far as the conflict between the United States and the Soviet Union is concerned—a détente which for many undermines the urgency and cogency of foreign aid as a Cold War weapon.

This national discussion of foreign aid does not lack for informed, articulate, and well-motivated spokesmen for a variety of points of view. Men such as Paul Hoffman, Gunnar Myrdal, Edward Mason and Frank Coffin have variously stated the case for a sustained and indeed accelerated program of assistance. Herbert Feis and others have chronicled the history and development of the program and its philosophy. Critics ranging from Hans J. Morgenthau, John Paton Davies, Jr., and Edward Banfield to the writers of journalistic exposés have attacked particular aspects of the program as well as many of its fundamental premises. Perhaps, then, the time has come to call a halt to new presentations of the issue and to speed up the process of national decision-making on the program's future.

Unfortunately, there is still a glaring gap in most discussions of the foreign aid problem, a gap to be found in discussions of American foreign policy generally: the absence of any adequate discussion of the moral aspects of foreign aid. This is not to say that existing formulations have entirely neglected the value implications of the subject, even less to assert that all sides of the argument have not made use of the moralistic rhetoric endemic to American political controversy. But there has been little attempt to examine systematically the foreign aid program, its justifications, and its effects from the viewpoint of the Judaeo-Christian moral tradition—which is still the central element in the moral consensus underlying American democratic institutions. It is the purpose of this essay to call attention to this gap and at least to suggest the nature of the moral dimension which so far has been largely lacking in discussions of the foreign aid program.

This is not a systematic moral treatise nor an attempt to discuss comprehensively all aspects of foreign aid problems—political, economic, and administrative. The author is neither a professional moralist nor a professional specialist in the field of foreign aid. But as a political scientist who believes that policy questions are a legitimate concern of his discipline, that it is impossible to discuss policy without discussing values, and that the foreign aid question is one of the most important policy questions facing the United States today, he has attempted to set forth what he considers to be the most important moral questions underlying the debate on foreign aid.

The Basis of Moral Obligation

No question has more engaged the attention of mankind throughout its history than the nature and origin of moral obligation. For most peoples, as for many schools of philosophy, questions of value cannot be separated from questions of fact. For them ethics and cosmology are congruent—the universe is a moral universe. It is a characteristic of modern thought that, especially in the post-Kantian period, the two spheres have been separated. Much of the political philosophy dominant in the Western world today is based upon this separation of facts and values.

The most important traditional expression of this political philosophy is found in the social contract theory in its various forms. The lowest common denominator of this theory, which for many people is the basis of modern democracy and international law, is that individual men are inherently free agents with no intrinsic obligations to anyone or anything outside themselves. Obligations can arise only as a result of consent. Where there is no agreement to an obligation there is no obligation. Rights and duties arise out of acts of gratuitous free choice or physical necessity and are operative only when there is formal and open agreement by the persons involved.

This concept of the nature of social morality coexists uneasily in the modern Western world with other older doctrines. There are many who still hold to the tradition of classical natural law, which maintains in effect that moral values are not arbitrary choices of the human will (as they essentially are in the contract theory) but are inherent in the very nature of man and of the world in which he lives. In this tradition, "is" does imply "ought," to the scandal of the theory's positivist critics. In the traditional view rights and duties stem from what one is and what the subjects of one's concern are. Reason, upon examining the nature of things, prescribes the nature of the morally admissible relationships.

Though there are many who would not accept this theory in its pure form, it is constantly recurring under various disguises: moral imperatives drawn from Marxian economic determinism, psychoanalytical definitions of mental health, and "functional" theories in the behavioral sciences, among others, tend to derive norms from the observed nature of things and to postulate what are in effect obligations arising from descriptive statements. However, such systems of morality, although they may provide the substance or content of the moral obligation, do not explain why the moral obligation binds in the first place. For if the contract theorist bases willingness to fulfill contracts merely upon personal honor or on the observable self-regarding consequences of the universal non-performance of contracts—in other words, appeals to passions and selfishness—the adherents of natural law and analogous theories have even less emotionally and intellectually satisfying motives for behaving acceptably.

The natural law theorist can say that it is contrary to reason to commit murder, but why *should* we always act rationally? Why *should* we seek to be in tune with the dialectic of history, or choose mental health rather than illness, or do what is functional rather than dysfunctional for our society? After all, there is a sense in which acting irrationally or unnaturally is part of the natural capacity of man.

It is here that the uniqueness of the position of the believer in supernatural religion and a personal God is most evident. The difference between the religious and the non-religious approaches to problems of morality is not, as some on both sides foolishly believe, primarily in the area of content but in that of motivation. The person who is guided in his personal and social behavior by religious norms believes that rights and duties are imposed upon him by his Creator. Even if these duties are implicit in the nature of things and discoverable through reason—as the natural law theorist holds—as well as through revelation, they are to be fulfilled not simply because they exist but because the Personal Being who has established them—by creating both the agent and the objects of moral choice—so desires. The oft-used expression, "The brotherhood of men under the fatherhood of God," is more than a cliché of rhetoric. It implies the proposition that one's obligations toward one's fellow men are based not on one's own desires, or even on the objective fact of the existence of these obligations, but upon the fact that a common Creator wishes these obligations to be fulfilled. They are obligations to Him, and they exist independently of the desires and deservings of either the subjects or objects of rights and duties.

This distinction between a religiously based and a non-religiously based morality is no mere extraneous excursion into moral or metaphysical theorizing. There may be considerable parallelism between the substance of the moral propositions held by persons of various religious faiths, and by non-believers who find in the natural law, custom or social contract the basis of obligation (indeed, there must be such agreement if pluralist democracy is to survive, especially in an increasingly global society), but the difference in the grounding of moral obligation is not a merely formalistic distinction. On occasion, differing beliefs about the origin of moral obligation can have logical and therefore practical consequences for substantive moral stands. These differences can enlarge or contract the nature, extent, and direction of one's obligations, the timing of their fulfillment, and the priority given to one over another. The fact that moral obligations are objective rather than subjective means that one may have obligations toward the spouse he no longer cares for and who no longer cares for him, toward the undeserving as well as the deserving poor, toward the madman who rejects our attempts to save his life.

The objective rather than the subjective nature of moral obligations is a major element in the justification of foreign aid programs. It is obvious that in accordance with the traditionally accepted norms of moral obligation within international society, obligations only exist when they are freely undertaken as the result of contractual agreement, as in the case of treaties, bilateral or multilateral. Rare exceptions exist in international law where standards are so universally accepted that for practical purposes they can be considered binding even on those nations that have not accepted them formally. Such instances usually are limited to semi-technical matters such as the offshore jurisdictions of states. However, in the nineteenth century the general revulsion against the slave trade led to attempts to suppress it on the high seas even when carried on by nations such as the United States which had not adhered to the relevant conventions. More recently, the Nuremberg trials represent a significant attempt to reintroduce a natural law concept of "crimes against humanity" into the working framework of international law.

Were formal convention (i.e., contract) the sole basis of obligation in the international sphere, it is obvious that the United States would have no obligation to aid any but those it chose to aid and on such terms as it chose. The obligations that arose out of foreign aid agreements would themselves then constitute moral obligations, but there would be no obligation to enter into such agreements in the first place. Although agreements entered into on the basis of self-interest could be morally good if all parties to the agreement benefited and no third parties were injured, it would be impossible to allege any other justification than self-interest for a nation's actions in the international realm; and it is doubtful whether self-interest alone can ever provide an adequate basis for an effective long-term foreign aid program, especially when the most evident early results of such a program are likely to be increased popular unrest, political repression, and growing ingratitude and resentment toward foreign benefactors. A recognition of our objective moral responsibility for the well-being of our fellow men may be absolutely necessary to sustain the kind of aid program which is required to create a world environment in which free societies may grow and flourish.

But do nations as well as individuals have God-given objective moral responsibilities? Is there not a difference between the system of moral obligations which bind individuals and the necessarily different system which obtains among nation states?

It is our contention that, rightly understood, the same moral obligations which bind men as individuals are also binding on them as members of a collectivity. Much confusion has been generated on this score in recent years as a consequence of the rise of Protestant "neo-orthodoxy" and its ideological derivative sometimes termed "Christian realism," which stresses the effects of original sin in the world and the consequent imperfectability of human society. According to the "realist" position there is such a radical dichotomy between the things of the natural and the supernatural world, and the natural world is so caught in the grip of evil, that there is little hope for virtuous acts taking place in the world, especially on a social level. Man may be capable of being moral on an individual level, but society as a collective is always immoral. This need not lead to a quietism, as some of the doctrine's critics might allege, since individuals must continue to promote justice when and where they can. But justice in this world will be hard to find and of short duration.

One of the consequences of this pessimism—a psychologically rather than a logically necessary consequence—is that one must accept the notion that persons acting through social groupings or governments will rarely be capable of living up to Christian norms. From this it follows, largely again for psychological reasons, that states must be judged not by religious moral standards but by standards of their own, standards of "this world." Individuals may be called upon to be truthful, magnanimous, and self-sacrificing, but not nations. If this were in fact the case then there would obviously be no possibility of justifying foreign aid on moral grounds or on any grounds other than the donor nation's own political, economic or military self-interest.

Attempts to get around this fact have led to more refined theories of self-interest, according to which generosity is good for the political and mental health of the nation which chooses to be generous. In brief, this theory holds that even if there is no moral obligation to aid other nations—that is, no moral obligation to them—such programs involve a moral obligation to ourselves. If we aid foreign nations simply on a directly interested, *quid pro quo* basis, it is argued, we demean ourselves; by giving generously of our resources even when there seems to be no direct benefit to ourselves we uplift ourselves morally. In other words, gratuitous and humanitarian foreign aid is good for our character. Max Millikan and W. W. Rostow claim that we need "the challenge of world development to keep us from the stagnation of smug prosperity." "Our duty to lighten the load of human misery is derivative from, indeed it is the reflex of our duty to ourselves as a great nation . . ." is the way that Professor Joseph Cropsey puts it.

This argument has some merits. Although it resembles the Puritan concept of morality as that which manifests the virtue of the saved, and is in this sense selfish, it is not completely incompatible with traditional Greek and Christian notions of virtue, in which inward states come to reflect outward actions even if originally our inward motivation was narrowly self-regarding. Such notions, however, suffer from the fact that they provide no clues as to how generous we should be, to whom, and under what circumstances. As long as we feel that inner glow we are all right, and the history of private charity on the domestic level suggests that that inner glow may come very cheaply indeed.

But, basically, for the "realist," Christian or otherwise, foreign aid like diplomacy and weaponry is one of the things of "this world," not subject to the standards of religious morality. It is the job of the statesman, according to Professor Edward C. Banfield, to risk his own moral health for the sake of society—to do "what by the standards of ordinary personal relations is evil in order to secure the public welfare." What is so pernicious in the "realist" dichotomy between the norms of individual and political morality is the simplistic view of individual morality itself which it implies. *Of course* no statesman is under the obligation to give his nation's wealth to poorer nations without stint, *but* neither is any father under an obligation to give to charity the money needed to pay for health insurance for the family, for the braces on Johnny's teeth, or even, ordinarily, for Susie's music lessons. *Of course* nations sometimes use force to counter aggression, *but* morality, as well as the law, permits the citizen to use violence on occasion to protect his property and personal rights as well as his person and that of his neighbor against marauders.

From the way in which some people hold to the conviction that the standards applicable to individual behavior cannot be applied to nations (Dean Acheson's harsh denunciation of the application of morality to foreign policy and to foreign-aid programs in particular as "misleading" and a source of confusion typifies this kind of criticism), one can only conclude that such persons also believe that all individuals are called upon by their religious principles to live according to the Counsels of Perfection—without family or property, eschewing all forms of force under all circumstances, and with a mission to tell the whole truth at all times even when the whole truth might seriously injure the listener or others. In fact, of course, the norms of morality generally accepted within the Judaeo-Christian tradition assume that it is the nature of man to live in society, with duties which differ in relation to different people and in different circumstances. Man's God-created nature necessitates his living in certain kinds of relations to others and the nature of these relationships implies particular patterns of rights and obligations.

The duties of states are simply the duties of citizens and statesmen in a particular context, and thus it is possible to judge the actions of states by the same standards that are used in judging the actions of individuals. The difference lies in the different relationships and contexts within which the actions occur. If one is telling the truth one tells it in relation to who has a right to what information in what context. If one is repelling violence one uses force to the extent necessary to establish or defend one's rights. If one gives aid to the needy, one does it in terms of the differential obligations one has to different human beings, based on the degree of the relationship and the extent to which one shares this obligation with other persons. The same considerations apply to a country's foreign policy.

If one accepts the principle that all human beings are obligated to seek to bring about a state of affairs on earth which is compatible with the objective canons of morality, then the people of every nation, including the United States, have an obligation to use whatever resources they have at their disposal to bring about that objectively desirable situation which might best be called the common good or the public interest of humanity. This international common good has many facets: an adequate standard of living, freedom from armed conflict, and respect for the rights and freedom of individuals, social groups, and states. That which contributes to these ends is a positive moral act. More than this it is, within the limits set by the powers of the actor and the situation in which he finds himself, a moral duty as well. The United States had and has a moral duty to do what it appropriately can to bring about the international common good.

Keeping in mind the dual principles that obligations are not arbitrarily chosen by the moral agent but derive from a divinely ordained moral code implicit in the nature of man and his environment, and that there is no radical difference between the moral obligations of men as individuals and as the members of political entities, we must now turn to an examination of the various aspects of America's contemporary foreign aid program, the justification for them advanced by their proponents, and the nature of the moral issues raised by the program.

Foreign Aid as a Defense Against Communism

The first major justification for our foreign aid program, at least as far as the American people and the American Congress were concerned, and the overriding justification even today, is its value as a defense against communism. This is true not only of directly military assistance but of economic assistance also. Although the Marshall Plan of 1948, from which our whole foreign-aid rationale as well as the current bureaucratic structure stems, was open to Communist as well as non-Communist countries (for a brief period Czechoslovakia and Poland hesitantly considered joining before being brought up short by the Soviet Union), the Marshall Plan cannot be considered outside of the context of the Truman Doctrine and the assumption of responsibility by the United States for the creation of situations of military strength and economic stability which would prevent further Soviet expansion in Europe.

Does this fundamental aim in and of itself present problems of moral justification? The answer obviously is no. Indeed—and this is an important because too often overlooked point—the answer is a definite and resounding no. The United States is certainly justified in protecting itself against the spread of a creed and system of government which it regards as threatening the continued existence of the United States as a political entity and as threatening the rights of man generally; indeed, it has a duty to do so. That duty stems from the very same moral principle of stewardship which is at the root of the American obligation to succor the needy of other nations in purely economic terms. Our obligation to aid nations to resist the economic and military pressure exerted against their national liberties by Communist states is simply a facet of our general obligation toward the international common good.

This simple fact has been obscured in discussion for a number of reasons. First of all many persons would deny, if only implicitly or at a subconscious level, that a world dominated by Communist states would be morally inferior to a world dominated by the United States or its allies. In part such denial stems from noble motives. The many political, social, economic and moral ills which exist in the non-Communist world are a responsibility of Americans and other non-Communists in a way that the ills of the Communist world are not, since they are ills which we can more readily do something about. There is therefore sometimes a natural tendency for us to judge ourselves more harshly than we judge the Communists, and thus to underestimate the differences in the character of life under the two systems.

A more important reason, perhaps, is the assumption made by many that since the taking of human life and the infliction of pain upon any creature is, in and of itself, an evil, therefore the use of the degree of violence involved in war and implicit in preparations for war can never really be morally justified. This is not the place to discuss the complex moral issues involved in war and the use of violence. Suffice it to point out that an implicit or unconscious pacifism (and sometimes a conscious one) has weighed heavily in the condemnation not only of military aid (where such pacifist attitudes would at least be germane, however correct or incorrect they might be intrinsically) but of all aid associated with countries or programs where considerations of military defense against the Soviet Union or mainland China were especially important. This of course has meant ignoring or downgrading whatever real, if subsidiary, merits such aid may have.

But most important of all in obscuring the moral quality of aid designed to help other nations resist Communist pressures has been a kind of moral stance which can only be defined as a degraded Puritanism or Manichaeanism. It is the political parallel of the feeling that whatever is pleasurable is bad and whatever is unpleasant is good, that anything you want is probably bad for you and that virtue consists entirely in self-denial and asceticism. The translation of this principle to the international order leads to the conclusion that actions taken in one's own interests are morally suspect, and that virtue consists solely in acting contrary to what one deems to be one's own self-interest. Although it is true that from the point of view of subjective individual moral dispositions, self-sacrifice has always been recognized by the religions of the West as an important element in moral training and action, and although the danger of serving oneself to the neglect of one's moral obligations is something against which nations as well as individuals must be on guard, nevertheless it certainly does not follow that what is objectively moral and ethically good automatically entails sacrifice or that the sacrifice of one's own interests is necessarily morally and ethically good.

Just because it is in the interest of the United States as a nation to strengthen other nations to resist Communist aggression does not mean that this is not also an objectively moral aim. In this case the interests of the United States and the international public interest in fact coincide; and an act which serves them both is not only morally permissible but morally good. Indeed, any acts which are mutually beneficial to two or more parties do not thereby become less acceptable ethically simply because they do not involve sacrifice on the part of one and direct benefit only to the other. International arrangements which serve the particular interests of their participants (provided of course they do not do so at the expense of third parties) are in an objective ethical sense good in themselves: international prosperity and order are intrinsically desirable, and actions which promote them are therefore good *per se*. There is a sense of course in which the sacrifices involved in certain kinds of foreign-aid programs may be of special personal spiritual benefit to the donors of such aid—at least to the extent to which they are conscious of them as sacrifices—but a program of aid given for purely humanitarian objectives is no more or less morally just *per se* than a mutually advantageous trade pact, nor (to return to our immediate context) any more so than a mutually advantageous military alliance.

If it is accepted that defense against communism—including defense by military means—is morally desirable in itself, then criticism of aid programs designed to promote resistance to Communist threats from within and without must be directed not against the ends of the programs but against the particular side-effects or over-all consequences of the programs.

The moral objections to aid given for limiting Communist expansion fall under two broad headings: the programs are said (1) to strengthen unpopular or undemocratic regimes, and (2) to encourage the involvement of otherwise neutral nations in the Cold War.

The granting of aid to undemocratic regimes is criticized mainly by those who regard themselves as liberals. Those raising this particular objection hold that military aid and related economic assistance to regimes which are not popularly chosen or which lack minimal public support is immoral in that it enables these regimes to stem the forces of popular discontent and thereby to keep themselves in power. In so far as we justify our opposition to communism by our belief in democracy, it is said to be hypocritical and self-defeating to defend democracy by supporting undemocratic political systems. Most moral criticism of our aid to South Korea, South Vietnam, Taiwan, and various military regimes in Latin America is based on these grounds. A paradoxically similar variant of this argument is proffered by critics of aid programs on the extreme right. They attack American aid to socialist governments, by which they rightly mean most of the regimes in underdeveloped countries, on the assumption that such regimes by stifling economic freedom are also anti-democratic.

To the extent that free political institutions are a requisite of the human dignity which is a natural right of man and which we are morally bound to help all men secure, to retard the development of free institutions anywhere is a moral evil. If our aid helps a landed oligarchy maintain itself in power, or enables a bureaucracy to inhibit the growth of a private sector of the economy which might provide the base for a meaningful political opposition, we have done the joint cause of freedom and justice, which is our own cause, a disservice. But to say that such effects of our action are wrong does not necessarily make the action of giving aid itself morally wrong. As individuals and as citizens we live in a world in which we are forced to choose between alternatives not of our own making. The only means of avoiding this dilemma is to enshrine one moral principle as an absolute and to give it priority in every situation: the defense of the free world against communism, for example, or the unity of the working class, or the abolition of armed conflict. But this means ignoring the claims of competing moral principles which may also be relevant to a given situation. To "do right though the heavens fall" when such a catastrophe might be averted is almost necessarily to do wrong. All actions have multiple consequences. Virtually no human act has unalloyed consequences for either good or evil. We are therefore forced to choose between greater and lesser goods, greater and lesser evils.

One reason that many have erroneously concluded that social morality is substantively different from individual morality is that the mixture of good and evil consequences is so much more apparent in the actions of states which perforce take place on a "broad screen," larger than ordinary life-size, involving more people and wider ramifications than the actions of individuals ordinarily do. But the general norms of morality apply to governmental as well as to private actions, which must ultimately be judged by their consequences, intended or unintended, insofar as these are known or knowable. One has an obligation in each individual instance to gain as much knowledge of and insight into the factual situation as possible. This done one must be guided by the dual principle that it is never permissible directly to perform an unjust act in order to gain any end, however just, and that that action is morally more just (compared either with other actions or with inaction) which brings about the greatest good.

This means in practice that in each case of foreign assistance designed to prevent the spread of communism one must ask whether any loss of freedom, prosperity or human dignity suffered by the population as a whole would be greater or less as a result of the granting of aid than it would be if the nation in question were allowed to fall under Communist domination and just how likely it is that the nation would in fact come under Communist domination without our help.

We also must ask whether or not the aid in question helps or hurts the cause of freedom in the world at large. It is not solely a question of whether the people of country X (now suffering under a military dictatorship) would be more or less free under a Communist regime but also whether the fall of country X to communism would be more deleterious to the over-all cause of freedom in the world than the continuance of an unpopular regime in that country. In each specific instance the United States and other nations giving foreign aid must do what they can to assure that foreign assistance does the cause of local liberty as little harm as possible, but they cannot make the facile assumption that every local or immediate increase in material prosperity or political freedom is automatically a blow for freedom in the long run or that no country is deserving of military or other aid until it has become a model society according to American standards.

At the same time that one engages in this essentially utilitarian calculus one must beware acts which constitute direct attacks on human freedom and dignity. For instance, American assistance which seeks to increase another nation's ability to resist internal subversion must not include direct support of or collaboration in activities which suppress the civil liberties of the population; and American aid which seeks to increase the over-all economic well-being of a recipient nation must never take a form which makes the rich richer at the expense of the poor. Such actions would be inherently unjust and even as means to a desired good end are never morally permissible.

The problem of military and economic programs with an anti-Communist intent which allegedly enlarge the scope of the Cold War is equally complex. The contention is that nations are put under subtle pressures to take sides in the Cold War in order to obtain economic assistance for development or to enhance their prestige or military power and that this constitutes an enlargement of the area of conflict and is therefore counter to the general international interest in peace. But actually the posture of neutralism assumed by many nations today is possible only because the strength of the non-Communist world balances Communist strength. The Cold War is a reality; it is not that it is extended by aid agreements but rather that the agreements take cognizance of it in a manner which makes it less likely that the Communists will win it by default.

Our discussion has so far centered upon aid given to non or anti-Communist nations to strengthen them militarily or economically against Communist aggression. In view of the origins of our aid program, the areas of activity of our basic foreign-aid agencies and the relative amounts spent in our overseas assistance activities, such an emphasis is natural. But what of aid given to nations that are already officially Communist? Such aid, though minimal in amount and marginal in significance, has already been given to Yugoslavia and Poland and may be given to other countries as well. Does it raise any special moral issues?

The answer would at first seem to be necessarily in the affirmative. After all, much of the moral rationale for foreign aid has been the defense of freedom in the Cold War, and at first glance Communist nations would hardly seem to qualify for aid so motivated. Even if one admits that Communist peoples too are our brethren, it could be cogently argued that compared with our other responsibilities, and considering the responsibilities which their own comrades have to these nations, there is no reason why our relatively limited resources should be used to aid these countries. In addition, the same arguments that apply against giving aid to right-wing dictatorships or doctrinaire socialist regimes that threaten the foundations of the political pluralism necessary to democracy would seem to apply with equal or greater force to outright Communist regimes. In their case the argument that a particular non-Communist dictatorship is likely to be more readily modified or less permanent than a dictatorship which is a member of an advancing Communist bloc would seem to have no force at all.

But in fact the situation is not this simple and the same arguments which apply to the morality of foreign aid in general apply to the morality of aid to Communist nations. If we believe in brotherhood as a motivation for aid, Communist nations are composed of human beings who are entitled to at least thoughtful consideration as possible recipients of such aid. More specifically, if aid is to be given to non-democratic states when and to the extent that it contributes to creating the preconditions of a more humane internal political order, then we must ask whether aid to Communist states in a specific case does or does not so contribute. Just as aid to a non-Communist dictatorship would be evil if it strengthened special economic and political privileges within the state, but not so if it made growth toward freedom possible, so aid to a Communist state would be justified or not by the same considerations. If states are aided because strengthening their economic and political stability helps keep them out of the Communist camp, one can justify aid to already Communist states if and to the extent it allows them greater flexibility within that camp. For our prime motivation in using aid as a weapon against communism is not our desire to lead an abstract ideological crusade but our desire to prevent a world situation in which a growing, increasingly united and hostile Communist bloc threatens world peace and our security. Economic or military aid which helps a nation, whatever its official ideology, to move further away from commitment to such a bloc is just as useful as aid which helps keep a nation from being compelled to join it.

One can argue that even if aid to a Communist nation does not strengthen the Communist power structure within the nation as such, it strengthens the nation as a whole, and makes a basically undemocratic system more viable. To some extent this is true, but this is just as true of aid given to many neutralist states which are, and are likely to remain, dictatorships directed by a narrow elite. If one puts aside the facile and false belief that economic development is in and of itself something which leads to a free political order, the situations are parallel and, *mutatis mutandis*, any arguments about the utility of economic assistance as a means toward democracy, stability and peaceful international conduct on the part of non-Communist nations apply with equal force to Communist ones.

Foreign Aid to Promote Economic Development

Economic aid is provided for a number of purposes and, as Professor Hans Morgenthau has suggested in his classic and influential article, "Preface to a Political Theory of Foreign Aid," it is important for us to distinguish among them.

Economic aid, as we have indicated in the preceding pages, is frequently a concomitant of military aid, in which case it is given primarily in order to strengthen a country to resist the expansion of aggressive communism. Economic aid may also be extended in order to keep from collapse a country which does not have the means for maintaining itself. France does this for some of its former African dependencies; the United States has done it for Libya and Jordan. Insofar as such aid prevents the disorder and suffering which presumably would follow governmental collapse it serves a moral purpose; however, if it serves merely to bulwark the status quo against a more satisfactory alternative it does the citizens of the aided nation a disservice.

Usually by economic aid is meant aid to promote the kind of economic development within a country which will provide it with a basis for self-sustaining economic growth. At first blush it would seem unlikely that there could be much in the way of moral objections to the granting of economic aid for development, but in fact both the nature of the aid provided and our motives for providing it raise a number of moral issues. This is especially true of the two aberrant forms of aid distinguished by Professor Morgenthau—aid for the purposes of prestige and bribery—which ordinarily masquerade as aid for the purpose of promoting economic development.

The first question which must be asked about programs designed to promote economic development is whether they are effective, and, secondly, even if effective, whether they sometimes have such seriously injurious side effects as to render them immoral.

It is important to know whether aid provided for economic development is effective or not, because if it fails to accomplish any useful purpose we certainly have no obligation to provide it. Indeed, it would be immoral to raise hopes only to disappoint them.

To answer the question of how effective economic aid is, it is important not to overestimate the actual capacity of underdeveloped countries to absorb economic assistance. Foreign capital and technical assistance cannot turn underdeveloped countries into modern industrial nations overnight. These infusions from without cannot substitute for (although they can assist in promoting) such prerequisite changes as those in education, traditional social structures and customs, and, perhaps especially, in personal attitudes. Because of the close interdependence of the many factors needed to create and sustain a modern economy, full development of underdeveloped countries will not be an accomplished fact for generations at least, even where the peoples involved are willing to take all the steps necessary to make this development possible. Nations are not simple entities which can be given gifts which will make them happier and better off. They are complex organisms with personalities and ways of life of their own, which are necessarily drastically altered by the process of economic assistance and development. To pour more capital into a country than it is ready to use effectively can result in unnecessary inflation which might further widen the gap between rich and poor or wipe out an independent middle class. In such cases this excessive foreign aid would be not only wasteful but clearly immoral.

On the other hand, the granting of too little economic assistance can be as undesirable as the granting of too much. To disrupt a country's traditional balance and way of life and encourage discontent and instability without being willing to commit the resources needed to bring the country to the point of self-sustaining growth would also be immoral.

Given the complexity, subtlety, and long-term nature of the problems involved, there would seem to be some question of whether one country should ever be dependent in large measure on the gratuitous acts of others for the course of its development. Would it not be more in keeping with their dignity as full members of the world community and with the human dignity of their citizens, if some means could be found to enable the underdeveloped nations to earn the funds necessary for their own development? Economic experts have estimated that from 50 to 100 percent of all foreign aid given to the developing nations over the last decade has been wiped out by changes in the terms of trade during the same period, largely as a result of the superior economic position of the industrially developed countries. Support for more favorable terms of trade for the underdeveloped world and for price stabilization agreements for the raw materials they produce might be a more moral approach to the problem of assisting their development than the constant provision of foreign aid as a dole.

Although the underdeveloped nations would still need help in the form of technical assistance, they would no longer be in the position of suppliants and it might be possible to avoid much of the rancor and bitterness which seems an inevitable concomitant of a lack of mutuality in a relationship—of an enforced position of dependency. Such an arrangement would have an additional advantage in that these countries would then have only themselves to blame for their own mistakes and might thus be more willing to take whatever remedial action might be necessary to reach the goals they seek. It is our obligation as moral beings to be aware of the subtlety and complexity of the issues involved in trying to help others and of the damage as well as the good that can result from intruding ourselves into their affairs.

But even with better terms of trade some form of foreign-aid program for the underdeveloped world is probably here to stay. Even were the Cold War (still the principal rationale for our aid program today) to end abruptly, world public opinion has come to take it for granted that the more favored nations have an obligation to help those in need of economic assistance. Infusions of capital and technical and administrative know-how from outside may help to cushion the shock of the economic and social transformation which the underdeveloped nations must undergo if they are to reach the goals they have set for themselves, but this outside interference can also serve to skew the workings of these societies in unforeseen and undesirable ways. Morality dictates not only that aid programs be based on the best knowledge available but that they be tempered with a goodly amount of humility and with respect for the judgment of others. Although we have a perfect right to refuse to support projects which, because of political, economic or administrative problems, do not seem to be useful means to the joint goal of national development, we cannot make our help contingent on the recipient doing things in exactly the way we might consider optimum. After all, the free activity and consequent growth in judgment of the recipient should be an integral part of any aid project. Besides we could be wrong. One of the reasons that the Peace

Corps has enjoyed greater popularity in most nations than other American aid ventures has been that the nature of its work and the level of its volunteers, acting in an operational rather than an advisory capacity and under the direction of the local community, have made them seem less like agents of moral colonialism.

But money and technical assistance alone cannot guarantee that a nation will be able to take on the characteristics of a modern state. It must first of all be willing to do and to suffer those things which are the necessary prerequisites of fully effective utilization of the capital and technical help needed for modernizing its economy. However, this does not mean that we can insist on moral grounds that countries must first completely overhaul their social and political structures as a condition of receiving aid (as we have tried to do in the Alliance for Progress). We cannot really expect a dominant class (one which, incidentally, tends to have a near monopoly on the skills needed to modernize their economy) to be enthusiastic about a program which is contingent on their committing suicide. As John Paton Davies, Jr. observes in his witty and perceptive little book, *Foreign and Other Affairs: A View from the Radical Center,* history suggests that economic development comes first, and only afterwards changes in the direction of democracy and stability, not the other way around.

The Western world has gained economic prosperity—at least for most of its citizens—by creating a particular social pattern. We are generally convinced that only societies with certain similar features can gain the economic growth which most of their inhabitants seem freely to want, and we are probably right. But which elements are essential to the pattern and just how similar must the pattern be? Until we know the answers to these questions we must proceed with caution and beware of trying to force others into our image as a result of pride in ourselves, failure to respect their national personalities, or sheer laziness or lack of imagination.

The moral justifications offered for foreign aid overlap each other considerably. As we have seen, a primary justification for foreign aid is its alleged efficacy as a means for stemming the spread of communism. Another major reason given is set forth as global economic development, often blurring the question of whether such development is a good in itself or good primarily because it stems the spread of communism, either directly or by promoting the cause of peace and democracy in the world. In the discussion of economic development this blurring serves the practical domestic American political purpose of enabling justifications to combine both selfish motivations (defense of American security against communism) and altruistic ones (helping other people economically), a kind of enlightened self-interest dear to the American heart. But does foreign aid given to promote economic development in fact also serve to promote peace and democracy?

Insofar as economic development stimulated by foreign aid does serve the cause of peace it is surely an unmitigated moral good. Peace is an intrinsic good which both parties to foreign-aid agreements cannot only agree on but share. It is a good which is not lessened by being shared by two parties but in a sense is increased. The discussion of peace as an end of foreign aid thus presents not so much moral as practical problems, but these practical problems themselves have moral dimensions.

The assumption is that economically developing nations will be less unstable than undeveloped ones and therefore less likely to become political power vacuums into which Communist powers might be tempted to move, with the attendant danger of direct confrontation of Communist and Western forces. It is also assumed that developing nations are less likely to cause local wars, which our foreign policy regards as bad in themselves as well as possible occasions for involvement of the great powers. The further assumption is made that economically developing nations are more likely to be democratic than they otherwise would be, and because they are democratic will be more likely to resist capitulation to Communist aggression and also more likely to refrain from attacking their neighbors, thus aiding peace on two counts. These assumptions cannot be accepted without question. Let us examine separately the two pillars on which this assumption rests: (1) that economic development means stability and therefore peace and (2) that economic development means democracy and therefore peace.

We must first of all bear in mind that we are talking about developing nations, not already developed ones. Nations with assured high standards of living may or may not have a propensity to peacefulness; being economically sated they probably do, though even they can be psychologically insecure and engage in wars to protect or enhance their status. But this is not the point. Here we are speaking of the nations of Asia, Africa, Latin America and the Middle East which have not yet attained the widespread high level of prosperity enjoyed by the developed nations.

The evidence seems to indicate that the process of development promotes instability rather than stability. An absolutely stagnant nation is quiescent, both in its internal and external relations. Yesterday's Yemen or Guatemala was no cause of difficulty. Internal political crises come about after the traditional social controls are strained or broken.

People see the possibility of a better life, yet the revolution of rising expectations outpaces real economic growth. Social unrest grows. Governments cannot keep the promises of prosperity for all that are implicit in their economic programs and even in the fact of newly won independence. The result is that political disquiet grows and the danger of Communist infiltration and situations tempting Communist aggression also grow. This explains the paradox that a little foreign aid—compared to need—is likely to bring about less rather than more stability.

In some cases this instability serves as a basis for Communist infiltration, as in awakening Latin America. In other countries this unrest may be vented by nationalistic governments which divert attention from unsolved or insoluble economic problems by foreign adventurism, as in the Arab pressures on Israel and the Indonesian attacks on Malaysia. This adventurism involves the threat of local wars and the danger that these may escalate into global ones. Economic development breaks the old mold; what the future holds—especially the immediate future—is not necessarily political stability and peace.

The case of democracy is similar. Economic growth may be a precondition of democracy, but it is not by itself sufficient to ensure democracy. Prosperous, economically developed nations may have a tendency to become democratic—though this is by no means certain —but here we are talking of nations still developing. Can you have a democratic resolution of the conflicts created in the process of modernization? Perhaps, but this is at least a moot question. The growth of "guided democracies" and of military and one-party dictatorships in Asia, Africa and the Middle East would suggest that it is not likely.

It is true that the people of these areas shout for freedom and democracy, but they define these terms differently than they are defined in the United States and the Western world generally. For them democracy means a government by people of their own race and color, seeking to satisfy their needs, primarily their desperate economic needs. It does not mean a government responsible to the people through regular institutionalized channels, one which allows opposition and civil liberties. In practice it means rule by a small revolutionary intelligentsia, seeking to develop the nation by centralizing power in their own hands. Such governments may find it expedient for the purposes of maintaining domestic morale, for keeping foreign powers on the hook, and thus enhancing their own power, to create situations of instability (witness the activities of Nasser, Nkrumah, Castro and Sukarno). Democratization or popular rule in the form it has taken in the emerging nations has not and will not necessarily contribute to peace.

What are the moral implications of all this? Although we cannot insist that other countries adopt exactly our form of government or economy we should attempt to be highly sensitive not only to the effect our aid programs have on the economic well-being of the countries aided but also to their effect on the status of civil and personal freedom within these countries and on these countries' attitudes toward their neighbors. It seems clear that morality dictates that whenever possible highest priority be given those programs which especially benefit that part of the population most in need and least able to help themselves, to programs which enhance the possibilities of responsible self-determination for individuals within the society, and to those which promote cooperation and unity among the countries within a given region.

To the extent that peace is a morally desirable end of foreign aid we must be cautious about extending aid to societies where such aid will have a disturbing rather than a pacifying effect. Difficult practical and moral choices will have to be made if the United States is called on to undertake an aid program which improves the standard of living of a nation but which may make it less free, more open to subversion, or more likely to embark on a dangerously adventurous foreign policy. If some nations demonstrate that for them economic development goes hand in hand with a general national aggrandizement which threatens the development of other nations and the peace and stability of their region and the world, it may be necessary to cut off aid to them entirely.

Some critics of our foreign-aid program and its rationale have complained that much needless difficulty has resulted from trying to subsume under the general heading of aid given for economic development grants which were really bribery or prestige aid. Such forms of aid certainly do exist, hidden in the interstices of the Program Books upon which our aid structure is based.

The notion of bribery immediately tends to conjure up an aura of immorality. Bad policemen and politicians take bribes as inducements not to do their duty, and it is the clear and universal judgment of moralists that to prefer one's private interests to one's duty to others is wrong. But discussions of the place of bribery in foreign aid tend to confuse the moral issue.

Bribes in the past were given to influential officials who regarded the nations under their influence as existing in large measure for their private profit. As far as the average subject or citizen was concerned, the results of most bribe-taking affected them little. Transfers of territory, even treaties of war or peace in many instances, did not affect their daily lives. In so far as the accepters of bribes acted counter to interests they had a duty to protect, including the interests of their sovereign, they acted immorally. But this was not always the case. The mere fact of money changing hands involves no wrong.

What of the moral position of the givers of bribes? If they were not inducing anyone to violate a duty to a third party they were not parties to any immoral act. But suppose they were? In such a case they would have to weigh the interests of their own nation or sovereign against the interest of the international community as a whole, which could not exist if the disloyalty of officials to their principals became universal; not only would bribery violate objective religious standards of morality but it would also be a violation of the natural law of Hobbes, since self-interest dictates that even in the state of nature the sanctity of certain kinds of contract must be observed.

Discussants of bribery in the modern context tend to be unclear about whether they are talking about the problem of giving to whole nations things which they cannot justify getting on the grounds of defense or development simply because they insist on them as a price for political support (for example, virtually useless roads built for a military ally and disguised as development aid) or about giving special assistance to individuals or groups within a recipient nation because they control a nations foreign policy and their support is supposedly necessary for the furtherance of our international political aims.

There is nothing intrinsically wrong with the United States government spending money to secure support for its political goals (assuming they are legitimate) from individuals and groups in foreign nations. But as has been noted it is a fundamental moral principle that one must take account of and responsibility for the consequences of one's actions. Numerous moral problems are presented by forms of assistance which tend specially to enrich or fortify the political position of dominant persons, classes, or cliques within a nation.

In and of itself the action of a foreign official or group in accepting what amounts to a bribe for advancing the United States' objective of keeping the country in question out of Communist hands is not wrong, and the objective consequences of such an act may be morally good. But there are several moral objections to bribing particular groups within foreign nations to commit their countries to support the positions of the United States in world politics. In the first place, the fact that those bribed are using their position for their own personal gain and have to be bribed in order to do what is objectively their duty indicates that the political process in the country involved is in an unhealthy condition. Even if one cannot expect underdeveloped nations to be politically democratic, one can hope that their political systems will be such that the rulers will at least give priority to national over purely personal interests. Insofar as we have an obligation to assist other peoples in attaining human dignity we are not contributing to that end by perpetuating and in many cases even reinforcing a situation in which whole peoples become the pawn of special interests.

In addition to strengthening political inequality, such aid often strengthens economic inequality as well. Both relative and absolute disparities in living standards may be increased. Moreover, bribes to special interest groups often have the consequence of directly undermining the future of free political development. One group that usually demands and receives a cut of such bribes is the secret police or similar agency of political repression, so that such aid often directly underwrites activities offensive to our moral principles.

Finally, such aid is frequently in large part diverted to armed forces which are oversized for the realistic security needs of the nation in question, thus initiating or expanding a local arms race contrary to our interest in peace in general and also, perhaps, to our local political interests in regional stability.

Bribery where the recipient is a whole nation rather than simply an irresponsible ruling class presents a less clear-cut case. There is no reason why a nation is not free to weigh its interests and seek to get some additional help by doing something which is not in itself intrinsically undesirable, e.g., supporting the United States in the Cold War. Rulers seeking to attract such bribes may well be acting in their nation's interest. In many cases the aid given is actually useful for such long-run aims as real economic development. What makes it a bribe is that it is given to this particular nation at a time and in quantities that might not be given if the question were treated as part of a world-wide program of economic development with world-wide priorities, indices of need and of capacities for use. In this case, the only interests which may be badly served are those of world development as whole. Given the lack of accurate measures on which to base priorities in real economic development programs the loss involved in using economic aid as a form of bribery may be marginal.

However, such aid can promote a frivolous and irresponsible attitude toward politics and economics on the part of the rulers and citizens of the nations concerned. It accustoms them to a false scale of values. Since such aid is given in accordance with political rather than economic priorities it is often unrelated to the country's real economic needs, and in any event it is difficult to ensure that such aid is properly utilized once given. When this type of bribery takes place, it tempts others with similar bargaining power to try to obtain similar plums; and the corruption of the aid process spreads.

Aid given for purposes of prestige raises considerations similar to those involved in the bribery of whole nations. Here the granting nation gives particular forms of aid which are justified not by the basic economic needs of the country involved but by their high visibility and the dramatic way in which they demonstrate the friendliness and economic power of the United States. The Soviet Union is often criticized for emphasizing this type of aid: for building great sports stadia, high-powered radio transmitters, unnecessarily elaborate schools or office buildings, paving the streets of the capital city—all things desired by the countries involved yet not contributing to their economic development as much as the humble irrigation projects or agricultural experiment stations the more virtuous United States is building in remote areas where few citizens will see them or become aware of their long-range significance for their country. Insofar as such prestige projects adversely affect the ability of the host country to solve its problems—if only by diverting funds and energies from more useful projects—providing them is as immoral in theory as it would be to corrupt youth by suggesting that they spend their money on flashy clothes and new cars rather than on necessary educational and medical expenses.

But nations, like men, do not live by bread alone. It is one of the paradoxes of modern history that in their aid programs the Communist materialists often seem more ready to recognize this than does the United States. One of the most basic problems of the new nations of the world is to create the civic morale that will give them the self-confidence and unity necessary to engage successfully in the arduous task of nation-building. Evidences of modernization such as paved streets, tokens of national existence such as presidential palaces, may in the long run be just as important to future development if not more so than fish hatcheries. One cannot endorse such show at the expense of absolutely needed economic growth measures, but few needs are absolute. One fears that much American criticism of such prestige aid projects is a Puritan carry-over, an international equivalent of the domestic attitude that families on relief should not be allowed to wear decent clothes or own television sets. In any event, if such aid increases the prestige of the United States and does not hurt the host country by diverting its attention and energies from other necessities, there can be no valid moral objection to it.

The Humanitarian Basis for Foreign Aid

Of the many reasons which have been advanced for an extensive program of foreign aid by the developed nations to the underdeveloped, none has more moral cogency than the humanitarian argument. Arguments based on the containment of communism and the related needs for world peace and stability are at bottom self-seeking. The argument that the United States and other nations should give foreign aid gratuitously, from motives of purest altruism, has an immediate appeal as apparently the most moral approach. Is this necessarily true?

Few attempts to justify our foreign-aid programs on altruistic grounds go beyond the mere statement of our duty to aid others, assuming it to be like a principle in mathematics—self-evident once stated. This lack of theoretical clarity opens the way to serious misunderstandings of the moral basis of foreign aid such as that evidenced by the argument of Professor Joseph Cropsey.

Professor Cropsey first attacks the notion that compassion, which for him is only a sentiment, can impose an obligation upon us to assist others, for reason, he says, must arbitrate among the sentiments. We cannot have a duty, he claims, to relieve sufferings which we have not caused. A universal duty to help those less fortunate than ourselves, he concludes, "would be to enslave the rational and industrious to the rest."

This argument is false on two counts—false theoretically in that it misconstrues the nature of compassion, and false empirically in that it ignores the social matrix which relates the wealthy nations to the rest of the world. Let us examine these errors in order.

First of all, the assumption that compassion is simply a sentiment is gratuitous. The classical doctrine of virtue developed by the Greeks and Romans, later made the basis of education in the Middle Ages, and surviving to our own day is a doctrinal system which involves dispositions of the will, not movements of the passions, to use the classical terminology. There is no assumption whatever of psychological affect in these dispositions. Compassion is one aspect of love. Love of one's neighbor in this tradition is not an amorphous "feeling" of the mind or "twinge" of the heart as the lyrics of a teen-age "rock and roll" hit might have it. It is a disposition of the will to do what the intellect rationally conceives to be best for the object of one's love. It is love in this sense which enables a parent to chastise a child, a teacher to give a student an honest grade, a doctor to watch a drug addict go through the agonies of withdrawal. Such actions may or may not be accompanied by pleasurable sensations in the performer, quite often they are not, but they have as their source not emotion but objective norms. The command to "love thy neighbor as thyself" invokes a duty, not an emotion.

This confusion of subjective disposition with objective duty is the crux of the misconception involved in the discussion of compassion from a purely naturalistic point of view. This approach assumes that acts of love are gratuitous because no duty is involved. Duty, according to such theorists as Professor Cropsey, is based upon responsibility. But responsibility is conceived of in purely causal terms, that is to say, he who is responsible for the ill is alone responsible for its remedy. Since Professor Cropsey holds that the destitution of underdeveloped nations is not our fault (an assertion which begs an important question of fact), we have therefore no duty to relieve it.

This concept of duty as being something created solely by the actions of autonomous human beings is reminiscent of and analogous to the concept of morality of the state-of-nature theorists, who begin by considering man as completely free and look upon his obligations as constituted solely by his own later actions. The major religions of the world, especially those in the Judaeo-Christian and Muslim tradition, have always taught otherwise. For them human beings have no rights to anything—not even their property or their lives—save as a Creator has delegated these rights to them. Obligations are objective because man is born not into a state of nature but into a divinely ordained society, whether this be thought of as local or world-wide in scope. Men may choose to incur additional special obligations to others, but the mere fact of a man's existence at a specific time and place already imposes duties upon him: children have obligations to parents, citizens to their sovereign, the rich to the poor, and so on.

The claim in the Declaration of Independence that it is self-evident that "all men are created equal" and that "they are endowed by their Creator with certain inalienable rights . . . [to] life, liberty, and the pursuit of happiness" is only a simplified Deist version of a generally held religious tenet. If others have rights this means, of course, that we necessarily have a duty to respect and to help implement those rights. A person has obligations which he does not create for himself. Paradoxical as it may seem to the naturalist theorists, it is not a question of whether compassion for the sufferings of others creates duties toward them, it is rather a question of the circumstances under which one has a duty to act compassionately.

Some commentators hold that carrying out the dictates of compassion would in practice make the more advanced nations the prey of the backward (a euphemism for saying that it would make the strong the prey of the weak), since those who were hardworking and prudent would be forced to support those who were neither. To the extent that nations which can help themselves fail to do so and choose to be what Professor Morgenthau has referred to as "bum and beggar nations" this would indeed be the case. But if others can help themselves but do not know how, love itself demands that they be taught to help themselves, since this is to do them a service. Love—the desire to be of service to the best interests of others—demands in such cases that one help the objects of one's love to grow in dignity and power rather than remain weak and dependent on others.

Some American aid programs seem ill designed to accomplish this end. A case in point is the Food for Peace Program, which is largely motivated by the desire to find a dumping ground for American agricultural surpluses (as is partially evidenced by the fact that Congressional jurisdiction lies with the Agriculture rather than the Foreign Affairs Committee). In a number of countries, most notably in Latin America, the effect of this program has been to reduce the amount of acreage under cultivation and thus make these nations less rather than more able to care for themselves.

But the desire to make others independent does not exclude the need to assist them to become so—indeed it implies it; nor does it free us from the obligation to succor those who cannot help themselves. No significant proponent of American foreign aid would hold that we should put on a dole those who can eventually be brought to the point of self-support. The real question is whether we have an obligation to render technical assistance, to lend "seed money" capital, and in other ways make eventual self-support possible. Clearly we have such an obligation. The revolutionary character of the parable of the good Samaritan lies in its extension of the social universe of those to whom one has a moral obligation, to persons outside one's own kinship group, one's own tribe, one's own nation: it takes for granted that one has an obligation to help one's own.

The division of the world into those who are capable and willing to help themselves, i.e., the strong, and those who are not, i.e., the weak—a division upon which is based the fallacious argument that the former can have no moral obligation to the latter—has a factual aspect which in turn has significant moral implications. In large measure this argument is the counterpart of the argument that relief and welfare benefits corrupt the recipients and victimize the provident. This argument is often, and rightly, condemned because it ignores the extent to which we are all part of the same economy and the degree to which the poverty of some may be the result of the very same social causes which have created the wealth of others. There is a symbiotic relationship between the poverty and ignorance of the migrant workers' settlement or the urban slum and the wealth and culture of millionaires' row or the suburbs.

Only overemphasis of the economic importance of national boundaries and of the legal construct of state sovereignty has been able to mask the fact that what is true of economic interdependence on the domestic scene is also true on an international level. There is no way, short of turning God into an accountant and asking Him for an annual report, to get a true picture of the international flow of works and rewards, but it is quite clear that the prosperity of the developed nations is in some part just as symbiotically related to the poverty of the underdeveloped countries as the rich are to the poor on the domestic scene. Economists have calculated that the greatest part of the aid given to developing nations over the last decade or so has been wiped out by changes in the terms of trade. In other words, what the developed nations have given in foreign aid with one hand—from charitable or other motives—they have taken away with the other. How much more was taken from these countries without adequate compensation before postwar foreign aid began? Even today, foreign-aid programs are so tied in with export and import policies and with the domestic economies of the countries giving aid (for example, in 1963, 90 percent of our foreign-aid commitments were used to purchase U.S. goods and services), that an intimate relationship has been created where the contributions to the economy by donor and donee are hard to separate. If one looks at the history of the past several centuries the argument can be made that much of the development of the Western powers has been made possible by those who are now the recipients of aid. What role did the cheap raw materials of Asia, Africa and Latin America play in creating the capital base for Western development? What role did their cheap labor play? What role, indeed, was played by the labor of millions of slaves transported to the new world?

To argue in this fashion is to assume that it is possible to talk of something resembling a "just price" for goods and services. While in both domestic and international economic exchange it is virtually impossible to attach any intrinsic value to goods and services other than that created by free exchanges in the market place, it is also possible to argue that any exchange—especially one in which one of the parties is dealing from a position of superior power, as for all practical purposes the developed nations do today—which leaves the stronger party better off and the weaker worse off almost certainly involves serious injustice. Since economists are not really in a position, either as regards data or methodology, to provide answers to questions about the justice of the terms of trade between underdeveloped and developed countries, it would be foolish to place too much emphasis on the argument that the poverty of the underdeveloped is a consequence of the wealth of the developed, but at least it appears to be incontrovertible that our world is in fact one world economically. There is and has been for centuries a world economy. If we are our brothers' keepers, the source of our obligation is not an arbitrary command of an omnipotent Creator, Who is the source of all morality, that we are to accept this responsibility, but the fact that He has created the world in such a way that it is impossible for us legitimately to deny our mutual involvement with our fellow men; and the only problem is not *whether* but precisely *how* and *to what degree* we are obligated by this connection. In other words, there is an international common good because there is an international community.

But if there is a universal, international common good, what are its features? The basic outlines are simple. A common good may be defined as a good which not only pertains to the whole to which it is common but in such a measure that the good of one part does not diminish the good of another. The common good of a symphony audience consists in enjoyment of the music: the pleasure of one cannot detract from the pleasure of another. A perverse individual who hates music and is accidentally present may find himself in opposition to the common good and prefer the concert to end early. In so far as he does so out of dislike of music he is an aberrant who need not be considered; his presence in the community is a contingent accident. If he wishes the music to end early in order to add to his pleasure in the music, the problem is more complex. Adjustments must be made, for what is common is not always uniformly distributed or distributable.

Similarly, at the level of the world or national community, peace and prosperity are assumed to be common goods. Those who seek discord or poverty are aberrant. But for some, the sight of the policeman is obnoxious, and the regulations necessary for peace, while acceptable, are burdensome; others feel insecure if laws and law enforcers are not highly visible. Not all can share identically in the specifics of prosperity, some gain more than others. What is necessary for the notion of a common good to have meaning is not that all share it equally or identically but that each be better off as the result of the existence of the good shared in common than he would be if this good did not exist.

The concept of an international economic common good has its basis in the belief that the human race is a natural unity and that national divisions are conventions, not necessarily contrary to nature but unnatural in so far as they involve a denial of common humanity. "The earth is the Lord's," and He has not given it to any one segment of the human race but to the race as a whole. The rights of possession of any part of the earth on a private basis, exercised by any segment of the race, are like the rights of individual private property, and derive from the fact that the earth must in most respects be cultivated and developed on a particular rather than a general basis. Each person or nation holds his portion of the earth's surface—and the talents relevant to developing that portion—in trust for the race as a whole.

What does this mean in practice? It means that access to the earth's resources must be equalized. Today minorities are in a position to defend their larger shares, and the complexity of the social matrix makes division by force undesirable. Presumably, under conditions of complete free trade, the combination of free movement of labor and of capital, combined with specialization of each area in producing what it could produce best, from oranges to bevatrons, would in theory give everyone equal access to the world's resources. But such an idealized condition has never existed for long. In any event it ignores the fact that over the course of time differences in the development of individual and group talents and organization have today become so entrenched that even under free trade certain groups would continue to have radically higher standards of living than others. How then can equal access of the peoples of the earth to the world's resources be achieved?

Some have simplistically suggested that all barriers to immigration be lifted and that the inhabitants of the less prosperous areas be free to migrate to the more prosperous. This is obviously impractical. Few "empty" spaces capable of supporting radically larger populations in the short run now exist on the earth's surface. Mass migration of different racial or cultural groups would create such severe social dislocations that they would almost certainly seriously damage or even destroy the political or economic mechanisms which were responsible for producing prosperity in the host areas in the first place.

Developed nations have shown themselves able to contribute to the standards of living of their less developed neighbors by allowing temporary immigration of labor. Irish migrations to England; Italian, Spanish and Turkish migrations to Germany and France; and Mexican and Puerto Rican migrations to the United States have played a part in easing discrepancies in living standards, but these may have reached the limits of the abilities of the host societies to sustain them without social dislocation so great as to imperil the basic communal bond.

Not only is migration socially disruptive to the host country, it is expensive. This is especially true if migrants are going to new, "unopened" lands, where the cost of creating homes and jobs for them would be greater than providing them a means of livelihood at home, where some of the economic costs are probably lower. Also, free migration might mean that the most ambitious, talented, and productive members of the population would decide to migrate, thus possibly leaving their homelands economically worse off than before. The obligation to share common resources must be met primarily by moving the resources, or the goods and skills created by them, rather than by moving people. In any event, not all underdeveloped nations are suffering from overpopulation; in some the reverse is true and underpopulation is an impediment to full resource development.

But foreign aid clearly cannot serve as the sole means to such redistribution. We have already indicated that in part the duty which is owed by the developed to the underdeveloped derives from the fact that the former have been able to increase their economic advantage over the latter by patterns of trade which have worked cumulatively to their advantage. Wealthy nations can offset this by doing more than simply making transfer payments in the form of foreign aid as normally conceived. The wealthy nations can and must help to right the imbalance in trade. Because the underdeveloped nations are now largely dependent on the export of raw materials for income, some kind of price stabilization for these commodities appears to be a current necessity. As the developing nations attempt to diversify their economies and thus improve their bargaining positions in international trade, they cannot be artificially denied the world markets necessary to do so. Tariff barriers and currency controls must be adjusted so that their manufactured and processed goods have an opportunity to compete in world markets with those of the developed nations. Only thus can wage rates and standards of living move toward equalization.

Such equalization will come gradually and need not—indeed probably will not—completely destroy the advantages which the developed nations have in comparative skills. What they will do eventually is to reduce differences to those created by relative levels of skill and willingness to work. Such a situation would not be one in which the more industrious are compelled to support the less so, as some moral critics of foreign aid have feared, but one in which all factors save the morally positive ones of application were minimized in the creation of relative standards of living.

To whom should humanitarian foreign aid be given? At first the answer would seem to be simple: to those that need it the most. But need itself is not a simple concept in this context. For if such aid has as a prime purpose helping others to help themselves, then need must also include the ability to use such aid. The poorest nation—that with the lowest standard of living—may not be the highest priority recipient. A nation less badly off with greater prospects for growth may be a better candidate. One feeds the starving before the merely hungry in a famine, but in a catastrophe one gives medical attention to those with a chance of recovering before providing palliatives for those for whom there is little hope.

But mere ability to utilize aid is not the only criterion. We are all brothers and live in one world community, but we are not thereby called on to be dessicated abstractions with no human ties. It is only natural that we should wish to give priority to aiding those who are closest by background—historical, linguistic, religious or cultural. In fact such aid may be more efficacious than that given to complete strangers whose needs and desires we may not understand as well and whose cooperation we may not be as readily able to acquire. In addition, as far as the developing nations of the world are concerned, most of them during their colonial period had especially intimate relations with particular developed nations. This not only provides a basis for understanding but also in all probability a debt which the mature power owes to the developing one. There is every reason to assume that Belgian aid to the Congo and American aid to the Philippines is likely to be more efficacious than vice versa.

Something can also be said for concentrating our aid in a few countries at a time. While it may seem unfair to help some to prosper while others stagnate, we have seen that the purpose of aid must be development whenever possible and that quite often small amounts of aid are enough to disrupt traditional and sometimes still viable ways of life and to cause social and economic instability without at the same time providing the basis for meaningful economic, political and social growth. Rather than creating a number of such situations, how much better it would be to provide simple subsistence aid for the less promising candidates for development—enough to prevent the most egregious human misery and political breakdown but little more—and to concentrate on helping a few nations reach the point where they would be capable of standing on their own feet. Not only would the direct benefit to human dignity be greater, but the nations which had made a breakthrough would be an inspiration to others entering the development cycle who could then perhaps profit from their mistakes and from their valuable technical assistance as well, just as some of them are today profiting from the technical help of Israel and Taiwan, both of which are heavy recipients of foreign aid of various kinds.

Unilateral Versus Multilateral Foreign Aid

One problem with respect to our aid program which has not yet been considered is the issue of unilateral versus multilateral aid. It is held by some that multilateral aid is morally superior to unilateral aid. This belief is based on two assumptions. The first is that multilateral aid, by which is almost always meant aid by international bodies representing both "East" and "West," is less likely to be a weapon in the Cold War and is likely to be more directly geared to economic development and/or humanitarian ends. Secondly, it is held to be more acceptable to the recipient nations because it imposes fewer psychic burdens upon them, since it does not make them the supplicants of another power. So runs the argument of such distinguished practitioners as Paul G. Hoffman.

To some extent both these contentions are true, and to the extent they are they have moral force. Multilateralism increases the humanitarian content of aid almost necessarily, by minimizing the ends of national self-interest which might be incompatible with purely humanitarian motives. Yet it must be recognized that to be truly multilateral, aid should be so in more than name. Even aside from the possibility that the personnel engaged in such multilateral activities have not yet become fully internationalist in spirit as well as in legal status and might seek (if only unconsciously) to win points for their homeland in the struggle for world public opinion, important problems remain. A scheme in which one power pays most of the bills, although credit and control are shared among many, may soothe the feelings of the recipient and please some of the nominal grantors of the aid, but it is a form of hypocrisy and to that extent immoral. To be truly multilateral, aid must call upon the resources of the donor nations equitably. The burdens of aid must be shared among all the prosperous or economically powerful nations to a greater extent than is true today, if they are to share equally in its control.

There are also practical reasons why unilateral aid is not to be dismissed. There are many programs where the day-to-day relationships of donor and donee must necessarily be so intimate that, if they are to succeed, unilateral aid is preferable because it creates fewer bureaucratic problems than would multilateral aid. Besides, in many areas of the world, long-time relationships make certain nations more logical donors of aid than others, especially if such aid programs must be integrated with long-run tariff and trade relationships.

On the whole, the moral benefits of multilateral over unilateral aid have been exaggerated in most discussions of the subject, and represent largely an emotional rejection of national identifications rather than a reasoned moral position on the part of the proponents of multilateralism.

Foreign Aid and Individual Rights

Our discussion so far has dealt almost exclusively with the moral obligations which the rich nations have toward the poor nations. It has been assumed that since the common teaching of the world's great religions is that God gave the earth to humanity as a whole, all groups and individuals have the right of equal access to its resources. It has also been assumed that nations, like individuals, have a moral obligation to comport themselves in conformity with this belief. If these contentions are accepted there would seem to be little room for argument about the morality of foreign aid.

But one major type of objection still exists. Not all citizens of the developed nations are Christians, believers in God, or humanitarians. Even among religious people in these countries some might not accept the line of reasoning set forth in our earlier discussion. What right has that segment of the population which accepts the moral obligation of foreign aid to use its influence to get the government to do what it believes the objective laws of God dictate? Does this not in an indirect way violate the rights of religious freedom of those individuals who do not accept these obligations in conscience? Does it not violate the bonds which hold American society together to force these dissenting individuals to give of their substance to those outside the American community? Can one speak of an act of morality when the wherewithal of foreign aid is taken from the taxpayers at large under compulsion? The temptation to identify one's own personal political and economic predilections with the will of God is an ancient and common one, a temptation against which all who moralize about public affairs must be on guard. These objections, raised by such cogent critics of our foreign aid program as Professor Edward C. Banfield and John Paton Davies, Jr., deserve serious consideration.

To answer the last question first: the issue of compulsion is essentially specious, though its variants are widespread. We have noted that morality is both subjective and objective. Subjectively, an act is perfectly moral if undertaken from the right motivation. The intention of the performer is important, and most religions assume that acts undertaken in good conscience, i.e., with proper intentions, are morally just as far as the individual is concerned. God will not punish the confused for their confusion. He rejects those who reject Him and His love by their improper dispositions. At the same time acts can be morally just in themselves even if the subjective intention of the person committing them may be improper or indifferent. If a citizen is forced to serve in the Army in a just war, he may gain no personal moral credit from doing so, but he is not acting unjustly—on the contrary. Neither does a restaurant operator who serves Negroes only because the law requires him to do so act unjustly. A citizen forced to contribute, through the taxes he pays to something which is for the common good—such as the schooling of his neighbors' children or the building of a hospital he may never choose to enter—may have his freedom curtailed from a certain point of view, but in so far as he wills that his society be a healthy and educated one he has willed these acts and certainly they do not lose their quality of contributing to the common good by his dissent. Justice has its own objective norms.

This being the case, to force a citizen to contribute to foreign aid on moral grounds which he does not share does not thereby make such aid immoral. His grudging acceptance of the social decision robs him of whatever credit he might have obtained from freely accepting his obligation, but it does not rob the decision of its objective moral correctness.

But what of his religious freedom? What right does that part of the American community which believes foreign aid to be a moral imperative have to force its judgment upon others? Aid given for reasons of national security would be one thing, but what of aid given for purely humanitarian reasons? Can we use the power of the state to force others to contribute to our charities? The simple answer traditionally given to similar questions through the ages has been to say "It is God's will" and to force conformity, as has been done in the institution of state churches, codes of public morals, and so forth. But respect for human freedom, freedom which is also God-given, forbids such a simple solution to our current problem.

To clarify matters we must return to a point made earlier. We saw that compassion and fellow feeling are not emotions, mere subjective movements of the passions. They are rooted in objective moral laws which impose duties. These duties are universal in that they apply to all, even those who refuse to recognize their moral origin or validity. Here we come again to the fundamental divide in political philosophy. On the one side is the individualistic social contract theory which says that all men seek self-aggrandizement and create societies so as to maximize these possibilities. Society exists only to protect them from the violence of others and to perform certain self-seeking acts—building of bridges, safety from brigands, protection against epidemics, etc.—which men as private individuals or groups cannot perform. This is the legacy of Hobbes and Locke. On the other side is the tradition, going back to the Greeks, that the purpose of society is to make possible the good life, that man fulfills his nature in society, and that the political community has not only the duty of preserving order and providing certain underpinnings for economic activity but also, through a myriad of activities, of aiding man to realize his highest potentialities in accordance with some objective norm.

Modern American society and Western society generally today embrace an uneasy mixture of these two norms, both in law and practice. Though many jurists and citizens hold to the former theory, there is still a firm belief in the latter. Education spurs the beautiful as well as the useful arts. Art and music may be a necessity for the good society, but they are not functional requisites for the survival of society.

Increasingly in the United States the courts are chipping away at the notion of the good society and reducing obligations to those necessary for simple societal survival. Recent rulings on obscenity and current challenges to zoning laws based on aesthetic norms testify to this. But a tremendous amount of governmental activity still exists simply because some of us think it improves the quality of our society, even if it is not necessary to keep society from falling prey to political anarchy, economic collapse, or epidemic. Governments in minor ways still subsidize less immediately useful aspects of education and the arts. They aid the indigent for motivations beyond that of preventing them from revolting and destroying the security of the propertied. They aid the sick and the weak in many ways. It is still possible to say that as a general rule society has the right to use the machinery of government to compel citizens, whether through taxes or enforcement of regulations against littering, to conform to someone else's standards of good.

Where these standards of good come from is immaterial. My selfish desire for beautiful public buildings or my emotional pain at the sight of an untended disease; your belief that God wills that buildings be beautiful and the sick cared for—these must stand equally before the bar of the Constitution and the social contract generally (assuming that no rights guaranteed by the Constitution are directly violated). The only practical question is whether enough citizens agree that something is desirable in order to be able to compel others to conform. Indeed, freedom of religion logically would seem to require that the religious or non-religious nature of the motivations of the proponents of any Constitutionally permissible activity not be a proper subject for inquiry. The justification of law applies to the actions it enjoins, not the motivation of its proponents. To force a fellow citizen to aid in a communal act to succor the weak at home or abroad does not force him to accept the religious creed of those proposing such actions, any more than fining him for littering forces him to accept the particular aesthetic creed of any individual who opposes dirty streets.

But perhaps this is only destroying a straw man. It is possible to argue that the American social contract contains more than the Lockean imperatives of protection of life, liberty, and property, that it involves a commitment to a common enterprise whose goal is a better life both for the citizens of the United States and for all mankind.

The Declaration of Independence says that all men are created equal and endowed with certain rights. The Liberty Bell is to proclaim liberty throughout the land and to all its inhabitants without qualification. Some commentators on the morality of foreign aid have denied that this language was intended to imply a commitment to any outside the basic national social bond. The empirical basis for such a contention is hard to find, however. America from the outset has been—rhetorically at least—a messianic nation. Those who condemn the rhetorical excess and moral interventionism of some of the new uncommitted nations of today could find parallels in early American history, when our constant proclamation was that the era of kings and prelates was over and that American independence was the first blow in a world revolution for freedom and prosperity. In the nineteenth century this idealism transformed itself into imperialism, but the sense of mission remained. It has continued to be apparent in Wilson's Fourteen Points and in Franklin Roosevelt's Four Freedoms and is still evident today.

It can be argued, therefore, that not only do the American people support foreign aid, as indicated by repeated public opinion polls, and not only do its proponents have some freedom in defining the ends of American society so as to include world prosperity, but that the basic social contract which binds us together has always had this world mission as one of its components.

Abraham Lincoln once said.

> "I have often inquired of myself, what great principle or idea it was that kept this Confederacy so long together. It was not the mere matter of the separation of the colonies from the motherland; but something in that Declaration giving liberty, not alone to the people of this country, but hope to the world for all future time. It was that which gave promise that in due time the weights should be lifted from the shoulders of all men, and that all should have an equal chance. This is the sentiment embodied in that Declaration of Independence . . . .

Those who have accepted the American social contract implicitly or explicitly have done more than agree to promote their own security and economic well-being, to create Plato's City of Pigs. They have signed aboard a vessel engaging in a perilous voyage of social discovery on behalf of all mankind. Unknowingly they have committed themselves in advance to such devices as foreign aid, devices which the American people view as necessary to build a world in which they can not only *be* but also *feel* secure, because they are at home there. Foreign aid is a moral commitment of the American nation, and no citizen is free to refuse his support because he does not share that commitment. He has signed up behind a stranger banner than he thought, one which proclaims that the cause is mankind.

Just War and Vatican Council II: A Critique

Robert W. Tucker

Our task in this paper is to examine the position on war and deterrence taken by the Second Vatican Council and to do so against the background of a general inquiry into efforts to adapt the doctrine of *bellum justum* to the nuclear age.

The significance of *bellum justum* is that in the history of Western thought it has formed the principal alternative to the ancient plea of necessity or reason of state. If the latter emanates from the state itself, the former has a source that is independent of and presumably superior to the state and its necessities. If the argument of necessity places no inherent restraints on the measures that may be taken to secure the state's independence and continuity, the doctrine of *bellum justum* insists that there are such inherent restraints—inherent not in the sense that they may not in fact be exceeded but in the sense that there can be no justification for ever exceeding them. Nevertheless, the observance of these restraints, whatever the circumstances, is not equated with the renunciation of statecraft. Now as in the past, the doctrine of *bellum justum* does not attempt to deal with the critical issue of means simply by abandoning statecraft. In most of its contemporary versions, as in its traditional versions, it seeks instead to square the circle by acknowledging that the state has its necessities and at the same time by insisting that the measures by which these necessities may be preserved must remain limited.

Modern Versions of the Just War

In considering contemporary versions of *bellum justum* it must be immediately observed that with respect to the justification for resorting to force there is little to distinguish these versions from contemporary developments elsewhere, notably developments in international law. Both in contemporary international law as well as in the prevailing twentieth century reconstruction of *bellum justum* war is no longer a means generally permitted to states for the redress of rights that have been violated. Still less is war considered a legitimate means for changing the *status quo*. To the extent that armed force remains a means permitted to states, it does so only to protect the state's self—its territorial integrity and political independence—against unjust attack.[1]

This restriction of the right of recourse to war in modern versions of *bellum justum* has been represented as a far-reaching change from the classic doctrine, though as we shall presently see the precise significance of the change is dependent upon the meaning and scope accorded to legitimate self-defense. In the classic doctrine the just war was a war of execution, an act of vindicative justice, taken to punish an offending state for a wrong done and unamended. But the rights in defense of which, or for the vindication of which, the traditional doctrine permitted states to resort to war, when alternative means of self-redress proved unavailing and unsatisfactory, were not restricted to the right of self-defense. Indeed, the "blameless self-defense" of the classic doctrine represented only one cause justifying the resort to war, and a cause the justice of which appeared so self-evident to the expositors of the doctrine as to scarcely warrant discussion. The primary concern was rather with the problem of "aggressive" or offensive war (i.e., aggressive or offensive in the sense of the initiation of force). The broad response of the classic doctrine to this problem was simply that aggressive war was justified when undertaken by constituted authority, with right intention and as a last resort, to restore the order of justice violated by the offending state.

If it is nevertheless said that the classic doctrine of *bellum justum* was, in principle, defensive, it was so in the sense that war was to be undertaken in defense of justice. It clearly was not defensive in any other sense; at least, it was not necessarily defensive. Not only was aggressive war permitted to redress an injury, to enforce one's rights, it was also permitted to forestall injurious action. The *bellum justum* could thus comprise a preventive war. Yet the "order of justice" in the defense of which aggressive or offensive war could be taken was

---

[1] The above statements no more than summarize the contemporary *jus ad bellum*. Some of the complexities and persisting ambiguities that attend this development are discussed in succeeding pages. Here it is sufficient simply to note that the formulation given in the text appears to represent the present consensus of Catholic and Protestant thought. The right of self-defense against unjust attack is complemented by the right of collective defense, i.e., the right of third parties to come to the defense of the party acting in legitimate self-defense.

never apparent. The rights in defense of which, or for the vindication of which, states might resort to war remained obscure, even among the expositors of the doctrine. Comprising both legal and natural rights, the just war in the classic doctrine was a war waged to enforce both positive and natural law. But there was no more assurance in an earlier era than today that law and justice would always coincide, despite the contrary assumptions of the classic doctrine.[2] When they did not, states might choose between the two. If the identification of positive right and its violation has always proven difficult, the identification of natural right in terms of the conflicting claims and aspirations of states has proven far more difficult. Given the circumstances in which they were applied, these features of the classic doctrine could scarcely constitute a serious restraint on state action. The criticism that has always been made with such telling effect against the argument of necessity may be made with equal effect against these features of the classic doctrine of *bellum justum*. As a justification of war the latter clearly must invite as much abuse at the hands of governments—and, it is only fair to add, not only at the hands of governments—as does the former. In this respect, at least, the contrast often drawn between *bellum justum* and reason of state seems unpersuasive; the one appears no less, or no more, subject to abuse than does the other.[3]

---

[2] The classic doctrine assumed not only the harmony of law and justice but the coincidence of peace and justice. In this view, peace is an ordered concord based upon justice. That a choice might have to be made between law and justice, on the one hand, or between peace and justice, on the other hand, was excluded by the classic doctrine. This equation of peace, order and justice continues to characterize contemporary versions of *bellum justum*, although it can scarcely be said to carry the same conviction today.

[3] It is significant that in a vast literature devoted to the problem of war in Christian thought, and particularly to the doctrine of *bellum justum*, there has been so little inquiry into the relation of doctrine to practice. It is only in recent years, and for recent wars, that such inquiry has been increasingly undertaken. For the most part, however, the literature of pure exegesis on *bellum justum* is as abundant as the literature on the practical uses to which the doctrine has been put in statecraft is scarce. That the doctrine has been abused on numerous occasions over the centuries, that it has been invoked time and again to justify policies of aggrandizement, is scarcely open to dispute. It may of course be argued that these abuses are without relevance to the intrinsic merits of the doctrine. But if this argument is employed in the case of *bellum justum* it must also be applied in the case of reason of state. To confront the theory of the one with the practice of the other clearly will not do. We can only assume that the historical fate of *bellum justum* forms as much a commentary on the doctrine as the historical fate of reason of state forms a commentary on the argument of necessity.

There is no need to labor the considerations that have prompted the change in the twentieth century reconstruction of *bellum justum*. In the main, the restriction of the just war to the war of self-defense rests on the presumption that war can no longer serve as an apt and proportionate means for resolving international conflicts. That presumption, in turn, presumably reflects our contemporary experience with war. There are dissenters from this reconstruction of the classic doctrine.[4] Their objections to restricting the just war to a war of self-defense are not unlike the objections raised by a number of jurists to restricting the legal war to a war of self-defense. In the absence of a society possessed of effective collective procedures for protecting the rights of its members as well as for changing conditions that have become oppressive and inequitable, it is argued that the attempt to deny states this ultimate means of self-redress—save as a measure of self-defense against attack—is bound to fail. Nor is it clear, in the view of some, that the attempt to proscribe "aggressive" war ought even to succeed, and this despite the destructiveness of war in this century, so long as those conditions persist that have always marked international society.[5] Whatever the merits of this view, and it is not to be lightly dismissed, the dominant position today is that armed force is forbidden except as a measure of legitimate self-defense.[6]

---

[4] Thus Paul Ramsey writes: "No sweeping proscription of 'aggressive' war can hope to stand, based as it is on the assumption that history can be frozen where we are, i.e., always in a relatively unjust *pax-ordo* or on the entirely erroneous assumption that any existing international organization is capable of introducing *fundamental* change into this order but in an entirely orderly fashion and by mutual consent. And in any case, aggression has to be defined so as to include within its meaning, not only the first resort to arms, but also any basic challenge to the security of a rival nation, to its *pax-ordo-justitia* and the laws of its peace, against which the only effective defense may be, and is known to be, a resort to armed force." *War and the Christian Conscience* (1961), pp. 89–90.

[5] The most persuasive presentation of the above view is the work of Julius Stone, *Aggression and World Order* (1958).

[6] These summary remarks on a critically important—if ultimately insoluble —controversy warrant some further discussion. Quite apart from the central question of the scope and meaning to be given "legitimate self-defense," this proscription of "aggressive" wars in the twentieth century reconstruction of *bellum justum* must encounter two difficulties. On the one hand, it can not be understood to imply that defensive wars are necessarily just wars. Clearly, the principle of proportionality applies to wars of "legitimate self-defense" as well, whatever the scope and meaning to be given the latter. Even a defensive war may not be an "apt and proportionate means"; even a defensive war, then, may be an unjust war if the good secured by such a war is outweighed by the evil attendant upon—or expected to attend—the conduct of war. This is precisely the

Does this change with respect to the justification for resorting to war permit a more persuasive contrast to be drawn today between *bellum justum* and reason of state than could be drawn in an earlier era? Does the twentieth century reconstruction of *bellum justum* thereby limit the "necessities" of the state in a way that the classic doctrine did not? The answer to these questions evidently depends largely upon the manner in which current versions of *bellum justum* circumscribe this one remaining cause justifying war. In fact, however, current versions of *bellum justum* do not appear to have a great

---

issue raised by the prospect of thermonuclear war; even if defensive in character, a thermonuclear war may nevertheless be an unjust war. On the other hand, if a defensive war may nevertheless be an unjust war, it does not necessarily follow from the principle of proportionality that under present conditions an "aggressive" war must be an unjust war. The presumption is not self-evident that war—any and all war—can no longer serve as an apt and proportionate means for resolving international conflicts. (Nor, for that matter, is it self-evident that war—any and all war—can no longer be waged with "right intent" and the proper means.) To say this is not at all to dismiss our experience with war in this century; it is simply to say that despite this experience, and despite the possible consequences of thermonuclear war, there may still be wars and wars. Our experience is neither so unambiguous nor our future so certain as to warrant making what is in effect an irrebuttable presumption. In his celebrated encyclical *Pacem in Terris*, John XXIII spoke of the "cruel destruction and the immense suffering" which the use of modern arms would bring to humanity and for this reason declared that "it is irrational to believe that war is still an apt means of vindicating violated rights." In taking this position John XXIII followed his predecessor, Pius XII, who also condemned the theory that war could serve today as an apt and proportionate means of state policy. Yet it is clearly quite possible to imagine that war might still serve in certain circumstances as an apt and proportionate means to repair injustice, although technically such a war would be an "aggressive" war. Moreover, as noted above, if the "aggressive" resort to armed force is always to be condemned on the basis of its disproportionality, the justice of defensive wars must also be seriously questioned. It is another matter to argue that while there may still be just "aggressive" wars, to proscribe any and all aggressive wars is nevertheless desirable given the conditions that have always attended the use of force in international society. On this view, whatever may be the merits of a particular case, the sum of our experience indicates that given these conditions force is more likely to promote injustice than justice, and that this expectation is very considerably strengthened by the novel conditions presently attending the use of force. The parallel argument in law must be that to permit states the right to use force as a measure of self-help to redress violations—or, rather, alleged violations—of their rights is more likely to promote disorder than order. It must be admitted, however, that this particular argument—whether undertaken on the moral or legal level—is inconclusive, even under present conditions. It depends, among other things, upon an interpretation of the history of state relations, past and present, that leaves ample room for uncertainty and disagreement.

deal to say about the meaning and scope of this one remaining justification for war. What they do have to say does not differ substantially from the more extended and detailed juristic analyses of the right of self-defense. In consequence, the same difficulties and ambiguities marking the concept of self-defense in contemporary international law also mark the concept of self-defense in most current versions of *bellum justum*. In the latter no less than in the former uncertainty and controversy persist over the vital issues of the rights on behalf of which, and the acts in response to which, forcible measures of self-defense may be undertaken.

The principal reasons for this persisting uncertainty and controversy are clear enough. What is at best a subordinate principle of order within the state must be something altogether different within a society that does not afford the measure of security normally afforded to individuals within the state. Given the conditions that have always characterized international society, it can hardly be expected that here the scope of the right of self-defense will be as narrowly defined or that the actual exercise of this right will be as severely controlled as within the state. Moreover, to the extent that the circumstances in which states may employ force generally as a measure of self-help are progressively restricted—if this progressive restriction is not accompanied by parallel change in the basic structural characteristics of international society—the significance attached to the right of self-defense must if anything increase. Force may be in principle forbidden to states, not only as a means for effecting change but as a means for the protection of established rights. At the same time, no viable and effective alternative to the institution of self-help may exist.[7] In these circumstances, the scope of the right of self-defense may largely determine the degree of security states enjoy, since a right of self-redress that nevertheless forbids the threat or use of force may prove insufficient to the task of preserving many of the rights on which the security of the state rests.

These considerations largely explain the controversies that have always attended interpretations of the critical provisions of the United Nations Charter, controversies that find an echo in the disparate interpretations of self-defense in current versions of *bellum justum*.

---

[7] The argument is no doubt true that the persistence of the institution of self-help must impede progress toward an effectively centralized juridical organization of international society. It is no less true, however, that the absence of such juridical organization must account for the persistence of states in retaining the right of self-help. Unfortunately, these truisms do not carry us very far.

A restrictive view of the Charter's provisions, in limiting the right to exercise force in self-defense to the sole contingency of a prior armed attack, is vulnerable to the criticism that, if adhered to, it might well result in defeating the essential purpose of this right.[8] To require that an armed attack must have actually begun before the right of self-defense may be exercised is to exceed even the requirements for exercising self-defense imposed by most municipal legal systems which permit acts in self-defense not only against on actual danger but also against one that is imminent. The restrictive view would therefore appear to place more rigid requirements on the right of self-defense precisely in those circumstances where this right must continue to afford the principal basis for security. More generally, however, the objection to the restrictive view is simply that a state may be unable to preserve its vital interests—above all its political independence— if self-defense is only legitimate where the measures taken to endanger the state's interests take the form of an armed attack. The measures that may jeopardize a state's independence need not involve armed force, though they may nevertheless be unlawful. To deny states the right to respond to such measures by employing, if necessary, forcible measures in self-defense may well result in turning the right of political independence into little more than a sham. Nor is it useful here to draw a parallel between the state and international society. Within the state a right of self-defense is denied the individual short of an armed attack or the imminent threat of armed attack precisely because the individual may seek and receive protection against other acts endangering his vital and legally protected interests. The same assurance evidently does not obtain for states in international society. To require of states what is required of individuals within the state is to ignore the disparate circumstances that make the employment of armed force a reasonable condition for the exercise of self-defense in the one case and an unreasonable condition in the other case.

---

[8] Even the restrictive view, however, would leave a substantial measure of uncertainty over the permitted scope of self-defense. In limiting the right to exercise force in self-defense to the sole contingency of an armed attack, it is still necessary to determine what constitutes an armed attack. Need an armed attack be "direct" before it may be responded to with forcible measures of self-defense? Those who respond affirmatively cannot rely upon the United Nations Charter, since Article 51 of the Charter does not require that an armed attack be "direct" before it may be responded to with force. It may of course be argued that the consequence of including indirect uses of armed force within the concept of armed attack is to expand this concept to a point where it may well become meaningless as a restraint. This may be true. Yet it is also true that a state's independence may be jeopardized by the indirect employment of armed force.

Although this criticism of the restrictive view of the right of self-defense is not without considerable merit, it is much easier to make than to suggest an alternative that is not equally vulnerable to criticism. However paradoxical the restrictive view appears in denying the legitimacy of anticipatory acts of self-defense, the explanation of this apparent paradox must be found in those very conditions that normally attend the exercise of self-defense in international society. The same conditions that do indeed lend support to the argument on behalf of anticipatory acts of self-defense also point to the considerable dangers of granting such a right. Nor does the nature of modern weapons substantially alter this conclusion. If the speed and destructive power of modern weapons may defeat the purpose of self-defense in the absence of a right to take anticipatory measures against an imminent attack, it is these same characteristics of modern weapons that must also render a right to take anticipatory measures particularly dangerous and subject to abuse.

Apart from the issue of anticipatory self-defense, if the restrictive view of the right of self-defense is considered inadequate and unacceptable, what is the alternative? The broad response given this question has been to insist that the resort to forcible measures of self-defense is legitimate not only to protect the state's territorial integrity, its "physical person" against armed attack; self-defense is equally legitimate when resorted to for the protection of those interests which collectively comprise the state's "existence" in the broader sense of political independence and which may be endangered by measures other than armed force. But if uncertainty has always prevailed with respect to the scope of the rights—the legally protected interests—that presumably comprise the state's security and independence, an equal uncertainty must prevail with respect to the scope of the right of self-defense. Given the congenital disposition of states to interpret their existence, and threats thereto, expansively, the claim of self-defense, even when limited to the protection of legal rights against delictual conduct, may come very close in practice to the more general claim of a right of self-help.[9]

---

[9] There is the further consideration that a state's independence may be impaired by acts that do not involve the threat or use of armed force. To the extent that unlawful intervention is held to encompass only those acts of interference in the affairs of another state that take an imperative or dictatorial form and involve the threat or use of force, the duty of non-intervention becomes irrelevant in dealing with behavior that may nevertheless effectively jeopardize political independence. If the right of political independence is held to justify the resort to forcible measures of self-defense, and if the right of independence

The immediately preceding considerations have assumed that, however ill-defined in their scope, the acts in response to which self-defense is presumably legitimate are at least clearly unlawful. Measures of self-defense are permitted, then, in response to unlawful acts which, at the same time, endanger another state's territorial integrity or political independence. It is clear, however, that a state's political independence, and the security on which independence rests, may be endangered by acts which are not forbidden—at least, not specifically forbidden—by international law. In recent years, the most dramatic illustration of this possibility resulted from the discovery in October, 1962, that the Soviet Union was secretly establishing missile sites on the island of Cuba. The action of the Soviet Government was interpreted by the United States, as well as by the Organization of American States, to constitute a threat to the peace and security—and accordingly, the political independence—of the states comprising the Western Hemisphere, thereby justifying the resort to forcible measures designed to prevent the further shipment to Cuba of missiles and aircraft having an offensive capability as well as to compel the withdrawal of such weapons as were already on the island. Yet in sending these weapons the Soviet Government acted with the consent and cooperation of the Cuban Government. There is no rule of international law that specifically forbids a state from giving arms to another state or from establishing military bases in the territory of another state, whether openly or in a clandestine manner, so long as this is done with the latter state's consent. Nor does international law forbid a state from attempting to alter the military balance of power in its favor, so long as this is done through actions which do not in themselves violate the rights of other states. To the extent that the forcible measures taken by the United States in response to the action of the Soviet Government are nevertheless justified as measures of legitimate self-defense, they afford a striking example of the claim to take measures of self-defense against acts which are not at least *prima facie* unlawful.[10]

---

is only given a sufficiently broad interpretation, the result must be to enlarge the scope of self-defense to a point where it is difficult to distinguish from the much more general claim of the state to possess the competence to take measures of self-help—including forcible measures of self-help—as a reaction to acts of other states which violate its rights. These considerations explain, in part, why the claim of self-defense in the customary law always bordered in practice on the much more general claim of a right to self-help.

[10] In undertaking the naval quarantine of Cuba, however, the United States did not attempt to justify the action as a legitimate measure of self-defense. Nor

It may of course be argued that acts which endanger the security and independence of other states are unlawful even though they are not specifically forbidden by international law. This is, it would appear, the implication of the claim that a state has the right to take forcible measures of self-defense, if necessary, against any and all acts which endanger its political independence. But if this argument is once granted, it is not easy to see wherein it differs from the traditional claim of a right to self-preservation, a claim the meta-legal character of which has always been practically indistinguishable from the classic plea of necessity. If the substantive rights in defense of which force may be employed remain both expansive and ill-defined, if all that can be said with assurance is that in some vague manner these rights encompass the security and independence of the state, it is not easy to see wherein the right of self-defense limits the "necessities" of the state.[11]

---

did the Organization of American States attempt to characterize the Soviet action as one giving rise to a right of individual and collective self-defense.

[11] Thus the authors of a recent study point out that claims of self-defense "are claims to exercise highly intense coercion in response to what is alleged to be unlawfully initiated coercion." Myres S. McDougal and Florentino P. Feliciano, *Law and Minimum World Public Order* (1961), p. 209. The legally protected interests for the protection of which measures of self-defense may be undertaken are summarized as "territorial integrity and political independence." Political independence is defined as that "freedom of decision-making or self-direction customarily demanded by state officials. Impairment of 'political independence,' as an attack upon the institutional arrangements of authority and control in the target state, thus involves substantial curtailment of the freedom of decision-making through the effective and drastic reduction of the number of alternative policies open at tolerable costs to the officials of that state" (p. 177). On this view, measures of self-defense are legitimate in response to acts of coercion by another state which impair or threaten to impair this "freedom of decision-making" of the target state, provided only that such measures are necessary in the circumstances and proportionate to the danger. Nor is it necessary that the acts in response to which measures of self-defense are undertaken be specifically forbidden by international law. They are unlawful, on this view, if only their effect is to endanger a state's political independence. It is difficult to see any substantial difference between this view of self-defense and the older—and avowedly political—doctrine of self-preservation. Professor McDougal confirms this conclusion, without admitting it, in his remarks on the Cuban quarantine. Cf. Myres S. McDougal, "The Soviet-Cuban Quarantine and Self-Defense," 57 *American Journal of International Law* (July, 1963), 597ff. For a candid reaffirmation of the right of self-preservation in the context of the Cuban quarantine it is necessary to turn from the international jurists to a former Secretary of State, who declares: "I must conclude that the propriety of the Cuban quarantine is not a legal issue. The power, position and prestige of the United States had been challenged by another state and law simply does not deal with such questions of ultimate power—power

These uncertainties marking the scope of self-defense in international law are equally apparent in current versions of *bellum justum*. They are scarcely overcome by other restraints placed on the exercise of self-defense. The lawful exercise of force in self-defense presumably requires that the danger giving rise to this right be immediate and of such a nature as to leave no reasonable possibility for recourse to alternative means of protection. Even then, the use of force in self-defense must prove reasonable, and it may prove reasonable only if it is proportionate to the end of protecting those interests that are endangered. Force in excess of this purpose is forbidden, since action taken in self-defense is held to have a strictly preventive character.

It is clear that these requirements of law still leave largely unaffected the vital issue of the rights on behalf of which, and the acts in response to which, forcible measures of self-defense may be undertaken. Even so, the interpretation to be given these requirements has never been free from substantial uncertainty. Thus it has never been clear whether the requirement of proportionality limits acts taken in self-defense to repelling the immediate danger or permits action directed to removing the danger. The latter interpretation is not unreasonable, given the circumstances attending the exercise of self-defense in international society. Within domestic societies the state assures that a danger once repelled will be removed. Hence the justification for the severe restriction of measures taken in self-defense. In international society this assurance evidently cannot be given to states. Hence an equally severe restriction of measures taken in self-defense may prove unreasonable in that it may defeat the essential purpose for which measures of self-defense are permitted in the first place. The argument is not without merit. Yet if it is once accepted, it must become increasingly difficult to set meaningful limits to the exercise of self-defense.[12]

---

that comes close to the sources of sovereignty. . . . No law can destroy the state creating the law. The survival of states is not a matter of law." Remarks by the Hon. Dean Acheson, Proceedings, *American Society of International Law* (1963), p. 14.

[12] The issue of proportionality arose in the Suez crisis of 1956. In attacking Egypt, Israel justified her action as a legitimate measure of self-defense, taken in response to a continuous series of armed raids on Israeli territory by fedayeen bands based in Egypt and in anticipation of what was alleged to be an impending attack on Israel by Egyptian forces. Quite apart from the issue of anticipatory self-defense raised by the Israeli action, the obvious and acknowledged intent of the Israeli action was to destroy the fedayeen bases in Egypt, that is, to remove this particular source of danger. At the time, the action was generally condemned,

In substance, the same requirements of necessity and proportionality are also held to govern the just exercise of force. In *bellum justum*, it is true, the requirement of proportionality possesses a broader meaning than does the requirement of proportionality in international law. In the latter, the proportionality required is little more than what may be termed proportionality of effectiveness. In the former, the proportionality required is both a proportionality of effectiveness and a proportionality of value. In *bellum justum* it is not enough that the use of force is proportionate, though no more than proportionate, to the effective protection of endangered interests or values. To this proportionality of effectiveness must be added a proportionality of value, requiring that the values preserved through force are proportionate to the values sacrificed through force. Indeed, if anything, it is the proportionality of value rather than of effectiveness upon which primary emphasis is placed in *bellum justum*. At the same time, the requirement of a proportionality of value can hardly be regarded as a very meaningful restraint, however great the emphasis placed on it. Devoid entirely of the element of specificity, it is a prescription that can readily be adjusted to the most varied of actions. It is not surprising that the requirement of a proportionality of value has been invoked with an apparent plausibility on all sides of the nuclear issue by Christian moralists. It illustrates that a prescription the converse of which is manifestly absurd can tell us very little that is meaningful about how men ought to behave.[13]

---

among other reasons, because it was considered disproportionate and unreasonable to the acts provoking the Israeli attack. In defense of the Israeli position, however, it may be contended that the action was without purpose or reason unless directed to removing this source of danger. In this respect, it is interesting to compare the position taken by Israel in 1956 and the position taken by the United States in the Cuban crisis in 1962. Much has been made of the proportionality and reasonableness of the Cuban "quarantine" in view of the considerable danger allegedly posed by the presence of Soviet missile bases in Cuba. It should be noted, however, that the declared policy of the American government was not only to stop the further shipment of missiles to Cuba but to compel the withdrawal of such weapons as were already on the island, and to do so by any and all means that might prove necessary. The proportionality and reasonableness of the American position can hardly be judged exclusively in terms of the measures that were actually taken; it must also be judged in terms of the measures threatened if the quarantine proved ineffective and the missiles were not removed.

[13] It must be emphasized that the principle of proportionality (of value) does not of itself confer a distinctive quality on *bellum justum*. This principle is implicit in almost every conceivable justification of force. Not only does it express what may be termed the "logic of justification," it is compatible with almost every justification—or condemnation—of force men have ever given. It is frequently

The Means of War; Do Limits Exist?

If we are to find a distintinctive quality in *bellum justum*, a quality that sets clear and meaningful limits to the necessities of the state, that quality simply cannot be found in the causes and ends of war. Nor can it be found in the general principles governing the conditions of war. If this quality is to be found at all, it must instead be found in the restraints placed on the conduct or means of war. To say this is not to imply that the doctrine of *bellum justum*, whether in its classic or in its modern versions, has indeed made the means of warfare the center of moral gravity.[14] On the contrary, it is in the

assumed that the difficulty in applying the principle of proportionality, and the limited utility of the principle when it is applied, result from men's inability to know all the facts of a situation and, above all, from men's inability to foresee the consequences of their actions. This is certainly true, but it is by no means the whole truth. Even if all the relevant facts were known, and all of the consequences of action (or abstention from action) foreseen, the application of the principle of proportionality would give rise to uncertainty and, in consequence, to disagreement. This is so for the apparent reason that the principle of proportionality is devoid of substantive content. The principle of proportionality prescribes that the good resulting from the use of force ought to outweigh, or to be proportionate to, the evil attending force. This is merely an elaborate way of saying not only what is evidently implied in the very task of justifying force but what all men can readily agree upon. There is no real consensus, however, among theorists of the just war with respect to the values that should form the content of the principle of proportionality. To be sure, there is agreement that the state, though it is considered an important value, cannot be considered the supreme value. Hence, the application of the principle of proportionality by theorists of *bellum justum* may lead to results that are different from the results of applying this principle by those who impute supreme value to the state and, accordingly, to the state's necessities. But this difference is scarcely sufficient to establish a meaningful consensus among the former with respect to the values that should form the content of the principle of proportionality. Moreover, even if we assume that men can know all of the consequences of their actions and can achieve meaningful agreement on the plurality of values the preservation of which may justify war, there is still no objective way of determining (calculating) whether the evil attendant upon the waging of war is justified in terms of the good obtained through war; reasonable men can, and will, reach quite disparate conclusions. Of course, the requirement of proportionality would give a distinctive character to *bellum justum* if it afforded a distinctive method of determining (calculating) a proportionality of value and one that somehow avoided these difficulties. This is admittedly not the case. The scales used by the theorists of the just war are the same scales used by others (though the weights are presumably different), and the results are quite as uncertain and subject to controversy. With respect to the manner of establishing either proportionality or disproportionality in war, then, there is little, if indeed anything, that is distinctive in *bellum justum*.

[14] Whether the theory of the just war *should* always have made the conduct of war the center of moral gravity is another matter. In this connection Paul

causes and ends justifying war that we must find the principal focus of the doctrine. It is true that in many contemporary analyses of the just war the means permitted in war have been given markedly increased attention. Even so, it would be rash to conclude that at present primary emphasis is placed on the manner in which war must be conducted. In this respect, as in many others, the evolution of *bellum justum* appears to parallel the evolution of international law. In both, it is the *jus ad bellum*, or, perhaps more accurately, a *jus contra bellum*, rather than a *jus in bello* that has formed the primary emphasis. Moreover, to the extent that the manner of warfare

---

Ramsey has written: "Since at least everyone seeks peace and desires justice, the ends for which war may legitimately be fought are not nearly so important in the theory of the just war as is the moral and political wisdom contained in its reflection upon the conduct or means of warfare. Unless there is a morality applicable to instruments of war and intrinsically limiting its conduct, then we must simply admit that war has no limits—since these can hardly be derived from 'peace' as the 'final cause' of just wars." "The case for making 'just war' possible," John C. Bennett, ed., *Nuclear Weapons and the Conflict of Conscience* (1962), pp. 146–147. Although Ramsey's latter assertion is an exaggeration, neglecting as it does the moderating effects limited ends in war may have on the conduct of war, even if it were accepted as true it would not follow that his former assertion must also be true. Nor can imaginative reconstructions of the *bellum justum* doctrine, such as Ramsey's (cf. *War and the Christian Conscience*), prove more than what the theory of the just war should perhaps have always had as its central emphasis, given the premises from which it starts. In fact, it is surprising how little emphasis was placed on the means of warfare by expositors of the traditional doctrine. It is this relative neglect along with the emphasis placed on the interpretation of war as an act of vindicative justice undertaken for the punishment of the wicked that has prompted critics to conclude that far from leading to greater restraint in the conduct of war the traditional doctrine had the contrary effect. Whatever the merit of this criticism, it is a matter of record that the greatest progress in the mitigation of war came in a period when the idea of the just war was in eclipse. No doubt, this progress cannot be attributed simply to the decline of *bellum justum*. Other and more important factors were at work in the eighteenth and nineteenth centuries which explain the limited wars of the period and the growing observance in war of the immunity of the civilian population. Even so, a persuasive case may be made for the position that the interpretation of war as a duel between equals significantly contributed to the humanization of warfare. There are perhaps no logical reasons why the interpretation of war as a duel between equals, rather than as the punishment of the wicked, should lead to greater restraint in the conduct of war, but there are very persuasive psychological reasons which suggest this result. These reasons are scarcely offset by the claim that the wicked are to be punished for love's sake, for the sake of a love that comprises the enemy but at the same time does not preclude—in St. Augustine's words—"a benevolent severity." For all his realism, Augustine's insistence upon the loving killer, or the loving avenger, who would vindicate justice though without passion and self assertion was not very realistic.

has been increasingly emphasized, the significance of this emphasis must largely be seen in the effects it has had in redefining the *jus ad bellum*.[15]

Despite these considerations, it is over the issue of the means permitted in war, or to deter war, that we must find, if anywhere, a significant conflict between the necessities of the state and the demands of *bellum justum*. The general nature that conflict must take is clear enough. Whereas reason of state must reject the claim that there are any inherent limits on the means that may be threatened or employed to preserve the state, *bellum justum* must insist that there are such limits and that whatever the circumstances they may never be transgressed.[16] The argument of necessity must reject the claim of inherent limits on the means of war not because it is informed by an "ethic of responsibility" and therefore requires the statesman to calculate and to weigh the possible consequences of alternative courses of action, but because it presupposes as an ultimate end the preservation and continuity of the state. The doctrine of *bellum justum* evidently cannot share this presupposition else it could not insist that there are means that may never be employed. At the same time, there is no denial here of the need to calculate and to weigh possible consequences of alternative courses of action. There is simply the insistence that whatever the results of calculation, certain limits must be imposed on the means permitted the statesman, limits that may never be transgressed.[17]

---

[15] That is, in restricting the circumstances or occasions in which the resort to armed force is considered justified.

[16] It must be made clear that this conflict is not over the proportionality or disproportionality of means, in terms of their effects, but over the means themselves. The distinction is a critical one, since it is not only over the issue of means, *per se*, that a clear conflict may arise between reason of state and *bellum justum*.

[17] The position taken in the text is at variance with what is perhaps the prevailing view of this conflict, a view that reflects the position taken by Max Weber in his now classic essay "Politics as a Vocation" (cf. *From Max Weber: Essays in Sociology*, H. H. Gerth and C. Wright Mills (1948), pp. 77ff.). In this essay Weber wrote: "We must be clear about the fact that all ethically oriented conduct may be guided by two fundamentally differing and irreconcilably opposed maxims: conduct can be oriented to an 'ethic of ultimate ends' or to an 'ethic of responsibility.' This is not to say that an ethic of ultimate ends is identical with irresponsibility, or that an ethic of responsibility is identical with unprincipled opportunism. Naturally nobody says that. However, there is an abysmal contrast between conduct that follows the maxim of an ethic of ultimate ends—that is, in religious terms, 'The Christian does rightly and leaves the result with the Lord'—and conduct that follows the maxim of an ethic of responsibility, in which case one has to give an account of the foreseeable results of one's actions." In con-

To the degree that *bellum justum* has a distinctive quality, then, this quality is to be found not merely in the significance given to the means of action but above all in the insistence that *bellum justum* is an "ethic of ultimate means." This quality is blurred, if not lost, if the problem of means is itself reduced to what is, in effect, another form of calculation. Thus it is not enough to argue that one may never do evil that good may come because the good will not come (only the evil), or that the evil act will corrupt the actor and thereby defeat his ends (however desirable in themselves), or that the means cannot be separated from the ends but are themselves the ends in the very process of coming into existence. It is not enough to argue in this manner if only for the reason that each of these familiar contentions is open to question. Whether the use of evil means will always and necessarily defeat the ends of action, if only by corrupting the actor, is not an issue that can be decided in the abstract. No doubt, the task of the moralist would be greatly simplified if it could be so decided. He would then enjoy the best of both worlds. If certain means are never to be employed, or threatened, it is not only because they are in and of themselves evil but also because they are, after all, imprudent, a mistaken form of calculation. Unfortunately, experience shows that good may come of evil, that the use of evil means does not always corrupt the actor and that it is much too simple to conceive of means as themselves the ends of action in the very process of coming into existence.[18] If certain means are to be absolutely forbidden

trasting an "ethic of responsibility" with an "ethic of ultimate ends," Weber presumably implies that an ethic of responsibility is *not* an ethic of ultimate ends. But this is not true—at any rate, it is not necessarily true. The statesman has as his highest moral imperative the preservation of the state entrusted to his care. If we say that he must act responsibly we mean that he must take all possible care to estimate the results or consequences of his actions. In saying this, however, we do not mean that the statesman has no ultimate end. Although the statesman must act prudently in preserving the state entrusted to his care, he must nevertheless preserve the state whatever the means. We might just as well say then that Weber's ethic of responsibility is an ethic of ultimate ends precisely because the statesman must—if necessary—subordinate the means to the ends of action. On the other hand, we might just as accurately call Weber's ethic of ultimate ends an "ethic of ultimate means." The statement that the Christian does rightly and leaves the results with the Lord means, if anything, that certain acts (means) are never to be employed whatever the consequences that may follow from their non-employment. The Christian does not feel "irresponsible" for the consequences any more than the statesmen feels "irresponsible" for the means. It is simply a question whether one accepts absolute restraints on action, whatever the ends sought, or whether one does not do so.

[18] Were the means employed by the Allies in World War II little more than the ends of action in the very process of coming into existence? Did they corrupt,

they must be forbidden quite apart from these considerations. If certain means are to be absolutely forbidden they must be so forbidden because of their intrinsic evil. If one may never do evil that good may come, it is not—or not primarily—because the good probably will not come but simply because one may never do evil.

Taken by itself, however, the bare assertion that there are absolute restraints on the means permitted even in war does not tell us what it is that is absolutely forbidden. Nor are we appreciably enlightened with respect to that conduct absolutely forbidden when we are further told that we may never do evil, or threaten to do evil, that good may come. If evil signifies that which is absolutely forbidden, we have simply been told what we already knew or should have known; that which is absolutely forbidden is evidently that which may never be done. The position that certain means may never be employed, or threatened, even to preserve the independence and continuity of the state does clearly mean that the state cannot be considered a supreme value for men. Moreover, if the survival of the state cannot serve to justify certain means, it follows that those values the state, and perhaps only the state, may serve to protect also cannot be considered supreme. But these conclusions, however significant they may be, still do not afford us much guidance with respect to that conduct which is absolutely forbidden.

It is another matter to identify the one restraint that in some form must be observed in war if this activity is to prove amenable to substantive limitation. Apart from the limitation the ends of war may impose on the conduct of war, it is apparent that this conduct can be significantly limited only by limiting those individuals who may be

---

as presumably they invariably must corrupt, the actors? It requires a very perverse reading of contemporary history to answer these questions affirmatively. Yet there are many Christian moralists who continue to insist that these questions must be answered affirmatively. To say this is not of course to justify the means employed in World War II. It is simply to say that the moralist who condemns certain means as intrinsically evil cannot expect to support his argument on every occasion by absolutizing what are in reality no more than prudential maxims. The temptation to do just this, however, is very great. Thus in recent years the condemnation by Christian moralists of policies of deterrence has often proceeded not only, and not even primarily, from the position that such policies imply the intent to do evil, and are accordingly to be considered in the same proscribed category as the doing of evil, but from the position that they are ultimately a form of bad calculation (i.e., either that they will issue in catastrophic conflict, or that they will corrupt the actors even if they do not issue in such conflict, etc.). As the age of deterrence progresses, the latter argument becomes less and less persuasive, even, one suspects, for those who advance it.

made the objects of attack. It is equally apparent that the only basis of the distinction to be drawn between those who may be made the objects of attack and those who may not be so made must rest upon the degree of involvement or participation in warlike activities. Historically, the importance of this distinction for the law of war is generally acknowledged. The development of a body of rules regulating, and limiting, the conduct of war has been largely synonymous with the development of the principle distinguishing between the armed forces (combatants) and the civilian population (noncombatants) of belligerents, and requiring belligerents both to refrain from making the civilian population the deliberate object of attack and to safeguard this population from injuries not incidental to operations undertaken against combatant forces and other legitimate military objectives. The decline in this century of the practices traditionally regulating the manner of warfare has also been largely synonymous with the decline of this principle.

It is the same principle that forms the main limitation on the just conduct of war. In the doctrine of *bellum justum,* however, the norm forbidding the direct and intentional attack on noncombatants represents an absolute injunction. At any rate, it is only with those versions of *bellum justum* which do so regard this norm that we are here concerned. For it is only where the prohibition against the deliberate killing of noncombatants is considered absolute that a clear conflict may arise between the necessities of the state and the requirements of an ethic which presumably sets limits to these necessities. In the theory of the just war the distinction in question is held to define the essential difference between war and murder; that is, the essential difference between the permitted and the forbidden taking of human life. It is the deliberate killing of the innocent that is always to be avoided, that may never be justified even as a reprisal measure taken in response to similar measures of an adversary. This is, in substance, the evil that may never be done, or threatened, that good may come.

Despite the absolute character given it, whether, and to what extent, the norm forbidding the direct and intentional attack upon the innocent does set significant limits to the necessities of the state are not self-answering questions. Restraints may be absolute in character yet innocuous in terms of the specific behavior they are interpreted to forbid. In forbidding the deliberate attack upon the innocent we must still determine who are the innocent and what constitutes a deliberate attack upon them. The answer to the first question does not present considerable difficulties provided only that the innocent are equated with noncombatants and the latter identified—as, indeed, they have been traditionally identified—by the remoteness of their relationship to warlike activities. Difficulties may of course arise, and persist, over the precise characteristics requisite for noncombatant status, but unless the very concept of noncombatant status is itself suppressed these difficulties are not likely to prove intractable.[19] The answer to the second question does pose very considerable difficulties, however, and it can scarcely be said that these difficulties have been any more satisfactorily resolved by theorists of *bellum justum* than by international jurists. That the former attribute an absolute character to the norm forbidding the direct and intentional attack upon the innocent only serves to accentuate rather than to resolve these difficulties.

In the practice of states the principle distinguishing between combatants and noncombatants has never been interpreted as giving the latter complete protection from the hazards of war. It has always been accepted that if war is to prove at all possible the immunity of noncombatants must be qualified, and substantially so. Thus the investment, bombardment, siege and assault of fortified places, including towns and cities, have always been recognized as legitimate meas-

---

[19] Even so, these difficulties do at least indicate that the absolute prohibition against attacking the innocent rests on a distinction that is far more relative and pragmatic in application than is commonly admitted. Theorists of *bellum justum* regularly point out that the concept of "innocence" corresponds to the concept of "noncombatancy" and, indeed, use these presumably coresponding terms interchangeably. In state practice, however, the distinction drawn between combatants and noncombatants has always had a relative character, in the sense that at the very least its application has been dependent both on the manner in which states organize for war and on the technology with which they conduct war. To this extent, then, it has always been true that the scope of noncombatancy could vary, and has varied, considerably; hence the scope of innocence could also vary, and has varied, considerably. Moreover, the relative character of the concept of noncombatant status is unavoidably a function as well of the degree of remoteness from warlike activities that is held to constitute this status. It is no doubt true that if the concept of noncombatant status is to be granted in principle, remoteness from warlike activities cannot be pushed beyond certain limits. Yet it must be admitted that what these limits are in practice is an issue over which reasonable men may differ and have frequently differed. Theorists of *bellum justum* sometimes assume that because the concept of innocence, like the concept of noncombatancy, depends upon objective behavior and not a subjective state of mind (i.e., personal innocence or guilt) that this concept is thereby susceptible to objective determination. But this is not true. Though the status of noncombatants, as well as the status of innocents, depends on objective behavior, the determination of either depends on a subjective appreciation of this behavior. In the subjective interpretation of this behavior there is no apparent reason for according greater weight to the insights of Christian moralists than to the insights of others.

ures of warfare, even though such places may contain large numbers of peaceful inhabitants. More generally, belligerents have never been required to cease military operations because of the presence of non-combatants within the immediate area of these operations or to refrain from attacking military objectives simply because of the proximity of military objectives to the noncombatant population. These qualifications to the principle of noncombatant immunity are to be explained in terms of military necessity, which permits belligerents to take those measures required for the success of military operations and not otherwise forbidden by the law of war (in this instance, not forbidden by some rule other than the principle distinguishing between combatants and noncombatants). To this extent, then, the scope afforded to the principle of noncombatant immunity has always been dependent upon the scope afforded to military necessity.

The same dependence upon military necessity is apparent in considering the concept of military objective. Time and again the attempt has been made to limit the concept of military objective by freeing it from the uncertainty and potential expansiveness of military necessity. Time and again the attempt has failed and has served only to emphasize the dependence in practice of the meaning given to military objective on the meaning given to military necessity. The essentially indeterminate character of the concept of military objective therefore reflects the essentially indeterminate character of the concept of military necessity, dependent as the latter is in any given period upon the manner in which societies organize for and conduct war, the technology with which war is waged and the ends for which war is undertaken. No doubt, it is true that if the principle of noncombatant immunity is to be retained at all in war there must be *some* limits placed on this relationship of dependency. Whatever the meaning given to military necessity, noncombatants cannot as such be considered a military objective. But short of the clear negation of the principle of noncombatant immunity, what these limits must be in practice has never been clear. All that can be said with assurance— all that could ever be said with assurance—is only that the scope of the immunity accorded the civilian population is largely dependent upon the meaning given to the concept of military objective and that the concept of military objective varies as the character of war—hence the character of military necessity—varies. Moreover, even if it were possible to resolve the uncertainty that marks the concept of military objective there would still remain the problem of determining the extent of the incidental or indirect injury that may be inflicted upon the civilian population in the course of attacking military objectives.

The answer to this latter problem, however, remains as uncertain and controverted as does the answer to the problem of what constitutes a legitimate military objective. To the extent the attempt has been made to answer it, the basis of that attempt has largely been through recourse to the very principle—military necessity—that accounts for the uncertainty attending the scope of military objective and that, in consequence, gave rise to the problem in the first place.

The general import of these considerations is clear enough. However critical the principle distinguishing between combatants and noncombatants may be for the regulation and limitation of war, this principle has always had a relative and contingent character in state practice as well as in the law that emerged from this practice. As such, the scope afforded it has always been subject to the imperious claims of necessity, the manifestations of which in the conduct of war are to be found in the claims of military necessity and of reprisal. Indeed, so pervasive is this subjection that belligerents have been able in practice to reduce the effective scope of the principle of noncombatant immunity almost to a vanishing point while nevertheless affirming the continued validity of this principle. Even where the attack upon noncombatants is openly avowed as direct and intentional, the continued affirmation of the principle of noncombatant immunity may be given a semblance of plausibility if the action is represented as a reprisal taken in response to similar behavior of an adversary.

In giving the principle of noncombatant immunity an absolute and unconditioned character, the doctrine of *bellum justum* presumably rejects this subordination to the claims of necessity. Since it may clearly do so only at a very high price, however, the temptation is understandably great to pose a rejection which, in terms of the specific consequences that may be drawn from it (hence the practical limits it imposes on military necessity), is more apparent than real. If *bellum justum* requires that the innocent may never be made the deliberate object of attack, the question nevertheless remains in what circumstances this absolute prohibition is deemed to have been transgressed. In answering this question the theorists of the just war have very little to say that is distinctive or instructive with respect to what constitutes a legitimate military objective. Apart from being told what we already knew, that noncombatants cannot as such be considered a legitimate military objective, we are left in quite as uncertain a position as before over what does constitute a legitimate military objective. Moreover, it must be made clear that no more than international law does *bellum justum* require a belligerent to refrain from attacking military objectives simply because of the proximity of these objectives to the civilian population. What *bellum justum* does require is that in attacking military objectives the death and injury done to noncombatants be beside the intention—at any rate, beside the direct or positive intention—of the attacker, that this death and injury done to noncombatants not constitute a means for achieving an otherwise legitimate military end and that, finally, the evil effect of the action not prove disproportionate to the good—or, at any rate, the morally sanctioned—effect.[20]

These requirements constitute the essential contribution of *bellum justum* to the vital issue of means. That they fail to provide a clear let alone a satisfactory solution to this vital issue is perhaps less a criticism of them than a testimony to the intractibility of the issue to which they are addressed. Nor is it the essential indeterminacy of intent that compels this conclusion, since *bellum justum* plainly requires more than subjective intention in judging the quality of action. Not only does it emphasize along with intent the objective consequences of action, for the most part it deduces intent from these consequences. Whether or not the actor is deemed to have intended to do evil is determined, in the absence of acknowledged intent to do evil, by inquiry into the character of the means he has chosen. The character of the means he has chosen is in turn determined

---

[20] The general principle involved here, and which comprises the above conditions, is commonly termed the principle of double effect. There are some variations in the formulation of these conditions. Thus it is often said that of the two effects of a permitted action, the first, and good effect is directly or positively intended while the second, and evil effect must be beside the actor's intention or only indirectly intended. In any event, the evil effect cannot be a means to the good effect. Hence, in the chain of consequences or in the order of causality—though not necessarily in order of time—the good effect must either precede or be immediate with the evil effect, else the evil effect would presumably cause, or be a means to, the good. The principle of double effect therefore attempts to reconcile the injunction against doing evil that good may come with the taking of certain acts that are known, and even known with certainty, to entail evil effects. In the case of war it is evident that this attempted reconciliation is mandatory if war is to be sanctioned at all, since evil effects of varying magnitude—i.e., the death and injury of the innocent—form an unavoidable effect of war. Of the three conditions set out in the text only the first two are examined in succeeding pages. The third requirement, that of proportionality, has already been discussed in relation to the justice of war in general. The indeterminacy of this test in a narrower context is almost as great as it must prove to be in a broader context, even though some writers attempt to reduce this indeterminacy by insisting that the effects, both evil and good, must be the "immediate" effects. No useful purpose is served by raising once again those considerations brought forth in earlier pages. Even so, the extreme limits to which the test of proportionality has been pushed by some moralists is significant and will be noted in a later connection.

by inquiry into the action itself, above all by inquiry into the consequences following from or the consequences that might have been
reasonably expected to follow from the action. Yet it is precisely this
dependence on the objective—indeed, on the quantitative—character
of action to which just war theorists are ultimately driven that lays
bare the largely relative nature of the judgments they must make.[21]
In practice, whether the death and injury done to the innocent is
directly intended or is beside the intention of the actor is determined
by the scope of this death and injury. But there are no objective
criteria for determining how much death and injury may be done to
the innocent while still preserving the right intention, or, conversely,
when such death and injury must establish the wrong intention. In
the absence of such criteria it is clear that the judgments men make
will be influenced in varying degree, whether consciously or unconsciously, by the claims of necessity. What was apparently excluded
at the front door is therefore admitted in large measure through the
back door.

Nor is this all. The attempt to reconcile the necessities of war—
of any war—with the injunction against doing evil that good may
come can be undertaken only by virtue of an implausible, or, at any
rate, an artificial, notion of means. If it is known with certainty that

---

[21] It is not enough to admit this dependence without drawing the full consequences from that admission. Thus Paul Ramsey writes: "It is the virtue, and
perhaps the irrelevance, of modern formulations of the rule of double effect in
the theory of the just war that, by requiring more than subjective intention, by
requiring that objectively also the intrinsically evil effect of the slaying of innocent
people be not a means to whatsoever military advantage, we are brought close
to the rejection of all modern warfare." *War and the Christian Conscience,* p. 64.
But how can we tell whether or not this slaying is a means rather than a second
or indirect effect? Surely we cannot do so through analyzing intentions as such,
since the indeterminacy of intent gave rise to the problem in the first place. Nor
can we do so through study of the sequence or order of action. The second effect
need not come later in time. Ramsey goes on to note: "It is a question of which
effect is, in the objective order, incidental to which, even when both effects are
produced at the same time from a single action." But this is clearly a matter of
quantity then—of objective consequences. Another writer, discussing the principle
of double effect in much the same terms as Ramsey, declares: "It is nonsense to
pretend that you do not intend to do what is the means you take to your chosen
end. Otherwise there is absolutely no substance to the Pauline teaching that we
may not do evil that good may come." G. E. M. Anscombe, "War and Murder" in
Walter Stein, ed., *Nuclear Weapons and Christian Conscience* (1961), p. 59. This
statement leaves in abeyance the critical issue: what are the means you take to
your chosen end? Are they determined by inquiry into the intention of the actor
or by inquiry into the nature of the end the actor seeks and the character of the
measures without which this end cannot be achieved?

in attacking a military objective death and injury will be inflicted upon the innocent, if it is known that two effects will follow inevitably from the action, the destruction of the military objective and the death and injury of noncombatants, is it still plausible to assert as theorists of *bellum justum* do assert that the one effect is a means while the other effect is not? Ordinarily, we regard a certain effect as a means to an end if that end cannot be secured without this effect, if the realization of the one is dependent, and is known to be dependent, upon the occurrence of the other. If this view is accepted, the death and injury inflicted on the innocent in the course of attacking a military objective is as much a means as is the destruction of the military objective. Whereas the one effect, destruction of the military objective, is a means to the end of victory in war, the other effect, the death and injury of noncombatants, is indirectly a means to the same end and directly a means to the end of destroying the military objective. Both effects, however, must be considered as means. It is true that one may avoid this conclusion, and thereby deny that the effect of inflicting death and injury on noncombatants is a means, by equating the notion of means with the question of intent. On this latter view, the one effect is a means because it is intended while the other effect, although it is foreseen, is not a means because it is presumably not intended, at least not directly intended, only reluctantly permitted. But this view not only must raise those difficulties attending the determination of intent considered above, it must also impute a meaning to intent that is very questionable. If it is known that an act will have certain evil consequences, and the act is nevertheless taken, it is plausible to contend that some of these consequences were not intended only if intent is made synonymous with wish or desire. This equation, however, accords neither with ordinary usage nor with common sense. We may not wish or desire something to happen, yet we may intend it to happen. The reason for this distinction is simply that to intend means to have in mind as something to be done or brought about. Thus we may not wish or desire a certain consequence of action and consider this consequence as tragic or as an evil. Even so, we intend this consequence if we know that it will result from a certain action and we nevertheless take this action.[22]

---

[22] There is a further point to be made in this connection. To say, as do the theorists of *bellum justum*, that an act must "positively intend only the good effect and merely tolerate the evil effect" is to give a moral significance to the notion of intent without resolving the real difficulty. Objectively, we still intend the one effect just as much as we intend the other effect. It does not alter matters to characterize the one effect as positively intended and the other effect as merely

It is altogether understandable that theorists of *bellum justum* have been so insistent upon tying an implausible notion of means to an equally implausible notion of intent, in view of the critical purpose this association serves. Once it is abandoned the attempt to reconcile the necessities of any war with the injunction that evil may not be done must also be abandoned. Yet to abandon this vain reconciliation is not also to abandon the position that means must remain limited; to acknowledge that it is not possible to wage war without doing evil is not thereby to open the door to any and every evil. There are still means and means, just as there is still evil and evil. If the issue that must be faced and somehow resolved is not whether one may do evil that good may come but rather how much evil one may do that any good may come, it is not for this reason without significance. There is surely a very important difference between the destruction of a city in order to destroy a military objective within or near the city and the destruction of the military objective, although destruction of the military objective inevitably involves inflicting some death and injury on noncombatants. There is still a very important difference even if we acknowledge that in both cases the death and injury done to the innocent is a means to the desired effect (end) and that in both cases this death and injury is intended. Whereas in the one case the death and injury done to noncombatants is, or may be, itself desired, in the other case it is not. If the one means is compatible with warfare that still retains significant limits, the other means is either not compatible or much less so. Above all, perhaps, is simply the difference in the objective consequences, the quantitative effects, of the two actions.

---

tolerated. Moreover, even the moral significance implied thereby is not without difficulty. When a military objective is attacked, death and suffering always result if only for combatants. De we "positively intend" this, is it a "good effect?" To the Christian moralist it would hardly seem so. From his point of view what we should "positively intend" is to repel injustice. The "good effect" is the repelling of injustice or perhaps the vindication of justice. The death and suffering inflicted on combatants is not as such a good effect. It too, is an evil that is tolerated, though only tolerated, in order to achieve a good end (effect). Of course, it is an evil that is far more tolerable than other evils, e.g. the death and suffering of noncombatants. Once again, the point must be stressed that at issue here is not whether one evil is greater than, or less tolerable than, the other evil but whether both evils (effects) must be considered as means. This issue cannot be resolved by endless, and inconclusive, discussion of the question of intent. Even if we were to concede that what is "indirectly intended," or "reluctantly permitted," is somehow different from what is "directly intended," or "positively permitted," it does not follow that the effect only indirectly intended is not a means. It too is a means, though it is a means that may be distinguished from the means that is directly intended or positively permitted.

There is no compelling reason, then, why we must accept the contention that if it is once accepted that evil must be done in war the issue of means is dissolved and any behavior sanctioned. This result *may* follow. The assumption that it *must* follow is no more compelling than the assumption that if men only believe that evil may never be done their behavior will thereby be restrained. Instead of restraining their behavior, the belief that evil may never be done may only strain their ingenuity. If evil may never be done, the practical significance of this injunction will still depend on the manner in which doing evil is conceived. Given sufficient ingenuity of conception, war takes on the character of an event in which ever greater evil effects may result yet apparently through no evil acts. In the most recent, and perhaps the most impressive, example of this ingenuity of conception it is argued that even the waging of a thermonuclear war need not imply the doing of evil so long as belligerents employ their weapons only against counterforce targets and other legitimate military objectives. The death and injury suffered by civilian populations would admittedly constitute a very great evil, but these evil effects might still be justified. At any rate, these evil effects, whatever might be said of their proportionality or disproportionality, would still not be the doing of evil. And if this use of nuclear weapons is not the doing of evil, it seems clearer still that the threat to use nuclear weapons against military objectives need not be considered forbidden.

Moreover, in order to remove lingering doubts about an intent to do evil, the threat to use nuclear weapons against military objectives may be attended by the express renunciation of an intent ever to use these weapons directly against a civilian population. In view of the magnitude of the expected destruction that would still be indirectly inflicted on the civilian population in the course of a direct attack on military objectives, deterrence would in all likelihood remain effective. Finally, however frequent and vehement the disclaimer of an intent directly to attack the civilian population of a potential adversary, even as a measure of reprisal in response to a similar attack, the character of nuclear weapons is such that an adversary can never be assured the weapons will not be used in this manner. This residual uncertainty results not only from the inherently ambiguous character of these weapons; it also, and perhaps more importantly, results from men's inability to predict with any real confidence what the consequences will be of using nuclear weapons and, indeed, whether their use can be reasonably controlled at all. This residual uncertainty forms the capstone of the deterrent system;

it cannot be removed from this system short of the dismantling of the system through destruction of the weapons themselves.[23]

It is roughly in this manner that the attempt has been made to bring both nuclear deterrence and even the waging of thermonuclear

---

[23] The position summarized above has been articulated at length by Paul Ramsey, *The Limits on Nuclear War* (1963) and "More Unsolicited Advice to Vatican Council II," in *Peace, The Churches and the Bomb* (1965). What makes Ramsey's writings of particular interest is not only the ingenuity with which he develops the argument for a just deterrent strategy and a just nuclear war strategy, should deterrence fail, but that he does so while remaining firmly committed to the more general position that the distinctive quality of *bellum justum* must be found in the restraints on the means of warfare, that there are certain means which because of their intrinsic evil may never be justifiably employed and that a largely teleological view of the Christian ethic, in refusing to place absolute limits on means, leads to the suspension—indeed, to the ultimate perversion—of an essential part of that ethic. This general position Ramsey set out in detail in his earlier study, *War and the Christian Conscience*. In the two later essays, cited above, he is concerned to show, first, that if war is to be a "rational politically purposive activity" it must be predominantly a "trial of strength" rather than a "test of resolve" or "battle of wills" and, second, that if war is so conceived it is possible to fashion a just—*and effective*—deterrent strategy as well as a just policy for waging nuclear war. Ramsey assumes that if war is a trial of strength it must thereby have limited means. If, however, war is a test of wills it must have essentially unlimited (and subjective) purposes; accordingly, it very probably must also be conducted by unlimited means. In terms of nuclear strategies, the former concept of war will go no higher than counterforce warfare whereas the latter concept may—and probably will—go to city exchanges (*The Limits on Nuclear War,* pp. 17–20). The argument is unpersuasive, however, because the essential distinction on which it rests is untenable. Will, or resolve, is a decisive ingredient in any "trial of strength." It is indeed difficult to imagine the character of a trial of strength that at the same time would not also be a trial of will or test of resolve. Of course, it is another matter to argue that the measures taken in war should be roughly commensurate or proportionate to the purposes of war, and, accordingly, that war *both* as a trial of strength and as a test of wills should reflect this commensurability. This counsel of perfection, which in practice men have seldom been able to meet, still says nothing about the nature of the purposes men should entertain in war. Instead, it merely says that whatever these purposes may be, the measures taken in war should be commensurate to them. Even so, one apparent qualification to this counsel is the sometimes advantageous tactic of attempting to obtain one's purposes either without a trial of strength altogether or with a minimum trial of strength by appearing more determined (resolved) than an opponent. If there are obvious limits to this tactic, they are very difficult to fix with any precision if only for the reason that the worth men set on the purposes or interests for which they fight and consequently the lengths to which they are prepared to go in order to obtain or to defend these purposes or interests, are difficult to fix with any precision. It is no adequate answer to this consideration to insert the antidote of common sense and to insist that some interests are still more

war into apparent conformity with the requirements on means laid down by *bellum justum*. The cumulative effect of that attempt is to reduce to a hollow shell the injunction against doing, or intending to do, evil that good may come. Not only does it strain the notion of

---

important than other interests, which is undoubtedly true, or that an opponent cannot be persuaded that all your interests are equally vital to you simply because you insist they are equally vital, which is also true. Despite these necessary, though obvious, limitations the fact remains that in most major conflicts there is a significant, and persistent, area of uncertainty in which one may obtain one's purposes by appearing more determined, and by being more determined, than an opponent. Moreover, there is the critically important consideration that the temptation to substitute a trial of wills for a trial of strength is roughly commensurate to the prospect of horrendous consequences issuing from a trial of strength. The relevance of this consideration in the case of almost any trial of strength between nuclear powers need not be labored. Indeed, to the extent that this prospect appears so horrendous as to render increasingly incommensurable the relation between the consequences of employing nuclear arms and the purposes or interests to be secured through such employment, to that extent the temptation, amounting almost to a compulsion, arises to substitute a trial of wills for what was heretofore a trial of strength and a trial of wills. In other terms, the trial of wills to which we give the name deterrence increasingly becomes the modern analogue of the wars of former periods; instead of "acting" out their conflicts, men are increasingly driven to "play" them out. In a nuclear age, then, the "spiritualization" of war appears inevitable unless nuclear powers are to abandon war altogether (i.e., in spirit and in form) in their mutual relations or to "conventionalize" nuclear wars. Ramsey's argument provides no persuasive considerations that the latter wars may prove feasible. Despite his sometimes all-too-confident statements about "limited counterforce warfare," his argument that just deterrent strategies are possible rests in part precisely on the uncertainty—indeed, the skepticism—that nuclear war can be so limited. Finally, in drawing his distinction between trials of strength and trials of wills, Ramsey neglects altogether the consideraiton that in any conflict, nuclear or otherwise, the importance of will depends upon the stakes of conflict. Thus in what is primarily a hegemonial conflict will becomes supremely important precisely because what is at stake is not whose will is to prevail in order to secure some other, and perhaps limited, objective but whose will is to prevail in order to prevail. Now one may refuse to consider this case, one may dismiss it out of hand as Ramsey is disposed to do simply by excluding it from the realm of "concrete policy," but in doing so one also dismisses the most important conflicts that arise among men. An analysis that declares in effect that it will not consider hegemonial struggles, that it will not deal with conflicts in which the motives of vain-glory and of survival are inextricably mixed yet all important, is largely irrelevant to the present period of state relations, not to speak of other periods. Nor can one get around this criticism by using such question-begging terms, as does Ramsey, as "*political* limits," "controlling objectives," "choiceworthy political effects," etc. If these terms are intended to rule out of order conflicts in which the desire to be first or in which the desire to survive are paramount, what point can they have when these are precisely the critical conflicts with which we must deal? And even if we take these terms seriously, to argue, for example, that

doing evil beyond reasonable limit, even on the basis of its own presuppositions it must rely on the threat to do evil. That this threat is for the most part implicit rather than explicit, that it largely inheres in the nature of the weapons themselves and men's inability to predict the consequences of using these weapons rather than in the overt threat to use them in a certain manner, does not alter matters. The expectations men entertain of the way in which nuclear weapons would be used if deterrence failed form as much a part of the reality of deterrence, so long as these expectations persist, as do the weapons on which such expectations rest. In consequence, whatever the express articulation of deterrent strategies, so long as men continue to entertain these expectations the effectiveness of the deterrent threat will continue to rest largely on what is interpreted as a threat to do evil. And given the novelty of the weapons that form the basis of deterrent systems there is, after all, quite as much to be said for the view that the use of nuclear weapons would not and could not be confined to military objectives as there is to be said for the contrary view.

To be sure, it may be argued that even if deterrent strategies rely on the threat to do evil, that threat still does not necessarily imply an actual intent to do evil. If what is evil to do must also be evil to intend to do, however small the chance that this intent will have to be carried out, it does not follow that what is evil to intend to do must also be evil to threaten to do. Nuclear strategies may therefore rely, it is argued, on a threat to do evil that still need not betray an actual intent to do evil. And even if the moralist may question the justification of threatening to do evil, though not intending to do evil, there is still a difference between a threat of action that carries no intent to act and a threat that does do so. But all this argument succeeds in establishing is a distinction which no one would care to deny, that is, that a threat to act may be distinguished from an intent to act. It does not indicate how the threat on which deterrence is based, if only by implication, can be effectively maintained without also maintaining the intent to carry out the threat if necessary. Still less, does it indicate how, in practice, an intentless threat may be distinguished from an intentful threat without putting the threat to the one and only reliable test. In the absence of this test, however, it must be admitted that the argument cannot be conclusively disproved. All that can be said, though it seems quite enough, is that in the absence of very strong

hegemony or survival are not "choiceworthy political effects" is, to say the least, a rather curious reading of history. If, however, we read history more normally they are not only the effects men have most desired, but also the effects which render the element of will supremely important.

evidence to the contrary, there is no reason to assume that a threat to do evil does not also imply an intent to do evil.[24]

The conclusion to which these considerations lead is that if we are not deliberately to press *bellum justum* into the mold of reason

---

[24] These remarks ought not to be interpreted as an acceptance of the view that what is evil to do is also evil to threaten to do, and to intend to do, whatever the consequences of refusing to threaten evil and however small the chance that the threat will ever have to be acted on. It is not self-evident why what must be evil to do must also be evil to threaten to do, and to intend to do, apart from the circumstances attending and the consequences following this threat. For the Christian moralist, however, it is self-evident. One must never intend to do evil simply because one ought never to entertain an evil intent. The view that if an act would be evil to do it must also be evil to intend to do may take several forms. In its pure form, one must never intend to do evil simply because one ought never to entertain an evil intent, and this quite apart either from the prospect that the intent will have to be acted on or from the consequences the intent (not the action) may have for those who entertain it. In its less than pure form, one must never intend to do evil because of the possibility that at some time, in some circumstances, one will do evil. Finally, there is the argument that even if the intent may never have to be acted on, one ought never to intend to do evil in view of the debilitating consequences that entertaining this intent will have for its possessor. In its pure form, then, the injunction against intending evil is evidently independent of calculation and consequence, whereas in its impure forms this injunction is just as evidently dependent on calculation and consequence. Moreover, in its impure forms this injunction is open to question when applied to a given situation precisely because it is dependent on calculation and consequence. Thus the condemnation of strategies of deterrence which are based on these impure, or less than absolute, versions of the injunction against doing evil are open to challenge and to possible rejection on their own chosen grounds. It may well be, for example, that the possibility of deterrent strategies breaking down is so small as to be negligible. And if this possibility is negligible, or is believed to be negligible, the consequences of holding this intent may not prove debilitating at all for the holders. Even if this possibility is not believed to be negligible, it may not prove debilitating. Indeed, what evidence there is seems to point to the conclusion that, on the whole, deterrent strategies have not proven debilitating for those societies maintaining them. At any rate, the argument from consequences is dependent on an examination of consequences, so far as we are in a position to do so, and a weighing of these consequences against the possible consequences of abandoning a deterrent strategy. By implication, it also involves a comparison of the values gained and sacrificed by each set of consequences and the making of a choice. But this must mean that the values involved, including the value of avoiding the intent to do evil, are only relative in character. In marked contrast, the Christian moralists who insist on the pure form of the injunction against intending to do evil must unreservedly condemn deterrent strategies, if the considerations put forth in the text above are sound. Even if deterrence is acknowledged as a means to a very desired end (world peace), and even if deterrence is acknowledged to operate with something akin to certainty, particularly if the threat is made sufficiently horrendous, it must nevertheless be con-

of state there is an irreconcilable conflict between the requirement of *bellum justum* and the requirement of deterrent strategies. This conclusion is not prompted in the first place by the unpersuasive character of the attempts that have been made to reconcile possible deterrent strategies with the requirements on means laid down by *bellum justum*.[25] Even if these attempts were more persuasive than they are they would fail in what must be their fundamental purpose, which is to show that in principle as well as in practice such reconciliation is possible. It is not enough to demonstrate that a hypothetical deterrent strategy or an equally hypothetical strategy for waging thermonuclear war may just possibly be made compatible with *bellum justum*. What must instead be shown is that the limiting conditions which may just possibly establish this compatibility can also be made, as a matter of principle and of practice, politically effective yet remain self-contained. No one has shown this, however, and it is altogether unlikely that anyone will be able to show this. All that can be shown is that the principal, and apparently the indispensable, sanction for the limits required of the just war, nuclear or otherwise, remains the meaningful threat of nuclear war which clearly exceeds these limits.[26]

---

demned if it implies the intent to do evil. Given the consequences that would probably follow from the condemnation of deterrence, if such condemnation were acted upon, the understandable reluctance on the part of many moralists to avoid that result has been productive of ingenuous efforts toward condoning deterrence yet insisting upon the pure form of the principle that evil may never be intended that good may come. The "psychology of deterrence" of course encourages such efforts. Thus, in addition to the distinction drawn between threat and intent, discussed above, it has been urged that deterrence requires us to distinguish between an interim and a final or ultimate intention. According to this argument, there is no ultimate evil intention involved in deterrence, only an interim intention to do evil. Paradoxically, one's ultimate intention can be free from evil only if cne's interim intention is evil. If I really intend to do evil, and the adversary knows I really intend to do evil, I will never have to do evil. My interim intent not only saves me from having to carry out this intent; the knowledge of this permits me ultimately not to intend to do evil at all.

There is no end to this sort of casuistry. However much these efforts may elicit our admiration, and even sympathy, they fail to persuade.

[25] We must emphasize the term "possible," since "actual" deterrent strategies are expressly based on the threat of attacking, if necessary, civilian populations. We have no reason to suppose that this threat does not correspond to real intent.

[26] A very different view of the possibility of reconciling the requirements of *bellum justum* with the requirements of nuclear deterrence is taken by Paul Ramsey, *The Limits of Nuclear War* and "More Unsolicited Advice to Vatican Council II." Ramsey believes such reconciliation is possible, if we distinguish with sufficient clarity between a "declared" and a "real" intention and if we assess correctly the "shared deterrence in the collateral damage inflicted by use of

There is no way, then, by which the present circle can be squared, no way by which the necessities of the nuclear power can be acknowledged yet the measures by which these necessities may be preserved always limited. In principle, there has never been a way by which the state's necessities can be acknowledged yet the measures by which these necessities may be preserved always limited. Nuclear weapons have not created this dilemma, they have simply illuminated it as never before and given it greater poignancy than men ever thought possible. Even so, whether and to what extent the require-

---

nuclear weapons over legitimate targets only." Although both points have been dealt with in the text, some additional remarks on the second point are in order. Ramsey's collateral damage is mainly the damage inflicted on noncombatants in the course of attacking military objectives. It is, in his view, not only an effective form of deterrence ("mutual and enough, without ever thinking of executing city-hostages") but a just form of deterrence ("Legitimate deterrence is the indirect effect of the unavoidable indirect effects [collateral civil damage] of properly targeted and therefore justly intended and justly conducted war in the nuclear age.") "More Unsolicited Advice . . .," pp. 46–47. We must ask, however, if purely counterforce deterrence has been "mutual and enough" why haven't nuclear powers been satisfied with it? The answer, it would appear, is that whereas the statesman knows that the limitation of violence is ultimately dependent on the threat of unlimited violence, Ramsey refuses to acknowledge this dependency. Besides, how limited is the nuclear war, hence the deterrent intent, Ramsey does consider compatible with *bellum justum?* Expert testimony indicates that between major nuclear powers a nuclear war limited to counterforces may still be expected to result in the deaths of perhaps a majority of the population of the participants. Even if we were to accept the view that this "indirect effect" of killing half a population would not be the doing of evil, there would remain the question of the proportionality of the action. Ramsey has correctly pointed out the indeterminacy of the test of proportionality. But if we are to retain this test at all, and we can scarcely discard it, the admitted indeterminacy of proportionality cannot be simply caricatured. If there is a point beyond which the sheer destruction of nuclear war becomes disproportionate to any good sought, where does Ramsey draw this line? To answer by declaring that the line cannot be drawn in advance is to permit, if only by implication, the death and injury of any portion of an adversary's noncombatant population so long as this death and injury is the presumed indirect effect of properly targeted weapons. Finally, and perhaps most importantly, the question arises whether Ramsey's use of "collateral" effects, in terms of indirect civil damage, is not a clear abuse of the principle of double-effect, in the sense that this principle is understood by Ramsey as well as by other Christian moralists. In a critique of Ramsey's position on collateral damage, Walter Stein correctly identifies this abuse: "The decisive flaw in Ramsey's position is the dependence of his supposed 'collateral deterrence' upon effects essential to the purpose of nuclear strategy, directly indispensable, radically wanted—and yet to be sanctioned as 'side-effects.'" "The Limits of Nuclear War: Is a Just Deterrence Strategy Possible?" in *Peace, the Churches and the Bomb*, p. 81.

ments of *bellum justum* are reconcilable in practice with the necessities of the state has always been conditioned by circumstances. When circumstance has permitted a reconciliation in practice, the reconciliation has nevertheless been made possible by the meaningful, if perhaps unobtrusive and unoppressive, prospect of conflict that must exceed the limits of the just war. The age-old institution of reprisal is but the most obvious illustration of this truth that the possibility of restraint in statecraft has been ultimately grounded in the possibility of a lack of restraint, or, in the terms of *bellum justum*, that the possibility of not doing evil has been ultimately grounded in the possibility of doing evil. Nevertheless, it is true that in the case of strategies of nuclear deterrence, the threat to do evil is more obtrusive and oppressive than ever before. It is also true that the dilemma which in practice could once be left in abeyance by those who insist that the state's necessities must always remain limited can no longer be left in abeyance.

Thus it is particularly in the nuclear age that it is the fate of *bellum justum* either to risk political irrelevance or to risk sacrificing its distinctive claim in order to remain politically relevant. If the injunction against doing evil that good may come is taken seriously the price is political irrelevance. If *bellum justum* is to remain politically relevant, the price is the erosion of the significance of "doing evil." For political relevance can be ultimately insured only by acceptance of the constituent principle of statecraft, which is that of reciprocity or retribution. Given the circumstances in which statecraft is conducted, the rejection of this principle is tantamount to the rejection of statecraft itself. Yet it is precisely this principle that *bellum justum* must reject if it is to set limits to the necessities of state. That the point in practice at which the latent antagonism between the injunction against doing, or threatening, evil and the principle of "like for like" must become overt cannot be determined in the abstract and with certainty does not mean that it cannot be determined at all. That it depends upon circumstances and a judgment that may always prove fallible does not warrant the conclusion that it is therefore non-existent. Whoever takes this position must refuse to acknowledge that in practice it is scarcely possible to identify the doing of evil at all.

The Just War and Vatican II

In the light of the foregoing analysis, what may we say of the statement on war in the Pastoral Constitution on "The Church in the

Modern World," adopted by the Second Vatican Council?[27] Our reply to this question can be summarily stated at the outset. The Council's position on war does not appear to deviate substantially from what has been earlier described as the prevailing twentieth century reconstruction of *bellum justum*. In consequence, the ambiguities inherent in this modern reconstruction are equally inherent in the position taken by the Council. Finally, the critical issues raised by the prospect of nuclear war and, more importantly, by existing strategies of deterrence are left by the Council largely as they were found.

This assessment of the Council's work will scarcely be challenged with respect to the position taken on the right of states to have recourse to armed force. The Council appears to adopt as its own the prevailing modern version of the *jus ad bellum* in declaring that: "As long as the danger of war remains and there is no competent and sufficiently powerful authority at the international level, governments cannot be denied the right to legitimate defense once every means of peaceful settlement has been exhausted." A literal interpretation of this right, it is true, does not exclude a measure of doubt over its meaning. A "right to legitimate defense" need not be construed as a right to have recourse to armed force only to protect the state's self— its territorial integrity and political independence—against unjust attack. A "right to legitimate defense" may be interpreted as a right to use armed force not only to defend the state's "self" but also to defend other rights of the state as well. Thus the statement may be understood to comprise a right to employ armed force not only as a measure of legitimate self-defense but, more generally, as a measure of legitimate self-help taken in response to other injuries done to a state, injuries in response to which alternative means of self-redress prove unavailing and unsatisfactory. But if this latter interpretation is not excluded, it is hardly a reasonable interpretation in view of the developments we have already noted. There is no sufficient reason to assume that the Council intended to arrest, and even to reverse, these developments by reaffirming, in effect, the *jus ad bellum* of the classic doctrine. Moreover, in a statement that shortly follows the statement quoted above, the Council speaks of being "compelled" to undertake an evaluation of war with an "entirely new attitude." In

---

[27] Cf. Second Vatican Council, *Pastoral Constitution on the Church in the Modern World, December 7, 1965* (National Catholic Welfare Conference, 1966). The Council's statement on war appears in Part II, Chapter V. In the following analysis we have chosen to concentrate on those issues developed in earlier pages. A number of significant issues raised by the Council's statement are thereby neglected.

part, at least, it seems clear that this "entirely new attitude" consists in restricting the just war to the war of legitimate self-defense.[28]

If the Council limits the just war to the war of legitimate self-defense, it does not have a great deal to say about the meaning and scope of this one remaining justification for war. The persisting uncertainty and controversy over the rights on behalf of which, and the acts in response to which, forcible measures of self-defense may be justly undertaken are scarcely considered. What the Council does address itself to are the general conditions or requirements that must be observed in exercising the right of legitimate defense. Although this right "cannot be denied" states, it may only be exercised "once every means of peaceful settlement has been exhausted." Since war, and particularly modern war, is an evil to be avoided whenever possible, this duty to exhaust every means of peaceful settlement must be taken with the utmost seriousness. Those who share public responsibility are therefore reminded that they have the duty "to conduct such grave matters soberly and to protect the welfare of the people entrusted to their care." If armed force nevertheless remains the only recourse open to a government, those who share public responsibility are further admonished that "it is one thing to undertake military action for the just defense of the people, and something else again to seek the subjugation of other nations. Nor, by the same token, does the mere fact that war has unhappily begun mean that all is fair between the warring parties."

These conditions of necessity, of right intention and of the limitation of means are also the conditions of war found in the traditional doctrine, conditions the traditional doctrine applied to just wars of "aggression" as well as to just wars of "defense."[29] The Council does not expressly refer to a further condition of the traditional doctrine and, of course, of modern versions of *bellum justum* as well, that is,

---

[28] Moreover, in a note to the Council's statement on undertaking the evaluation of war with an "entirely new attitude" the following statement from John XXIII's *Pacem in Terris* is cited: "Therefore in this age of ours which prides itself on its atomic power, it is irrational to believe that war is still an apt means of vindicating violated rights."

[29] In part, of course, a change has occurred in the meaning given to right intention. Although it is true that the *recta intentio* of the traditional doctrine proscribed what the Council statement proscribes ("to seek the subjugation of other nations"), it permitted, and even stressed, the desire to punish the wicked. This punitive element no longer characterizes modern versions of *bellum justum*. If anything, this element is expressly disavowed in the contemporary reconstruction of the doctrine.

the condition or requirement of proportionality. There is no apparent reason for assuming that this omission of an express reference to the principle of proportion is significant. Perhaps the Council considered this condition so self-evident as not to require express reiteration. Perhaps the Council considered that the principle of proportion was implicit almost throughout the Council's statement on the avoidance of war, that it implicitly formed a large part of the rationale on which the Council's statement rested, and for this reason needed no explicit reference. Whatever the reason, the omission is interesting, if not significant, in view of the prominence usually accorded the principle of proportion in previous utterances of the Church and, more generally, in the writings on war of Christian moralists.

We have earlier argued that if we are to find a distinctive quality in *bellum justum*, a quality that sets clear and meaningful limits to the necessities of the state, this quality must be found in the restraints placed on the conduct or means of war. Whereas reason of state must reject the claim that there are inherent limits on the means that may be threatened or employed to preserve the state, *bellum justum* must insist that there are such limits and that whatever the circumstances these limits may never be transgressed. The Council, too, places great emphasis on the intrinsic limits that men must observe in their actions, including—or especially—their actions in war, in declaring that: ". . . the Council wishes, above all things else, to recall the permanent binding force of universal natural law and its all-embracing principles. Man's conscience itself gives ever more emphatic voice to these principles. Therefore, actions which deliberately conflict with these same principles, as well as orders commanding such actions are criminal, and blind obedience cannot excuse those who yield to them."

This is, indeed, a very uncompromising statement of principle. It reasserts, and reasserts in the most emphatic manner, that there are limits to the necessities of the state, limits that may never be transgressed. How is this statement of principle applied to the conduct of states, particularly in war? Does it set clear and meaningful limits to the measures men may take, whatever the circumstances and whatever the alleged necessities of the state? Does it forbid, is it interpreted by the Council to forbid, the doing, or the threatening, of evil that good may come?

There is no simple answer to these questions. There is no simple answer largely for the reasons that there was no simple answer to the same questions when considered in an earlier context. However uncompromising the statement of principle made by the Council, in itself this statement does not afford us much guidance with respect to the conduct which is absolutely forbidden. Genocide apart,[30] there is one, and only one, action that elicits the Council's unqualified moral condemnation. It is set forth in these words:

> . . . this most Holy Synod makes its own the condemnations of total war already pronounced by recent popes, and issues the following declaration:
>
> Any act of war aimed indiscriminately at the destruction of entire cities or extensive areas along with their population is a crime against God and man himself. It merits unequivocal and unhesitating condemnation.

How are we to interpret this most solemn declaration by the Council? What is the behavior or action that is forbidden and why is it forbidden? The two questions are, of course, closely related. In neither case, however, is the answer altogether clear. This uncertainty is particularly apparent when we examine the rationale for the Council's declaration. To be sure, for those who interpret the Council's declaration to mean the reassertion of the moral immunity of non-combatants from direct attack, the why of this declaration is entirely clear. On this view, the Council has simply and forcibly reaffirmed the essential difference between war and murder; it has said that the deliberate killing of the innocent must always be avoided, that this killing may never be justified even as a reprisal measure taken in response to similar measures of an adversary. But if this interpretation is correct why did the Council not affirm the rights of the innocent even more simply and directly by stating in traditional terms the principle of noncombatant immunity from direct attack? That principle may surely be violated, and seriously violated, by acts which fall well short of the indiscriminate destruction of "entire cities or extensive areas." Moreover, if the Council simply intended by this most solemn declaration to reassert the principle of non-combatant immunity, one might not unreasonably have expected it to go a good deal beyond this in the acts it condemned, and to do so even in the context of a discussion of the "horror and perversity" of modern warfare. That the Council does not do so leaves open the possible interpretation that it condemns total war and any act of war aimed indiscriminately at the destruction of entire cities or extensive areas primarily for the reason that these acts violate the requirement of proportionality, that the evil attending the commission of these acts

---

[30] The Council does not actually use the term genocide. Instead, it condemns as the "most infamous" among the actions which deliberately conflict with universal natural law those actions "designed for the methodical extermination of an entire people, nation or ethnic minority."

is disproportionate to the good resulting from them. It is also possible to interpret the Council's condemnation to imply that the acts condemned are so condemned because their commission, in addition to violating the principle of proportion, is not compatible with a defensive war. On this latter view, total war and acts aimed indiscriminately at the destruction of entire cities must be condemned for the additional reason that even though subjectively undertaken only in self-defense their objective effect is to lead either to the subjugation or the annihilation of the adversary.[31]

There are, then, at least three possible interpretations of the rationale for this most solemn declaration by the second Vatican Council. Even if we accept the first interpretation as the most plausible, there remains the question of the significance of this presumed

---

[31] The Council introduces the declaration under discussion by the words "with these truths in mind." In doing so, the Council evidently refers, in large part, to these statements made in an immediately preceding paragraph: "The horror and perversity of war is immensely magnified by the increase in the number of scientific weapons. For acts of war involving these weapons can inflict massive and indiscriminate destruction, thus going far beyond the bounds of legitimate defense. Indeed, if the kind of instruments which can now be found in the armories of the great nations were to be employed to their fullest, an almost total and altogether reciprocal slaughter of each side by the other would follow, not to mention the widespread devastation that would take place in the world and the deadly after-effects that would be spawned by the use of weapons of this kind." In introducing its most solemn declaration with "these truths in mind," the Council provides further support for the possible interpretation that the acts in question are condemned not only, and not even primarily, because they violate the principle of noncombatant immunity but because they violate the requirement of proportionality and go beyond the bounds of a defensive war. — It is also worth noting that one of the "truths" endorsed by the Council is not always true except in a definitional sense. If "legitimate defense" is understood to imply defense by certain means and not by others, and if the means excluded are acts inflicting "massive and indiscriminate destruction," then it is by definition true that acts inflicting such destruction "thus" go beyond the bounds of legitimate defense. It is doubtful, however, that this is all the Council intended to say. More probably, the Council intended to imply by its "truth" that acts inflicting massive and indiscriminate destruction are neither legitimate (in the definitional sense) nor defensive (in the sense of ever proving necessary for a state's defense). This latter contention is not always true. A state may employ forbidden means—including the means in question—and nevertheless wage a war that, in terms of causes and ends, is strictly defensive. If the just war must now be a war fought only in self-defense against unjust attack, it does not necessarily follow that a strictly defensive war, in terms of causes and ends, is a just war. The Council does not quite face up to the difficulties these considerations must raise. Instead, it manages to avoid them by presenting the limiting case in which war would be neither defensive nor just.

reassertion of the principle of noncombatant immunity in terms of the acts that are absolutely forbidden. Literally, what is condemned by the Council is not any act that involves the direct and intentional attack on the innocent. Nor is it even true to say that what is expressly condemned is an indiscriminate act of war. Apart from "total war," what the Council expressly condemns is not indiscriminate action as such but "any act of war aimed indiscriminately at the destruction of entire cities or extensive areas along with their population."[32] We cannot but call attention to these words: "entire cities" and "extensive areas." Is this the simple and forcible reassertion of the moral immunity of noncombatants from direct and intentional attack or is it the near emasculation of this immunity?

It may of course be argued that these considerations, and the criticism they evidently imply, miss the point. In expressly forbidding what it does expressly forbid, and forbids absolutely, the Council's declaration should not be interpreted as permitting any and all actions that fall short of these forbidden actions. What the Council does not expressly condemn it does not, for that reason, thereby permit. What men do in war, no less than what they do in peace, is subject to, in the Council's words, "the permanent binding force of universal natural law and its all-embracing principles." If one of the most important of these universal and all-embracing principles is the prohibition of murder—the deliberate killing of the innocent—the Council can hardly be criticized for not having expressly condemned behavior it evidently intended and must have intended to condemn. But even if we accept this argument, we are still left with all of the issues raised in earlier pages. Apart from condemning what it does expressly condemn, the Council does not address itself to these issues. Instead, it has for the most part simply left these issues where it found them.

These considerations should not be pushed too far. If the Council has not simply and forcibly reasserted the principle of noncombatant

---

[32] We do not seriously consider a further ambiguity in the declaration, an ambiguity that is almost certainly the result of technically poor drafting or of an inadequate translation of the original text. The Council forbids "any act of war aimed indiscriminately at the destruction of entire cities . . ." Logically, this leaves open the possibility that any act of war "aimed discriminately at the destruction of entire cities" may not be forbidden, unless, of course, the destruction of cities is, by definition, an indiscriminate act. If it is so defined, and we may assume that this definition is implied, then the statement as it stands in its English version is simply redundant rather than ambiguous. Instead, it should have read: "any act of war aimed at the destruction of entire cities . . . is indiscriminate and is a crime against God and man himself."

immunity from direct and intentional attack, it also has not abandoned that principle. If the Council has not reconciled the necessities of any war, and particularly of nuclear war, with the injunction against doing evil, it has insisted that there are at least some necessities that can never be justified, some means that may never be permitted, and accordingly, some evil that may never be done. It may be true that the acts the Council condemns are of such a character that their condemnation can hardly afford much comfort. The fact remains that these acts may express, and in certain circumstances undoubtedly do express, the necessities of the nuclear Power. Moreover, the Council, while clearly not condemning the use of nuclear weapons and other "scientific weapons," goes very far in expressing its skepticism that these weapons can in actual practice be justly employed.

The Council does not content itself merely with pointing out that these weapons "*can* inflict massive and indiscriminate destruction" but goes on to state: "The unique hazard of modern warfare consists in this: it provides those who possess modern scientific weapons with a kind of occasion for perpetrating just such abominations [i.e., the indiscriminate destruction of entire cities or extensive areas]; moreover, through a certain inexorable chain of events, it can catapult men into the most atrocious decisions." What can this passage mean save that scientific weapons severely limit the freedom men formerly enjoyed in war, a freedom to control and to limit their actions, and that they do so not because, or not primarily because, of their nature but because of man's nature. The "kind of occasion" these weapons provide their possessors, if once employed, does not constitute a necessity in the literal sense. It is a kind of occasion, however, which in practice might well prove indistinguishable from just such a necessity.

The weapons that provide a "kind of occasion" for perpetrating abominations in war also provide a way by which, in the Council's words, "peace of a sort" can be maintained. What has the Council to say about this peace of deterrence? The importance of the Council's position on deterrence need not be labored. Nuclear war is a possibility and increasingly in the view of most observers only a remote possibility. Deterrence is the reality in which we live at present and the reality in which we are very likely to continue living for a considerable time. The necessities of the nuclear state do not find their principal manifestation today in that dreaded, but hopefully remote, possibility of nuclear war. They do find their principal manifestation in deterrence. It is clear, then, that the significance of this most recent expression of the Christian response to the ancient plea of reason of state must largely be found in the Council's position on deterrence, the substance of which is found in the following paragraphs:

> Scientific weapons, to be sure, are not amassed solely for use in war. Since the defensive strength of any nation is considered to be dependent upon its capacity for immediate retaliation, this accumulation of arms, which increases every year, likewise serves, in a way heretofore unknown, as a deterrent to possible enemy attack. Many regard this as the most effective way by which peace of a sort can be maintained between nations at the present time.
>
> Whatever be the facts about this method of deterrence, men should be convinced that the arms race in which an already considerable number of countries are engaged is not a safe way to preserve a steady peace, nor is the so-called balance resulting from this race a sure and authentic peace. Rather than being eliminated thereby, the causes of war are in danger of being gradually aggravated. While extravagant sums are being spent for the furnishing of ever new weapons, an adequate remedy cannot be provided for the multiple miseries afflicting the whole modern world. Disagreements between nations are not really and radically healed; on the contrary, they spread the infection to other parts of the earth. New approaches based on reformed attitudes must be taken to remove this trap and to emancipate the world from its crushing anxiety through the restoration of genuine peace.

The reader can only sympathize with the hardships under which the drafters of this statement labored to reconcile positions that are, in the last analysis, irreconcilable. At the same time, he must remain frustrated by the studied ambiguity that appears to characterize the result of these labors. The Council declares that "many regard" the accumulation of arms for immediate retaliation against aggressive attack "the most effective way by which peace of a sort" can presently be maintained. Does the Council share this regard? It will not say so. Yet it does say that this accumulation of arms serves as a deterrent "in a way heretofore unknown." Does this imply indirect acceptance of what "many regard"? One cannot be sure. The Council disavows knowledge of the facts of deterrence ("whatever be the facts about this method of deterrence"). Yet it declares that "men should be convinced that the arms race . . . is not a safe way to preserve a steady peace . . ."[33] Why should men be so convinced, whatever be

_____
[33] The sense of this statement is, in any event, far from clear. Is the Council merely saying that there are, in principle, safer ways to preserve a steadier peace? If so, the point seems curiously out of place, since it borders on levity. On the other hand, if the Council is saying that in the world in which we presently live, a world the Council describes elsewhere so profoundly, there are available safer

the facts? Again, the Council implies that "this method of deterrence" prevents war while aggravating the causes of war, that deterrence both lessens and increases the dangers of war. This analysis may very well be true, though one may still seriously question whether sums spent on new weapons prevent an "adequate remedy" for the "multiple miseries afflicting the modern world" just as one may question whether these multiple miseries constitute a significant cause of the war men hope to avoid. But how can the Council know all this without also knowing the facts about "this method of deterrence"?

It is not with the ambiguities marking the Council's analysis of deterrence that we are primarily concerned, however, but with its judgment of the morality of deterrence. Whatever be the facts about this method of deterrence, what is the Council's position on the legitimacy of this method? In refusing to condemn the possession of nuclear weapons, does the Council thereby approve, however reluctantly, the possession of these weapons for deterrent purposes? It would seem so. Nor is this all. In failing to condemn strategies of deterrence that rest, and that are known to rest in the ultimate resort, upon the threat of destroying "entire cities," does the Council thereby approve, however reluctantly, these strategies? Again, it would seem so. If this is the most reasonable interpretation of the Council's position on the morality of deterrence, the substance of this position is that the means that may never be employed and the evil that may never be done may nevertheless be threatened.[34] Thus does the Coun-

---

ways to preserve a steadier peace than the peace of deterrence, this is an altogether different point and a point that many, including the present writer, would seriously controvert. Again, it is quite another matter to insist that what we presently have is not a "sure and authentic peace." That the "so-called balance" resulting from the arms race and deterrence is not a "sure and authentic peace" follows from the Council's definition of a sure and authentic peace. It is painfully clear that the peace of deterrence is not a peace that is the fruit of mutual trust and of justice, let alone of love. In this sense, of course, no peace men have known has been a sure and authentic peace. Moreover, in the relations of states such peace as men have known has nearly always been based on this "so-called balance" that the Council contrasts with a sure and authentic peace. These considerations apart, it probably remains true that the peace of deterrence represents the polar extreme when compared with the peace that is based on mutual trust and a shared sense of justice, for the peace of deterrence forms the classic —one is almost tempted to say the perfect—example of the peace that is based on the principle of retribution.

[34] This interpretation of the Council's position will be contested by many. Clearly, the Council neither expressly condemns nor expressly approves the possession of nuclear weapons. It is possible, then, to interpret the Council either as implicitly condemning or implicitly approving the possession of nuclear weapons.

cil retain political relevance for *bellum justum* in an age dominated by the peace of deterrence. Thus does the Council attempt to reconcile the irreconcilable, the requirements of *bellum justum* and the necessities of a nuclear Power. And thus does the Council demonstrate once

---

(We exclude the possibility that the Council neither implicitly condemns nor implicitly approves the possession of nuclear weapons. Quite apart from the logical difficulties this alleged possibility must raise, it suggests that the Council refused to take any moral position on what is perhaps the most important issue of the day and the most important issue that confronted the Council. We do not enter the charge, indeed we reject it, that the Council thus shirked its duty by refusing to provide men with moral guidance on this critical matter.) There is very little support for the position that the Council implicitly condemned the possession of these weapons. True, the Commission responsible for the drafting struck out the statement on the next to final draft that "the deterrent possession of such arms cannot be said to be illegitimate." That statement appeared to some to come very close to expressly sanctioning the possession of these weapons and was therefore resisted. It requires a curious interpretation of the omission of that statement, however, to conclude that the Council thereby implicitly condemned the possession of nuclear weapons. Indeed, the omission of that statement from the final text does not significantly alter the meaning of the text.

If the Council implicitly approved of the possession of nuclear weapons it must be further assumed that it implicitly approved, in principle, of deterrent strategies which have their basis in these weapons. The question that arises, then, and it is the central question, is whether or not the Council implicitly approved of deterrent strategies which threaten, in the last resort as a measure of reprisal, the destruction of "entire cities." Those who argue that the Council cannot be interpreted as approving such strategies point to the Council's solemn and unqualified condemnation of "total war" and of "any act of war aimed indiscriminately at the destruction of entire cities or extensive areas . . ." If the Council condemns these acts, it is contended, then it must also be understood to condemn the threat to carry out these acts and, of course, the intent to do so. We do not deny that this argument is a possible interpretation of the Council's position. We do assert that it is not the more plausible interpretation of that position. If the Council wished to condemn deterrent threats of an indiscriminate nature, why did it not do so? Nothing would have been easier than to have made a statement in the context of deterrence parallel to the statement made in the context of war. But the Council did not do so, and it did not do so knowing that strategies of deterrence rest, in the final resort, on the threat of counter-city warfare. How are we to interpret a statement that condemns, and condemns absolutely, acts which form only a hopefully remote possibility yet is silent on threats which form the reality in which we daily live?

The answer to this question, it would seem, is that the Council Fathers were faced with a true moral dilemma. The issue of deterrence raised conflicting moral demands. As between these conflicting moral demands the Council remained uncertain, hence the Delphic character of its statement on the morality of deterrence. At least, this would appear to be a reasonable interpretation of the Council's statement on deterrence. Nevertheless, it will be resisted by those moralists, and particularly by Catholic moralists, who refuse to accept the possi-

again that there is no way by which the circle can be squared, that there is no way by which the injunction against doing, or threatening, evil that good may come can be reconciled with the constituent principle of statecraft.

---

bility of true moral dilemmas arising. From this viewpoint, moral choice may be extremely difficult but it never gives rise to a true dilemma, the essence of which is the inability to justify a choice between moral claims that, although regarded as equally compelling, have become irreconcilable. But this viewpoint assumes that men have, or may always have, a clear hierarchy of values and that the significance of this hierarchy of values is always apparent in practice. There is no persuasive reason, however, for believing that this must always be so. Nor, indeed, does experience indicate that it is always so. Moral dilemmas may, and do, arise because men are often unable to order their moral life as neatly as this view assumes. Not only do they often give equal significance to certain ends which circumstances have made irreconcilable, they are often confronted with situations in which it is next to impossible to determine the effects of a choice, any choice, on the values they do hold.

Modern War and the Pursuit of Peace

Theodore R. Weber

Introduction

The notion of justified war implies that freedom is a condition of all human action including political action, and that all action in freedom is subject to moral limitations. It is opposed to naturalistic interpretations of war, which deny accountability and the power of contrary choice, and to *realpolitischen* interpretations, which deny responsibility beyond the interests of the parochial political community. However, despite its moral intentions, the notion of justified war always has been a severe problem for the Christian conscience. The reasons for its problematical character are well known. Christian discipleship in its purest and most primitive model is defined in terms of total reliance on the providence of God and unqualified love for the neighbor. In this model, one who has been drawn out of his old existence into a new creaturely relationship to God through Jesus Christ is non-resistant and self-sacrificial. He suffers harm but does not inflict it, and he renounces every inclination to rely on force for the achievement of his goals and the fulfillment of his responsibilities. Supported by the authority of this model, Christian pacifists always have argued that the development of the just war concept represents a degeneration of Christian witness and commitment, that it baptizes war rather than preventing it, and that it is but a transitional stage to the intolerance and inhumanity of the crusade.[1]

These objections notwithstanding, the just war concept in one form or another is and has been the principal moral theory with which most of the communions of Christendom in most of the centuries of Christian history have wrestled with the problems of war and peace. In specifically Christian usage, as distinguished from its roots in classical antiquity, it is as old as the fourth century A.D. In its breadth of acceptance it is Protestant as well as Catholic, the doctrine of Luther as well as of Thomas Aquinas. References to the "scholastic just war tradition" are references to but one just war tradition — perhaps the most thoroughly developed one, but by no means the original or only one. The original formulation for just war deliberation was laid out well in advance of the rise of Scholasticism by St. Augustine, who, after St. Paul, was the great seminal theologian of both Catholic and Protestant theology.

Of course, to cite the antiquity and wide acceptance of the just war concept is not to prove that those who have employed it as an instrument of moral analysis and decision have been right in doing so. Certainly pacifism has a better claim both to antiquity and to correspondence with the primitive form of Christian witness. On the other hand, just war Christians never have looked upon the concept as merely a concession to human sinfulness or as merely a means of applying restraints to arrogance, malice and selfishness. Rather, they have believed it to be a necessary instrument of life lived in faith in God and loving service to the neighbor under conditions in which the hopes for radical eschatological transformation of the world have lost the power of immediacy. The problem with the "primitive form of Christian witness" is that it assured that the world was passing away in some radical and total manner. When the world refused to pass away but insisted on enduring through generations and centuries of Christian history, the "primitive form" became less suitable as a means of defining Christian vocation. To the contrary, most Christians found it necessary to face the world forthrightly as the theater in which the vocational commitment was to be acted out. And when they did so, they had to find some way of choosing among worldly alternatives under the discipline of faith and love. The intention of the just war theory was to provide criteria for guiding the choices in cases where the alternatives posed the problem of the instrumental necessity of using military force. Therefore, the just war theory was understood to be a necessary device for implementing Christian vocation in a fallen world, and not — as its critics contend — a way of baptizing man's sinful inclination to greed and violence.

Two issues in particular have seemed to demand the use of the just war theory as an inner-worldly instrument of discipline and guidance. First, the just war criteria have helped to show the moral limits of the divinely given obligation to obey the ruling authorities. Christians always have known that they are to "be subject to the governing authorities for they are ordained of God" (Romans 13:1) — although they are inclined to forget their major political tradition in a liberal democratic society and to reject it in a revolutionary age. And they always have known that they "must obey God rather than men" (Acts 5:29) — which is a way of saying that theologically grounded political authority is not absolute, precisely because it is theologically grounded. However, they have not been able to develop any universally acceptable formula for deciding exactly when the command of the ruler was contrary to the command of God. Once they concluded that the command to participate in war was not *per se* contrary to the command of God (because the rulers needed to defend the political society in order to fulfill their divine commission), they needed some device for determining the justification of particular occasions of resort to war. The just war theory — inevitably imperfect — was intended to be that device. Christians must obey the command to participate in justified wars — or at least in those not known to be unjust. Justified wars are those which are waged as a last resort by competent authority for a just cause and toward a just end, which enjoy a reasonable hope of success, which probably will produce no greater harm than that represented in the injury which provides the just cause, and which are conducted with discriminate and proportionate means.

Second, the just war theory helps to determine the concrete meaning of love for the neighbor. If love always means "never do anyone any harm," it allows no room for the concept of justified war. If, on the other hand, love requires us to meet the needs of the neighbor, it cannot exclude altogether the use of force. Many of the most important needs of human beings can be met only in the context and through the agency of political society, and political institutions always require some component of force. And yet the use of force cannot be permissible in any and every situation nor by any and every means and quantity of administration. The just war theory intends to perform the strange work of making force a disciplined instrument of love.

Basic Assumptions of Just War Theory

These explanatory comments establish the character of the just war theory as a form of political-moral theory. Its peculiar moral concern is with definitions of political responsibility, especially at those points where the discharge of political responsibility requires the use of military force. Particular determinations of justice or injustice in the use of military force are made by means of applying the just war criteria, but the criteria are only instruments of the just war theory and are not to be equated with the theory itself. The really fundamental elements of the theory are to be found in certain assumptions concerning the nature of inter-group conflict and the normative role of force in such conflict. These assumptions and the political character of the theory must be kept in mind in any effort to assess its contemporary relevance. As we consider the following assumptions, we should remember also that they are distillations from the tradition as a whole and may not be altogether characteristic of the position of any particular just war thinker.

1) Moral inquiry into the problem of war should begin with political rather than with military considerations, and the exercise of military power always should be subordinated to the determinations of political responsibility. It is no accident that the essentially political criteria of just cause, just intention and competent authority constituted the basis of the original Augustinian formulation, and that concern for the conduct of warfare emerged into full view much later in the history of the theory.[2] Whatever other reasons may be given for this chronological priority, it reflects the logical priority in moral analysis. The basic question of just war deliberation is not, "How can the war be conducted justly?" but "How can incumbent political responsibilities be discharged under conditions which require the use of military force?"

2) The justified war is political and not religious in its character and its objectives. It is not a holy war between the godly and the ungodly. "Just" and "unjust" are predicates of the positions taken and the methods employed — not essential distinctions between the one side and the other. It is not a war on behalf of the religious purposes or ecclesiastical interests of the church. The issues over which the contest takes place are those which concern the sustenance and advancement of the earthly *polis*. For those reasons they are important, and they may indeed be sufficiently important to justify the use of force for their prosecution. But they are not the ultimate issues of the Kingdom of God. To confine the military struggle to a level of political reference is important for two principal reasons: (a) when a military conflict takes on a religious or holy, i.e. a crusading, character it tends to become a war of extermination unrestrained by any sense of moral limits; (b) where the interests are religious rather than political the possibility of rational compromise is lost, because there can be no compromise with falsehood and evil.

3) The requirement of justice towards the opponent implies a fraternal connection between the belligerents which transcends their

political separation. This fraternal connection is clearly present in both the Stoic and the Christian versions of the just war theory, and it distinguishes both of them from the Aristotelian concept of the just war. In Stoicism the connection is grounded in common possession of rationality, and thereby in common participation in the divine being. Fraternity, along with liberty and equality, is one of the direct inferences from the rational nature of all human beings. In Christianity the connection is discerned in the common status of friend and foe in the grace of God. Jesus Christ died for the sins of the whole world — therefore the enemy is a brother for whom Jesus Christ died and one towards whom the Christian is directed in his divinely given ministry of reconciliation. Aristotle, by contrast, defined the justified war as one conducted for the purpose of enslaving those who by their nature are slaves.

Fraternity among the belligerents as a philosophical or theological condition of inter-group conflict is doubtless the most significant assumption of the just war theory. Not only does it demand respect for the life and personality of the opponent; it also sets moral limits to the value and the pretensions of the particular political community and asserts the ontological reality of a community transcending and including the particular communities. It does not deny that the particular communities are important for both the sustenance and the historical character of human life and personality, but it does deny their sufficiency and finality for individual existence and self-realization — and thereby it denies the basic presupposition of the ancient city-state and the inherent goal of the modern nation-state with regard to this level of community. The parochial political community is absolute neither in value nor in authority. Its commands do not override all moral reservations. Even the basic questions of its survival and independence do not justify unlimited and indiscriminate uses of force.

In practice, the just war theory depends on the sociological reality and not only on the ontological reality of the transcendent community. That is, it depends on the actual existence of connecting tissue among the belligerents, on common elements of culture, common institutions, common values. The more community really exists among the belligerents the greater is the common will to observe the moral limits. The less it exists the greater is the risk taken by any particular belligerent in attempting to observe them.[3]

4) Political authority is the basic political-moral category of just war theory. This means that the right to exercise political power must be established before the instrumental right to take human life by

military force can even be considered. The central problem involved in establishing authority lies in the fact that authority is a function of community, and no integral international community exists to authorize the exercise of power in international relations. How then can a state authoritatively use power and justifiably take human life in international conflict?

In centuries long since past some just war thinkers supposed that this difficulty could be covered by the criterion of competent authority, because they thought of warfare primarily as a problem of strife within the Christian empire, and they assumed that competent authority would be the pope or emperor as impartial judge. If this supposition ever had any realistic foundation, it ceased to have it when both pope and emperor became parties to conflicts among Italian city-states, and even more so when the nation-state emerged as a discrete and integral political unity independent of the moral and religious authority of the papacy and of the political and legal authority of the empire. Where princes or parliaments functioned as competent authority, the most that they could claim on the basis of community authorization was the authority to exercise power on behalf of their political community. They could not justifiably claim jurisdiction over other peoples.

Of course, the absence of integral and authoritative international community produced a situation in which the need to exercise power on behalf of particular communities tended to create the authority to exercise it. Usually this exercise was justified as an extension of domestic police power into external affairs, a characterization which implied that enforcement of law was the role of such power and impartiality the presupposition of its operation. The more conservative of these interpretations justified only such "police power" as was necessary to secure the rights and interests of the particular society. The more ambitious ones claimed that in the absence of a world ruler the princes qualified as "competent authority" for the purpose of enforcing the universal moral law. That is, they claimed that the princes had an implied status as officers of a wider political community — one which existed necessarily and ontologically if not legally and sociologically. If the more ambitious interpretations invited extravagant and arrogant pretensions to exercise power with no real authority, even the more conservative ones represented cases of rulers and states acting as judges in their own causes.

More recently the development of international organizations like the League of Nations and the United Nations has opened the prospect of bridging this gap and creating instruments for the genuinely authoritative exercise of power in international politics. But thus far such organizations have very limited authority, and their enforcement powers are far weaker than those of the political system itself.

Political authority remains the basic political-moral category of the just war theory, but its problems have not yet achieved satisfactory resolution.

The Crisis in the Relevance of Just War Theory

We now have set forth four basic assumptions of just war theory: the primacy of political over military considerations, the political and not religious character of the conflict, the implicit if not explicit bond of community among the belligerents, and the need to establish the authority to exercise power. All of these assumptions must be operational in any attempt to make a valid application of just war criteria to particular situations of conflict. However, just war theory is in a state of crisis vis-à-vis modern warfare and means of warfare precisely because of threats to these assumptions posed by certain conditioning factors in contemporary international relations. Three factors in particular are major sources of difficulty: (1) the development of weapons of mass destruction and their companion delivery systems; (2) the decline of Christendom as the cultural and religious context of international conflict, and the emergence of severe religious, cultural and ideological divergences in the midst of international conflict; (3) the emergence of revolutionary-interventionary wars as the principal nonnuclear form of conflict in the international system.

The crisis in the relevance of the just war theory is produced by these factors in the following way:

1) Modern weapons technology has reversed the standard procedure for deliberating the justifiability of war. From the beginning the procedure was to ask the question of justifiable cause and then proceed through the consideration of other criteria until finally the questions of the means of warfare was reached. This sequence helped to maintain the primacy of the political character of the conflict.

With the advent of nuclear weapons, however, the means rather than the causes and ends have become the prime data of inquiry. The reason for this reversal is that modern weapons systems have called radically into question the qualifying assumptions under which the possibility of justifying and regulating the conduct of war could be entertained. Preeminent among these assumptions are the following: that meaningful distinctions between combatant and non-combatant could be made and sustained both in strategy planning and in combat, that weapons were subject to the rational control of the persons using them or ordering their use, and that disproportionate uses of military force were the results either of malice or of miscalculation but not of the nature of the weapons themselves. Now all of these assumptions have been shaken if not altogether repudiated by the almost incredible destructive power of the newer weapons, the near impossibility of containing the destructive effects to spatially and temporally limited targets, the development of swift and long-range delivery vehicles, and the separation of man from weapons by technological control systems.

This state of affairs makes it necessary to establish the moral possibility of using requisite means before the ends themselves can be certified for prosecution with the means of war. To do this requires a heavy concentration on the problem of the means, and this concentration tends to over-emphasize the military aspects of policy to the neglect of the political aspects. It tends also to over-emphasize the critical and discontinuous aspects of international relations to the neglect of the more stable and systemic aspects. That is, it is inclined to be crisis-oriented — to deal with the "hot spots" of international politics and to neglect the health of the less visible and fascinating political structures which keep most problems from coming to crisis level and which attempt to manage active crises with institutional means.

Even if these were the only consequences of the reversal of the ends-means relationship, they would seriously threaten the conditions of just war theory relevance. What is most serious, however, is that the problem of the means not only displaces the problem of just cause in priority of attention but also threatens to eliminate the criterion of just cause altogether. Already there is consensus among just war thinkers that the prospects for "total war" and the implications of modern weapons systems have reduced the category of just cause to the single justifiable cause of defense against aggression. Other causes are important, but only the irreducible values of national survival and independence are considered strong enough to bear the risks and, if necessary, the costs, of nuclear warfare. But can even this cause escape the logic of this reductionism? Is the cause of defense able finally to justify the risks and the costs? Is it possible to target nuclear weapons in such a way that they do not violate the principle of noncombatant immunity? And if so, is it possible to hold the weapons at a level adequate for effective deterrence yet not disproportionate in terms of prospective damage?

For purposes of discussing this issue at its frontier I shall defer to William O'Brien in his contention that an effective defense policy presupposes a strategic nuclear deterrent, and that the execution of such a deterrent — and therefore the will to execute the deterrent — inevitably violates the principle of noncombatant immunity.[4] If adherence to that principle is a necessary condition of just conduct in war, we may go no farther in considering defense within the framework of just war theory. We are already in the ranks of the nuclear pacifists. If it is not a necessary condition — and O'Brien claims it is not — we may proceed with him to consider the morality of nuclear deterrence on the basis of the right of self-defense.[5]

But even assuming that O'Brien is right in relativizing the authority of the principle of noncombatant immunity, can the right of self-defense serve as just cause *vis-à-vis* the risks of nuclear warfare? The possibility that it might do so fails on three counts. First, a strategic nuclear deterrent defends only so long as it deters. If and when it fails to deter, the decision-makers are confronted with the choice of declining to execute the deterrent — an alternative presumably tantamount to surrender — or of executing it and very likely involving the society in a war of mutual destruction. The deterrent willed into action is self-contradictory: it draws upon the home base destruction greater than that which would have occurred had there been no deterrent. Second, the prospect of submission to Communist rulers is not demonstrably worse — or even demonstrably as bad — as the prospect of a major nuclear exchange. In stating the case thusly let us remember that the comparison is not between life under communism and life in our present society. It is between life under communism and the experience and aftermath of nuclear war, that is, the experience of megaton blasts, of fire storms, of radioactive clouds of dust, of a hundred million or more deaths, of a totally ruined society. Granting that none of us wants to live under communism, how does one determine that that would be worse than nuclear war? Third, under the terms of the criterion of just intention, as well as of the Christian mission of reconciliation, it is not morally permissible to destroy or threaten to destroy an entire political society. Yet that consequence is what is implied in the will to execute a strategic nuclear deterrent.

The conclusion is that the right of national self-defense cannot bear the weight of moral responsibility placed upon it by the need to use nuclear means for its fulfillment. And if this is the fate of the last remnant of just cause, then the just war theory itself is relevant to modern warfare — at least among nuclear-equipped powers — only as its negation.

Nuclear confrontation, however, is not the only situation of modern warfare which poses the problem of the priority of the means. It is posed also by revolutionary-interventionary warfare, although the issue is different. In this case the critical element is not the probable inherent immorality of weapons but the fact that the nature of the struggle seems to require conditions and methods of warfare which violate either or both of the criteria of just conduct.

Insurgency warfare is fought among and through the people rather than on battlefields between organized units. This style of warfare inevitably makes civilian areas the targets of counter-insurgency attack, and it raises the question whether effective counter-insurgency action can be mounted without necessarily violating the just war principle of noncombatant immunity.[6] Paul Ramsey has argued that attacks which intend to destroy the insurgent element in these mixed targets do not violate the principle of noncombatant immunity even though the village itself be destroyed.[7] The village or the area is an "enlarged military target," and the moral responsibility for having enlarged the target rests with the insurgents, not with the counter-insurgents. Ramsey denies, however, that this placement of guilt with regard to noncombatant immunity leaves the counter-insurgents morally free in every case to launch attacks which will produce major civilian damage. The attacks still must be judged by the principle of proportionality, and it may well be that they must be rejected as disproportionate. The difficulty here is that the criteria for determining proportionality are very subjective and elusive. An occasional attack of the type that destroys a whole village which also is a guerrilla base may conceivably find proportionate justification, but can the practice be justified when the nature of the conflict requires it as a matter of standing policy?

A further level of difficulty is reached when the insurgents begin to draw support from the populace, e.g., when some of the peasants become daytime farmers and night time guerrillas, or when the people, because of effective intimidation, cooperate with the insurgents in concealment, deception, logistics, and information. Combatant-noncombatant becomes a distinction of roles in the same person rather than a distinction between persons. For military purposes it is justifiable to say that the acceptance of the belligerent role even as only one role makes one liable to attack, but the camouflage provided by the duality of roles makes it difficult and sometimes impossible to know whether the target is a military one at all. Can this situation, too, be covered by the notion of the "unjustly enlarged target"?

Problems of the conduct of revolutionary-interventionary warfare are not as intractable, morally speaking, as are problems of upper level nuclear deterrence. Because the actual weapons still are conventional weapons, they cannot be charged with being inherently immoral, and it may be possible to find ways of mounting a successful counter-insurgency campaign without inevitably violating the criteria of just conduct. Nevertheless, the two sets of problems bring into focus the same crisis in just war theory, namely, that just war thinking about these questions must first establish that the means are not immoral in themselves before it can argue that certain justifiable causes and goals be allowed to guide and determine policy.

2) Modern conflicts tend to have a mixed political-religious character. We can make this statement about some important conflicts — such as those between India and Pakistan and between Israel and the Arab states — even by restricting the term "religious" to its more common and traditional usage. However, we see the full scope of the problem only when we include the influence of ideological, cultural and racial factors, which tend to function as religious elements in a power struggle. These factors foster the inclination to treat the issues as ultimate issues rather than proximate ones, to attribute cosmic and moral significance to the distinctions among the contestants, to dehumanize the opponents with unflattering stereotypes, and to conduct military struggles as wars of righteousness. Generally speaking, the revolutionary struggle is religious in character. Its aim is not merely to change the personnel of government or even to redistribute the assets of the society — although it has both of these aims. Its more profound intention is to reconstitute the society as a righteous and just society, to create a new type of man, to cooperate with the forces of history, and to destroy the diabolical elements which prevent the fruition of the dream. When equipped specifically with an ideology like Marxism, it offers a secular plan of salvation. And when the revolutionaries conceive and conduct the struggle in ultimate terms they tend to evoke a corresponding response. Those who react against the revolution interpret it as an ultimate threat to be met with ultimate weapons if necessary. Both communism and anti-communism in their more extreme forms are primarily religious rather than political phenomena. Both are crusades against evil; neither is consonant with the political assumptions of just war theory.

Looking at the matter in broad perspective, however, we can see that it would be a mistake to regard the modern conflicts as altogether religious and not at all political. Their character indeed is mixed, and political elements such as the interests of nations continue to show the capacity to exert themselves against religious-ideological drives even in the more ideologically oriented societies. This resiliency of politics is a sign of hope for peace, stability and justice. Nevertheless, the functionally religious tendencies press against the political like the jungle crowding in on the cleared land, creating a situation in which the political character of international politics is ground which daily must be won and held against the contrary tendencies. The greater the ascendancy of the religious element in the struggle, the smaller the possibility of prosecuting the struggle on the assumptions of just war theory. There is more than enough evidence in our own Western history, particularly in our experience of the Wars of Religion and their aftermath, to document the following claim: that when wars are fought over religious questions, or when political struggle takes on a religious character, the moral limits fall away and force proceeds to its task without restraint. The recovery of moral limits requires the secularization of the struggle.

3) The bond of community among belligerents is threatened both in its sociological character and in the assumptions about its onto-logical character by the scope and nature of modern conflicts. This problem of contemporary just war relevance is related intimately to the preceding one in that the emergence of serious religious differences threatens to destroy existing elements of community, and changes in the sociological context of struggle permit greater influence to divisive religious loyalties.

Let us note three of the ways in which communal assumptions and conditions of political struggle have been altered. *First,* the expansion of international politics from a European system to a world system has produced much greater heterogeneity in the moral, religious and cultural foundations of international politics. We speak in cautious comparative tones of "much greater heterogeneity," because much of the world accepts, at least formally, the essentially Western assumptions and elements of the Charter of the United Nations and wants to make Western technology its own. Also because we cannot make extravagant claims for the homogeneity of Europe and "Western civilization." We must reckon, after all, with the dissolution, secularization and particularization of whatever unity existed in the West — with the aforementioned Wars of Religion, with the idolatrous tendencies of the modern nation-state, with the ideological dislocations of the French Revolution, and with the emergence of communism and of fascist racism and nationalism on Western soil. However, in spite of these reservations we recognize that the West has a common memory, whereas the world as such does not. Its religious conflicts take place within Christendom, and therefore with some common points of referennce. Its legal differences and legal violations are set against the background of common belief that there is Law, and that Law has become incarnate in the legal history of the civilization. Its members often abrogate the rules of the game, but they know what the rules are and what they mean. These communal conditions do not hold true for contemporary world politics.

Second, the horizontal divisions of class struggle cut across the vertical divisions of nation and culture, and the struggles for national interest and identity divide the revolutionaries. The revolutionary is brother to the poor and oppressed of other lands but not to the affluent and powerful of his own land. The Black Power advocate asks why he should go fight the enemy in Vietnam when the real enemy owns the shack where he lives and the store where he trades. Marxism has a vision of universal brotherhood, but universality as the Marxist understands it is the outcome of the struggle and not a presupposition of the struggle between the classes. Universal brotherhood is achieved by purgation, not by reconciliation. Yet the revolutionary appeals also to national sentiment, and when he comes to power his responsibility for governing tends to create patterns of conflict with his ideological brethren of other nations.

Third, a nuclear defense strategy which requires something more than proportionate counter-forces targeting implicitly denies any fraternal connection with the aggressor. This is so because a level of deterrence which exceeds the counter-forces level implies the intention to destroy the society of the opponent and not only his military forces. Where there is the will to destroy the opposing society there can be no serious assertion of common humanity or any will towards reconciliation. To will to destroy another society in order to preserve one's own is to decide in faith that the parochial political community is the ultimate human community.

4) The perennially unresolved problem of authority for the use of power is worsened, not improved, by the conditions of modern warfare. Each of the two major cases which we have considered complicates the difficulty in its own characteristic way. Nuclear defense policy draws its authority from what it takes to be a direct and visible threat to national survival and independence. Assuming that the threat is real, there is no denying the right to maintain a defense.[8] However,

if a nuclear deterrent ever is drawn into actual use to force an attacker to stop his attacks, the effects of the weapons will not be confined to the target. Even if the missiles are controlled exactly to the targets, the radioactive fallout will be carried around the world. Does the right of defense confer authority to use defensive power which will have seriously damaging effects on people unrelated to the conflict and remote from the hostile areas?

Authority for intervention in revolutionary struggles or so-called "wars of national liberation" is difficult to establish because the grounds of authorization are in a fluid state. Authorization may be given in the form of an invitation to intervene from the official government of the society where the struggle is taking place. But the authority of the host government is the central issue of the struggle, and the fact that it must draw upon outside support seems to underscore the claim of the revolutionaries that it has lost the support of its own people — if indeed it ever had it.

Of course, a *status quo* power like the United States is unlikely to intervene in what it believes to be a purely domestic conflict, that is, one in which it sees no interest of its own at stake. That being the case, much of the burden of authorization shifts to the identification of national interests affected by the revolutionary struggle and its international implications. But the problem of establishing presence or absence of national interests is not so simple as either the proponents or opponents of intervention appear to believe. On the one hand, the threats to national security are vague and indirect by comparison with the clarity and immediacy of the threat posed by a nuclear strike force. This is not to say that the threats are unreal, but only to say that it is more difficult to prove their reality and seriousness. It certainly would make no sense to suggest that a morally justifiable defense begins only when hostile gunboats begin a pre-invasion bombardment of our coastal beaches, but if the line cannot reasonably be drawn at that point, where can it be drawn? The use of the "Munich analogy" and the "domino theory" for justifying the Vietnam intervention is an attempt to show how and why a geographically distant war is a real threat to the United States and must be taken seriously. What they mean to say is that if certain initial steps are permitted to be taken, then certain disastrously negative consequences are sure to follow, and the most responsible use of limiting power is to be made at the beginning of the chain of events rather than at the end. As the debate over the intervention shows, the analogies are not immediately convincing. But their inability to convince does not make any less real the need to define the outer limits of defense.

On the other hand, the problem of defining the national interest is controlled to a large extent by the condition of the international system. "National interest" is defined concretely not only by what the nation has and wants and needs, but by what it has and wants and needs within the prevailing system of power relationships, and by what the system permits to it and requires of it. When the system is stable, the concrete determinations of interests are fairly definite and well-known. When the system is fluid the definition of national interest is fluid, and it must be recreated and reshaped as part of the process of recreating and reshaping the international system. The prospective shape of the international system is a national interest, and it is also the context for future particular definitions of national interest. Therefore, when one nation believes that it ought to intervene in the internal struggles of another nation its external justification is developed less by reference to what the national interest has been than by reference to what national interest is becoming through the role of national power in the reshaping of the international system. Needless to say, this "role" is not assigned by any impartial international agency. But neither is its assumption wholly arbitrary, for each nation-state has international responsibilities beyond the contribution to international order made by tending properly to its own domestic affairs. However, the more fluid the system the more unilateral and subjective is the task of defining the role.

We have now shown how each of the four major assumptions of just war theory has been qualified if not entirely discredited by conditioning factors in contemporary international relations. All four of these difficulties come to focus, directly or indirectly, in every serious conflict in international relations, and their live combination shows the crisis of just war theory relevance in its fullest dimensions. However, if we are asking what United States foreign policy morally may do and may not do, we need proceed no farther than the first point: the implications of modern weapons technology have destroyed the possibility of a justifiable cause for deploying force adequate to cope with the most fundamental threat to American societal existence. Of course, there are non-nuclear situations where force may be applied with discrimination and restraint, and here the just war criteria would seem to have some utility. But the force that is used is part of a system that rests on a nuclear foundation, and the non-nuclear situations are not so disengaged from the more comprehensive realities of world politics that they could not in any sense threaten escalation to the nuclear level. The inference is clear: regardless of the values at stake, under present conditions of international politics the direct application of just war criteria to the United States military system *per se* yields only prohibitions and not permissions.

But that is only one side of the difficulty. The other is represented in the certainty that any attempt on the part of the United States to abdicate its position of power in the world (an unlikely occurrence in any case) would produce more serious international tension and more likelihood of nuclear war than would the maintenance of its nuclear armaments in a state of wartime readiness. The fact which cannot be ignored is that United States military power is the most important stabilizing element in world politics. To be sure, that power sometimes is used arrogantly and foolishly, but it serves nevertheless to deter aggression and to relieve smaller and/or weaker states from the need to build up their own nuclear weapons systems. Any serious signs of intention to withdraw from that role would place the Russians especially and also the Chinese under enormous pressure and temptation to improve their power positions even at the risk of war, and it would set off a scramble for nuclear weapons systems on the part of states that could foresee the loss of their protection. Before this could take place, however, reactions within the United States itself almost certainly would deliver the military capacity of the country into the hands of those persons most likely to make direct and extensive uses of nuclear weapons. The moral option of advocating unilateral disarmament on nuclear pacifist premises seems to be discredited by the likelihood that it would contribute to the evocation of precisely those results which it intends to avoid. To show that this is not idle speculation, we point to the responsibility which American and British pacifism of the 1930's bears for helping to create the political vacuum which contributed to the onset of World War II.

Persons who become pacifists as a result of applying just war criteria to contemporary conditions of defense and warfare do not necessarily seek to make their convictions public policy. That is, they may decide that it is inadvisable or too unpromising to encourage the government to take up a policy of unilateral disarmament. Their pacifist witness takes a different form: one that abandons responsibility for policy determination, accepts its part of the corporate guilt, seeks other means of responsible service, prepares to suffer for its witness, and leaves the outcome in the hands of Almighty God. One should not regard lightly the moral courage of persons who take this position, but neither should one describe the position without calling attention to some of its moral and theological limitations. In the first place, it is increasingly difficult to justify "leaving the results to God" in a world that more and more is subject to human mastery and control.

The world is our responsibility as God has given it to us. It is not impossible to draw the world back from the brink of disaster, and so long as it remains possible we have the responsibility for attempting to do so. In the second place, this "just war pacifism" cannot appeal to the vocational dualism employed by the older forms of consistent and categorical pacifism. That is, it cannot assume that non-Christians are fulfilling a divine commission to govern the world with the norms and instruments of civil justice while Christians witness to the justice of the Kingdom of God. The reason is that just war theory assumes that war *may* be a means of expressing moral responsibility for the Christian as well as for the non-Christian. When one turns towards pacifism on the basis of just war principles, what he means to say is that war and defense are not justifiable either for the Christian or for the non-Christian. In the third place, a just war pacifist who makes this form of witness must be serious about renouncing attempts to influence public policy. If he cannot keep his hands off policy advocacy, he must either show that unilateral disarmament will not have the negative consequences which we have suggested, or else return to the problems of an ethic for the management of nuclear power.

We have come to a point where the just war theory as it is commonly used breaks down as moral theory because it fails to maintain the unity of responsibility and possibility. The major alternatives — pacifism, crusading anti-communism, one-dimensional national interest politics — are unacceptable for a variety of reasons, not the least of which is their inability to provide an adequate framework for dealing with the central problem of the threat of nuclear war. We cannot, however, escape the responsibilities of political existence at this point in time and history. Therefore, we must ask whether the just war theory as political-moral theory provides any guidance for the recovery of the possibilities of responsibility.

Recovering the Relevance of Just War Theory

To recover and restate the relevance of just war theory to problems of modern warfare it is necessary to reverse the usual pattern of moral inquiry into the limits and possibilities of the use of military force. Customarily, the procedure is from politics to war. War is the "last resort" when the attempts to secure justice through political means have failed. And as "last resort" it must yet be conducted justly. Now we must proceed from war to politics, because both "last resort" and the violation of just conduct are present in principle in the countervailing weapons systems of major nuclear powers. Moral permission to make overt and direct uses of nuclear weapons is not an open question; the limit of permission already has been reached and exceeded. The only route that remains open, morally speaking, is the one that leads back to politics.

To move from war to politics is to move from the conflict to the political system, that is, to the international system. What this means in the first place is that particular conflicts must be recognized and dealt with as problems of the international system and not only as local problems. To be sure, the conflicts are local problems and they have a local character, but they are demonstrably elements in a larger system of interrelationships — which they affect and by which they are affected. It is possible to have really "localized" conflicts only when the international system in whole or in part is sufficiently stable to isolate some conflicts. At a time like the present, i.e. when the system is unstable and is changing shape, it is next to impossible to regard any given occasion of socio-political conflict as purely "local." The struggles in Vietnam and the Middle East obviously are disruptions of the international system as a whole, but so also are riots in Detroit, a *coup d'état* in Yemen, or the agitations of the copper miners in Bolivia.

Now if this be true, namely, that particular crises are problems of the system, what follows is that the attempt to deal with the crisis must look broadly at the system and not only at the particular trouble-spot. What also follows is that the international system must be strengthened in all its parts and processes as the primary instrument for handling its own systemic crises. We are dealing not with the individuated power of this or that nation or group of nations but with a system of power relationships, i.e., a comprehensive system of relationships of reciprocal influence and control. The task, therefore, is primarily the management and administration of the system of power itself and only secondarily and instrumentally of the power of the particular states. The inclusive problem and the systemic interrelated-ness of power and political existence are expressed, for example, in the attempt to get an effective treaty preventing the spread of nuclear weapons. If non-nuclear states are willing to sign such a treaty, they probably will do so only if the international power system is reshuffled in such a way as to provide them the guarantee of security which the possession of nuclear weapons presumably would afford. When the United States extends the rationale of its nuclear deterrent system to provide those guarantees to states which expect them from the United States, it makes its own power more directly and deliberately an instrument of international order and not only of the national interest.

When we speak of "maintenance" and "administration" of the system we foresee a work of stabilization but not a condition of staticity. The problems of injustice and desperate need as well as the problems of insecurity must be resolved if the system is to have the stability requisite to its function. Moreover, the tasks of maintenance and administration cannot be expressed permanently and entirely in terms of an effective deterrent. Other forms of power must be brought into prominence, international institutions must be developed and strengthened, the political and legal transcendence of sovereign national power must advance.

All of this is to say that the return to politics requires the activation or creation of a field of political relationships which is more inclusive than the nation-state and more than simply a contingent creature of the will of the nation-states. It requires, in other words, the development of an international community with enough self-identity to give meaning and authority to the moral limits of power. We need not distract ourselves with the question whether a community with that degree of integration ever will exist. The international political system is before us in its concreteness, and it performs many of the tasks of integral community and world government in their absence. Under these conditions, the just war theory discloses the shape of political responsibility to be the bringing of national power to a greater recognition of its obligations and limitations in relation to the governing functions of the international system, and the consequent strengthening of the system so that the functions may be more rationally, effectively and equitably performed.

In discussions of morality and international politics it is common to hear someone say, "At this point the moral issue enters." Presumably the "moral issue" had not been present up to that point. What is implied in this view of the moral-political relationship is that "moral issues" arise when a state's use of power to pursue its own interests issues in conflict with the interests or rights of other states or persons. Moral decision takes place by way of applying moral principles either to certify and limit this use of power or to deny it. Understandably, the principles are comparatively ineffective in their limiting and negating functions, because they are not supported with social authority from an inclusive and integral community. There are more problems in this view than we need to analyze at the present time, but the basic one surely is that it fails to recognize that moral responsibility and political responsibility are coeval and coterminous. Political responsibility is a form of moral responsibility, and it is moral responsibility because it has to do with the stewardship of an office and of the power that goes with the office. "Just war" is not the point at which morality "enters." It is a specification of the standing concern to exercise power justifiably within a system of power relationships.

In order to continue our inquiry into the relevance of just war theory to modern warfare, we must explore this concept of "office" in relation to the role of national power in international politics and in particular to the problem of moving from war to politics.

One way to approach the question is to define the office of national power in terms of its service to the interests of the persons who are members of the particular political society. Statesmen exercise responsibility when they use the national power to secure the national interests. They would be irresponsible if they failed to do so, and they would not be worthy occupants of their office if they sacrificed those interests to "moral" considerations. The movement from war to politics is served in part by refining the concrete definitions of national interest and using national power *only* for those purposes which clearly are cases of national interest. We say "served in part" because, as was pointed out earlier, the definitions of national interest are *historical* rather than *natural*. They tend to change with major changes in the international system. It may indeed be helpful to make parsimonious definitions of national interest when the system is in turmoil, but it seems unlikely that under such conditions a state could avoid expanding the scope of national concern to include the emerging shape of the system as a whole. It is tempting to suppose that the dislocations of the system can be acknowledged adequately with an act of faith in *laissez faire*, i.e., with the argument that if each state were to pursue its own interests in limited and enlightened fashion the interests of all would be served by the resultant condition of international equilibrium. However, a more realistic politics will relate the office of national power deliberately to the structures and processes of the international system as a necessary expression of its service to the national interest.

In the second approach the office of national power is defined in terms of the location and function of the nation-state within the sets of relationships that make up the international system. The perspective on the relationship of state to system is different. In the first case the system was viewed from the state as something external to the state with which the state had to contend. In the second case the nation-state is viewed as within the system, integral to the system, with power that serves both the state and the system. Ideally, the dimensions and responsibilities of the office should correspond to the state's legal jurisdiction. In that situation the state would fulfill the duties of its office by minding its own (internal) business. But the ideal is not realizable apart from the existence of an inclusive world government able to assume the international responsibilities. At present the dimensions of office in the system correspond to the effective power of any state in the system rather than to its legal jurisdiction. And that means that in the absence of a central and dominant agency it is the office of the great powers to provide for much of the management of the international system in addition to minding their own (internal) business. The "in addition" qualification makes it clear that the national interest is not set aside in this approach. What happens is that it is seen as having an integral and not an accidental relationship to the interests of the other states and to the international system. The primary question of moral inquiry is not "What is the responsible role of national power in relation to the national interest?" but "What is the responsible role of national power within the prevailing and developing power structures of the international system?" With this approach the "moral issue" arises not with conflict of interest but with entrance into political existence. Morality is the meaning of the constantly responsible exercise of legal and at times extra-legal power in relation to the needs and problems of the international system — and therefore to the needs and problems of the particular nation-states.

The conceptualization of the role of national power as that of an office within the international system seems presumptuous and arbitrary, because the office is not formally and impartially delineated and the working definition must be made by the nation-state itself. But it is not wholly presumptuous and arbitrary. The smaller nations of the world recognize that much of the management of world affairs is provided by the stronger nations acting beyond the limits of their legal jurisdiction. Ideally they may wish that it were not so, and in particular cases they will protest against the heavy-handedness, the arrogance, the insensitivity of great-power action. But they call upon and rely upon this form of management often enough to convey to the great powers their understanding that the office corresponds more to the power than to the legal jurisdiction. Moreover, the principle does have some formal and legal standing in the fact that the major powers at the end of World War II were given permanent membership and veto power in the Security Council of the United Nations.

The present absurdity of the Taiwan veto and the vast difference between the power of the United States and the Soviet on one side and that of France and England on the other does not alter the principle.

Granted the dangers of the concept of "office," it yet is less dangerous than either isolationist withdrawal from the responsibilities of power or the ambitious and unstructured exercise of power with no real sense of the extent and limits of responsibilities. By asking the major powers to recognize their office in the international system we are not inviting them to expand their interventions but rather to regularize and submit to discipline what they are already doing. Any state that wants to be aggressive and expansionist and to reshape the international system in its own image will in any case invent whatever justification it needs — if it feels that justification is important. The concept of "office" as it has been developed here is intended for those states that want to know the limits as well as the extent of their responsibilities. It is for those states which participate in the management of the international system and want authority to sustain that participation. They cannot have authority from the international community without accepting limits to the exercise of national power.

Of the two approaches to the question of the "office" of national power, the second is more congenial to the task and viewpoint of this paper. It sees the nation-state as more completely and more integrally a "social self" within the international system, and it commits the state more deliberately and thoroughly to international responsibility and to the development of an authoritative international community. Using the second approach as the framework of moral inquiry, we now must ask how the just war criteria can instruct and guide the office in the task of moving from war to politics.

The New Role of Just War Criteria

The just war criteria have a new and more comprehensive role in the modern context of the conduct of foreign policy. Traditionally they were used to judge actual and prospective uses of military force. Their application to these occasions of the use of force was enabled and authorized by the assumptions of just war theory which we have enumerated and discussed. Now, however, the assumptions themselves have been undermined, and with that change in operating conditions the primary role of the just war criteria has become that of providing guidelines for the recovery of the assumptions. All foreign policy deliberation and execution — all forms of national power and not only military power — are put under the discipline of promoting the restoration of the operational status of the just war assumptions. The just war criteria instruct this disciplined action, and they deny the morality of all uses of power which merely express the absence of the assumptions. We now shall look briefly at several of the major just war criteria in order to determine their relevance to the problem as we have presented it.

1) *Just intention.* Under present conditions, in which the qualifying assumptions of just war theory have been dissipated or destroyed, just intention becomes the primary just war criterion. This is so because just war deliberation presupposes the acceptance of the following working premises: that all belligerents possess a common humanity, that the right of the opponent to exist politically must be recognized, that unqualified, unlimited violence against his person and property is not permitted, that the belligerents must develop a *modus vivendi* within a common set of political relationships. Where these premises are in abeyance, just war limitations usually cannot be sustained. In medieval Christendom, for example, wars against the infidels were considered to be justified (i.e., to the Christians) by definition, and moral restraints on the conduct of such wars tended to lose their compulsion. The present political situation bears many similarities to that one. The criterion of just intention is founded on the acceptance of these premises and it attempts to bring them to concrete expression by limiting war with the fraternal and structural elements of political existence. War must not intend vengeance toward nor dispossession of the enemy, and in particular it must not intend to destroy the enemy's society. War must be conducted in such a way as to point towards and permit the restoration of peaceful political relationships. That is, it must be conducted within the limits imposed by the prospects of re-establishing a working international system. If these premises are not currently the premises of the conduct of foreign policy, "just intention" requires both a renewal of acceptance and the effort to restore the political conditions of their efficacy. Now that politics has become global and the divisions within international politics represent more than the disintegration of Western political community, just intention requires not only the restoration of community and struc-

ture but also the creation of community and structure where none have existed. Specifically, it implies the following:

a) *Secularization of the conflict.* Just intention requires the reduction of the mixed religious-political character of international conflict to its basic political elements, and therefore it implies the necessity of dethroning ideology where it reigns over politics. This argument usually is made against the tendency to define the rationale of United States foreign policy primarily as opposition to the spread of communism. It is supported by the claims that Communist states are guided in their foreign policy more by consideration of national interest than of ideology, that revolutionary movements are manifestations less of conspiracy than of the dislocations and injustices of the modern world, that foreign policy should show initiative and not only counter-action, that foreign aid should concentrate on development by economic means and not on prevention of change by military means. Of course, the justice of these claims should not lead to the underrating of the importance and the compelling power of ideology. Ideology represents a demand for the realization of denied values, in interpretation of the meaning of the conflict and of history, a vested interest of those who have institutionalized the ideology and achieved power with it. And yet precisely because it is all of those things, ideology is a threat to rational and limited political action. As the absolutization of a relative perspective it distorts both value and truth, and it must be relativized in the interest of an accurate understanding of the elements of the conflict, of the fulfillment of its own demands, and of the setting and maintaining of just limits to the use of force. To submit foreign policy to the discipline of just intention means to require it to examine international conflict with less and less ideological distortion, and also to attempt to make the conflict itself more "this-worldly" — and yet to do so without discounting either the general problem of ideological struggle or the specific problem of political communism.

b) *Humanization of the conflict.* Just intention requires the constant renewal of sensitivity to the human suffering and deprivation which creates the conditions of war and which war itself imposes. It requires also the destruction of stereotypes — "commie," "Jap," "nigger," "honky," "fascist" — which depersonalize the opponent and deny his essential and existential humanity. The main objection to these stereotypes is not that they are unflattering but that they enable us to destroy the opponent — noncombatants as well as combatants — with a clear and even righteous conscience. If the enemy becomes real to us as a human being, and therefore not as monster or as refuse, we shall consider much more gravely the cause and the means of our strife with him.

c) *Institutionalization of the conflict.* Just intention requires perseverance in the search for means to transfer the conflict from violent to non-violent, from military to legal, modes of resolution. The development of institutions around common interests, differences and threats is part of the effort to build up the integrity and authority of the international system.

2) *Just cause.* Questions of just cause for the use of force in international politics now must be asked within the framework of managing the power relations of the international system and not within that of the right of national self-defense. National power serves national interest, to be sure, but national interest is the penultimate rather than the ultimate justifying and limiting factor. When national power is put under the discipline of its office in the international system it may be able to serve the national interest in ways that could not be justified by national interest alone. However, it may also be that some clear cases of national interest will be denied the support of national power by the same discipline.

Earlier in the paper we delineated the dilemma of nuclear deterrence policy, namely, that an effective nuclear deterrent cannot be justified morally by the right of national self-defense, but that total unilateral nuclear disarmament by the United States would be morally irresponsible by virtue of its implications for increasing the likelihood of nuclear war. Now, however, we can see the way to overcome this division between possibility and responsibility by setting the question of "just cause" within the context of international rather than national necessity. The fundamental premise of every foreign policy in our time is that the world must be spared a nuclear war, and that all planning and execution of foreign policy must contribute to the avoidance of nuclear war. The task of avoidance must reckon with two basic facts: first, man knows the secrets of nuclear power and rapid delivery and he will not forget them. He cannot walk away from his technology but must find the means to control it. To use the now-famous phrase of Professor Weizsäcker, he must learn "to live with the bomb." Second, the non-nuclear nations which have the capability to build nuclear weapons feel the threats to their national security more immediately than they feel the threat of nuclear war, and they will acquire the weapons — even at great cost to their vitally necessary programs of national development — if their security is not otherwise provided for. When these two facts are taken together they define the problem of management of power which must be carried through in the international system. Whatever justification a national nuclear weapons system may have derives from its participation in the management of this problem by providing defense or credible suggestion of defensive help for non-nuclear powers and thereby preventing aggression and insecurity from developing into nuclear war. Of course, the defense interests of the nuclear provider also are served thereby, but it is not its own national defense which alone justifies the deployment of nuclear power. The justification is found in protecting the international system as such against nuclear war, and in providing the conditions for moving towards political control of the national nuclear weapons systems.

3) *Competent authority.* The standing problem of authority for the use of national power in international politics appears to us in this form: We are tempted by the existence of international institutions to suppose that the only authorized way to use power to resolve international conflicts (except for clear cases of self-defense) is through multilateral action approved and directed by these institutions. The political reality is that while the members of international organizations are debating what course, if any, they should take, significant changes in the international order can be made by way of direct or indirect aggressive action and then presented to the members as a *fait accompli.* That being the case, the most necessary service to international order, justice, and peace may be rendered by unilateral action which either violates international law or else operates in a gray legal area where anyone can make his own legal points. This perennial problem of political authority is not resolved by setting it within the covering framework of the international system, but it does acquire meaningful shape and direction therein.

In any setting a use of power which claims justification even though it violates or seems to violate the limits of legal jurisdiction should be defined in such a way as to draw authority to itself. It should conform as closely as possible to the interests of other nations, and involve other nations, if possible, in the decision and the action. Although violating international law and usage at some point, it nevertheless should be aligned with them as closely as it can be. The national interest involved should be defined narrowly and explicitly, and the resolution of the problem should allow for flexibility and adjustment.

In the setting of moral analysis which we have defined here, the use of power should contribute as directly and intentionally as possible to the development of an international system which increasingly will have the integrity and capacity to authorize particular uses of power. Any uses of power which constantly and directly frustrate the possibilities of developing authoritative centers of political jurisdiction are unjustifiable. A consideration of alternatives for United States policy in the Far East will serve to illustrate the principle. Let us assume for purposes of argument that mainland China is indeed an expansionist threat to Southeast Asia, and that the principal justification for the presence of American power in that part of the world is to contain that threat. The United States could propose to accomplish its purpose either (a) by establishing a ring of military and naval bases — a "Western defense perimeter" — running from Korea through Taiwan and South Vietnam at least as far as Thailand, or (b) by assisting the various states of Southeast Asia to prepare their own defense of the area — largely by means of economic and social reforms designed to promote national viability and make the national society largely immune to insurgency warfare. These alternatives are not mutually exclusive, but there is a significant difference represented in the question concerning which would be instrumental to the other. The second alternative would confer substantially more authority on the role of American power than would the first. It would make the defense of the area the responsibility primarily of the states in that area, and would require the leaders to seek more authority for their own rule by meeting the needs of their people and attending to the tasks of modernizing their societies. It would place American intervention on a transient and retractable rather than a permanent basis. It would not be as provocative and threatening to China as would the first alternative, and therefore it would serve to stabilize the international system by improving the prospects for regularizing Chinese-American relationships.

4) *Just conduct.* Questions of the just conduct of war, including the justice of mounting a nuclear deterrent system, require the application of both just conduct principles, i.e., proportion and discrimination. Arguments against the moral authority of noncombatant immunity on the grounds of its comparatively late historical development are irrelevant.[9] Romantic love and companionship were fairly late additions to the institution of marriage, but that only means that the insight of earlier generations into the nature of marriage was inadequate. If the issue is approached from the standpoint of just war theory rather than just war history, one can see that the principle of noncombatant immunity is implied in the criterion of just intention.

Just intention forbids the intent to destroy the enemy's society, and that is what the noncombatants represent, namely, the enemy's society, as distinct from his military capacity. To intend to attack noncombatants directly, especially with nuclear weapons, is the equivalent of intending to destroy the society.

In the total exercise of moral-political responsibility, the principles are used not only for making particular moral judgments, but also for guiding the return to politically usable force by subjecting questions of targeting to moral analysis and by attempting to recover for policy the distinction between counter-forces and counter-peoples targeting. One of the serious risks of counter-forces targeting is the likelihood of seeing wartime uses of weapons escalate beyond what was intended and targeted in the deterrent. One who agrees to the deterrent must accept moral responsibility for the likely consequences even though they are not intended, and this extension of responsibility to probabilities requires acceptance of the implicit violation of noncombatant immunity or else rejection of the deterrent. Actually, however, this way of posing the problem is an abstraction. The probability of escalation is a risk, not an intention. And it is to be judged not as an extension or condition of intention but in comparison to the alternative risks. On the basis of risk-comparison I would judge a discriminatingly targeted deterrent to be justified by the office of national power in supporting the stability and security of the international system but not by its office of securing the national defense. In the former case it is ultimately an instrument for preventing nuclear war and proximately an instrument for preventing aggression. In the latter case it is proximately an instrument for preventing nuclear war and ultimately an instrument for preventing aggression. The risks of escalation involve the devastation we are likely to suffer as a nation and the devastation we are likely to inflict as a nation. They cannot be justified by defense against aggression, however threatening to basic values the aggression may seem to be. But precisely because they are so serious they justify the mounting of a discriminating deterrent which intends to serve the primary purpose of prevention of atomic war, not the primary purpose of national self-defense.

We must append some notes to the discussion in this section for purposes of emphasis and for avoiding — hopefully — the more likely misunderstandings. With regard to the movement from war to politics we must underscore two points: first, the way leads back to politics, not to disarmament (where the opponents never were). This does not mean that disarmament is altogether undesirable and should never be attempted. It does not mean that the United States should not perhaps attempt some limited unilateral steps towards disarmament which would signal a desire to relax international tensions but would not compromise the credibility and effectiveness of the deterrent. It *does* mean that disarmament plans or treaties can be safely and responsibly considered only within a context of political arrangements for the disposition of power and the guarantee of security. Second, the way back is not a new non-political, non-military way, but a retracing of steps through the power arrangements that presently exist. Our situation is like that of a man who inches along the ledge of a skyscraper to rescue a would-be suicide, and who must move back along the ledge to the safety of the window after he has his quarry firmly by the arm. The new role of the just war theory is that of showing us how to use nuclear power arrangements to bring nuclear weapons under control.

The way back to politics is a stage in the way forward to international community. Just war theory as moral-political theory requires the effort to bring the international community increasingly into existence. However, the future which it faces is more immediate than remote — less the dream of world government than the hope of transcending present conflicts by building on the substance of community already in existence. There is no leap from politics to law and organization, only the patient work of strengthening international institutions and giving them tasks commensurate with their authority and power, of assisting the weaker societies to achieve dignity through competence and self-reliance, of encouraging the major powers to learn how to live in the same world. This work is the office of national power in the international system.

To conclude, we assert that just war theory finds its relevance in our time in helping to conceptualize and guide the task of civilizing the vast and often arbitrary power that is present in the international political system. To civilize power is to make it an instrument of the *civitas* of the nations, the international community which is present in hope if not altogether in substance. But to civilize power is also to create the *civitas*, to give it will and reason, continuity and depth, structure and process. And this work of creating community and civilizing power, of transcending through policy and practice the deepest divisions of mankind, of incarnating the hope, is a response to the divine work of reconciliation disclosed in Jesus Christ and carried on in our history. Those Christians who enter politics with this understanding of their work are as much ministers of reconciliation as are their clergymen. Their vocation is peace — active, dynamic, creative peace that transcends the Roman model of *pax* and approaches the Augustinian model of *concordia*. The requirements are as Pope Paul VI described them in *Populorum Progressio*: "Peace cannot be limited to a mere absence of war, the result of an ever-precarious balance of forces. No, peace is something that is built up day after day, in the pursuit of an order intended by God, which implies a more perfect form of justice among men."

NOTES

[1] The best historical survey of Christian attitudes towords the problem of war is Roland Bainton's *Christian Attitudes Towards War and Peace* (New York: Abingdon Press, 1960).

[2] Augustine's admonitions on the conduct of war are made within the framework of the criterion of just intention, and they define a general approach or orientation rather than definite rules. The aim of war is peace, and the conduct of war should show the restraint necessary to permit this aim to come to fruition.

[3] Bainton comments: "Another rule of warfare became prominent in the Maccabean struggle — the Jews would not fight on the Sabbath. When consequently they were butchered, the rule was relaxed until it prohibited attacks but not defense upon that day. The Romans, discovering no resistance on the Sabbath desisted from warfare until the morrow and spent the intervening time in erecting earth works with which the Jews did not interfere but adhered to their scruples to their own hurt." *op. cit.*, p. 43.

[4] *Nuclear War, Deterrence and Morality* (New York: Newman Press, 1967). Although O'Brien does make the usual and necessary (according to just war theory) distinction between "counter-city" and "counter-forces" warfare and deterrence, he apparently is using the term "strategic nuclear deterrence" to refer to counter-city deterrence. In doing so, he does not mean to say that an effective nuclear deterrence policy must be primarily a counter-cities policy — like that, for example, of President de Gaulle. What he does mean is that a limited nuclear deterrent is not a clear alternative to counter-cities deterrence. The possibility of effective lower-level and counter-forces deterrence is created not by the determination to maintain the limits but by the apparent willingness to go to higher levels of retaliatory destruction if that should prove necessary to deter.
The willingness to execute that level of deterrence violates the principle of noncombatant immunity. But the principle is violated also, he argues, by the level of strictly counter-forces targeting necessary to deter a nuclear-equipped foe which really is determined to commit aggression. There are, he concedes, some conceivable uses of nuclear weapons which would not violate the moral immunity of noncombatants from direct and intentional attack. But such uses are isolated instances, and to cite them does not get to the real problem, namely, that deterrence is a system — not an aggregate of individually targeted weapons — and the projected damage of the system in execution is so great as to eliminate meaningful distinctions among targets. Unintended but unavoidable civilian damage is to be covered, morally speaking, by the principle of "double effect," but the projected

damage of an otherwise justifiably targeted deterrence system strains that principle past the breaking-point. An effective nuclear deterrent becomes morally possible only if the absoluteness of the principle of noncombatant immunity is given up.

O'Brien's position agrees with that of the nuclear pacifists on this point: that when nuclear weapons are deployed in such manner and quantity as to provide effective deterrence they are inherently indiscriminate. That is, they cannot make any significant distinction between military and civilian targets. The nuclear pacifist would insist — and O'Brien apparently would agree — that a city cannot be a justifiable target even though it may be the site of or in close proximity to a major military installation. Any attack on a military force or installation which also would destroy a city must be ruled a violation of noncombatant immunity. Under modern conditions of warfare, a nuclear deterrent which covered the major military targets would threaten destruction of cities as well. Therefore an effective deterrent would violate the principle of discrimination before the question of proportion even could be raised. This conclusion is responsible for the nuclear pacifist's being a nuclear pacifist, but it leads Dr. O'Brien to question the authority of the principle of discrimination. A contrary position is taken by Paul Ramsey in *The Limits of Nuclear War* (New York: The Council on Religion and International Affairs, 1963). Ramsey argues that a direct attack on a city does not violate the principle of noncombatant immunity if the opponent has made the city a military target by placing significant military installations in or near it. To exclude cities on principle would allow the opponent to make most of his military capacity morally immune from attack by giving it an urban address. Attacks on cities that are not military targets do, of course, violate the principle, and attacks on cities that *are* military targets *may nevertheless be unjustifiable by virtue of violating the principle of proportion.* I agree with Ramsey on this definition of targeting, but I believe also that no considerations of national interest alone ever could confer proportionate justification on this level of nuclear destruction.

5 His argument is outlined in *ibid.*, pp. 82-84. His main points are that the principle was comparatively late in its development, that it is a customary principle of municipal and international law and not self-evidently of natural law, that "there is not a single explicit reference to it in the principal papal and conciliar statements on nuclear war," and that under present conditions it contradicts the right of defense — which is clear and explicit both in the tradition and in papal and conciliar statements. His objection, however, is only to the absoluteness of the principle, and he agrees that it is "a preferred goal, a guideline to belligerents, which they are morally obliged to respect."

6 Insurgency and counter-insurgency warfare characteristically raise numerous problems related to the principle of noncombatant immunity. Insurgency by its very nature seems to violate the principle, because the insurgents usually attempt to avoid direct confrontation with military forces and to attack instead the civil structure of the society. They murder village chiefs, doctors, school teachers, agricultural experts and others whose services might improve the society and thereby reduce the presumed need for violent revolutionary change. Their acts of terrorism — intended to under-

mine public confidence in the government by showing its inability to pro-vide protection — are directed mainly against civilian targets and therefore manifest an inversion of the principle of noncombatant immunity. Terrorism of this type is less of a moral problem for the counter-insurgents, not because they are more inclined to show moral restraint than are the insurgents, but because actions against the civilian population by government forces work against the government rather than for it. Torture is a temptation to both sides because of the high premium placed on fresh and accurate information in this type of warfare.

[7] "Can Counter-insurgency War Be Conducted Justly?" Unpublished study paper prepared for the American Society of Christian Ethics, meeting in Evanston, Illinois, January 21, 1966.

[8] This statement does not contradict the argument made earlier about the inability of the right of national self-defense to bear the burden of justifying a strategic nuclear deterrent. The state has the right to use military power in its own defense, but the right is limited — not absolute. At issue in this section is one of the questions about where the limits of this right are to be found.

[9] In addition to O'Brien's arguments, see also Richard Shelly Hartigan, "Noncombatant Immunity: Reflections on Its Origins and Present Status," Review of Politics, XXIX (April, 1967), pp. 204-20.

Is Gradualism Dead? Reflections on Order, Change, and Force

Denis Goulet

Two Forms of Gradualism

As a doctrine, "gradualism" is roughly synonymous with incrementalism or evolutionism. Common to all is the central tenet that necessary social changes can and ought to be pursued by successive degrees and within legal bounds, not by abrupt mutations or in violation of procedures defined by law. Its opposite is the doctrine of revolution which advocates a sharp break from present structures, and operates outside the law if necessary, even at the risk of much violence to persons and property. Nevertheless, the term "gradualism" is not applied solely to a doctrine of social change. Besides designating a particular viewpoint on change, it also describes the specific incremental processes by which such change sometimes takes place.

No one can assess the ethical worth of change processes unless he adverts to the initial and terminal conditions lying at either end of change. At the risk of over-simplifying admittedly complex issues, I wish to state clearly which social changes I deem necessary. They are necessary because, in their absence, social justice and authentic development for all mankind are unattainable. Major institutional changes in world order are essential. No less crucial are drastic domestic alterations within the United States and other countries, developed and underdeveloped alike. Something much broader is meant by the term "development" than mere economic progress or even the collection of general goals social scientists frequently label "modernization." Rather, as economist Benjamin Higgins has written, "development is the human ascent, the ascent of all men in their quintessence of humanity, including the economic, biological, psychological, social, cultural, ideological, spiritual, mystical and transcendental dimensions."[1] Thus viewed, economic and social development are but means for reaching the good life and the good society. This pursuit is situated no doubt in a twentieth-century context marked by multiple technologies and interdependencies among social systems, as by almost instant reaction by subjects to all important

---

[1] Benjamin Higgins, *Economic Development, Problems, Principles & Policies*, rev. ed. (New York, 1968), p. 369.

social stimuli and responses. Idyllic simplicity is forever out of reach: complexity has now become "the name of the game."

One may ask at this point what traits would "authentic development" possess? The late L. J. Lebret, a French development theorist and practitioner, has summarized them in terms borrowed from the report on development in Iranian Beluchistan prepared by Italian expert Giorgio Sebregondi in 1954. According to Sebregondi, sound development must display five characteristics: (1) finalization by larger goals; (2) coherence; (3) homogeneity; (4) self-propulsiveness; and (5) indivisibility.

1. These *larger goals* refer to the human welfare factor in all social categories, for mere improvement in material well-being is not enough: We must seek optimum fulfillment of all human potentialities. In Sebregondi's words, "the transition which is required in underdeveloped countries is not a passage from one technical level to another, but rather from one stage of civilization to another."[2] However, to profess lofty goals is futile unless adequate measures are adopted to reach these goals. Developers must choose or devise means which are proportionate to their declared objectives or else the development they achieve will be fragile or mythical.

2. *Coherence*, Sebregondi's second trait of sound development, calls for recognition of the necessarily complementary dimensions of development: the biological, cultural, technical, economic, ethical, political, administrative, and still others. Even when planners deliberately foster strategic imbalances in order to create greater dynamism, they must, over time, define some desired pattern of coherence among the diverse aspects, sectors, and branches of activity.

3. *Homogeneous development* is that process in which even revolutionary activity builds on real history, not on imaginary futures. There is a limit beyond which one cannot, to use Régis Debray's phrase, "free the present from the past." It is no small part of the wisdom of China's present leaders to have understood this and to have grafted their cultural revolution onto ancient deviant streams of Buddhist and Hindu values in their massive effort to subvert traditional Confucian attitudes. In a more practical vein, Chinese human resource planners have skillfully upgraded traditional medicine so as to begin modernizing health practices in the countryside.

4. *Self-propulsiveness*, the capacity to sustain growth, is develop-

---

[2] Giorgio Sebregondi, "Le développement harmonisé. Notes pour une théorie," *Economie et Humanisme*, No. 84 (March-April, 1954), p. 68.

ment's most important trait. It presupposes the association of elites and populace in the creation of new structures. True development is never some "gift" from above or a handout from a benefactor, but the exercised capacity of multiple human agents to promote their own creativity.

5. *Indivisibility* means that apparent gains are not genuine unless they contribute to growth at all levels. [3]

Once it is admitted that authentic development is desired, one is forced to conclude that existing institutions are not adequate to obtain it. The institutions in greatest need of reconversion are precisely those which govern access to world resources (including human knowledge and research capacities) and to decision-making as to the use of resources and power. Dissatisfaction with present arrangements has led scholars like Tinbergen, Myrdal, Perroux and others to conclude that some form of *world planning* must eventually come into being. Equally urgent are: *curtailments in the exercise of national sovereignty;* the institution of *new global financing arrangements;* and the creation of a *world-wide technological* pool at the service of mankind's priority needs. [4]

Still another major innovation required for development, in addition to the four just mentioned, is a *cultural revolution* in the world's developed societies. Unless basic changes in operative values take place within the United States and other high-income nations, indispensable cultural revolutions within underdeveloped nations will be impeded from bearing fruit.

This means, specifically, that unless the attitudes of the United States populace toward mass consumer goods changes, the American economy will continue to be obliged to waste scarce resources voraciously. Worse still, unless America's image of itself and of its "civilizing" role is modified, its foreign policy will continue to be oppressive

---

[3] L. J. Lebret, *Dynamique Concrète du Développement* (Paris, 1961), pp. 75-83.

[4] Limitations of space prevent me from expounding in detail which need priorities ought to orient the use of world resources. Nor can I here explain in what essential respects needs of the first order differ from other categories of needs: enhancement needs, luxury needs, and shibboleth needs. (For a discussion of these points the reader is referred to my forthcoming book, *The Cruel Choice: A Normative Theory of Development.*) Nor can I here undertake to list the economic policy implications which flow from such a theory of needs. For present purposes it suffices to say that once the distinction among these needs is admitted and once we recognize a certain priority among them, we must conclude that suitable instrumentalities must be created, if they do not already exist, in order to meet mankind's needs.

and structurally paternalistic. Unless technology's processes are mastered and subordinated to human purposes domestically, technical transfers practiced by the United States will necessarily remain manipulative and ethnocentric. The kind of development the United States has set out to achieve for itself constitutes in truth anti-development, which is a major obstacle to the conquest of genuine development by many other societies.[5] This is why I contend that a cultural revolution in values inside the United States of America is no less necessary than a value revolution among Indian peasants or Bolivian tin miners.

An obvious objection to the second of these five innovations presents itself, namely, that many people find it difficult to admit the possibility of "curtailing sovereignty." The difficulties experienced by "advanced" European countries in limiting sovereignty, even within the framework of an economically advantageous Common Market, give pause to any congenital optimists on the matter. Yet unless sovereignty is curbed, catastrophical results will ensue: the oceans will be irrevocably handed over to bellicose and depleting purposes; the very ecological safety of the planet will be endangered; and the "development" of most Third World nations will perforce remain satellitic to that of a few technological metropolises. It is utopian to expect powerful countries to abdicate their own absolute sovereignty freely. Fragile polities, on the other hand, may need to experience a period of intensive nation-building in order to gain minimal strength to bargain with established nations. The powerful countries must therefore be pressured into abdicating partial sovereignty. The United Nations is attempting to do just this in the specific domain of ocean legislation.[6] Moreover, coalitions of underdeveloped countries, notably within UNCTAD (United Nations Commission on Trade and Development), are exercising pressure in the same direction. By judicious group action, Latin American countries might achieve further new bargaining strength vis-à-vis the United

---

5 On this, cf. Denis A. Goulet, "The United States: A Case of Anti-Development," in *Motive* (January, 1970), pp. 6-13. The article states that in America itself, development concentrates unduly on providing goods, while neglecting to enhance esteem and freedom for men, and that U.S. aid and assistance programs abroad reflect the same narrowness of perspective. Anti-development, in short, is that appearance of development which, upon more critical examination, proves to be a sham. Genuine development optimizes life-sustenance, esteem, and freedom for all, it does so in a manner which is based on a sound theory of priority needs, which fosters (even when conflict occurs) universal solidarity — all this in a non-elitist mode.

6 Cf. Elizabeth Mann Borgese, *The Ocean Regime*, Occasional Paper, Center for the Study of Democratic Institutions (October, 1968).

States were they to implement suggestions recently made by Harvey Perloff.[7] The rule of thumb in world-wide development politics is that politics can no longer be the "art of the possible." Instead it must aim at creating new frontiers of possibility. Apparent by now should be the difficulty of transcending "present conditions" and the bankruptcy of all thinking which starts with the assumption that only "under present conditions" can solutions be envisaged.

Substantial progress on all these fronts is clearly not feasible, however, through any single revolutionary program or even any possible combination of programs. Indeed, revolutionary action leaves unsolved a score of monumental questions affecting our fate: how to prevent nuclear war, how to avert ecological catastrophe, how to gain human control over mass technology, how to devise an education for all which will not be a massive brainwash? The answers to such questions demand patient inquiry, debate, professional knowledge, and long-term social experimentation, all of which transcend the reach even of successful revolutionary action. Of course, certain problems are amenable to revolutionary solution. It may even be that they cannot be solved otherwise. Where conditions are suitable and leverage exists, revolutions may prove desirable. Nonetheless, innumerable obstacles, large and small, must be removed before life on this planet can be fully humanized. Consequently, even ardent revolutionaries, who by definition tend to scorn piecemeal change, must stock their quivers with incrementalist arrows. The reason is that many social changes can come only via a series of cumulative partial steps. The burning question now becomes: Can basic structural mutations be achieved incrementally, that is, by a series of cumulative steps? Or does gradualism remain at the surface of things? Does a gradual process ineluctably transmute all innovations into sheer palliatives?

My own view is that what at first glance appear to be identical measures at times constitute mere palliatives whereas, in different circumstances, they creatively expand possibilities for future change. In short, two opposing kinds of incrementalism can be identified: the one palliative, the other creative.

Palliatives prevent deep change by lulling people into accepting minor gradual improvement instead of adequate responses to fundamental problems. As time passes, however, palliatives always worsen the condition they mean to cure—by raising hopes they cannot satisfy or

---

[7] Harvey S. Perloff, *Alliance for Progress, A Social Invention in the Making*, (Baltimore, 1969), ch. 10 and 11.

tinkering with defective social mechanisms, thereby postponing treatment until the disease becomes incurable. Creative incremental measures, on the contrary, are designed to open new possibilities for subsequent radical change even though at the moment of adoption they appear modest. Such measures contain a latent dynamism which propels society beyond immediate problem-solving and renders new futures possible. John Wilkinson, a physicist and philosopher, aptly remarks that the "potential energy of a rock that has been sitting on top of a hill for a million years is harmless to anyone. Only when its energy can be made kinetic by some random push can it cause a new situation to arise." As with energy, contemplated social measures are endowed with a greater or lesser potential for generating major transformation. A good strategist of induced social change must learn to discern which measures have but a palliative potential, which a creative potential. All latent social energy remains fruitless until it is kineticized. Of course, the total consequences of a given measure cannot always be assessed before the fact. Randomness or serendipity can transform "safe" concessions into explosively revolutionary instruments. Nonetheless, sensitive change agents can appeal to subjective and objective criteria when they attempt to assess the change potential contained in contemplated moves.

Even revolutionists who shrink from violent methods have lost their faith in the capacity of *existing institutions* to produce required changes in piecemeal fashion. If, therefore, they feel compelled to resort to seemingly incremental tactics, they always do so in the hope that today's modest moves will open the door to deeper mutations tomorrow. Consequently, all specific recommendations made by change agents need to be evaluated in the light of the long-term intentions of those same agents. An illustration may help. We may suppose country "A" favors creating an international ocean regime having sole authority over all seabeds and committed to using the oceans' resources exclusively for peaceful development purposes. Let us further assume that country "A" adopts this scheme because it considers an international ocean regime to be a first step in the direction of abolishing national sovereignties and creating world political responsibility. That country's leaders may reach the practical judgment that the cause of world government is advanced if global control over the oceans can be established before sovereign nations acquire uncontested rights over them. In this case, the measure is not merely palliative: subjectively at least, it is perceived as capable of creating new leverage for a more profound institutional change later.

The identical ocean regime, however, may be supported by country

"B" for quite opposite reasons. Country "B" may oppose the prospect of world government and fear the eventual demise of national sovereignty. Nevertheless, the country might wish to curb military or commercial exploitation of the ocean floor by powerful nations to the detriment of poorer nations. Relative to world government, the final objective, "B's" support of an international ocean regime, must be considered mere palliative. In both cases incrementalism is clearly at work, but a subjective criterion helps us discern whether the same measure constitutes palliative or creative incrementalism.

Proponents of radical change sometimes contend that they should publicly portray all measures they advocate in the guise of modest problem-solving moves. By so doing, it is argued, they can disarm the fears of those who mistrust their ulterior subjective intentions. It is not my intention to engage in this debate. More important, even in political terms, is to inquire whether any *objective* criterion exists for distinguishing between incremental steps which are mere patchwork and those which genuinely expand future possibilities.

British scientist Denis Gabor, author of *Inventing the Future,* is convinced that palliative solutions to social problems, however attractive or adequate they appear at the time of adoption, inevitably worsen the ills they seek to cure. According to Gabor, non-palliative measures, when programmed in a computer designed to isolate the consequences of a contemplated course of action, can be shown in simulated exercises which portray hypothetical possible futures to result in better conditions. The opposite also holds true: palliatives, once played out, make matters visibly worse. If this be so, one can distinguish palliative from creative incremental measures *without appealing to ideological norms.* Such norms remain decisive, of course, for true believers whether the objective of their faith is free-enterprise or Marxist socialism. For them there exists one unmistakable criterion of discernment which they allege to be "objective," namely, the degree to which the measure envisaged strengthens or weakens the social system they champion. Great wisdom would doubtless be required of the programmer if he is to assesses all important factors correctly in his computer-programming exercise. Nevertheless, if Gabor is right, it becomes at least theoretically possible to judge the change potential of prospective measures. In fact, one can create a scale on which to measure the potential transformation value of all steps proposed.

It is my belief that the five institutional reconversions advocated above are creative, not palliative, incremental measures. The reader will recall that these proposals are: the institution of a world development plan, the curtailment of national sovereignties, the creation of new global financing institutions based on ground rules different from those now prevailing, the pooling of technological capacities at the service of mankind's priority needs, and the launching of a cultural revolution within developed societies to create requisite conditions for a successful change of values in the Third World. This judgment is made in the light of a form of universal development based on a hierarchy of priority needs, development which enhances men in all their dimensions and in a non-elitist mode. The measures proposed above are incremental because, by themselves, they do not suffice to generate authentic development. They are not sheer palliatives, however, because they remove obstacles impeding authentic development and create new possibilities of moving men toward the eventual obtention of such development.

A word must be added to explain why palliative solutions to social ills are so pernicious. Such solutions do not root out the causes of social ailments but merely tamper with symptoms. Politically speaking, they are designed to "buy off" potential agents of deeper change with social bribes, in the form of visible benefits. Yet, the way in which development is obtained determines whether men will be liberated or alienated at the end of the development road. The manner itself is as decisive as the matter. Many of development's benefits can be obtained in an elitist, technocratic, oligarchic mode even under the ostensible banner of greater freedom and democracy. Behind the scenes, however, may lurk deterministic forces manipulating mass opinion and desires. To achieve the benefits of development while sacrificing human freedom and critical intelligence is, however, to negate the very good life and good society development professes to nurture. Palliative measures may solve problems or settle issues, but they cannot foster those qualities in life which are the terminal goal of development itself.

Because anything less than basic reconversion of the world's institutions is sheer palliative to the evils of world underdevelopment, the crucial task incumbent upon social change agents is to devise bold measures consonant with feasibility and creativity. Ultimately, development is not some "art of the possible" but rather of creating new possibilities. Critical debate over the ethics of development is, however, but a preliminary step: it merely traces normative boundaries of what must be rendered possible if development's global promises are not to be betrayed.

Conflicting Images of Change

Social change does not occur in a vacuum but in specific settings wherein societies and their members entertain quite precise images of change. Diverse levels of consciousness regarding change are a crucial ingredient of change itself. As Harvard economist Albert Hirschman has explained (in *The Strategy of Economic Development*), some images of change are better suited than others to induce change itself. Exclusively ego-focused images of change are unsatisfactory because they violate certain requirements of social solidarity. On the other hand, unduly group-focused images of change impede innovation by stifling creativity. Hirschman concludes by advocating a hybrid ego-and-group-focused image of change as being most suitable. Although useful, this distinction is not adequate to explain the dynamics of change. Also required is critical reflection on which social changes are under discussion.

For example, most of the social changes now being deliberately planned in the world have development as their goal. Clearly, however, planned changes take place only within a larger historical context which includes many unplanned changes of an ecological and symbolic nature. These flow in large part from unpredictable effects of mass technology. Overshadowing these large considerations is the fact that the poor world wants development and it wants it fast.

As early as 1956 Nehru declared: "We are not going to spend the next hundred years in arriving gradually, step by step, at that stage of development which the developed countries have reached today. Our pace and tempo of progress has to be much faster."[8]

Former United Nations official Raul Prebisch, an Argentine economist, speaks for most of his fellow Latin Americans when he asserts that "profound transformations of our economic and social structure are necessary to facilitate the appearance of means suited to accelerating the rhythm of economic and social development . . . these transformations are urgent."[9]

---

[8] Cited in Gunnar Myrdal, *Asian Drama* (New York, 1968), Vol. II, p. 716.

[9] Raul Prebisch, "Aspectos Economicos da Aliança Para o Progresso," in *A Aliança Para o Progresso*, ed. John C. Dreier (Rio de Janeiro, 1962), p. 55.

In short, as one development economist once privately declared: "The West does not shove development down the Third World's throat; rather, its leaders are hell-bent on getting it."

So the Third World is hell-bent on development. But in what manner is the desire to be fulfilled? What ends should be kept in sight?

Even within "developed" countries such questions cause tension between social critics and militant reformers, who tend to nourish different goals for development (and of course between these two groups and those people who like things as they are). Perhaps the most important and divisive issues concern the institutions required to control technology and the instruments society can devise to assure non-elitist decisions. In short, questions relating to dehumanized existence and exclusion from meaningful decision-making.

Within developed and underdeveloped countries alike, *how* change is obtained is as crucial as *what* benefits change will bring. The Third World, in all its diversity, nourishes at least one common hope: to obtain Bread plus Dignity. It seeks, therefore, a way of getting its bread without having to forfeit dignity. Similarly, increasing numbers of Americans, dissatisfied with mere affluence or guaranteed success, are demanding control and participation. This common concern for the *how* suggests, if it does not demonstrate, an important nexus between perceptions of change in advanced countries and those found in Third World countries. According to World Bank economist Barend A. de Vries, "The richest communities which demonstrate awareness of their own internal development needs also show most understanding of the needs of other communities. This is not merely a question of balancing domestic against foreign objectives. Rather, a country's attitude toward the development problem of others, and toward what is commonly called development assistance, is closely akin to the attitude toward its own development needs."[10]

One inadequate model of the manner in which to dispense foreign aid is offered by Neil H. Jacoby, a former economic advisor to President Eisenhower, who pleads for a business-like partnership between donor and recipient nations. For him it is "constructive to think of the relationship between aider and aided as a partnership venture entered into for mutual advantage. Each partner contributes to the enterprise and hopes to gain therefrom. The aiding agency, committing itself to assistance over an extended period, agrees to provide physical and human resources in

---

[10] Barend A. de Vries, "New Perspectives on International Development," *Finance and Development* (No. 3, 1968), p. 26.

the form of machinery, commodities, and technical assistance needed for development. The aided country contributes its commitments to undertake measures of self-help and to bring about necessary economic and social reforms. A long-term program of development is agreed upon with targets to be reached at specified points of time. As long as goals are met and each partner honors his commitments, the relationship continues. In the event of material default by either partner, or a severe falling-short of the accepted goals, the relationship is reconsidered and either revised or terminated."[11]

The defect of such imagery is that it glosses over structural inequalities existing between partners and assumes that social reform is needed in recipient, but not in donor, nations. Such language tends to reinforce structures of paternalism and fosters the "domestication" of recipient countries' development efforts.

Of course, within underdeveloped societies there are also conflicting images of the constituents of progress. Among the competing notions one invariably finds some version of the "salvation by redistribution" image versus the "salvation by the overflow from increased productivity" image.

Not surprisingly, analogous polarizations regarding needed change are discernible within the United States as well, where many argue that racism, social injustice and poverty can be abolished only by making America's ongoing and successful enterprise more ongoing and more successful. But numerous others, on the contrary, despair of the capacity of present ground rules operative in society to satisfy the needs of blacks, migrant workers, and Appalachian poor. Proponents of both views nourish competing images as to the meaning of the changes now taking place in the United States, and more importantly, as to the shape of desired changes in the future.

Theorists of social change have long debated the respective importance to be attached to so-called objective and subjective conditions of change. Political scientists have had the issues thrust upon their attention in dramatic revolutionary terms by the writings of Che Guevara and Régis Debray. According to both authors, Cuba's revolution provides evidence that the subjective conditions — in the form of a dedicated and active revolutionary focus or nucleus — can make up for the seeming absence of putatively necessary objective conditions.

Even in non-revolutionary contexts, however, parallel arguments

---

11 Neil H. Jacoby, *The Progress of Peoples*, Occasional Paper, Center for the Study of Democratic Institutions (June, 1969), pp. 10-11.

are heard. Most gradualists contend that certain prerequisites for social change are indispensable: high literacy in citizens, modern bureaucratic institutions, and honest government practices; or perhaps political independence or relative democracy, and the like. Others plead for the very antithesis of a "stages of growth" approach, stressing instead autonomous cultural creativity, rapidly achieved. They point to such examples as Tanzania's policy of self-reliance, and China's insistence on historical contemporaneity and revolutionary consciousness.

Nevertheless, sociologists like Orlando FalsBorda, Irving Louis Horowitz and others have shown that a man's preferred categories of analysis correlate highly with his position on a ladder of political, economic and cultural influence. Quite predictably, therefore, scholars and government officials from developed countries have legitimized models of social change which treat transformation in functional and behavioral terms. With equal predictability large numbers of analysts and practitioners from the Third World view the problem in terms of gaining some mastery, or at least some voice, in the ground rules governing access to resources and to significant decision-making. What they stress are the structures of domination and dependence which govern the exchange of goods, of men and of ideas throughout the world.

The importance of these correlations is evident. Each moral evaluator is heir to certain biased interests and viewpoints. It would be illusory, therefore, for him to imagine that he can gain even some relative measure of objectivity in his vision of social change without extreme critical effort. His heritage, vested interests, social roles, and personal options all strongly incline him to place his stakes in one particular image or other of social change.

In his landmark study on the *Social Origins of Dictatorship and and Democracy*, Barrington Moore has analyzed the historical distortions produced by dominant Western biases. His conclusion compels attention. "For a Western scholar to say a good word on behalf of revolutionary radicalism is not easy because it runs counter to deeply grooved mental reflexes. The assumption that gradual and piecemeal reform has demonstrated its superiority over violent revolution as a way to advance human freedom is so pervasive that even to question such an assumption seems strange. In closing this book I should like to draw attention for the last time to what the evidence from the comparative history of modernization may tell us about this issue. As I have reluctantly come to read this evidence, the costs of moderation have been at least as atrocious as those of revolution, perhaps a great deal more.

"Fairness demands recognition of the fact that the way nearly all history has been written imposes an overwhelming bias against revolutionary violence. Indeed the bias becomes horrifying as one comes to realize its depth. To equate the violence of those who resist oppression with the violence of the oppressors would be misleading enough." [12] Moore further declares that gradualist myths have been shattered and that the costs of going without a revolution are sometimes greater than those incurred in a revolution.

It is significant that the author of these lines should be a meticulously professional historian at Harvard, and not some undisciplined polemicist. As thoroughly as he refutes gradualism, however, Moore rejects the simplistic revolutionary argument on the grounds that its claims rest on promise rather than on performance. What is pertinent here, however, is the pervasiveness of anti-revolutionary biases as we read history and examine the contemporary scene.

The central question now becomes: Are we capable of rising above our ethnocentric and particularistic vision? At the very least, we must listen attentively to spokesmen of underdeveloped countries, especially when they draft a formal list of complaints. A representative list can be found in the "Charter of Algiers," a document prepared on October 24, 1967, by the signatories of seventy-seven underdeveloped nations. This report, which summarizes trends and problems in world trade and development, stands as a major position paper submitted to the second UNCTAD meeting held in New Delhi in 1968. Its twenty-nine pages speak of the international community's obligation to rectify unfavorable trends and "to create conditions under which all nations can enjoy economic and social well-being, and have the means to develop their respective resources to enable their peoples to lead a life free from want and fear." More importantly, the Algiers document asserts that "traditional approaches, isolated measures and limited concessions are not enough. The gravity of the problem calls for the urgent adoption of a global strategy for development requiring convergent measures on the part of both developed and developing countries." [13]

Americans will doubtless find it painful to alter their cherished images of the deep meaning of social changes occurring throughout the world. Robert Heilbroner, among others, has explained how America's special vantage point in appraising world-wide social changes produces gross distortions in the vision of reality it nourishes. He confesses

---

[12] Barrington Moore, Jr., *Social Origins of Dictatorship and Democracy* (Boston, 1966), p. 505.

[13] Charter of Algiers, UN Document MM/77/I/20, 30 October, 1967, p. 5.

that he does "not know how to estimate the chances of affecting such deepseated changes in the American outlook. It may be that the pull of vested interests, the inertia of bureaucracy, plus a certain lurking fundamentalism that regards communism as an evil which admits of no discussion — the anti-christ — will maintain America on its present course with consequences that I find frightening to contemplate. But I believe that our attitudes are not hopelessly frozen."[14] Heilbroner rests his hopes on a United States rapprochement with the Soviet Union and the capacity of United States humanitarian currents to assert themselves over the mainstream United States fear of communism's triumph in underdeveloped regions. Whatever be the prospects, however, it is certain that America's perceptions of change have gone awry. Moralists have no reason to evince surprise. They have always known, or should have known, that structures of power and structures of wealth tend to corrupt structures of ideas. Great wealth and great power do indeed, as Alfred Marshall expressed it, greatly impede understanding. But neither wealth nor power as such are proper scapegoats, for somewhere in the world certain societies and certain categories of men will hold power and possess wealth.

The choice between gradualist and non-gradualist solutions to grave social problems requires, in final analysis, the intervention of human wills. Consequently, decision-makers must become acutely conscious of their responsibility for validating or legitimizing for themselves any particular image of change they entertain. Shakespeare's dictum is fully applicable here: the wish *is* father to the thought. Statistically, one can predict with surprising accuracy that those in whose interest it is to cherish a gradualist image of change will, by and large, do so. Conversely, those who stand to gain most by adopting a non-gradualist image of change will probably do so, provided their level of critical consciousness has reached a certain minimal threshold. The impasse can be broken only by those who are willing—the term is used advisedly since an act of will is required—to settle issues in broader terms than those dictated by their limited interests or those of their nation, social class, professional category or ideological confession. This is no doubt a task of monumental difficulty. French economist François Perroux evokes the stigma which will long remain attached to men who place the interests of all mankind above those of their own person, nation or society. He fears that spokesmen from any given nation will deprive

---

[14] Robert L. Heilbroner, "Counterrevolutionary America," *Commentary* (April, 1967), p. 38.

themselves of immediate influence if they speak on behalf of an experience or an ideal which transcends mere national interests or myths. Nevertheless, he concludes, it is precisely such vicious circles which threaten the destiny of all mankind and are preparing the death of the entire species. He ends by appealing for a tacit alliance of all the "heretics" of the world to shatter the orthodoxies of limited viewpoints.[15]

Psychologically speaking, there is a danger that such "witnesses of the human species" (Perroux) will undergo a severe process of uprooting, fraught with dangers of insecurity and disintegration of character. Yet Karl Mannheim does well to remind us "that what we pejoratively call 'uprooting' has its positive aspects both for personality formation and the construction of world community. Uprooting, viewed positively, might be called emancipation. Hardly anybody will doubt that the establishment of larger communities — possibly a world-wide community — is possible only if people overcome the state of unconditional subservience to the power demon of national sovereignty and aggressive nationalism. Partial uprooting, emancipation, is therefore necessary and is indeed achieved by progressive men."[16] It is to such emancipation that the wills of men are summoned if development is to become feasible.

To sum up, it is clear that in America gradualism is not dead: for many individuals and interest groups gradualism remains a very desirable model of social change. But it is equally clear that the ranks of those who have lost faith in gradualism are swelling. This fact itself seriously affects the viability of gradualist models of change. For there comes a point in all societies beyond which legitimacy is transferred from within the boundaries of the law to an arena outside those boundaries. When this happens, gradualism loses all relevance.

Order, Change and Force

Under "normal" circumstances, legitimacy is the attribute of a politically established order which enjoys a monopoly in the lawful use of force. Where far-reaching institutional changes are sought by large numbers of subjects, however, the legal order faces serious challenges from below. Its capacity for change may be doubted and its

---

15 François Perroux, *La Coexistence Pacifique* (Paris, 1958), Vol. III, p. 623.

16 Karl Mannheim, *Freedom, Power and Democratic Planning* (London, 1951), p. 62.

very legitimacy questioned. More important, its monopoly over force risks being broken. For this reason it is useful for us, at this point, to inquire into the precise relationship which links order to force and change. We cannot do so without first clarifying the precise meaning attached to these three terms.

"*Order*" must here be understood in its societal sense: it signifies all lawful and enduring arrangements for reaching social decisions. These arrangements regulate exchanges and implement norms imputed to law and justice. Inasmuch as social order is itself relative, however, it cannot be judged substantively except by some appeal to criteria transcending order. Over varying time spans, diplomatic practice as well as moral judgment ratify facts, even when these are not considered by the sanctioning agents to be legally valid or morally good. I am here referring, evidently, to diplomatic recognition when *de facto* control is exercised by a government, irrespective of its *de jure* status. Similarly, ethics invoke the prescription principle to ratify, on grounds of effective control over goods and persons, the rights of usurpers. The existence of these practices suggests an important truth, namely, that order expresses the particular conception of legitimacy which those who wield power can effectively enforce. This is why no basis can be found for attributing absolute ethical value to order.

There are times when order validates privilege, stagnation, obscurantism, manipulation, or provincialism. In happier circumstances, it may legitimize a high measure of relative justice and dynamic responsibility, along with genuine cultural progress in freedom and respect for universalizable values. From the mere fact that it exists, therefore, order enjoys no antecedent claim on the moral allegiance of citizens. Quite the opposite may be the case for technologically developed societies where citizens have special reasons to be skeptical of appeals made in the name of order. This is so because those who wield political power systematically manage information in ways calculated to engineer consent — or at least minimize dissent. Such management has become, in the contemporary technological world, an essential instrument used by men in power to legitimize their decisions. Not surprisingly, therefore, even a traditional moral philosopher such as Father Pie Régamey, the French Dominican, insists on the obligation incumbent upon citizens *not* to make a presumption in favor of governmental decisions. After alluding to the "essentially inhuman character of the modern state," Régamey asks whether modern governments, instead of pursuing a work of *reason* in the Aristotelian sense, are not rather involved in the *rationalization*, in the psycho-analytical sense, of their own irrationalities and egoism. The classical presumption in favor of constituted authority, he adds, is not "a presumption of moral rectitude." Rather, a citizen, and above all a Christian, must maintain a stance of *radical suspicion* vis-à-vis established authority. The reason is that the state so easily betrays essential human value and so readily enters into complicity with crime.[17]

The world is now alerted to the shocking immorality contained in Eichmann's obedience to orders and in his fidelity to order. Although his case is admittedly an extreme one, it dramatizes the permanent danger of immorality inherent in all large-scale administrations based on the principles of efficiency. There can be no doubt that the critical contestation both of the claims of order and of the validity of orders is the enemy of efficiency. And who can deny that efficiency ranks high on the scale of public values? Nevertheless, all citizens and men of influence—in particular, government officials, professional men, business executives and others—have no right to abdicate their moral responsibility of being critical and skeptical. The burden of proof lies with existing *order* because its operative structures institute a built-in bias in favor of efficient solutions to problems, not to morally good solutions. Not that efficiency is unfit to be a moral goal, of course, but rather that it is a subordinate, not a superordinate goal.

Psychologist Erich Fromm asserts that the flight from freedom by most individuals is a major reason why collective crimes (usually sins of omission or connivance with lesser justice) are so frequently committed by official agents of established orders. At the very least, therefore, moral realism dictates that we purge our minds of the biases induced by inertia and custom in favor of a just order. Indeed wherever order is structurally unjust, disorder is a prerequisite of justice.

Change Is Necessary. Most gradualists agree with revolutionists that social change is needed. They part ways, however, in their appraisal of how urgent change is, what quality of change is most desirable, and how suitable is one procedure for obtaining it as compared to others. Nevertheless, it is worth noting that revolutionary solutions to grave

---

17 P.R. Régamey, *La Conscience Chrétienne et la Guerre* (Paris, n.d.), pp. 43-44.

social problems are always desperate final solutions to an impasse. Ferhat Abbas, first president of the Provisional Government of the Algerian Republic in exile, has been nicknamed the "Reluctant Revolutionary" because he supported the *fellagha* guerrilla movement for independence only after losing faith in legal channels. Mohammed Khider, Belkacem Krim, and Messali Hadj are other Algerian nationalist leaders who "opted" for revolution because with the passage of time no other way was left open to them.

The rapid evolution in the thought of Camilo Torres, the rebel priest killed in ambush in the mountains of Colombia in 1966, further illustrates this point. In 1963 Torres condemned revolutionary violence on the grounds that it was incompatible with Christian morals. Within three years, however, he was publicly declaring that "the people do not believe in elections. The people know that legal paths have been exhausted. The people are in a state of despair and are resolved to risk their lives so that the next generation of Colombians will not be slaves . . . Every sincere revolutionary has to acknowledge that armed combat is the only alternative that is left."[18]

Even as he preached black emancipation from the secular tutelage of "whitey," Malcolm X never failed to remind his listeners that, ultimately, it rested with white America to determine whether black freedom would be attained with or without bloodshed.

A final example is supplied by that paragon of the confirmed revolutionary activist, Che Guevara. He does not hesitate to write, in the opening pages of his manual on guerrilla warfare: "Where a government has come into power through some form of popular vote, fraudulent or not, and maintains at least an appearance of constitutional legality, the guerrilla outbreak cannot be promoted, since the possibilities of peaceful struggle have not yet been exhausted."[19]

Only when they despair of obtaining necessary changes via legal gradualist methods do reformers find revolutionary procedures seductive. This is why any moral appraisal of the means of change must also look not only to the goals of change, but to the nature of change processes (dialectical, conflictual, non-linear) and to the world-wide matrix of change (structures of dominance and dependence) as well.

---

[18] *Camilo Torres*, SONDEOS Collection, No. 5, CIDOC (Cuernavaca, Mexico, 1966), pp. 116, 374.

[19] Che Guevara, *Guerrilla Warfare* (New York and London, 1967), p. 16.

Historical options are open at one moment, closed at the next. Accordingly, typologies of change situations, such as those formulated by Brazilian economist Celso Furtado or by Harvard's Albert Hirschman, throw light on the relative viability of several options. Furtado asserts, in short, that revolutionary change is regressive in those cases where political and social structures are not inflexibly rigid. On the other hand, gradualism is inadequate where rigid privilege structures prevail. The difficulty faced by Brazil in 1963, Furtado explains, was that the southern states were sufficiently advanced to progress better by evolutionary patterns, whereas the wretched northeast needed a radical restructuring of its basic institutions. Hirschman in turn considers revolution by stealth or reform-mongering, as he calls it, to be an intermediate option between ineffectual gradualism and destructive revolution. According to him, decentralized, unrequited and problem-solving violence practiced by revolutionaries can allow shrewd reformists to gain support from non-revolutionary interests for revolutionary programs.[20]

The aim of this essay is not to analyze these and other theories of change, but merely to emphasize that major changes are necessary. If, therefore, existing world and domestic orders prove incapable of generating required change, one must look beyond order, and beyond gradualism.

The Inevitability of Force. A final clarification deals with force, which I consider to be inevitable. "Force" is a narrower term than "power," which can be physical or moral, coercive or persuasive, etc. Physical force usually designates the ability, by arms if necessary, to impose compliance with positive injunctions and to restrain performance of prohibited actions. In contexts of broad social change, physical force can sometimes be countered by political and moral power. This occurred when India had recourse to massive civil disobedience in its campaign to win independence from Britain. There is clearly an inverse relation between the need of an established *order* to use force and the ability of that *order* to assure necessary change. When the existing *order* is powerless to effectuate or permit required change, it uses force to preserve order, to stifle change, or to channel change into domesticated paths. In such cases the likelihood of counter-force being used by change

---

[20] Albert O. Hirschman, *Journeys Toward Progress* (New York, 1965), Ch. 5 "The Contriving of Reform."

agents increases proportionately. Violence in turn is a particular kind of physical force which violates human life or damages property.

At the heart of the present argument is the historical fact that Western moralists throughout the centuries have condoned the use of force for purposes of coercion or defense and to assist allies. Their stand unequivocally implies, therefore, that force is not immoral *per se*. Consequently, once we accept the purely relative merits of any given *order*, there is no reason on principle for condemning the use of force against order, where order is unjust or is guilty of omission in the pursuit of the common good. Force is sometimes — I would say, usually — on the side of order. At times, it is on the side of change. More rarely, it is on the side of both; this happens when the existing order is compatible with necessary change.

The real question, in final analysis, is not whether the use of force or of counter-force is legitimate, but rather: Which kind of order is being served by the force employed? And which norms set limits to the use of force?

Is the order one defends that of a Salazar regime, of a Stalinist regime, or a Batista regime? On the world scene, is it the order of a *Pax Americana*, of a United States/Soviet spheres of influence model, or some other?

To challenge any given *order* is obviously tantamount to contesting the legitimacy of the values defended by that same order. The final chapter of Fanon's *The Wretched of the Earth* is entitled "Colonial War and Mental Disorders." There Fanon describes the medical visits he received both from French police torturers and from Arab victims of those very tortures. Psychiatrist Fanon at that time was employed by the French Ministry of Health. This explains why he was sought out by French and Arabs alike to confer good conscience on those who administered violence and to salvage the identity of those who suffered it.

Unless we can answer to our own satisfaction all the questions just raised about force, there is something hypocritical about using a double standard either to approve or to condemn force. The champions of law and order approve the force used by government, at times even by self-appointed Minutemen, but denounce that resorted to by social protestors. Some social dissenters, in turn, denounce on high moral ground the use of force against them, but contend that use of force by them is acceptable. The central problem abides, however: Which values are served by force, how and by whom is it employed, at whose expense? There is also the problem of how force is used. The use of force, whether legally or illegally, usually places agents in a situation of moral distress. When he finds himself in such straits, the ethical agent faces a dilemma: regardless of his choice, he is unable to predict or fully control the outcome of his moral options. Thus the revolutionary violence he could perpetrate in the name of justice can lead to repression under the facile pretext of "eliminating counter-revolutionaries" or "saving the revolution." But to abstain from revolutionary activity, once antagonisms have sharply polarized, may be nothing more than cowardly collusion with structural injustice. Paradoxically, even non-violence practiced for love's sake can pave the way for that greater violence which is born of the desperation of oppressed men. There is no way to avoid risking the subversion of one's most precious moral values. If one is lucid in such cases, his conscience is in distress. Not that all choices are morally equivalent, or that pure subjectivity can dictate the practical stance to be adopted. Yet, with the exception of certain rare cases of ethical heroism (embodying perhaps the living precept of Buddhism — "Hatred does not cease by hatred, but only by love" — or of Christianity — "Love those who hate you, do good to those who injure you"), most men find themselves in a condition where no certainty can be had as to what is the ethically good course of action. Perhaps the only honest advice moralists can offer in such cases is that submitted by Domenach, who writes: "Carry on your revolution if you wish; in the extreme case, wage your war if you wish. But stop preaching someone else's war. When the moment comes to take up guns, then let the intellectual resort to arms, but not to words which place bullets inside guns at a distance! . . . What weight can we give to the bad conscience which preaches war without waging it — or the good conscience which preaches peace and justice without forging the means to establish them."[21] The war one preaches or wages must always be his own war, not someone else's. This is why we can take Guevara or Mao seriously but not those who merely instigate others to carry on revolution.

---

21 Jean-Marie Domenach, "Un Monde de Violence," in *La Violence, Recherches et Debats* (Paris, 1967), p. 7.

Conclusion: Incrementalism and Revolutionary Changes

The stewards of social order are ethically bound to create conditions which render the use of force as little necessary as possible. This is the reason why politics cannot properly be defined primarily in terms of using power, but rather in terms of wider social goals. As sociologist Irving Louis Horowitz has aptly written: "The study of power is the beginning of sociological wisdom — but the essence of that wisdom is that power resides in men. Hence the existence of power is a less significant area of study than the human uses made of power. Men define power; they are not necessarily defined by it."[22] Most especially in change situations, politics is not the art of the possible but the art of redefining the limits of possibility. The task of ethics is indeed, to paraphrase Croce, to create new facts. The present world is characterized by massive underdevelopment and structural inequities among classes and nations. That is to say, the international common good is not being achieved by the custodians of world order and of domestic national orders. Morever, comprehensive social changes are now consciously perceived to be necessary by large numbers of men. Consequently, opposing conclusions will be reached as to the capability of existing social orders to achieve needed change *under present ground rules.* This means that the revolutionary potential in the world, and more particularly in certain portions or sectors of the world, is high. It also suggests the possibility at least that revolution in many areas may also be supremely moral. Yet, as noted earlier, no single revolution or combination of revolutionary programs can suffice to create a valid world order and sound arrangements for social justice within nations. Consequently, partial reliance at least must be placed on gradualist or incrementalist measures.

Earlier in this essay I attempted to explain the difference between palliative and creative incrementalism. Any realistic appraisal of future probabilities leads us to conclude that some form of gradualism will

---

[22] Irving Louis Horowitz, editor's "Introduction" to *Power, Politics and People, The Collected Essays of C. Wright Mills* (New York, 1963), p. 11.

continue to be advocated as a doctrine and practiced as a policy. Most of the time I fear it will be palliative gradualism, the kind which simply connives with that institutionalized violence of the established order analyzed by Barrington Moore. Such gradualism has the innate tendency, over the long term, to elicit the very anti-thesis of gradualism, namely, the violence of rebels who despair and who must affirm their dignity, even at the cost of failure to achieve valid social objectives.

The major responsibility of decision-makers, therefore, as distinct from that of social critics or dissenting activists, is to devise creative incremental measures. Hirschman suggests (in *Journeys Toward Progress*) that what is needed are revolutionaries without revolution. Such revolutionaries must engage in problem-solving, decentralized, unrequited violence. The threat posed by the possible escalation of their violence will, he hopes, spur those in power to conduct audacious reform-mongering or revolution by stealth. Their aim is to win support, even from enemies of reform who fear the supposedly "greater evil" of a complete revolution. However esthetically appealing it may be, however, Hirschman's model is inapplicable to many situations. And one may doubt whether profound changes can truly be achieved by people who fear an imagined "worse alternative." Frei's performance in Chile leaves us skeptical to say the least. In my view, unless the ground rules of production and decision-making are profoundly altered within the United States, a world order of authentic development has no chance to be born. Thus, at the very least, a major cultural revolution is needed in the United States. Recent political history suggests, however, that most Americans are not prepared to give up their illusions and myths. Consequently, the cultural revolution is unlikely to take place. And I fear that gradualism as palliative is not dead. But it ought to be, and we should bury it as quickly as possible.

Its opposite, gradualism as creative incrementalism, is, of course, not dead. The problem is that it has not yet been born on a wide scale. Morever, it could succeed only if non-gradualist measures also remain possible.

Certain moral compromises are involved in all these stances. It is either naive or hypocritical to assume that righteousness is the exclusive prerogative either of those who defend order or of those who contest it. Similarly, it is sheer mystification to condemn the counter-violence of revolutionaries while closing one's eyes to the oppressive force employed by those who legitimize their actions by appealing to order.

My own perspective on history and social change is dialectical. Thus, I believe that even solidarity must often be conquered through conflict. Lest this view appear too dismal, however, let me add that in dialectics the boundaries separating gradualism from non-gradualism are destined to disappear. Gradualism reaches a point where one more quantitative increment leads to a qualitative change. This is the proverbial "straw that breaks the camel's back," the point where one more palliative results in an order's loss of psychic legitimacy. And once this legitimacy is lost, the use of legitimate force summons up counter-force. On the other hand, even revolutionary changes are in some sense gradual and incremental. Notwithstanding Régis Debray's fervent voluntarism, men can never completely free the present from the past or the future from the present.

In a world grown so disconcertingly complex, we need not lament over the demise either of palliative gradualism or of simplistic revolutionism. But the sheer existence of China, of Cuba, and of black militants within the United States demonstrates that revolutionaries need not be simplistic. Conversely, the measures advocated by the Charter of Algiers or within Tanzania by Nyerere prove that creative incrementalism is also possible.

To conclude, let me return to a point made earlier. Some men have vested interests in keeping gradualism alive, others in doing it in. At some ultimate point, the scales will be tipped by the intervention of human wills. The sobering truth is that our own wills will help tip those scales.

Appendix: The Meaning of the Term "Ethics"

Since the days of early Greek philosophers, ethics has meant the reflective study of what is good or bad in that part of human conduct for which men have some responsibility. Contemporary ethical theories focus, it is true, on how to explain the "oughtness" in human experience, whereas older viewpoints centered more directly on how man could best live and act so as to reach his final objective. Nevertheless, as one historian of ethics has recently explained, "This contrast between the older and the modern viewpoints is a matter of different emphases and not an absolute shift in the meaning of ethics."[23]

In general parlance, however, far removed from the tangled vocabulary of specialists, the dominant ethical stress is placed on the body of norms which regulates action. We see little critical examination of the ends themselves. For many observers, ethical choices are no different from empirical statements about alternative ways of reaching the same objective. Goals themselves, however, can be endowed with varying moral qualities. Aristotle noted centuries ago that some ends are good because they are intrinsically noble, others because they are useful, a third category because they cause pleasure. Accordingly, Morris Ginsberg rightly insists that "reason has not only a regulative but a constitutive function in relation to the ends of action. A rational ethic must assume that there is such a thing as rational action, that intelligence has a part to play not only in cognition, but volition . . . It is concerned also with the relative worth of the different ends in relation to the costs involved in attaining them, and this task it cannot fulfill adequately without inquiry into the basic human needs and grounds of our preferences and choices."[24]

Ethical specialists doubtless acknowledge the existence of esthetic, utilitarian, emotional, and other values. Although none of these are reducible or assimilable to ethical values, ethics does arbitrate among them by appealing to norms of "oughtness." These norms, it must be noted, are neither initially given nor self-evident. Rather, they are perpetually conditioned historically, socially, psychologically, culturally and biologically. Even norms themselves must be subjected to rational critique and judged in the light of other values. By reason of their "oughtness," however, ethical norms can exist only where freedom and accountability are present. The very possibility of ethics is annihilated if full determination or complete irresponsibility prevails.

In ideal terms, ethics has several roles to play:

a. It teaches men by making them critically aware of the moral significance of their choices. It is a pedagogue.

b. To the extent that it commands good and forbids bad actions, ethics is coercive.

c. It confers bad conscience upon exploiters and provides exploited victims with rational grounds for revolting against their lot.

d. It helps build institutions because, in the long run, norms need to be embodied visibly in rights, duties and laws.

Because it "lives, moves and has its being" in shifting historical processes, social ethics cannot be based on any Kantian imperative or fixist natural law. Ultimately, social ethics is the pursuit by human intelligence of leverage to act with varying degrees of freedom and responsibility in social universes where multiple and complex determinisms, as well as irrationalities, are powerfully at work. The very possibility of ethics is conditioned by a prior possibility of freedom and accountability. Yet, the accountability here invoked need be only to

---

[23] Vernon J. Bourke, *History of Ethics* (New York, 1968), p. 8.

[24] Morris Ginsberg, *On Justice in Society* (New York, 1965), p. 29.

reason itself. No extrinsic source of morality is necessarily presupposed, nor, on the other hand, excluded on principle.

The term "ethics" has been employed in the present essay to mean those conditions without which men can exercise no genuine choice, either of ends or of means. Certain of these conditions are cognitive — men must know certain things. Others are structural: men must not be fully determined by the social forces which impinge on them. Still others are deeply subjective, grounded on diverse levels of self-awareness. Stated differently, "ethics" is that realm of judgment concerned with the goodness and badness of human actions. There are three requisites for ethical discourse. The first is some attributable measure of freedom to choose on the part of human agents. The second is some mode of accountability for choices made. The third is some standard of oughtness in the light of which goodness and badness are assessed.

It follows, therefore, that human acts (including internal acts of mind and will) lie outside the pale of ethical judgment if they are totally determined, flow from non-responsible agents, or cannot be referred to some norm of goodness. Nevertheless, even ethically neutral events may have clear ethical consequences for human beings, quite apart from the ethical intentions of their originators.

Still another clarification may be useful here. Ethical discourse about good and evil is not always, and need not always be, intellectually disciplined or conceptually rigorous. Moreover, such discourse sometimes deals primarily with collective societal decisions, at other times with personal choices. It should be manifest to the reader of this essay that my generic usage of the term "ethics" — whether overt or merely implicit — embraces all these spheres of meaning. No less worthy of note is the fact that whether a human agent appeals to God as the ground of "oughtness," to Marxism, Social Utilitarianism, or to some other doctrine, to private intuition, to a pragmatic calculus of probable consequences, or even to purely gratuitous subjective impulses, he is nonetheless appealing to some *norm* of oughtness. In short, most human choices fall ineluctably within the arena of ethics.

Human Rights and Foreign Policy

Hans J. Morgenthau

A professor of law at Harvard at the beginning of the century said that, with the exception perhaps of theology, there is nothing about which so much nonsense has been written as international law. One could add to this statement or one could modify this statement by extending it to international morality. There has been recently a flood of statements, some of them on the highest authority, that have very little to do with a philosophic or even pragmatic understanding of international morality. Let me say first of all, in criticism of those who deny that moral principles are applicable to international politics, that all human actions in some way are subject to moral judgment. We cannot act but morally because we are men. Animals are limited by their own nature; they don't need and they don't have moral limitations, normative limitations that restrain their actions. But man, exactly because his imagination soars above natural limits and his aspirations aim at certain objectives that are not naturally limited, must submit *as man* to moral limitations that may be larger or more narrow as the case may be, but which exist.

Take an example from the conduct of foreign policy and you will see right away that this cannot be otherwise. At the Conference of Teheran in 1943, in the presence of Roosevelt and Churchill, Stalin suggested that the German general staff be liquidated. I quote now Churchill's report:

> The whole force of Hitler's mighty armies depended upon about 50,000 officers and technicians. If these were rounded up and shot at the end of the war, German military strength would be extirpated. On this I thought it right to say the British Parliament and public will never tolerate mass executions even

if in war, in war passion, they allow them to begin. They would turn violently against those responsible after the first butchery had taken place. The Soviets must be under no delusion on this point. Stalin, however, perhaps only in mischief, pursued the subject. "Fifty thousand," he said, "must be shot." I was deeply injured. "I would rather," I said, "be taken out into the garden here and now and be shot myself than sully my own and my country's honor by such infamy."

Obviously, here you have as clear an example as one can wish of a moral reaction to a particular course suggested in foreign policy. Whenever we are face to face with a situation in which a statesman could perform a certain action that would be in his interest and he refrains from doing so, he acts under a moral compulsion. Take any number of examples from history and you will see that time and again statesmen have refrained from certain actions on moral grounds, actions they could have taken physically and which would have been in their interests.

Take, for instance, the sanctity of human life in peace, which we today take for granted. This is a development that is relatively new and didn't exist, for instance, in the fifteenth or sixteenth centuries. At that time it was common to kill foreign statesmen who were particularly obnoxious to oneself. The republic of Venice had a special official, the so-called official poisoner of the republic of Venice—we have the records, everything was written down, because obviously they were not afraid of congressional investigations—and we can read that one poisoner was hired on probation and was assigned Emperor Maximilian and tried five times to kill him without success. The record does not show whether he was hired or let go.

In any event, at that time the killing of foreign statesmen or foreign diplomats was as common a practice among nations as is today, let me say, the exchange of notes or summit meetings. Until very recently we have refrained from such practices. We have witnessed in this particular and in other respects a moral improvement in the behavior of nations—which, it is obvious, is in the process of disappearing. That is to say, we are living today in a situation in which the moral restraints that in the eighteenth and nineteenth centuries contributed greatly to the civilized relations among nations are in the process of weakening, if not disappearing.

Let me give you another example, an obvious one. Take the distinction that has been made in the eighteenth and nineteenth and the beginning of the twentieth century between combatants on the one hand and noncombatants on the other. The Hague and the Geneva conventions laid down intricate legal rules of conduct, which in turn are a reflection of moral rules of conduct to the effect that only soldiers ready to fight shall be the object of belligerent action but that soldiers who want to surrender, or who are incapacitated, and civilians altogether shall be exempt from warfare.

In the First World War it was still regarded as outrageous that certain armies would deal harshly with certain groups of the civilian population. Still, at the beginning of the Second World War an outcry of indignation swept through the Western world when the Germans bombarded Coventry, Rotterdam, Warsaw. At the end of the Second World War we accepted the destruction of the major German cities and of Hiroshima and Nagasaki with considerable equanimity. Here again what you see is a decline in the adherence to moral values in general. But in any event it cannot be doubted that the conduct of foreign policy is not an enterprise devoid of moral significance. That is, like all human activities, it partakes of the judgment made by both actor and the witnesses to the act when they perceive the act. To say this is perhaps to belabor the obvious.

To conclude from this omnipresence of the moral element in foreign policy that a country has a mission to apply its own moral principles to the rest of humanity or to certain segments of humanity is quite something else. For there exists an enormous gap between the judgment we apply to ourselves, our own actions, and the universal application of our own standards of action to others. Take again so elemental and obvious a principle of action—obvious at least and elemental for us—as the respect for human life and the refusal to take human life except under the most extraordinary, exculpating circumstances. There are obviously civilizations and even groups within our own civilization that have a much less strict conception of the sanctity of human life, that are much more generous in spending the life of others than we would be and would have been under similar circumstances.

So there exists of necessity a relativism in the relation between moral principles and foreign policy that one cannot overlook if one wants to do justice to the principles of morality in international politics. The relativism is twofold. It is a relativism in time (to which I have already referred), when certain principles are applicable in one period of history and not applicable in another period of history, and it is a relativism in terms of culture—of contemporaneous culture— in that certain principles are obeyed by certain nations, by certain political civilizations, and are not obeyed by others.

That consideration brings me to the popular issue with which the problem of morality in foreign policy presents us today, and that is the issue of what is now called human rights. That is to say, to what extent is a nation entitled and obligated to impose its moral principles upon other nations? To what extent is it both morally just and intellectually tenable to apply principles we hold dear to other nations that, for a number of reasons, are impervious to them? It is obvious that the attempt to impose so-called human rights upon others or to punish others for not observing human rights assumes that human rights are of universal validity—that, in other words, all nations or all peoples living in different nations would embrace human rights if they knew they existed and that in any event they are as inalienable in their character as the Declaration of Independence declares them to be.

I'm not here entering into a discussion of the theological or strictly philosophic nature of human rights. I only want to make the point that whatever one's conception of that theological or philosophical nature, those human rights are filtered through the intermediary of historic and social circumstances, which will lead to different results in different times and under different circumstances. One need only look at the unique character of the American polity and at these very special, nowhere-else-to-be-found characteristics of our protection of human rights within the confines of America. You have only to look at the complete lack of respect for human rights in many nations, or in most nations (consider that there is only one black country in Africa with a plural political system; all others are dictatorships of different kinds) to realize how daring—or how ignorant if you will, which can also be daring—an attempt it is to impose upon the rest of the world the respect for human rights or in particular to punish other nations for not showing respect for human rights. What we are seeing here is an abstract principle we happen to hold dear, which we happen to have put to a considerable extent into practice, presented to the rest of mankind not for imitation but for acceptance.

It is quite wrong to assume that this has been the American tradition. It has not been the American tradition at all. Quite the contrary. I think it was John Quincy Adams who made the point forcefully that it was not for the United States to impose its own principles of government upon the rest of mankind, but, rather, to attract the rest of mankind through the example of the United States. And this has indeed been the persisting principle the United States has followed. We have made a point from the very beginning in saying that the American Revolution, to quote Thomas Paine, ''was not made for America alone, but for mankind,'' but that those universal principles the United States had put into practice were not to be exported by fire and sword if necessary, but they were to be presented to the rest of the world through the successful example of the United States. This has been the great difference between the early conception of America and its relations to the rest of the world on the one hand and what you might call the Wilsonian conception on the other.

For Wilson wanted to make the world safe for democracy. He wanted to transform the world through the will of the United States. The Founding Fathers wanted to present to the nations of the world an example of what man can do and called upon them to do it. So there is here a fundamental difference, both philosophic and political, between the present agitation in favor of human rights as a universal principle to be brought by the United States to the rest of the world and the dedication to human rights as an example to be offered to other nations—which is, I think, a better example of the American tradition than the Wilsonian one.

There are two other objections that must be made against the Wilsonian conception. One is the impossibility of enforcing the universal application of human rights. We can tell the Soviet Union, and we should from time to time tell the Soviet Union, that its treatment of minorities is incompatible with our conception of human rights. But once we have said this we will find that there is very little we can do to put this statement into practice. For history has shown that the Soviet Union may yield under certain conditions to private pressure (and I have myself had certain experiences in this field; the agitation in which I was involved, for instance, in favor of the dancers Panov had a great deal to do, I think, with the final release of that couple). There are other examples where private pressure—for example, the shaming of public high officials in the Soviet Union by private pressure—has had an obvious result. But it is inconceivable I would say on general grounds, and more particularly in view of the experiences we have had, to expect that the Soviet Union will yield to public pressure when public pressure becomes an instrument of foreign policy and will thereby admit its own weakness in this particular field and the priority of the other side as well. So there is, I think, a considerable confusion in our theory and practice of human rights, especially vis-à-vis other nations in the field of foreign policy.

There is a second weakness of this approach, which is that the United States is a great power with manifold interests throughout the world, of which human rights is only one and not the most important one, and the United States is incapable of consistently following the path of the defense of human rights without maneuvering itself into a Quixotic position. This is obvious already in our discriminating treatment of, let me say, South Korea on the one hand and the Soviet Union on the other. Or you could mention mainland China on the one hand and the Soviet Union on the other. We dare to criticize and affront the Soviet Union because our relations, in spite of being called détente, are not particularly friendly. We have a great interest in continuing the normalization of our relations with mainland China, and for this reason we are not going to hurt her feelings. On the other hand South Korea is an ally of the United States, it is attributed a considerable military importance, and so we are not going to do anything to harm those relations.

In other words, the principle of the defense of human rights cannot be consistently applied in foreign policy because it can and it must come in conflict with other interests that may be more important than the defense of human rights in a particular instance. And to say—as the undersecretary of state said the other day—that the defense of human rights must be woven into the fabric of American foreign policy is, of course, an attempt to conceal the actual impossibility of consistently pursuing the defense of human rights. And once you fail to defend human rights in a particular instance, you have given up the defense of human rights and you have accepted another principle to guide your actions. And this is indeed what has happened and is bound to happen if you are not a Don Quixote who foolishly but consistently follows a disastrous path of action.

So you see that there are two basic logical and pragmatic hindrances to a consistent policy of the defense of human rights. On the one hand you cannot be consistent in the defense of human rights, since it is not your prime business as a state among other states to defend human rights, and second you cannot pursue human rights without taking into consideration other aspects of your relations with other nations, which may be more important than those connected with human rights.

Where does it leave us in the end? I think in this consideration of the relations of foreign policy and morality we are in the presence not of a peculiar, extraordinary situation but of a particular manifestation of a general human condition. As I said at the beginning, we are all moral beings because we are men. And we all try to a greater or lesser extent—to a better or worse extent one might say—to realize the moral principles with which we are identified. We find that we are faced with contradictions, with difficulties—logical, pragmatic, moral difficulties themselves. And so the best we can do is what Abraham Lincoln asked us to do. He warned us first against the exaggeration of moral virtue we claim for ourselves, and next he outlined the limits within which man can act morally and at the same time have a chance for success. Lincoln's statement was made during the Civil War and is a reply to a petition by a delegation of ministers who asked him to emancipate all slaves forthwith. Here is what Lincoln said:

> In great contests each party claims to act in accordance with the will of God. Both may be and one must be wrong. God cannot be for and against the same thing at the same time. I'm approached with the most opposite opinions and advice and that by religious men who are equally certain that they represent the divine will. I'm sure that either the one or the other class is mistaken in that belief and perhaps in some respects both. I hope it will not be irreverent for me to say that if it is probable that God would reveal his will to others on a point so connected with my duty it might be supposed he would reveal it directly to me. For unless I am more deceived in myself than I often am it is my earnest desire to know the will of Providence in this matter and if I can learn what it will be I will do it. These are not, however, the days of miracles and I suppose it will be granted that I am not to expect a direct revelation. I must study the plain physical facts of the case, ascertain what is possible and learn what appears to be wise and right.

Contributors

John C. Bennett was president of Union Theological Seminary from 1964 to 1970 and served with Reinhold Niebuhr for many years as co-chairman of the editorial board of *Christianity and crisis.*

Victor C. Ferkiss is a teacher and one-time director of a training program for the International Cooperation Administration and a consultant to the Peace Corps. He is the author of numerous works, including *Africa's Search for Identity.*

Robert Gordis, even in retirement, continues to teach at the Jewish Theological Seminary of America, where he was associate professor of biblical exegesis, and to edit the quarterly *Judaism.* He served for many years as rabbi of Temple Beth-El, Long Island.

Dennis Goulet holds the O'Neill Chair in Education for Justice, University of Notre Dame. He is a pioneer in a new discipline that deals with the ethics of development. In addition to teaching and writing, he has worked as laborer and factory hand in Madrid and areas of central France and has shared the life of nomadic tribes in the northern Sahara and of Amazon Indians in Latin America.

Manfred Halpern is professor of politics, Princeton University, and a staff member of Princeton's program in Near Eastern Studies and the Center of International Studies. From the late 1940s to the late 1950s he worked in the Department of State, where he was special assistant to the chief in the Division of Research and Analysis for the Near East, South Asia, and Africa, and received the department's Meritorious Service Award.

Hans J. Morgenthau held the chair of Albert A. Michelson Distinguished Service Professor at the University of Chicago and was named Leonard Davis Distinguished Professor at the City College of the City University of New York. He also served as visiting professor at Harvard, Yale, Columbia, and Berkeley. His numerous publications include *Politics Among Nations*, which remains the basic textbook in the philosophy of international relations.

John Courtney Murray, S.J. is one of the most distinguished of contemporary American Roman Catholic theologians. He was the editor of *Theological Studies* and a member of the faculty of Woodstock College.

Paul H. Nitze is the U.S. representative for the INF negotiations. He became director of the State Department's policy planning staff in 1950 and served as president of the Foreign Service Educational Foundation. He was appointed assistant secretary of defense for international affairs in 1961 and served as secretary of the navy in the Johnson administration.

Paul Ramsey is Harrington Spear Paine Professor of Religion Emeritus, Princeton University. Among his many publications is *War and the Christian Conscience*.

Kenneth W. Thompson is Commonwealth Professor of government and foreign affairs at the University of Virginia and director of its White Burkett Miller Center of Public Affairs. He is author and editor of more than a score of books, including the most recent *Cold War Theories*, vol. 1. He was vice-president of the Rockefeller Foundation and a member of the *Christianity and Crisis* editorial board unitl 1982.

Robert W. Tucker is Edward B. Burling Professor of international law and organization and acting director of American Foreign Policy at the School of Advanced International Studies, Johns Hopkins University. The present essay includes material that later appeared in the volume *Force, order, and Justice*, of which he is a coauthor.

Theodore H. Weber is professor of social ethics at the Candler School of Theology, Emory University.

Gordon Zahn is professor emeritus of sociology, Boston University, and is associated with the Pax Christi USA Center on Conscience and War, Cambridge. He works include the pathbreaking sociological study *German Catholics and Hitler's Wars* and *In Solitary Witness*, an account of the life of Franz Jagerstätter—a German pacifist during World War II.

180 5658 7